Dear Dorothy:
Thanks so much!
All my best,
Kunal
04/2011

Common Law, History, and Democracy in America, 1790–1900

This book argues for a change in our understanding of the relationships among law, politics, and history. Since the turn of the nineteenth century, a certain antifoundational conception of history has served to undermine law's foundations, such that we tend to think of law as nothing other than a species of politics. When law is thus viewed, the activity of unelected, common law judges appears to be an encroachment on the space of democracy. However, Kunal M. Parker shows that the world of the nineteenth century looked rather different. Democracy was itself constrained by a sense that history possessed a logic, meaning, and direction that democracy could not contravene. In such a world, far from seeing law in opposition to democracy, it was possible to argue that law – specifically, the common law – often did a better job than democracy of guiding America along history's path.

Kunal M. Parker is Professor and Dean's Distinguished Scholar at the University of Miami School of Law. He was previously the James A. Thomas Distinguished Professor of Law at Cleveland State University and has held fellowships at New York University Law School, Cornell Law School, Queens University in Belfast, and the American Bar Foundation. Professor Parker has served on the editorial boards of *PoLAR: Political and Legal Anthropology Review* and *Law and Social Inquiry*. His writing focuses on U.S. intellectual and legal history, the philosophy of history, the history and theory of immigration and citizenship law, and the history of law in colonial India.

Cambridge Historical Studies in American Law and Society

SERIES EDITOR

Christopher Tomlins, *University of California, Irvine*

PREVIOUSLY PUBLISHED IN THE SERIES

Andrew Wender Cohen, *The Racketeer's Progress: Chicago and the Struggle for the Modern American Economy, 1900–1990*
Davison Douglas, *Jim Crow Moves North: The Battle Over Northern School Segregation, 1865–1959*
Tony A. Freyer, *Antitrust and Global Capitalism, 1930–2004*
Michael Grossberg, *A Judgment for Solomon: The d'Hauteville Case and Legal Experience in the Antebellum South*
Rebecca M. McLennan, *The Crisis of Imprisonment: Protest, Politics, and the Making of the American Penal State, 1776–1941*
David M. Rabban, *Free Speech in Its Forgotten Years*
James D. Schmidt, *Industrial Violence and the Legal Origins of Child Labor*
Robert J. Steinfeld, *Coercion, Contract, and Free Labor in the Nineteenth-Century America*
Michael Vorenberg, *Final Freedom: The Civil War, the Abolition of Slavery, and the Thirteenth Amendment*
Jenny Wahl, *The Bondsman's Burden: An Economic Analysis of the Common Law of Southern Slavery*
Barbara Young Welke, *Recasting American Liberty: Gender, Race, Law, and the Railroad Revolution, 1865–1920*
Steven Wilf, *Law's Imagined Republic: Popular Politics and Criminal Justice in Revolutionary America*
Michael Willrich, *City of Courts: Socializing Justice in Progressive Era Chicago*

Common Law, History, and Democracy in America, 1790–1900

Legal Thought before Modernism

KUNAL M. PARKER
University of Miami School of Law

CAMBRIDGE
UNIVERSITY PRESS

CAMBRIDGE UNIVERSITY PRESS
Cambridge, New York, Melbourne, Madrid, Cape Town,
Singapore, São Paulo, Delhi, Tokyo, Mexico City

Cambridge University Press
32 Avenue of the Americas, New York, NY 10013-2473, USA

www.cambridge.org
Information on this title: www.cambridge.org/9780521519953

First published 2011

Printed in the United States of America

A catalog record for this publication is available from the British Library

Library of Congress Cataloging in Publication data
Parker, Kunal Madhukar, 1968–
Common law, history, and democracy in America, 1790–1900 : legal thought before modernism / Kunal M. Parker.
p. cm.
(Cambridge historical studies in American law and society)
Includes bibliographical references and index.
ISBN 978-0-521-51995-3 (hardback)
1. Common law–United States–History. 2. Justice, Administration of–History. 3. Progressivism (United States politics)–History. 4. United States–Politics and government–19th century. I. Title. II. Series.
KF395.P37 2011
340.5′70973–dc22 2010037104

ISBN 978-0-521-51995-3 Hardback

Contents

Acknowledgments

I have many people and institutions to thank for this book. It is a sincere pleasure to acknowledge them all here.

This book began as a doctoral dissertation in the Department of History at Princeton University. While I was a graduate student at Princeton, each of my advisors – Hendrik Hartog, Anthony Grafton, and Daniel Rodgers – did individual reading courses with me, taking time out of their busy schedules every week to walk me through scholarly literatures and to respond to my concerns and queries. Dirk's, Tony's, and Dan's generosity speaks volumes not only about their extraordinary commitment to graduate students, but also about the very special culture of the Department of History at Princeton. This generosity continued while I was writing the dissertation and after. Dan Rodgers and Dirk Hartog both read the book manuscript at a late stage. Dirk, in particular, offered detailed and characteristically challenging comments. I know I am not the only one of Dirk's graduate students to feel overwhelmed by his generosity with his time. I cannot thank him enough.

A few more individuals deserve to be identified. Over the years, Christopher Tomlins has been a supporter and a friend. He encouraged me to go to graduate school in history and wrote me reference letters; he recognized the worth of this project when it was in its earliest stages; he shepherded it through to what it has now become; and he offered innumerable points of advice and suggestion. Annelise Riles, whom I met when we were both first-year students at the Harvard Law School, has taught me an immense amount over the years. Especially worthy of mention is that she arranged for me to spend a year at Cornell University in

2003–2004, which is where my dissertation began. Bill Nelson offered me the Samuel I. Golieb Fellowship at New York University Law School in 2006–2007, which allowed me to finish my dissertation. Barbara Quint gave me heavily subsidized housing during that crucial last year. Two individuals, with whose ideas this book engages, have been incredibly generous in their reading of my work: Bob Gordon and Dorothy Ross. I have learned much from their framing of issues. Clayton Koppes agreed to read the manuscript as it was close to completion and offered the valuable (and much desired) feedback of a non–legally trained historian. The editorial team at Cambridge University Press has been wonderful. I thank them all.

I have presented papers drawn from this book at the Benjamin N. Cardozo Law School, Case Western Reserve University Law School, the Cleveland-Marshall College of Law, Cornell Law School, Emory Law School, New York University Law School, Northwestern Law School, Queens University Belfast, the University of British Columbia, the University of California at Irvine, the School of Oriental and African Studies at the University of London, the University of Miami School of Law, the University of Oregon School of Law, the University of Southern California Law School, Villanova Law School, and at various annual meetings of the American Society for Legal History, the Law and Society Association, and the Association for the Study of Law, Culture and the Humanities. I thank audiences, commentators, and fellow panelists at all of these venues for their engagement.

I would also like to acknowledge the valuable research support of the Cleveland-Marshall College of Law and the University of Miami School of Law. The libraries of both institutions have been admirable in responding to my requests. Jessica Mathewson, Barbara Cuadras, and Sue Ann Campbell have gone above and beyond what one might reasonably expect of librarians. At both institutions, assiduous research assistants – Frank Wardega, Chris Valley, Justin Wales, and Eliot Williams – have helped make this book a better one. The William Nelson Cromwell Foundation offered me a welcome dissertation writing grant.

It is also a pleasure to name a number of friends and interlocutors who have helped in different ways to refine my thinking over the years: David Abraham, Anita Bernstein, Ritu Birla, Linda Bosniak, Christina Burnett, Marianne Constable, Charlton Copeland, Patti Falk, Zanita Fenton, Martha Fineman, Michael Froomkin, Rachel Godsil, Reg Graycar, Ariela Gross, Patrick Gudridge, Laura Hengehold, Gloria Howard, Dan Hulsebosch, Nancy Khalek, Amy Levine, Christine McBurney, Pat

McCoy, Michelle McKinley, Renisa Mawani, Hiro Miyazaki, Mae Ngai, Bill Novak, Mariana Ortega, Ishita Pande, Daria Roithmayr, Teemu Ruskola, Yumna Siddiqi, Frank Valdes, Mariana Valverde, and Barbara Welke.

Lastly, I want to acknowledge the support of my family, in both India and the United States. I want particularly to thank my mother, whose support has never faltered even as, over the years, my interests have changed.

1

Introduction

Common Law, Democracy, History: a Modernist Tradition of Reading the Past

From the American Revolution until the very end of the nineteenth century, the common law was considered an integral mode of governance and public discourse in America. The vital presence of the common law might seem odd in a country that was premised in so many ways on breaking with its European past and on assuming political control of its own destiny. After all, the common law had originated in, and remained closely identified with, England. It was ideologically committed to upholding precedent and to repeating the past, claiming as it did so to embody the "immemorial" customs of the English, customs so old that their origin lay beyond "the memory of man." It consisted of judicial, rather than legislative, articulation of legal principles. For all these reasons, one might expect Americans, who were intensely proud of their republican experiment, to have rejected the common law.

Instead, until the very end of the nineteenth century, the common law was widely – although never universally – claimed and celebrated. In 1826, in the first volume of his celebrated *Commentaries on American Law*, the "American Blackstone," James Kent, delivered the following breathless paean to the common law that captures how many nineteenth-century American lawyers thought about it:

> [The common law] fills up every interstice, and occupies every wide space which the statute law cannot occupy.... [W]e live in the midst of the common law, we inhale it at every breath, imbibe it at every pore; we meet with it when we wake, and when we lie down to sleep, when we travel and when we stay at home; and

it is interwoven with the very idiom that we speak; and we cannot learn another system of laws, without learning, at the same time, another language.[1]

We might account for the longevity and resilience of the common law tradition in nineteenth-century America by advancing at least two reasons, both well known. First, the common law came with heavy ideological freight. Since the early seventeenth century, English common lawyers had resisted the encroachments of would-be absolute monarchs in the name of England's "ancient constitution," an agglomeration of immemorial, endlessly repeated, common law freedoms. Americans had thoroughly absorbed this learning. The American revolutionary struggle was fought to a large extent to vindicate what colonists considered their common law rights and freedoms. As a result, many prominent American legal thinkers from the late eighteenth century on considered the written U.S. Constitution to be informed by, and indeed to be incomprehensible without reference to, the common law.[2] Second, throughout the nineteenth century, the American state – whether at the federal, state, or local level – did not play nearly as significant a role in economy and society as it would in the twentieth century. The gap it left was filled by common lawyers, who played a correspondingly larger part in articulating law for America's vibrant and multiplying polities and economies. Even as they were accused of political bias, nineteenth-century American common lawyers took this role extremely seriously. More than a quarter-century ago, Morton Horwitz detailed the considerable creativity of American common law-

[1] James Kent, *Commentaries on American Law* (4 vols.) (New York: E. B. Clayton, 1840) (4th ed.; 1st ed., 1826), Vol. 1, p. 343. It is noteworthy that Kent makes an argument that many contemporary sociolegal thinkers would recognize, namely that law is utterly constitutive of our lives, down to their most mundane, routine, habitual aspects. For contemporary legal scholars, the authoritative work on the constitutive nature of law is Robert W. Gordon, "Critical Legal Histories," *Stanford Law Review* 36 (1984): 57–125.

[2] The contemporary American legal scholar most clearly associated with identifying the common law sources of the revolutionary struggle is John Phillip Reid. See John Phillip Reid, *The Ancient Constitution and the Origins of Anglo-American Liberty* (DeKalb: Northern Illinois University Press, 2005). See also Reid's multivolume *Constitutional History of the American Revolution*. John Phillip Reid, *The Constitutional History of the American Revolution: The Authority of Rights* (Madison: University of Wisconsin Press, 1986); *The Constitutional History of the American Revolution: The Authority to Tax* (Madison: University of Wisconsin Press, 1987); *The Constitutional History of the American Revolution: The Authority of to Legislate* (Madison: University of Wisconsin Press, 1991); *The Constitutional History of the American Revolution: The Authority of Law* (Madison: University of Wisconsin Press, 1993).

yers as they reshaped English doctrines of tort, contract, and property to suit the needs of the nineteenth-century American economy.[3]

But there was more, and it is this that forms the subject of this book. Throughout the nineteenth century, the common law, history, and democracy were imagined to coexist in ways very different from the way we (or at least many of us) are now wont to imagine them. These nineteenth-century ways of imagining the relationships among the common law, history, and democracy go a long way toward explaining why the common law tradition survived for as long as it did as such a vital part of American governance and public discourse. They reveal different conceptions of how law, history, and democracy related to one another, different modes of historicizing law, and different ways of thinking about history itself.

For all their importance in their own time, however, these nineteenth-century ways of conceiving of the relationships among the common law, history, and democracy have been largely obscured from our view – or, alternatively, caricatured – by a powerful and still authoritative late-nineteenth- and early-twentieth-century modernist tradition of thinking about law, history, and democracy. In order to recover the ideational world of the nineteenth century and to rediscover the ways in which it might speak to us, it is therefore necessary to understand the modernist tradition that still largely occludes it. Accordingly, it is to this modernist lens through which we continue to read the past that I first turn. We need to understand how we have been reading the past, I submit, in order to see the past differently and to learn from it.

Less than a century after Kent penned his extravagant paean to the common law, it would become impossible for most serious American legal thinkers to express quite such an enthusiastic endorsement of the common law tradition. Around 1900, the common law tradition, so ardently claimed by American lawyers for so long, began to experience a loss of prestige. Furthermore, while it is emphatically not the case that the common law faded from the twentieth-century American legal landscape, its decline as a mode of governance and public discourse – relative to the twentieth-century regime of state-generated law, codes and regulations, bureaucratic experts, and administrative agencies – seems unquestionable. What happened?

The standard account runs as follows. By the end of the nineteenth century, massive transformations in American life – urbanization,

[3] Morton J. Horwitz, *The Transformation of American Law, 1780–1860* (Cambridge, Mass.: Harvard University Press, 1977).

industrialization, capital–labor conflict – seemed to necessitate ever greater democratic, collective, directive, and expert control over law. Calls for reform were everywhere. Common law notions of contract, property, and tort were entirely unable, it was maintained, to deal with the grave problems of America's industrial economy. Indeed, the common law, especially as it was joined to the U.S. Constitution and applied by the federal courts, was widely considered a bastion of past-oriented conservatism, threatening the viability of urgently needed social democratic legislation. The activities of the U.S. Supreme Court seemed to confirm such critiques. In the notorious case of *Lochner v. New York* (1905), the Court effectively read common law freedoms into the U.S. Constitution's Due Process Clause when it struck down as unconstitutional a New York maximum-hours law intended to regulate working conditions in bakeries on the ground that the law interfered with the right to contract.[4]

The *Lochner* decision, and others like it, incensed Progressive Era critics. The common law's conservative and individualistic orientation toward contract and property, to the extent that it was used to overturn or subvert reformist, redistributive, social democratic legislation, was read as profoundly antidemocratic. In order to restore to democratic majorities their rightful role in giving themselves their own laws, there began a long, complex, and contradictory assault on the common law extending all the way to the New Deal, which ended in the common law's retreat. *Lochner v. New York* rapidly became, and has remained, a symbol of judicial overreaching, a nadir in the history of the U.S. Supreme Court. Law in the twentieth century increasingly became a matter of state-generated law.

Beneath this factual account of how the forces of democracy defeated a reactionary common law lies the modernist account of the relationships among democracy, law, and history to which I have referred. This modernist account arose in the late nineteenth century. It provided the critical intellectual underpinnings for the Progressive Era assault on the common law tradition and remains extremely influential in our own understanding of the relations among democracy, law, and history.[5]

4 *Lochner v. New York*, 198 U.S. 45 (1905).

5 The standard and important work on legal modernism is David Luban, *Legal Modernism* (Ann Arbor: University of Michigan Press, 1994). Luban's own understanding of "modernism," while not at odds with anything I say, is too specific for my purposes. For a discussion of modernism that is closer to the one I advance here, see Dorothy Ross, "Modernism Reconsidered," in Dorothy Ross, ed., *Modernist Impulses in the Human Sciences, 1870–1930* (Baltimore: Johns Hopkins University Press, 1994).

In order for the forces of democracy to defeat the common law, law had to be convincingly represented as a species of politics, its foundations as law undermined. It was only when law could be successfully represented as a species of politics that common law judges could be represented as *illegitimately* usurping the realm of democratic politics. To be sure, as I will show, democratically oriented American critics of the common law had been attacking the common law as a species of politics from the American Revolution on. But the decline in the prestige of the common law in the early twentieth century and into our own time emerges in important part from this specific modernist tradition of thinking about democracy, law, and history. This modernist sensibility is discernible in the writings of America's most famous late-nineteenth-century critic of the common law tradition, Oliver Wendell Holmes, Jr. Although Holmes's role as a critic of the common law is well recognized – and widely celebrated – by American legal scholars and intellectual historians, it is not always sufficiently appreciated that his critique emerges out of a modernist historical sensibility.[6]

"Modernism," Peter Gay has argued, "is far easier to exemplify than to define." While it is beyond the scope of this book to come to terms with the various meanings of modernism as a cultural and intellectual phenomenon, it is significant that Gay identifies as the key attributes of modernism "the lure of heresy," on the one hand, and "a commitment to a principled self-scrutiny," on the other[7]; for it is precisely these two features of modernism, as Gay defines them, that were part of what I would characterize as a special kind of awakening to history revealed by Holmes's writings. (Later in this book, I will argue that much of Holmes's historical sensibility is shared with his late-nineteenth-century contemporaries.) For Holmes, in the spirit of heresy or iconoclasm, history would serve to tear down the suprahistorical foundations – logic, morality, and so on – of law. In sweeping away such foundations, history would invite critical self-reflection, new ways of imagining the future. The result would be an erosion of the boundary between law and politics.

[6] David Luban also takes Holmes to be the first major American legal modernist. As he puts it, "To see these modernist themes at work in legal theory close up, we need go no further than the writings of Oliver Wendell Holmes, whom I propose to take as a case study of the modernist predicament in law." Luban, *Legal Modernism*, p. 28. Luban, to be sure, recognizes the significance of what I would call historical thinking in his rendering of legal modernism.

[7] Peter Gay, *Modernism: The Lure of Heresy from Baudelaire to Beckett and Beyond* (New York: Norton, 2008), pp. 1, 3–4.

In a series of oracular texts, Holmes faulted the common law tradition for being insensitive to history. First, at the opening of his now little read classic, *The Common Law* (1881), Holmes makes an iconoclastic statement that has since become a mantra, if not a cliché, of modernist, pragmatist legal thought:

> The life of the law has not been logic: it has been experience. The felt necessities of the time, the prevalent moral and political theories, intuitions of public policy, avowed or unconscious, even the prejudices which judges share with their fellow-men, have had a good deal more to do than the syllogism in determining the rules by which men should be governed. The law embodies the story of a nation's development through many centuries, and it cannot be dealt with as if it contained only the axioms and corollaries of a book of mathematics.[8]

Holmes was arguing that legal thinkers had begun erroneously to believe that the common law could be understood as a matter of ahistorical logic, such that legal results would follow automatically from initial premises. But the common law, Holmes suggested, was ultimately irreducible to logic. Logic was not its foundation. Like all law, the common law had to be seen, instead, as the product of *nothing* but history, as something that had arisen and developed in time, as something without ahistorical foundations.[9]

Second, even as he insisted that the common law was not logic but instead the product of nothing but history, Holmes argued that the common law was excessively wedded to repeating the past for its own sake. In a celebrated essay entitled "The Path of the Law" (1897), Holmes famously declared that the mere passage of time, or antiquity, was an insufficient basis for endowing a rule with legal weight and significance. He put it thus:

> It is revolting to have no better reason for a rule of law than that so it was laid down in the time of Henry IV. It is still more revolting if the grounds upon which it was laid down have vanished long since, and the rule simply persists from blind imitation of the past.[10]

[8] Oliver Wendell Holmes, Jr., *The Common Law* (Boston: Little, Brown, 1881), p. 1.

[9] The phrase "nothing but history" comes from Benedetto Croce's *La storia come pensiero e come azione* (translated as *History as the Story of Liberty*). It has been popularized by David D. Roberts, *Nothing but History: Reconstruction and Extremity after Metaphysics* (Aurora, Colo.: Davies Group, 2006) (1995).

[10] Oliver Wendell Holmes, Jr., "The Path of the Law" (1897), in *The Collected Works of Justice Holmes: Complete Public Writings and Selected Judicial Opinions of Oliver Wendell Holmes* (Chicago: University of Chicago Press, 1995) (5 vols.) (Sheldon Novick, ed.) (hereafter "*Collected Works*"), Vol. 3, p. 399.

Antiquity, something that had long served as a ground of the common law's legitimacy, was thus as illegitimate a foundation for law as was logic. For law to be justified, it had to be justified in the present as a matter of critical self-reflection. A mere "blind imitation of the past," of the kind common lawyers allegedly engaged in, would not do. If we are to repeat the past, Holmes tells us, we must choose to do so now and with utter self-consciousness.

Holmes's twin critiques of the common law are superficially opposed. How could the common law simultaneously be accused of being excessively wedded to an ahistorical logic and excessively wedded to repeating the past for its own sake? Holmes was, in fact, pointing to different aspects of the common law tradition. The logic-oriented tradition was the product of a scientific orientation to the common law of relatively recent vintage. It had been developing around the Harvard Law School at the time Holmes came of age intellectually. The precedent-oriented tradition, in which the legitimacy of the common law rested upon repeating the past, went back centuries. It had been articulated authoritatively in the early seventeenth century and had been repeatedly reaffirmed.

What unifies Holmes's twin critiques of the common law is his modernist conception of history. For Holmes, history is the heretical or iconoclastic practice of revealing the merely temporal origins of phenomena in order to dismantle the foundations upon which such phenomena rest, whether those foundations be the logic allegedly underlying law or the accumulated weight of law's past that authorizes its own repetition. Once the temporal origins of phenomena have been identified and their foundations undermined, however, no underlying order, instantiated in an unfolding historical time, becomes visible. In other words, history possesses no necessary or coherent direction or meaning. It simply sweeps away foundations, clears ground, and invites self-reflection. Law's foundations may be dismantled in the name of history, but we are given no substitute foundations. We are told to think about what we might want law to be.

Holmes himself was no unambiguous partisan of popular democracy. Indeed, his modernist, antifoundational view of history could as readily be turned on the foundational philosophies of democratic majorities as they could on foundational theories of law. Nevertheless, Holmes's view of history as a ground-clearing gesture, when turned on law specifically, played an important role in breaking down the always tenuous distinction between law and politics. If law's foundations could be shown up as thoroughly temporal, as arising in historical time, contingent, and revisable, how could one distinguish meaningfully between law and politics? Was not law just another way of doing politics? Where the law in question was not the direct result of the activity of democratic majorities, as was so clearly the case with the judicially articulated common law, did this then not render law an illegitimate way of doing politics? Although they have not always adequately underscored the modernist historical sensibility that is such an important part of Holmesian thought, American legal historians have frequently placed Holmes at the origin point of the "discovery" that law could be collapsed into politics. At the end of a brilliant and detailed discussion of Holmes, for example, Morton Horwitz puts it thus:

> [H]olmes pushed American legal thought into the twentieth century. It is the moment at which advanced legal thinkers renounced the belief in a conception of legal thought independent of politics and separate from social reality. From this moment on, the late nineteenth century ideal of an internally self-consistent and autonomous system of legal ideals, free from the corrupting influence of politics, was brought constantly under attack.[11]

The Holmesian breaking down of the wall between law and politics, itself part of a much wider modernist political, intellectual, and artistic "revolt against formalism" throughout the Western world, provided a critical intellectual underpinning for the early-twentieth-century Progressive assault on the common law.[12] Indeed, Holmes became the darling of democratically inclined, scientifically oriented Progressive Era critics of the common law precisely for having reduced law to politics. These critics actively claimed Holmes as an intellectual forebear, even though only a few subscribed in a philosophically rigorous way to all aspects of his particular brand of modernist, antifoundational, skeptical historical thought. Many of Holmes's insights were taken up, repeated, and deepened. Following in Holmes's footsteps, Progressive Era thinkers railed against the common law's late-nineteenth-century formalist orientation. For example, in his celebrated *Economic Interpretation of the Constitution of the United States* (1913), the historian Charles A. Beard deplored "[t]he devotion to deductions from 'principles'... which

[11] Morton J. Horwitz, *The Transformation of American Law, 1870–1960: The Crisis of Legal Orthodoxy* (Oxford: Oxford University Press, 1992), p. 142.

[12] G. Morton White, *Social Thought in America: The Revolt Against Formalism* (New York: Viking Press, 1949); James T. Kloppenberg, *Uncertain Victory: Social Democracy and Progressivism in European and American Thought, 1870–1920* (Oxford: Oxford University Press, 1986).

is such a distinguishing sign of American legal thinking."[13] Progressive Era thinkers also followed Holmes in attacking the common law's more traditional backward orientation, its commitment to repeating the past. Law was increasingly thought of as something that had to be made in the present, with full awareness of its contingency, provisionality, and revisability. This present-focused law had to rely, furthermore, on the latest expert knowledge of non-lawyers. As John Dewey put it in a little 1941 essay describing his philosophy of law, law required that "intelligence, employing the best scientific methods and materials available, be used, to investigate, in terms of the context of actual situations, the consequence of legal rules and of proposed legal decisions and acts of legislation."[14] Various early-twentieth-century schools of legal thought – Sociological Jurisprudence, Legal Realism, and so on – flourished at least in important part on the basis of Holmesian insights. To be sure, not all twentieth-century legal thinkers subscribed to the Holmesian reduction of law to politics in the name of antifoundational history. Considerable intellectual labor would be expended in the twentieth century in the attempt to retrieve a conception of law from the rubble produced by this reduction. Even if legal thinkers ultimately rejected Holmes, however, they had first to confront the challenge he posed.

Within contemporary American legal history, what started more than a century ago as an erosion of the boundary between law and politics has become fully authoritative, indeed entirely traditional. Following patterns set in the Progressive Era, histories of American law that reveal its underlying politics abound (although contemporary American legal historians, far more sensitive to trends in the discipline of history, have been offering more richly contextualized histories than ever before). Over the years, we have learned how the nineteenth-century common law was Americanized and instrumentalized and formalized in the service of politics; how it was used to promote capitalism or to block redistributive legislation; and how it created or transformed relational identities (employer–employee, husband–wife, master–slave, etc.).[15] We are often left with the uneasy sense that something illegitimate transpired, that common law judges were engaged in

[13] Charles A. Beard, *An Economic Interpretation of the Constitution of the United States* (New York: MacMillan, 1935) (1913), p. 9.

[14] John Dewey, in *My Philosophy of Law: Credos of Sixteen American Scholars* (Boston: Boston Law Book, 1941), p. 83.

[15] See William Nelson, *Americanization of the Common Law: The Impact of Legal Change on Massachusetts Society, 1780–1860* (Cambridge, Mass.: Harvard University Press, 1975); Horwitz, *The Transformation of American Law, 1780–1860*; Horwitz, *The Transformation of American Law, 1870–1960*; William M. Wiecek, *The Lost World of*

overreaching, that they were doing something deeply political, that democracy was being subverted by law. At the close of *The Transformation of American Law, 1870–1960* (1992), Morton Horwitz captures perfectly this modernist tradition of looking at America's past. He exalts the modernist moment of law – one might legitimately label it a Holmesian moment – as a triumph for history *and* democracy, even as he recognizes that that triumph never became complete in twentieth-century America:

> Only pragmatism, with its dynamic understanding of the unfolding of principle over time and its experimental appreciation of the complex interrelationship between law and politics and theory and practice has stood against the static fundamentalism of traditional American conceptions of principled jurisprudence.
>
> Until we are able to transcend the American fixation with sharply separating law from politics, we will continue to fluctuate between the traditional polarities of American legal discourse, as each generation continues frantically to hide behind unhistorical and abstract universalisms in order to deny, even to itself, its own political and moral choices.[16]

If this still vital modernist account of the collapsing of the law–politics distinction in the name of antifoundational history is taken as an object of faith (as indeed it continues largely to be), we are left with a number of questions. Were American common law thinkers throughout the nineteenth century condemned to oscillate between a naive "blind repetition of the past" and a kind of surreptitious politics? Or did nineteenth-century American common law thinkers also conceive of law in history as they engaged in what we have long known to be a creative reshaping of common law doctrines? If nineteenth-century American common law thinkers did conceive of law in history, what did their historical sensibilities look like? Did they avoid collapsing law into history, and hence into politics, as we – living, teaching, and writing after Holmes – now do so automatically? What were the relationships among history, democracy, and law *before* the Holmesian modernist moment that has been so critical to twentieth-century understandings?

Classical Legal Thought: Law and Ideology in America, 1886–1937 (Oxford: Oxford University Press, 1998). On labor law, see Christopher Tomlins, *Law, Labor and Ideology in the Early American Republic* (Cambridge: Cambridge University Press, 1993); William E. Forbath, *Law and the Shaping of the American Labor Movement* (Cambridge, Mass.: Harvard University Press, 1991). On the law of marriage, see Hendrik Hartog, *Man and Wife in America: A History* (Cambridge, Mass.: Harvard University Press, 2000). On the law of slavery, see Thomas D. Morris, *Southern Slavery and the Law, 1619–1860* (Chapel Hill: University of North Carolina Press, 1996).

16 Horwitz, *The Transformation of American Law, 1870–1960*, 271–272.

At stake in posing and answering such questions are our understandings of the historical relationships among American democracy, law, and history, which might serve as important explanations of the vitality of the common law tradition in nineteenth-century America. However, the answers might transcend the American context itself, speaking more generally to philosophical concerns about the status of foundational thinking after modernism. Philosophers of history have recognized that, since the late nineteenth century, we have been living in a world "after" metaphysics, where the world is nothing but history and seems "ever-provisional." Recognizing what Holmes recognized a century ago when he sought to tear down the foundations of law in the name of history, Benjamin Barber has written: "[P]olitics is what men do when metaphysics fails." Democracy, David Roberts writes, "is the form of interaction for people who cannot agree on moral absolutes."[17]

In seeking to re-create the ideational world of nineteenth-century common law, historical and democratic thought, I am seeking to reconstruct the world *before* this modernist intellectual crisis. At stake is not only an appreciation of the dynamism, sensitivity, and richness of nineteenth-century legal, historical, and democratic thought, something that has hitherto remained largely hidden from view because of the modernist lens through which we read the past, but a "provincializing" of the Holmesian, modernist tradition of thinking historically to which we are heirs.[18]

Nineteenth-Century Common Law Thought, the Historical Imagination, and American Democracy: a World before Modernism

In order to begin exploring the relationships among democracy, law, and history before modernism, one has to distance oneself from one of the critical assumptions of modernist historical thought, namely that an iconoclastic dismantling of the foundations of phenomena through the technique of revealing their temporal origins will clear ground, enable critical self-reflection, and open up the world for reimagining and remaking. To this day, I submit, this is an integral feature of our (now more "postmodern") historical method, obsessed as we are with demonstrating the

[17] Benjamin Barber, quoted in Roberts, *Nothing but History*, pp. xvii–xix.

[18] The standard text on "provincializing" Europe as a subject of history is Dipesh Chakrabarty, *Provincializing Europe: Postcolonial Thought and Historical Difference* (Princeton, N.J.: Princeton University Press, 2000).

contingency of things, of emphasizing that nothing had to be the way it turned out, that things could have gone differently, that alternative choices and possibilities necessarily crowd the past, present, and future. Thinking this way implies that the subject – whether an individual, a democratic majority, or a society – can be rendered radically unconstrained and unencumbered, a blank slate from which thoroughgoing personal or democratic or societal reimagining might somehow begin. However, barring exceptions, this was not the ideational world of eighteenth- and nineteenth-century Americans.

Instead, the nineteenth century was a world in which the notion of *given* constraints was very real indeed. One undoubtedly valid explanation for the persistence of a sense of the givenness of constraints is that, even though Americans had long ceased to enact biblical strictures as law, this was a society that remained overwhelmingly religious.[19] However, the presence of religion in nineteenth-century American thought, if offered up as a definitive and all-encompassing explanation for the givenness of constraints, risks becoming monolithic and reductionist. It often fails to capture the changing, proliferating, and complex ways in which nineteenth-century Americans went about constructing their worlds and naming its limits and constraints. In what follows, I begin by offering a sense of how nineteenth-century Americans imagined the scope of political democracy, the formal sphere of the political. The formal sphere of the political, which would be called upon to do so much work in twentieth-century America, was often imagined as constrained. But it is the kinds of limits that were imagined, and the ways in which those limits were made to interact with each other, that are ultimately of interest.[20]

When it comes to nineteenth-century understandings of political democracy, it is important to keep in mind a cardinal fact. From the American Revolution into the twentieth century, throughout the Western

[19] For an article on the issue that adopts a comparative perspective and introduces the reader to much of the relevant literature, see Richard J. Ross, "Puritan Godly Discipline in Comparative Perspective: Legal Pluralism and the Sources of 'Intensity,'" *American Historical Review* 113 (October 2008): 975–1002. A good starting place is George L. Haskins, *Law and Authority in Early Massachusetts: A Study in Tradition and Design* (New York: Macmillan, 1960).

[20] I am not talking about constraints on political democracy in the narrow sense of Lockean natural rights, but about a broader set of constraints that operated, at a philosophical level, as given. Indeed, my argument about the givenness of constraints supports, rather than contradicts, William Novak's discussion of nineteenth-century America as a "well-regulated society." See William J. Novak, *The People's Welfare: Law and Regulation in Nineteenth Century America* (Chapel Hill: University of North Carolina Press, 1996).

world, political democracy, even as it was an aspiration for millions, was new and exceptional and not necessarily viewed as a prerequisite to national prosperity or prominence. The explosive eruptions and vicissitudinous careers of various revolutions – the late-eighteenth-century American, French, and Haitian Revolutions, the Latin American struggles, the revolutions of 1848, and the Paris Commune, to name just a few – underscored political democracy's instability, unpredictability, violence, and dangerousness.

It should not be surprising, then, that political democracy was the object of deep, ongoing suspicion. This suspicion was at the heart of the republican tradition that gave rise to the elaborate structure of checks and balances in the U.S. Constitution. But it continued into the nineteenth century long after the preoccupation with republicanism waned. Thinkers strove mightily to ponder political democracy's limits, to conjure up truths that the democratic subject, in his arrogant assertion that he could remake his world through self-conscious political activity, would be unable to tamper with. The midcentury Scottish romantic conservative historical thinker Thomas Carlyle offered the catchiest formulation, one that enjoyed considerable currency throughout the English-speaking world. Carlyle compared the nation to a ship that had to round Cape Horn. Was the establishment of political democracy among the crew of the ship sufficient to negotiate this confrontation with an inexorable and limiting nature? Carlyle's answer was unequivocal:

> Your ship cannot double Cape Horn by its excellent plans of voting. The ship may vote this and that, above decks and below, in the most harmonious exquisitely constitutional manner: the ship, to get round Cape Horn, will find a set of conditions already voted for, and fixed with adamantine rigour, by the ancient Elemental Powers, who are entirely careless how you vote.... *Ships accordingly do not use the ballot-box at all; ... one wishes much some other Entities, – since all entities lie under the same rigorous set of laws, – could be brought to show as much wisdom, and sense at least of self-preservation, the first command of Nature.... [Democracy is] a very extraordinary method of navigating, whether in the Straits of Magellan or the undiscovered Sea of Time* [emphasis added].[21]

"Nature" or "ancient Elemental Powers," in Carlyle's formulation, consisted of "a set of conditions already voted for, and fixed with adamantine rigour" that operated as an absolute limit on political democracy.

[21] Thomas Carlyle, "The Present Time," *Latter-Day Pamphlets* (New York: Scribner's, 1901) (1850), pp. 19–21.

But one should not imagine that the world of the nineteenth century was one in which limits to political democracy were necessarily self-consciously conjured up only by those ideologically opposed to it. What we might take to be a limiting or cabining of political democracy was in fact often merely taken to be an actually existing feature of political democracy, nothing other than the order of things itself. Throughout the nineteenth century, American political and legal thinkers were acutely aware of political democracy's manifest – and, to many, necessary or inevitable – incompleteness, even in those very few countries, such as the United States, that claimed to be democracies. They were fully aware, for example, that large segments of the native American population – a changing group that included women, minors, African Americans, Native Americans, property-less white males – were not full participants in the polity but were nevertheless subject to its laws. They were also aware that only a limited number of even those Americans entitled to vote actually voted in elections. They were conscious of how much of the rest of the world was non-self-governing. While some saw this as the basis for demanding an extension or deepening of political democracy, others did not think this incompletion made American political democracy less democratic, but instead that it underscored the fundamentally or essentially nondemocratic nature of law. This in turn fed the sense of constraints on political democracy, a Burkean inevitability of subjection to a governing order that one had not chosen. Did the fact that women were constrained to obey laws they had had no part in making not imply that *everyone* was, in some profound sense, similarly constrained?

This sense that the world was, in crucial ways, beyond the power of the democratic subject to remake, that it was subject to laws not of his making, imbues nineteenth-century American political and legal discourses. It allowed political democracy to coexist with various kinds of constraints or limits, most of which we would today reject. As a result, the politicolegal sphere was crowded with times ahistorical and historical, times with mysterious origins, times with a given logic and direction and meaning that democracy was declared unable to subvert. For our purposes, two different kinds of *given* times that enjoyed currency as limits to the sphere of political democracy are the nonhistorical premodern times of the common law, on the one hand, and the changing teleological and foundational times of nineteenth-century history, on the other. The creative and productive ways in which these times intersected, I argue, should lead us to provincialize our post-Holmesian thought and to render its reign less tyrannical and belittling as we look back on the nineteenth century.

Let me begin with the nonhistorical time of the common law. As I will set forth in much greater detail in Chapter 2, from the seventeenth century on, the common law tradition claimed for itself the self-consciously nonhistorical time of "immemoriality." The origins of the common law were said to reach back to a time "beyond the memory of man," a time self-consciously set beyond historical specification or determination. It was precisely this resistance to history that common lawyers relied upon to claim legitimacy for the common law. Freed from the strictures of a law that could be pinned down in chronological, historical time, common lawyers could claim a diffuse, imprecise, and mysterious antiquity on behalf of the common law. This special antiquity allowed them to claim superiority vis-à-vis lawgiving acts that could be located in chronological time, such as acts of monarchs or legislatures. Such temporally delimited acts of monarchs and legislatures, common lawyers argued, could never possess the wisdom of a law that embodied the wisdom of multiple generations going back into the mists of time.

But the "immemoriality" of the common law did not mean that the common law was immune to change. Even as they maintained that the common law was "immemorial," seventeenth-century common lawyers hailed the common law's ability to respond to changing circumstances through recourse to the time of "insensibility." The common law changed so "insensibly," it was argued, that it could never be seen to change. This was, in other words, also a time impervious to chronological or historical specification or determination. The precise moment of the common law's changing could never be located in chronological time; change could only be inferred from comparing origin and end points. And once again, common lawyers used this time as proof of the common law's superiority. Because it was "insensible," whatever change the common law brought about was less abrupt, less disruptive, and less violent, they argued, than the sudden and ill-conceived changes introduced by monarchs and legislatures.

It was precisely the indistinctness and imprecision of these times of "immemoriality" and "insensibility" – times that could easily crumble under the magnifying glass of modernist historical thought and its obsession with identifying the temporal origins of things – that American lawyers claimed, albeit in complicated ways, throughout the nineteenth century. It was precisely these times that gave the common law its authority. To nineteenth-century American common law thinkers, the Benthamite charge that common law judges made law as they pleased was an illegitimate aspersion. To them, the common law was an inherited body of "immemorial" doctrine that commanded a measure of fidelity because of its antiquity and its association with Anglo-American freedoms. But this was never a blind fidelity. Above all, the common law was a method – indeed, the best, most scientific, and least despotic method – of "insensible," step-by-step lawmaking. The common law judge was uniquely privileged, far more so than any elected legislature, to "read" the community that presented itself to him in his courtroom. When the common law judge spoke, in other words, the common law corresponded perfectly to the actually existing state of the community. This was a view that had emerged in seventeenth-century England and that was held by prominent American common law thinkers throughout the nineteenth century, from Joseph Story to Thomas Cooley to the younger Oliver Wendell Holmes, Jr. Furthermore, the common law judge decided case by case, unwilling to turn his back on the past or to plunge headlong into the future. As such, the common law judge was committed to a careful calibration of the competing claims of the past, the present, and the future, of maintaining the identity of society over time even as he was committed to change. This was also a view repeated by nineteenth-century common law thinkers, from Francis Lieber in Jacksonian America to James Coolidge Carter at the end of the nineteenth century. When these features of the common law method were combined, it was democratically elected legislatures rather than common law judges that appeared "unscientific" in their lawmaking. Nineteenth-century American political democracy shared space, as it were, with a law that began but could not be seen to have begun, that changed but that could not be caught in the act of changing, that always embodied the current needs of the people even as it reflected the wisdom of an illimitable past.

The second kind of time that limited the scope of nineteenth-century American political democracy was the time – or rather times – of teleological and foundational history. Through much of the nineteenth century, history was not self-consciously antifoundational as it would become with Holmes and his modernist, pragmatist champions. When one contemplated the historical world, one did not see it, as many historians are now accustomed to seeing it, as a product of nothing but history, as one historically locatable phenomenon giving way to another. One saw it instead in terms of the logic of a number of "firsts" that underlay the passage of time and that gave it meaning: God, "spirit," "laws," "life," and so on. There has been a powerful tradition in American intellectual history that has charged American historical thought with inadequacy or insufficiency or weakness. Eighteenth- and nineteenth-century

Americans were too mired in a sense of their own exceptionalism, we have been told, to understand their historical world as genuinely historical, that is, as devoid of foreordained directionality.[22] This sense that eighteenth- and nineteenth-century Americans were committed to teleological and foundational conceptions of history is largely correct. But to say this does not capture the richness of nineteenth-century historical discourses. Regardless of the overwhelmingly foundational and teleological nature of nineteenth-century history, discussions about history, and about America's place in history, were vigorous. They were also decidedly not provincial: they employed vocabularies and structures that were in use in Europe as well. Furthermore, even though nineteenth-century Americans organized the historical world in terms of firsts and foundations, they did not necessarily agree with one another about what constituted the logic of history. There were many accounts of what history was about, of where it was headed. Finally, for all Americans, the actually existing world was unambiguously complex, crowded not only with different logics but also with what had to be recognized as exceptions to them.[23]

Teleological and foundational ideas of history were applied to American democracy from the American Revolution going forward. Even as many in the nineteenth century saw democracy as furnishing the logic of history, to the extent that history was imagined to possess an underlying logic and meaning and direction, it could equally serve as a check on democracy. If history was going somewhere, in other words, it was possible to judge the activities of a democratically elected legislature in terms of that logic. Thus judged, a legislature could be "wrong" in the sense that it was guilty of flouting the logic of history. Let us take the example of slavery. Proslavery thinkers in the mid-nineteenth century believed that slavery instantiated the natural "law" of subordination of blacks to whites. History proved this natural law. One could look at the subordination of blacks to whites across temporal and geographic contexts and conclude this. But it also implied that American democracy could *not* violate this natural law. Antislavery legislation was thus represented as an exception to this law, as something that went against the logic of history

[22] See J. G. A. Pocock, *The Machiavellian Moment: Florentine Political Thought and the Atlantic Republican Tradition* (Princeton, N.J.: Princeton University Press, 1975). The authoritative work for the nineteenth century is Dorothy Ross, *The Origins of American Social Science* (Cambridge: Cambridge University Press, 1991).

[23] For my attempt to discuss the intellectual aesthetic of "complexity," see Kunal M. Parker, "Context in Law and History: A Study of the Late Nineteenth Century American Jurisprudence of Custom," *Law and History Review* 24 (2006): 473–518.

itself. Antislavery thinkers employed the same logic, but to the opposite end. On both sides, the space of democracy was cabined or limited, in other words, by the logic imagined to imbue history.

Thus far, I have been arguing, political democracy in nineteenth-century America coexisted with two sets of constraining or limiting times, those of the common law and those of history. It is in the intersection of these times that we see how common lawyers made out the case for the centrality of the common law as an important mode of governance in America. We see that common lawyers were engaged neither in a "blind imitation of the past" that Holmes accused them of nor in a surreptitious or unthinking political reshaping of common law doctrine, but were openly, articulately, vigorously, and self-consciously trying to fit the common law to the imperatives of history as they and their contemporaries saw them, imperatives that were imagined to constrain American democracy itself. This common lawyerly turn to history was not just a defensive strategy against the common law's many critics (although it was also that), but a deeply felt position. Where legislatures seemed unable or unwilling to guide America along history's imagined path, or simply as lacking the expertise to do so, common lawyers would do the needful.[24]

I do not claim that the flourishing of the common law in the nineteenth century is due entirely to common lawyers' skillful mobilization of the times of history. That would be a crude idealist argument as easily rejected as a crude materialist one. The absence of an extensive state structure and a large number of organized voices calling for state intervention, which did not occur until the end of the nineteenth century, counts for much. At the same time, however, nineteenth-century lawyers' turn to history contributed powerfully to the vitality of the common law tradition as a mode of governance and public discourse in nineteenth-century America.

Nineteenth-century American common lawyers' turn to history reveals possible relationships between history and law that are occluded by the Holmesian, modernist antifoundational turn to history. In order to see

[24] Certain scholars have discussed nineteenth-century lawyers' turn to history. A major early work in this vein is Perry Miller, *The Life of the Mind in America: From the Revolution to the Civil War* (New York: Harcourt, Brace & World, 1965). More recent work, albeit with orientations different from mine, include David Rabban, "The Historiography of Late Nineteenth-Century American Legal History," *Theoretical Inquiries in Law* 4 (July 2003): 541–578; Stephen A. Siegel, "Historism in Late Nineteenth Century Constitutional Thought," *Wisconsin Law Review* (1990): 1431–1547; and Steven Wilf, "The Invention of Legal Primitivism," *Theoretical Inquiries in Law* 10 (2009): 485–509.

this, let us explore the mechanics of how nineteenth-century American lawyers combined common law and historical sensibilities.

Armed with the indistinct common law times of "immemoriality" and "insensibility," convinced of the superiority of the common law method over that of legislatively generated law, nineteenth-century American legal thinkers turned to the common law tradition to make sense of pressing issues ranging from labor to crime, commerce to slavery, marriage to local government, contract to tort. It is important to emphasize that the nineteenth-century common law was by no means the exclusive preserve of pro-commerce or laissez-faire legal conservatives (although such conservatives were overwhelmingly pro–common law). In the slavery debates, for example, common law ideas sustained both anti- and proslavery positions. During the years of the Civil War, when Americans had to rethink the very nature of their political system, the common law tradition could even provide a legal framework for the prosecution of the War. Indeed, we need to think of the common law tradition as a tradition of thought in and of itself, encompassing ideas about time, law, society, and government, to which American legal thinkers turned again and again.

Even as they turned to the common law tradition, however, nineteenth-century common lawyers turned to the varying times and logics of history. And it is here that the conjoining of common law and history reveals something interesting.

In the first instance, the bringing together of the times of the common law and the times of history served to subject the common law to history. From the eighteenth century on, English and Scottish political and legal thinkers were acutely aware that the old common law had developed in a land-based feudal society. Their challenge was to fit this law to the needs of eighteenth-century Britain's commercial society. History was thus imagined as a move from the feudal to the commercial. In the late eighteenth and early nineteenth centuries, American political and legal thinkers continued this trend of subjecting the common law to the imperatives of history imagined as a move from feudal to commercial. Political democracy played a complicated role in this regard. Scottish Enlightenment thinkers had posited foundational and teleological historical laws – such as the shift from feudal to commercial – in a world constrained by monarchs and aristocrats. Democracy was supposed to imply a lifting of the constraints of the feudal such that the laws of society and nature would have free reign. But as I will show, political democracy in the imaginations of late-eighteenth- and early-nineteenth-century

American political and legal thinkers remained constrained by the Scottish narrative of a historical shift from feudal to commercial, even as thinkers came up with shifting and contradictory ways of relating America's present to its British past. As the nineteenth century wore on, the imperatives of history changed. By the mid-nineteenth century, American political and legal thinkers were no longer preoccupied with plotting a relationship to a prerevolutionary, feudal past. The specter of British influence, so prominent in Jeffersonian and Jacksonian America, waned. At the same time, political democracy, once seen as at least potentially able to allow the laws of nature and society to flourish, came increasingly to be seen as itself a potentially serious obstacle to the flourishing of natural and social laws. First the slavery crisis, and then the centralizing impulses of federal and state regulation, brought about new, but equally constraining languages of history, whether Comtean languages of underlying invariable natural and social laws or Darwinian–Spencerian ones that plotted history as a slowly but constantly evolving "life." These new historical languages would also, as had been the case in earlier decades, be used to make sense of the common law. From the time of the American Revolution going forward, then, American common lawyers judged the common law rigorously in terms of various prevailing vocabularies and logics of history. Thus judged, parts of the common law were declared obsolete and excised, others systematized, yet others reformed or revived.

American common lawyers' critical use of these historical languages reveals something significant, I maintain, about the relationship between the foundational histories of the nineteenth century and the antifoundational modernist history that emerged with Holmes. From our post-Holmesian perspective, it is antifoundational modernist history that is invested with the ability to allow us to see bits of law as contingent and therefore as subject to reform. But nineteenth-century common law thinkers were equally able to render bits of law contingent and therefore subject to reform. The only difference is that they did it from the perspective of a history that was explicitly, even exuberantly, foundational, a history that had a meaning, logic, and direction. This suggests something that might be unnerving. Although the difference between foundational history ("their" history) and antifoundational history (supposedly "our" history) might appear enormous at first glance, upon reflection, it might be less significant. "Religious faith is so little at variance with skepticism," the philosopher Karl Löwith observed a half-century ago, "that both are rather united by their common opposition to the presumptions of a settled knowledge."[25] If I understand this statement correctly, Löwith is arguing that religious faith (which might be a stand-in for the foundational and teleological histories of the nineteenth century) and skepticism (which might be a stand-in for modernist antifoundational history) are *both* opposed to a settled knowledge. *Both* are techniques for unsettling knowledge, for seeing things as contingent and therefore as changeable. In being brought to bear upon the common law, the foundational and teleological histories of the nineteenth century were no less effective than their early-twentieth-century modernist counterpart.

Even as they subjected the common law to history, however, nineteenth-century common law thinkers could argue that the common law, occasionally as doctrine but more often as method, itself realized and embodied the logic, meaning, and direction of history. It is important here to emphasize that, because nineteenth-century common law thinkers were not using history to pull down foundations generally in the manner of Holmes, the common law was never dissolved into history and reduced to politics. The times of the common law and the times of history brushed up against each other, informed each other, constituted each other, without destroying each other. History produced a perspective on the common law, but at the same time the common law produced a perspective on history. Nineteenth-century American common law thinkers reveal themselves, in other words, to have been able simultaneously to inhabit two different types of time, the nonmodern times of the common law and the varying times of nineteenth-century history. Of course, as I will demonstrate, holding on to two utterly different kinds of time, setting them in relationship to one another, required considerable intellectual labor. How might one maintain simultaneous affiliations to a legal tradition that had emerged in the seventeenth century and to the historical imperatives of the nineteenth century? Common lawyers' answers to this question form a large part of the subject of this book.

As already suggested, the common law tradition that common lawyers drew upon and defended so vigorously throughout the nineteenth century could not have survived in the way it did had it not been constantly updated, constantly reinvigorated, constantly re-presented in terms of the historical consciousness of the period. At the same time, and just as important, arguing that the common law itself embodied the logic, meaning, and direction of history secured a place for the common law in

25. Karl Löwith, *Meaning in History: The Theological Implications of the Philosophy of History* (Chicago: University of Chicago Press, 1949), p. viii.

America. Political democracy was incomplete, crowded with given limits, constrained by history. The state was often inept. When the common law was joined to history, common lawyers were able to argue that they – rather than democratically elected legislatures or bureaucratic departments or commissions – were better able to take American society in the direction in which history was pointing, better able to embody history's meaning and logic. These arguments were made over and over throughout the nineteenth century. When history ceased to have a necessary direction, as was the case when a modernist, antifoundational history appeared to triumph around 1900, the common law could be made to look like "mere" politics by its influential opponents. Until then, common law thinkers could argue that they had a vital role to play in America's development.

This is not to suggest, as I will argue in conclusion, that the triumph of modernist antifoundational history around 1900 meant that foundational and teleological histories were forever banished from the American political and legal landscape. Holmes's own historical sensibilities – important as they were to the erosion of the boundary between law and politics – were not shared by many of those who claimed him as an intellectual forebear in the twentieth century. Indeed, they would use the breakdown of the law–politics distinction to advance different foundational histories, to instantiate different political perspectives as law, to create an administrative state, to undo America's legacy of institutional racism. Legal thinkers – including those very thinkers who had attacked the nineteenth-century common law tradition – would respond by returning to the common law tradition. The history of the relationship between history and the common law in the twentieth century remains to be written, but I have been struck by the impress of older common law ways of thinking in some of twentieth-century America's most prominent legal thinkers.

The Structure of the Book

The reader should be clear about what I am arguing. I do not deny the significance of the modernist turn in historical and legal thought that took place around 1900. Indeed, I take very seriously the reduction of law to politics that took place as a result of that turn, not just because of its enormous impact on the evolution of twentieth-century law, but also because of its impact on how historians have read the common law in the nineteenth century. However, at the same time, in seeking to reconstruct the ideational world of nineteenth-century lawyers, I seek not only to put before my readers the sophistication and sensitivity of nineteenth-century legal, historical, and democratic thought, but also thereby to provincialize the modernist turn in history and law. I attempt to show that history was something eighteenth- and nineteenth-century common lawyers were doing all along, that history permitted them to render bits of common law contingent, that history informed their reformist efforts even as the fusion of the common law with history allowed them to argue that the common law was itself an agent of history. In other words, I am simultaneously attempting to illustrate the difference between nineteenth- and twentieth-century legal thought and to flatten that difference. This simultaneous emphasis on and erasure of differences tracks the way nineteenth-century common lawyers plotted the relationship between history and the common law, alternately distancing the one from the other and collapsing the one into the other.

A simultaneous emphasis on and erasure of differences is embodied as well in the structure of the book. The changing historical imaginations, vocabularies, and structures that American common lawyers inhabited from the American Revolution to about 1900 – and according to which the book is organized – were utterly different from one another, but nevertheless utterly equivalent in their ability to generate complex meaning for their adherents and to produce perspectives vis-à-vis the common law. In each case, even as the dominant historical imagination changed, what it did for its adherents remained similar. Common lawyers were able to use the relevant historical imagination to contextualize the common law, even as they were able to argue that the common law realized the logic of that same historical imagination.

Each chapter begins with a discussion of the dominant historical imagination of a particular period. After introducing the relevant features of this dominant historical imagination, each chapter explores how a range of legal thinkers used that historical imagination in different contexts, from labor prosecutions to vested rights to commerce to slavery to codification. In every chapter, there is also a discussion about the relationship between the U.S. Constitution and the common law. The reader should see each chapter as an illustration of the relationship between common law thought and a particular historical imagination: the range of contexts simply illustrates the pervasiveness of a particular historical vocabulary. It is important to keep in mind that this is emphatically not a book about doctrine (and as such does not attempt to make a contribution to the history of legal doctrine), but a book about the relationships among law, history, and democracy.

To be sure, identifying the "dominant" historical imagination for any given period is fraught with perils. Over the course of the nineteenth century, there were many ways of conceiving of the movement of history. Each of the periods I identify contains many different historical logics, some pointing backward to earlier periods, others anticipating future periods, yet others simply different from one another. Each period, in other words, is inevitably complex. One would expect no less. The point of identifying a period for me, then, is not to make an argument about periods, but to identify a historical imagination, unarguably influential at a particular time, and to show how it was shared, appropriated, and transformed by legal thinkers. My technique has been to work back from the principal legal texts, to rely upon the historical imagination of legal thinkers as a guide to reconstructing the historical imagination of any given period.

2

The Creation of Times

Custom and History in the British Background

The Historical and the Customary: Two Legal Times

All over Western Europe, the political and religious upheavals of the sixteenth and seventeenth centuries compelled legal thinkers to reflect upon the temporality of law. When, where, and how had law arisen? If one could identify law's temporal origins, did that mean that law could be remade? If so, by whom? In pondering such questions, early modern legal thinkers accomplished a range of objectives. They bolstered or diminished the claims of nations, monarchs, popes, parliaments, and judges; reinforced or fractured the holism of medieval legal thought; and juggled multiple political, religious, legal, and intellectual constituencies. We can trace to their efforts the appearance of two distinct and powerful temporalities as ways of thinking about law: the historical and the customary.[1]

European countries with strong Roman law traditions appear to have been at the forefront of the emerging historical thinking about law. According to Donald Kelley, the earliest modern attempts to historicize law – which began as efforts to fit bits of law into temporal

[1] For important works on the relationship between the historical and the customary in early modern Europe, see Constantin Fasolt, *The Limits of History* (Chicago: University of Chicago Press, 2004); Donald R. Kelley, *Foundations of Modern Historical Scholarship: Language, Law and History in the French Renaissance* (New York: Columbia University Press, 1970); J. G. A. Pocock, *The Ancient Constitution and the Feudal Law: A Study of English Historical Thought in the Seventeenth Century* (Cambridge: Cambridge University Press, 1987) (1957). For an account of historical thinking in early modern Europe, see Anthony Grafton, *What Was History? The Art of History in Early Modern Europe* (Cambridge: Cambridge University Press, 2007). In this chapter, I have relied heavily upon the writings of Pocock.

context – grew out of Renaissance philology. From a deep commitment to language and rhetorical style, the fifteenth-century Italian humanist and legal scholar Lorenzo Valla sought to demonstrate how the Latin language had changed over the centuries by dating shifts in usage. In tracking linguistic and stylistic changes in Latin, and in relating such changes rigorously to legal doctrine, Valla was able to reveal the transformations that Roman law had undergone. Valla's work was part of what became a growing intellectual trend in early modern Roman law studies toward differentiating between new and old, pure and corrupt, original text and subsequent annotation. This philological-historical study of Roman law continued as the center of legal and historical studies shifted in the sixteenth century from Italy to France.

The very success of the philological-historical study of Roman law, combined with the rise of national sentiment and religious schism, appears to have driven sixteenth-century French humanist legal scholars in the opposite direction, away from Roman law and toward indigenous legal materials. French Protestant scholars such as François Hotman, hostile to Roman influences, self-consciously inaugurated the study of French customs and institutions. And this gave rise to the invigoration of a customary temporality attributed to law that was at odds with the ongoing historical ways of thinking about Roman law. Paradoxically, then, even as French humanists were fitting Roman law into historical context, they turned to custom as a way precisely of eroding the gap between new and old that they had themselves opened up through their historical techniques. J. G. A. Pocock suggests that this was a pan-European phenomenon:

> [The humanist] appeal from written to customary law is part of a fairly widespread reaction that was going on in sixteenth-century juristic thought; and one of the attractions of custom was precisely that it offered a means of escape from the divorce of past and present threatened by the criticisms of the historical school. Because Roman law was written and unchangeable, it could be subjected to grammatical analysis and proved to belong to a past state of society, but because custom was by its nature unwritten law, the usages of the folk interpreted through the mouths of judges, it could be argued with some plausibility that it could never become obsolete.[2]

In "never becom[ing] obsolete," custom came to be possessed of a nonhistorical temporality denied Roman law. It could resist, in other words, the historicization of moments of origin and change to which the Roman law was increasingly subjected.

[2] Pocock, *Ancient Constitution*, pp. 14–15.

Early modern France thus witnessed the attribution of both historical and customary temporalities to different components of its legal tradition, the Roman and the indigenous. Matters in England, a country that had never had a comparably developed Roman law tradition, would necessarily be different. There, the interplay between historical and customary temporalities would play out in fierce seventeenth-century contests between monarch and Parliament, on the one hand, and in less anguished but ongoing tussles between statutory law and judicially declared law, on the other. Ultimately, these different temporalities would account for the unique place of the common law in the English (and later American) politicolegal tradition.

This chapter is not meant to be a contribution to the historiography of British legal thought. It serves, instead, to draw attention to the profound continuities between the rhetoric of seventeenth- and eighteenth-century British common lawyers and their nineteenth-century American counterparts. It illustrates how British common lawyers skillfully combined customary and historical temporalities in their representations of the common law. Such maneuvers anticipate the ways American common lawyers would effortlessly shuttle back and forth between historical and customary temporalities during the nineteenth century.

The chapter begins with a discussion of two of the most important seventeenth-century sources of common law thought, the writings of Lord Coke and Sir Matthew Hale. The reader is urged to pay attention to the utter self-consciousness with which Coke and Hale attribute the nonhistorical temporalities of "immemoriality" and "insensibility" to the common law as they attempt to defend England's "ancient constitution" against the encroachments of the monarch, to guard the common law from legislative tampering, and to bolster the monopoly of common law judges in declaring the law. Neither Coke nor Hale was at all unaware of the possibility of thinking historically about law. The debates of the time made that impossible. Hale in particular was especially sensitive to the changeability of the common law, to its necessary correspondence to changes in society, and to the possibility of pinning down changes in the common law in historical time. Despite this acute sense of history as a way of thinking about law, however, both Coke and Hale insisted upon alternative, nonhistorical temporalities for the common law, underscoring the fact that such temporalities were temporalities imagined and constructed by common lawyers for themselves and deliberately set against other, potentially more destabilizing ways of thinking about law that would have had the effect of concentrating the authority to declare law in the hands of monarchs.

By the eighteenth century, historical thought had become a powerful mode of imbuing time with meaning, logic, and direction. Although various strands of historical thought flourished in the eighteenth century, the two most important from the perspective of late-eighteenth- and early-nineteenth-century American legal thinkers were republicanism and the philosophies of history associated with the Scottish Enlightenment.[3] In the remainder of the chapter, I discuss the writings of three prominent British eighteenth-century legal thinkers, each widely read by Americans. The first, Viscount Bolingbroke, is an exemplar of the republican thought that would animate the revolutionary generation. The second, Lord Kames, is an exemplar of the highly influential philosophy of history of the Scottish Enlightenment. The third, Sir William Blackstone, represents mid-eighteenth-century orthodox English common law thought and would be the most widely read of the three. In Blackstone's writings, we observe how the intellectual trends of the mid-eighteenth century infiltrated common law thinking. Each of these legal thinkers, as we shall see, performs a complex shuttling between the times of history and the times of law, conceiving of the common law in terms of history and simultaneously arguing that the common law effectuates history.

Common Law, History, and King in Seventeenth-Century England

"Immemoriality" as Resistance to the Sovereign: The Early-Seventeenth-Century Writings of Lord Coke

In the early seventeenth century, the English idealization of the common law was part of a pan-European effort to check the claims of increasingly powerful monarchs seeking greater directive control of polity, economy, and society. James I had argued that "kings were the authors and makers of the Lawes and not the Lawes of the kings."[4] Such a statement, insofar as it placed front and center the idea that law could be made at discrete points in time by a succession of lawful sovereigns, might itself be seen as partaking of the emerging historical sensibility of early modern Europe. A century or more of historical thinking about Roman law had taught legal thinkers

[3] As I suggest later in this chapter, a sharp distinction between republican thought and Scottish Enlightenment thought might not always be easy to maintain. I am not suggesting, of course, that various kinds of Christian eschatological thought did not continue to remain important to eighteenth-century Americans.

[4] Charles H. McIlwain, *The Political Works of James I* (Cambridge, Mass.: Harvard University Press, 1918), p. 62.

to reject the idea of law as a continuous, temporally undifferentiated fabric. If law could be broken up and set in discrete bits of time, did that not imply that it arose, and therefore could be made, in discrete bits of time?

In response, early-seventeenth-century English common law thinkers advanced a complex of ideas about the common law designed to limit the lawgiving powers of England's monarchs, to concentrate the ability to declare law in the figure of the common law judge, and to identify the common law with the people. It is important to keep in mind that early-seventeenth-century common law thought was to a large degree a gesture of resistance, an insistence on fragmenting power in light of the perceived threat of royal absolutism. For heuristic purposes only, I disaggregate the complex of early-seventeenth-century common law ideas into the following: (1) notions of legal temporality; (2) ideas about the appropriate division of roles between sovereign, legislature, and judge when it came to speaking the "reason" of the law; and (3) claims associated with the freedoms of the people and England's "ancient constitution." Within early-seventeenth-century common law discourses, there was an easy shuttling among these different ideas, each of which implied the others.

First, early-seventeenth-century English common law thinkers reworked the medieval idea that law could not be made, but only discovered and declared. Where medieval legal thinkers had argued on the basis of timeless, discoverable, universal, and rational principles, early-seventeenth-century common lawyers attributed a special nonhistorical temporality to the common law, one that saw the common law as possessed of a deeply temporal fabric even as it explicitly denied the possibility of disaggregating that temporal fabric in the way scholars of Roman law had increasingly been thinking of that body of law. According to the theory, the common law as declared by the common law judge stood not for universal principles, but for the "immemorial" customs of the English nation. "Immemoriality" implied that the English common law stretched back to a time beyond "the memory of man" or to a "time out of mind." These phrases, the "memory of man" and "time out of mind," stood for a formal legal test. There was an assigned legal cutoff date, 1189 C.E., the beginning of the reign of Richard I, such that everything *after* 1189 was deemed within the "memory of man" or on this side of "time out of mind," and hence not "immemorial."[5]

[5] Additional proof of the common law's self-representation as "immemorial custom" lies in the test articulated during the seventeenth century for judicial recognition of customs at variance with the common law. In addition to the *general* or *common* customs declared

One might assume that the idea of "immemoriality" was simply a kind of crude historical dating device, telling us where chronology might operate and where it might not. But "immemoriality" operated very differently from any historical dating device we might imagine. Early-seventeenth-century English common lawyers such as Lord Coke (1552–1634) were not unaware of history as a way of setting phenomena in chronological time and of distinguishing between old and new. Notwithstanding their knowledge of history as a technique, they refused to surrender control of the common law's temporality to non-lawyers. In other words, they invoked "immemoriality" self-consciously. The whole point was to defy the chronology that was such an important part of early modern historical and legal thought and to insist upon the extended and continuous temporal fabric of the common law. As Pocock puts it:

> Coke not only accepts a legal judgment dating a law from time out of mind as historically valid, but he regards such statements as better historical evidence than those made by chroniclers. Where the courts have adjudged an institution immemorial and a historian alleges that it was set up in such a king's reign, Coke leaves little doubt that we are to think the historian wrong, and he urges the historiographers of his own day to consult a lawyer before making any statement about the history of the law.[6]

Insofar as the temporality of "immemoriality" was self-consciously set in opposition to historical chronology, it became possible to *attribute* "immemoriality" to the common law *tout court*, without asking troublesome questions about when this or that bit of law had arisen. Regardless of when it might actually have arisen, in other words, all existing common

by the common law judge, which were simply assumed to be "immemorial," customs in England could also be local, specific to regions or trades. But practices on behalf of which litigants sought judicial recognition as local customs had to meet a set of requirements that reflected and reinforced the common law's self-understanding as "immemorial." These requirements were antiquity, continuity, certainty, and reasonableness. The requirement of antiquity was that a practice should have existed from a "time whereof memory of man runneth not to the contrary," in other words, that it should have existed "immemorially." The requirement of continuity was that a practice should have been exercised without interruption by a number of individuals, any significant interruption constituting proof that the practice had never been a custom at all. The requirement of certainty was that the practice be definite – and hence limited – in scope. Finally, the requirement of reasonableness was that the practice not fall afoul of what the common law considered reasonable. A practice would be absorbed into the wider common law only if it met these requirements. For a discussion of the test, see Andrea C. Loux, "The Persistence of the Ancient Regime: Custom, Utility, and the Common Law in the Nineteenth Century," *Cornell Law Review* 79 (1993): 183–218, at 192–195.

[6] Pocock, *Ancient Constitution*, pp. 40–41.

law was assumed to be without an original locatable act of foundation, and as such cloaked in the "immemorial."

This cloaking of the common law with "immemoriality" translated into a specific common lawyerly way of reading historical records. For example, the beginning of the records in the king's courts in the twelfth century was read not as proof that those courts had begun at that time, but rather as evidence of an older "immemorial," hence unspecifiable, origin. In the hands of common lawyers, the written record, one that historical thought might see as evidence for pinning something down in the chronological moment to which the record itself pointed, became a way of pointing to an ever more remote origin that precisely could not be pinned down and, hence, to a way of invoking a time that could not be disaggregated.

As a check on the lawmaking ability of England's monarchs, the indistinct temporality of "immemoriality" needed to rely upon more than imprecision. It had to be filled out with content. Common lawyers would argue that the temporality of "immemoriality" embodied the undifferentiated collective wisdom of multiple generations, reaching far back into the past and stretching far out into the future. This ability of the common law to embody a multigenerational wisdom is what placed it beyond the reach of monarchs. An important aspect of the claim was that past and future generations were simultaneously present in each pronouncement of the common law judge. By contrast, acts of the monarch were mere specks of time, temporally delimited acts of individual human will or reflection. In his discussion of Coke, Pocock puts it as follows:

> The law which the judges declare is unwritten and immemorial.... It embodies the wisdom of generations, as a result not of philosophical reflexion but of the accumulations and refinements of experience.... [W]hat speaks through the judge is the distilled knowledge of many generations of men, each decision based on the experience of those before and tested by the experience of those after, and it is wiser than any individual – even James I – can possibly be.[7]

Thus, "immemoriality" was a specific way of embracing the weight of the past to limit the possibilities open to the monarch in the present.

Second, and following from the preceding discussion, ideas about the "immemoriality" of the common law, and the allied claim that the common law embodied the undifferentiated collective wisdom of multiple generations, translated into arguments about who was best suited to declare the common law. Even as the common law was placed

[7] Ibid., p. 35.

beyond the reach of the monarch, common law thinkers argued that only the common law judge was possessed of the necessary qualifications to declare what they called the "reason" of the common law. The resistance to monarchical power was, therefore, an assertion of judicial power.

"Reason" in early-seventeenth-century common lawyers' rendering was in a very important sense indistinguishable from the undifferentiated collective wisdom of bygone generations, the distilled learning of a diffuse past that gave the time of "immemoriality" its content. In early-seventeenth-century common law thought, only the common law judge was possessed of the special ability to declare "immemorial" customs, to produce a continuous legal fabric effortlessly binding past, present, and future, to embody the wisdom of past generations, and hence to speak "reason." All others lacked the necessary knowledge and the requisite solicitude for the past and concern for the future. It is in this sense that Coke famously described the common law as being possessed of an "artificiall perfection of reason," something inaccessible to the untrained non-lawyer, who possessed only the "naturall reason" available to every man. As Coke put it:

> [R]eason is the life of the law, nay the common law itselfe is nothing else but reason; which is to be understood of an artificiall perfection of reason, gotten by long study, observation, and of experience, and not of every man's naturall reason.... This legall reason *est summa ratio*.[8]

As such, the common law judge's arrogation of the right to declare law was a claim not only against monarchical encroachment, but also against legislative tampering. Common law thinkers frequently criticized the lawgiving efforts of non-common lawyers. The preface to Coke's *Fourth Reports*, for example, lists many statutes that have injudiciously altered the common law and hence have been subsequently repealed, a complaint that would be heard repeatedly in later centuries. Coke's well-known opinion in *Bonham's Case* (1610), although it established only the narrow proposition that common law courts could not remedy the statutory monopoly of the London College of Physicians, even suggested that the common law might limit the reach of statutes. According to Coke, "[W]hen an Act of Parliament is against common right and reason, or

[8] Sir Edward Coke, *The First Part of the Institutes of the Laws of England; or A Commentary Upon Littleton* (2 vols.) (reprint of the 1832 ed.; J. & W. T. Clark, London) (New York: Garland, 1979), Vol. 1, L.2.C.6 Sec. 138.

repugnant, or impossible to be performed, the common law will controul it, and adjudge such Act to be void."[9]

Finally, if the common law was possessed of "immemoriality" and rendered the special preserve of the common law judge who possessed "artificiall perfection of reason," it was also invested with the ability to embody the unique and precious freedoms of Englishmen. In this regard, the common law could simultaneously operate at distinct levels or scales, ranging from an unmediated reflection of the day-to-day practices of the people to an instantiation of the political practices of the people in the form of the "ancient constitution" of the English. The association of the common law with the freedoms of Englishmen implied two things: first, that the common law was ultimately a self-given law rather than one imposed from above; and second, that the freedoms of Englishmen as embodied in this self-given law were temporally continuous, knitting past, present, and future together, freedoms of inheritance rather than of precipitate creation or abstract reflection. Monarchical and even legislative assertions of power, imposed from above, could thus be construed as attempts to rend the essential continuity, and hence the inherited freedom, of the people.[10]

We see the common law powerfully associated with popular freedom in early-seventeenth-century texts. For example, in his *Irish Reports* dedicated to Lord Chancellor Ellesmere in 1612, Sir John Davies, then attorney general for Ireland, put it thus:

> For the *Common Law of England* is nothing else but the *Common Custome* of the Realm: and a Custome which hath obtained the force of a Law is always said to be *jus non scriptum*: for it cannot be made or created either by Charter, or by Parliament, which are Acts reduced to writing, and are alwaies matter of Record; but being onely matter of fact, and consisting in use and practice, it can be recorded and registered no-where but in the memory of the people.
>
> For a Custome taketh beginning and groweth to perfection in this manner: When a reasonable act once done is found to be good and beneficiall to the people, and agreeable to their nature and disposition, then do they use it and practise it again and again, and so by often iteration and multiplication of the act it becometh a *Custome*; and being continued without interruption time out of mind, it obtaineth the force of a *Law*.

[9] *Bonham's Case*, 77 Eng. Rep. 646, 652 (C.P., 1610).

[10] As Coke put it in the preface to his *Report*, the "ancient and excellent laws of England are the birthright, and the most ancient and best inheritance that the subjects of this realm have, for by them he enjoyeth not only his inheritance and goods in peace and quietness, but his life and his most dear country in safety." Sir Edward Coke, *The Reports of Sir Edward Coke, Knt* (6 vols.) (London, 1777 ed.), Vol. 3, Pt. 5, Preface, p. iii.

> And this *Customary Law* is the most perfect and most excellent, and without comparison the best, to make and preserve a Commonwealth. For the *written Laws* which are made either by the Edicts of Princes, or by Councils of Estates, are imposed upon the Subject before any Triall or Probation made, whether the same be fit and agreeable to the nature and disposition of the people, or whether they will breed any inconvenience or no. But a *Custome* doth never become a Law to bind the people, until it hath been tried and approved time out of mind, during all which time there did thereby arise no inconvenience: for if it had been found inconvenient at any time, it had been used no longer, but had been interrupted, and consequently it had lost the virtue and force of a Law.[11]

As already mentioned, the mere existence in the present of a "use or practice" was sufficient for common lawyers to attribute to it the temporality of "immemoriality." But Davies's paean to the common law reveals that it was possible to attribute even more. The claim that the common law arose spontaneously from the people by dint of repetition made it possible to argue, without the need to offer any special evidence, that the common law was undergirded by popular consent and that it was supremely well suited to the people because every "inconvenience" had been ironed out in the mythic time of "immemoriality." Once these arguments were in place, it was possible to conclude that the common law was freer and less oppressive than any law generated by a monarch or legislature, which Davies tells us are "imposed upon the Subject, before any Triall or Probation made, whether the same be fit and agreeable to the nature and disposition of the people, or whether they will breed any inconvenience or no."

In its claim to embody what Davies called the "use and practice" of the people, the common law was also projected onto a much wider screen, that of the "ancient constitution" of England. Coke himself was an important defender of the rights of the Commons as part of England's "ancient constitution." To the extent that the temporality of "immemoriality" implied a continuous temporal fabric, one that resisted identifiable breaks and founding moments, the Norman Conquest of 1066 had to be shown to be more or less irrelevant. Coke thus insisted, as the Normans had themselves insisted, that all the laws and institutions introduced by the Normans either were only continuations of the laws of Edward the Confessor or had been otherwise prefigured in pre-Conquest law. For

[11] Unpaginated preface dedicatory to *Irish Reports (Les Reports des Cases & Matters en Ley, Resolves & Adjudges en les Courts del Roy en Ireland. Collect & digest per Sir John Davis Chivaler, Atturney Generall del Roy en cest Realm)* (London: E. Flesher, J. Steater & H. Twyford, 1674).

Coke, Latin charters referring to juries, sheriffs, Chancery, and escheat for treason "prove that the common law of England had been time out of minde of man before the Conquest, and was not altered or changed by the Conqueror."[12] In his 1610 history of "our *English Brittish* Law," the jurist and parliamentarian John Selden wrote that the Norman conqueror "bestow[ed] upon the yielding conquered Nation the requital of their ancient Law."[13] In Coke's hands, such interpretations easily became an assertion of complete identity over time. Thus, he could argue that "the grounds of our common laws at this day were beyond the memory or register of any beginning, and the same the Norman conqueror then found within this realm of England."[14]

But intense seventeenth-century debates about the historical origins of the House of Commons would soon make it difficult to make such assertions about the complete identity of the common law over time. The writings of Sir Matthew Hale reveal how common law thinkers in the later seventeenth century came to terms with such challenges.

"Immemoriality" and "Insensibility" in the Writings of Sir Matthew Hale: Common Law Responses to Seventeenth-Century Historical and Positivist Thought

As part of England's seventeenth-century constitutional crisis, there arose a range of challenges to the idea of the "ancient constitution." Many of these involved the fixing of the temporal origins of Parliament. Through the efforts of antiquaries such as Sir Henry Spelman, feudalism was beginning to be conceived of as a distinct historical phenomenon. The result was a growing sense of difference between pre- and post-Conquest politicolegal structures, which pushed thinkers to conceive of law in historical time. Spelman shattered the idea of an ancient Parliament with the Commons "immemorially" represented. Instead, he argued that Parliament had begun as a supreme curia, a council to the king, in which only the king's chief vassals had been permitted to participate. Those who had attended Parliament had done so, in other words, by virtue of duties toward their lord. The Commons had come into existence only at a much

[12] Sir Edward Coke, *The Reports of Sir Edward Coke, Knt* (London: Joseph Butterworth & Sons, 1826) (1602), Vol. 2, Pt. 3, Preface, p. xiii.

[13] John Selden, Preface to *Jani Anglorum Facies Altera* (London: Thomas Basset & Richard Chiswell, 1682) (1610).

[14] Sir Edward Coke, *Reports of Sir Edward Coke, Knt* (London: Joseph Butterworth & Sons, 1826), Vol. 4, Pt. 8, Preface, p. iv.

later date as lesser tenants evolved into freeholders through a commutation of their feudal obligations. The conclusion was that Parliament was not "immemorial" and had not always included commoners.

Although written in the 1620s, Spelman's works were not published until the 1660s and 1670s. Ideas of the "ancient constitution" continued relatively unchallenged, therefore, until the Exclusion Crisis of 1679, at which point the debate over feudal history acquired an explicitly partisan cast. The Tory medievalist Sir William Dugdale commenced the party controversy in the 1670s and 1680s by claiming that the House of Commons was little older than the reign of Henry III. Not surprisingly, Dugdale's Whig opponents responded by reasserting the "immemoriality" of the Commons. In his *Ancient Rights of the Commons of England Asserted* (1680), the Whig William Petyt answered Dugdale with the proposition that the Saxon parliamentary institution of Witenagemot, with commoners represented, had persisted throughout the Middle Ages. The Norman Conquest had represented no serious disruption. Whig texts were in turn answered in the early 1680s by Dr. Robert Brady, who marshaled Spelman's findings into the service of the royalist cause. Brady's arguments were similar to Spelman's, denying the Whig claim that a class of Anglo-Saxon freeholders had survived the Conquest and attributing English politicolegal arrangements to the Conquest and its legacy. Parliament had grown, Brady contended, out of the king's feudal council. Like Spelman, he suggested the emergence of the Commons out of lesser tenants. Magna Carta, a keystone in the Whig understanding of the "ancient constitution," had represented only a demand for the relaxation of feudal services and the implementation of feudal privileges. As such, it had stood for no appeal to any older, pre-feudal law. Brady's history was advanced explicitly to "teach the people loyalty and obedience and frustrate the designs of the seditious."[15]

Although the royalist cause of Dugdale, Brady, Filmer, and others was defeated in 1688, the politicolegal crises of the mid-seventeenth century gave rise to a series of important theoretical meditations on law and its temporality. Some of these shared Tory historical sensibilities, even as they advanced general ideas that extended to the common law as a whole. Perhaps the most famous explicit meditation on common law thinking was Thomas Hobbes's (1588–1679) *A Dialogue Between a Philosopher and a Student of the Common Laws of England*, first published in 1681, although the exact date of its composition is a matter

[15] Quoted in Pocock, *Ancient Constitution*, p. 194.

of speculation.[16] Staged as an exchange between a "Philosopher" and a "Lawyer," the *Dialogue* takes up themes familiar from Hobbes's better-known works, *Leviathan* and *Behemoth*.

Alarmed by the splintering of community that had attended the English Civil War and Revolution, Hobbes sought to fix law in the authority of the king, an authority that was not only grounded in, but also limited by, universally valid, general, and timeless precepts of reason and laws of nature. The mere antiquity of any human arrangement was powerless against such precepts or laws. As Hobbes put it, "[W]hatsoever is against reason, though it be reiterated never so often, or that there be never so many precedents thereof, is still against reason, and therefore not a law of nature, but contrary to it."[17] Not surprisingly, Hobbes was utterly dismissive of the common law's claim to rest its authority on an "immemorial" custom that embodied an "artificiall perfection of reason." Reason was natural, the possession of every man. Far from being associated with antiquity, natural reason acted as a check on common law arrangements hallowed by antiquity:

> Now as to the Authority you ascribe to Custome, I deny that any Custome of its own Nature, can amount to the Authority of a Law: For if the Custome be unreasonable, you must with all other Lawyers confess that it is no Law, but ought to be abolished; and if the Custom be reasonable, it is not the Custom, but the Equity that makes it Law. For what need is there to make Reason Law by any Custom how long soever when the Law of Reason is Eternal?[18]

Ultimately, for Hobbes, it was the king who decided in the present who should be judge and which customs should be picked up for recognition and which discarded. To the extent that multiple generations spoke in the law, these were generations represented by kings, each speaking, as it were, in the present, unfettered by solicitude for the common law's "immemoriality."

The impact of these various historical and positivist intellectual challenges to common law thought might be discerned in the reformulation of common law theory in the late seventeenth century. As an exemplar of common law thought that absorbs and responds to these challenges, I turn to Sir Matthew Hale's (1609–1676) *History of the Common Law of*

[16] Thomas Hobbes, *A Dialogue Between a Philosopher and a Student of the Common Laws of England* (Joseph Cropsey, ed.) (Chicago: University of Chicago Press, 1971) (1681).

[17] Thomas Hobbes, *The Elements of Law, Natural and Politic* (Ferdinand Tönnies, ed.) (Cambridge: Cambridge University Press, 1928) (1650), Pt. I, Ch. 4, Sec. 11.

[18] Hobbes, *Dialogue*, pp. 96–97.

England, a text that Sir William Holdsworth called "the ablest introductory sketch of a history of English law that appeared till the publication of Pollock and Maitland's volumes in 1895."[19] As chief justice of the King's Bench, Hale upheld the common law throughout the Protectorate. In Hale's writings, one remarks, to an extent unrecognizable in the writings of Coke, not only a self-conscious mingling of the distinction between custom and statute, law generated on the basis of repetition and law generated as a product of sovereign will, but also an acute sense of the changeability and historicity of the common law. We also discern, however, the appearance of rhetorical strategies through which the nonhistorical temporality of the common law is reaffirmed even as the common law is historicized.

At the very outset of the *History*, Hale distinguishes between *lex scripta*, the written law (statutes), and *lex non scripta* (unwritten law or common law). The point of the distinction is not that the former, as distinguished from the latter, is expressed in writing, but rather that, when it comes to the *lex non scripta*, the laws "have not their Original in Writing; for [they] have obtain'd their Force by immemorial Usage or Custom."[20] From this rendering, one might surmise that statutes, insofar as they are originally written, are locatable in chronological time, whereas the common law, insofar as it rests upon "immemorial Usage or Custom," is not so locatable. However, Hale promptly offers us a series of deconstructions of the distinction between statute and common law.

According to Hale, some statutes – which by his definition originally exist in writing – nevertheless form part of *lex non scripta* because they were made "before Time of Memory." The "Time of Memory," as stated earlier, is established in terms of the cutoff date of the beginning of the reign of Richard I. Thus, Hale continues:

[19] Hale's *History of the Common Law of England* was printed three times (1713, 1716, and 1739). I have consulted a reprint of the 1713 edition. Sir Matthew Hale, *The History and Analysis of the Common Law of England* (Union, N.J.: Lawbook Exchange, 2000). The quote from Holdsworth comes from John Clive's preface to the 1971 reprint of the third edition, Sir Matthew Hale, *The History of the Common Law of England* (Charles M. Gray, ed.) (Chicago: University of Chicago Press, 1971), p. ix.

Hale wrote an undated response to Hobbes's *Dialogue*. See "Reflections by the Lrd. Cheife Justice Hale on Mr. Hobbes His Dialogue of the Lawe," reproduced in W. S. Holdsworth, *A History of English Law* (9 vols.) (London: Methuen, 1973), Vol. 5, pp. 500–513. The arguments in Hale's response to Hobbes are better articulated in the *History of the Common Law*.

[20] Hale, *History of the Common Law*, p. 3.

And therefore it is, that those Statutes or Acts of Parliament that were made before the Beginning of the Reign of King Richard I. and have not since been repealed or altered, either by contrary Usage, or by subsequent Acts of Parliament, are now accounted Part of the *Lex non Scripta*, being as it were incorporated thereinto, and become a Part of the Common Law; and in Truth, such Statutes are not now pleadable as Acts of Parliament, (*because what is before Time of Memory is supposed without a Beginning, or at least such a Beginning as the Law Takes Notice of*) but they obtain their Strength by meer immemorial Usage or Custom [emphasis added].[21]

In this paragraph, Hale tells us that the distinction between *lex scripta* and *lex non scripta*, statute and custom, rests not only on a definitional difference (having or not having an original source in writing), but also on whether they fall on one side or another of a clean legal dividing line, the year 1189. That legal dividing line itself has no particular relationship with whether one can *actually* locate a law's chronological beginnings. The point is rather whether something does or does not have "such a Beginning *as the Law Takes Notice of*." Thus, if some statutes, despite being chronologically locatable acts of writing, were promulgated before 1189, they will nevertheless be treated as if they have no locatable chronological beginning. We see clearly that "immemoriality" is simply a time given by the common law to itself.

However, striking a distinctly Hobbesian note, Hale goes further. He observes that large areas of the common law might actually have emerged from statute, that is, from acts of sovereign will rather than spontaneously from the people: "And doubtless, many of those Things that now obtain as Common Law, had their Original by Parliamentary Acts or Constitutions, made in Writing by the King, Lords and Commons."[22] One might expect this to be true of statutes promulgated before 1189. However, this observation is extended even to those statutes promulgated *after* 1189, that is, those from the reigns of Henry III, Edward I, and Edward II. Some of the statutes from these reigns were made to affirm existing common law doctrines. In other words, custom underlies acts of sovereign will, which merely reflect it. However, Hale argues, others "made a Change in the Common Law," but were so ancient "that they now seem to have been as it were a part of the Common Law."[23] The effect is to deconstruct the division between law as custom and law as sovereign will yet again.

[21] Ibid., p. 4.
[22] Ibid.
[23] Ibid., p. 7.

Hale also reveals himself to be acutely conscious of the fact the common law has changed at a greater or lesser pace in different periods or, in other words, that various aspects of it can be pinned down in historical time. For example, describing legal developments in the reign of Edward I, Hale describes "the great Advance and Alteration of the Laws of England in the King's Reign, over what they were in the Time of his Predecessors."[24] Hale attributes changes in the common law not only to those statutes passed during the reign of which there are records, but also to "considerable Alterations and Amendments made by those [statutes] that are not extant, which possibly may be the real, tho' sudden Means" of the change."[25]

Notwithstanding an acute sense of the complex relationship between statute and custom, a sense of the constructedness of the temporality of "immemoriality," and a sense of the changeability and historicity of the common law, Hale continues to adhere to the myth of the common law as a self-given law that acquires force through repetition. He insists throughout the *History* that "the formal and obliging Force and Power [of the Common Law] grows by long Custom and Use."[26] There is no effective distinction to be made, in other words, between the common law and the people. Thus, the common law "is not only a very just and excellent Law in itself, but it is singularly accommodated to the Frame of the *English* Government, and to the Disposition of the *English* Nation, and such as by a long Experience and Use is as it were incorporated into their very Temperament, and, in a Manner, become the Complection and Constitution of the English Commonwealth."[27] How does Hale secure his sense of the common law as an unbroken temporal fabric emerging through repetition notwithstanding his acute sense of the changeability and historicity of the common law, the fact that it might actually be a creature of statute as much as the product of repetition?

Hale relies, I suggest, on a crucial analogue to the temporality of "immemoriality," the temporality of "insensibility." Unlike Coke, Hale admits freely that the common law – and, as we shall see, the "ancient constitution" – has changed and will change. This is part of his claim

[24] Ibid., p. 8. Later, describing the reign of Edward I, Hale says, "Yet the Laws did never in any one Age receive so great and sudden an Advancement, nay, I think I may safely say, all the Ages since his Time have not done so much in Reference to the orderly settling and establishing of the distributive Justice of this Kingdom, as he did within a short Compass of the thirty-five Years of his Reign, especially about the first thirteen Years thereof" (p. 101).

[25] Ibid., p. 8.

[26] Ibid., p. 17.

[27] Ibid., p. 30 (emphasis added).

about its essential fitness to the condition of the people, which he recognizes as changing. But, for Hale, common law change is so "insensible" – so difficult to grasp in the moment – as to restore a sense of the common law's essential continuity and its resistance to historical specification:

From the Nature of Laws themselves in general, which being to be accommodated to the Conditions, Exigencies and Conveniencies of the People, for or by whom they are appointed, as those Exigencies and Conveniencies do *insensibly* grow upon the People, so many Times there grows *insensibly* a Variation of the Laws, especially in a long Tract of Time; and hence it is, that tho' for the Purpose of in some particular Part of the Common Law of England, we may easily say, That the Common Law, as it is now taken, is otherwise than it was in that particular Part or Point in the Time of Hen. 2. when Glanville wrote, or than it was in the time of Hen. 3. when Bracton wrote, yet it is not possible to assign the certain Time when the Change began; nor have we all the Monuments or Memorials, either of Acts of Parliament, or of Judicial Resolutions, which might induce or occasion such Alterations; for we have no authentick Records of any Acts of Parliament before 9 Hen. 3 [emphasis added].[28]

It might appear as if it is the absence of "authentick Records" or "Monuments or Memorials" that makes it necessary to insist upon the "insensibility" of the common law's changeability. However, it turns out that the common law's "insensible" changing is not so much a consequence of a lack of supporting documents as an assertion about how the common law changes in general – in short, about its method. It is the gradual and partial nature of its changes, a step-by-step process in which identity and difference are collapsed, more than the absence of records, that makes it meaningful to describe the changeability of the common law as "insensible." Thus, Hale continues in a well-known passage:

But tho' those particular Variations and Accessions have happened in the Laws, yet *they being only partial and successive*, we may with just Reason say, They are the same English Laws now, that they were 600 Years since in the general. As the Argonauts Ship was the same when it returned home, as it was when it went out, tho' in that long Voyage it had successive Amendments, and scarce came back with any of its former Materials; and as Titius is the same Man he was 40 Years since, tho' Physicians tells us, That in a Tract of seven Years, the Body has scarce any of the same Material Substance it had before.[29]

"Insensibility" does the critical work, then, of recognizing difference and change and yet insisting on identity and continuity. After the challenge of

[28] Ibid., pp. 39–40.
[29] Ibid., p. 40.

historical thought to the orotund common law pretensions to "immemoriality," "insensibility" allows the common law to be always different from itself and yet always the same.[30] Hale has thus recognized the significance of chronology (as is apparent from his deconstruction of the difference between common law and statute), but has nevertheless transcended it.

Hale's use of the temporality of "insensibility" is apparent when he deals with the highly politicized question of the impact of the Norman Conquest. Like many common law thinkers committed to the idea of the common law as an essentially unbroken continuity synonymous with the freedoms of Englishmen, Hale was at pains to "wipe off that false Imputation upon our Laws, as if they were the Fruit or Effect of a Conquest, or Carried in them the Badge of Servitude to the Will of the Conqueror, which Notion some ignorant and prejudiced Persons have entertain'd."[31] What ensued was a whole range of arguments aimed at limiting the scope of the Norman Conquest to the legal acquisition of the Crown and eliminating the possibility that it involved a conquest of the people. Nevertheless, in keeping with the historicizations of feudalism and the Conquest swirling around him, Hale argues that the Norman Conquest "might easily have a great influence upon the Laws of this Kingdom." This argument is, however, instantly undermined. This "great influence" of the Conquest is rendered "insensible," impossible of easy identification. Thus, the Norman Conquest is characterized as having "*secretly and insensibly* introduce[d] *New* Laws, Customs, and Usages" into England, with the overall effect being one akin to the intermingling of rivers.[32] At the same time, Hale describes a mutual exchange of customs and people between England and Normandy that took place so "insensibly" that the identities of people and laws became blurred.[33]

As we leave the seventeenth century for the eighteenth, we might draw some general conclusions about the state of common law thinking. Early-seventeenth-century common law thinkers such as Coke were

[30] Hale resorts to corporal metaphors to account for the common law's gradual ironing out of inconveniences: "Insomuch, that even as in the natural Body the due Temperament and Constitution does by Degrees work out those accidental Diseases which sometimes happen, and do reduce the Body to its just State and Constitution, so when at any Time through the Errors, Distempers or Iniquities of Men or Times, the Peace of the Kingdom, and right Order of Government have received Interruption, the Common Law has wasted and wrought out those Distempers, and reduced the Kingdom to its just State and Temperament, as our present (and former) Times can easily witness." Ibid., p. 30.

[31] Ibid., p. 48.

[32] Ibid., p. 42 (emphasis added).

[33] Ibid., p. 72.

well aware of historical ways of conceiving of law, but nevertheless insisted upon nonhistorical ways of doing so as strategies of resisting England's monarchs and staving off legislative tampering. Over the course of the seventeenth century, however, positivist and historicist thinking compelled recognition and made it much harder to insist upon the common law's unbroken continuity over time. This was especially true when the common law was identified with the "ancient constitution." However, these intellectual developments did not mean that the essential contours of common law thought were abandoned. In the later seventeenth century, as illustrated in the writings of Sir Matthew Hale, the formal legal concept of "immemoriality" was openly recognized as a legal construct, the distinction between statute and common law blurred, and the historicity and changeability of the common law acknowledged. Yet the essential ideas associated with the common law survived. An addition to common law theory that was critical to this survival was Hale's conception of the "insensible" changing of the common law, the temporality of its method, rather than of its substance. The essentially ungraspable nature of the way the common law changed in time – "insensibility" – made it possible to insist upon continuity even as one recognized changeability. If Coke's common law had been possessed of identity over time as a matter of assertion, Hale's common law, equally as a matter of assertion, recognized difference, but subsumed it into identity.

Common Law Thought and the Historical Imagination in Eighteenth-Century Great Britain: Three Legal Thinkers

Over the half-century following the Glorious Revolution of 1688, change in Great Britain was nothing short of dramatic. At the level of constitutional structure, there was the rise to prominence of Parliament, the Act of Settlement (1701), and the Act of Union (1707). The threat of royal absolutism that had driven common law thinkers such as Coke had largely dissipated. At the same time, there was considerable growth in Great Britain's commercial, military, and imperial power. As commerce developed within Britain and across its empire, land ceased to be the sole source of power and wealth. There was increasing pressure to render economic resources, including land, the subject of market transactions.

These transformations brought about intense historical reflection on relationships among Britain's past, present, and future. Unlike many of their seventeenth-century counterparts, eighteenth-century British thinkers moved beyond chronology as a technique of situating – and hence questioning – existing politicolegal arrangements. They increasingly thought of history as something imbued with logic, meaning, and directionality (it is no accident that the term "philosophy of history," coined by Voltaire, comes to us from the eighteenth century). Armed with a historical perspective, such thinkers sought to judge existing politicolegal arrangements in terms of history, identifying certain aspects of such arrangements as belonging to a superseded past and others as heralding an imagined future.

Feudalism and commerce played a crucial role in eighteenth-century philosophies of history. Feudalism, something that seventeenth-century antiquaries had begun to recognize as a historical epoch, was now universally acknowledged to be a distinct part of Europe's past, albeit one that continued to cast its troublesome shadow on the present, most notably in a law of real property that hindered the free alienability of land. Feudalism's legacy was thus widely seen as standing in the way of the development of commerce. But the commercial was itself seen as beset with dangers: corruption, the besmirchment of citizenship, the tarnishing of liberty. From the perspective of eighteenth-century British legal thinkers, convinced as they were of the common law's roots in feudalism, there were also difficult questions about how to bridge the gap between the feudal and the commercial.

Each of the three thinkers explored here – Bolingbroke, Kames, and Blackstone – offers a distinct approach to questions of feudalism and commerce, to the relationships among the past, present, and future. All three recognize feudalism as a superseded historical epoch. The common law legacy, at the level of the "ancient constitution" and legal doctrine, must be understood in terms of the new epoch that they are living through. But Bolingbroke, Kames, and Blackstone have different perspectives on the rise of the commercial. The republican polemicist Bolingbroke sees the commercial, at least insofar as it is intertwined with the corruption and faction of the early-eighteenth-century Walpole ministry, as jeopardizing the liberties embodied in England's "ancient constitution." Thoroughly in the grip of Scottish historical thought, Kames embraces the shift from feudal to commercial. He is committed to excising all traces of feudal land law and to ushering in the commercial. An orthodox and conservative common lawyer, Blackstone recognizes the advent of the commercial with less anguish than Bolingbroke, but also with much less ardor than Kames. But he is unwilling to consign

England's feudal past, as Kames might be, to the dustbin of history. Even as Blackstone recognizes the advent of the commercial, his world is a world dense with overlapping, plural, "immemorial" customs and conventional rights.

In the different attempts of these thinkers to think historically about law, we notice something else. Even as the common law is subjected to history, it is represented as the motor of history. For Bolingbroke, if history is driven by the struggle between the "spirit" of liberty and the "spirit" of faction, the "ancient constitution" of the English *is* the "spirit" of liberty, even though Europe is understood to be in a historical epoch very different from its predecessors. For Kames, it is the judge, not the legislature, who is to bring about the shift from feudal to commercial. Even as he derides the English for their conservatism and past orientation, he admires the incremental nature of common law change. Blackstone goes even further, celebrating the hard work of the common law judge in conjuring fictions that bridge the gap between England's feudal past and its eighteenth-century present. The hard work of the common law judge, Blackstone argues, allows the Englishman to enjoy a law that fits his present even as he experiences his past as utterly continuous. This is, of course, nothing other than the temporality of common law "insensibility," put to work for the eighteenth century.

Republicanism, Feudalism, Commerce, and the "Ancient Constitution": The Writings of Bolingbroke

In *The Machiavellian Moment* (1975), J. G. A. Pocock offers a masterful account of the neo-Machiavellian ideas that eighteenth-century British opposition thinkers employed to make sense of the legal, political, and economic transformations under way around them. Itself in part a response to the political and economic corruption associated with the rise of commerce, eighteenth-century British republican thought imagined history in terms of the following: the decline and regeneration of republican polities through an abandonment of, or a return to, fundamental principles; the need to maintain a balanced government; the struggle between virtue and corruption; the contrast between liberty and faction; the contest between Court and Country parties; the controversy over standing armies; and so on.[34] Taking this rich account as a point of departure, I attempt here to draw attention to an influential

[34] Pocock, *The Machiavellian Moment*.

strand of Augustan historical thought often seen as a simple extension of seventeenth-century common law thinking on the subject of England's "ancient constitution." I focus on the writings of the Tory polemicist Henry St. John, Viscount Bolingbroke (1678–1751). Even though he was a Tory, Bolingbroke would be claimed by writers in the Whig tradition. As Isaac Kramnick has observed, what is unique about the conflict between the Tory Bolingbroke and the Whig Walpole is that "the champion of the Tory opposition ... wrapped himself in the noble flag of Whiggery and covered the Whig Walpole with the ignominious standard of Toryism." "In their attitudes to English history," Kramnick argues, "Bolingbroke was the true disciple of Coke and Sydney while Walpole was the follower of the Royalist Tory Dr. Robert Brady."[35]

In the political and economic restructuring that followed 1688, fears and threats that virtue would be overwhelmed by corruption seemed greater than ever. While the formal post-1688 constitutional structure remained in place, the rise of commerce, the extreme corruption of the Walpole ministry, and what was perceived as the *sub rosa* increase in the power of the Crown made it important to delve *beneath* the surface of laws to get to the truth of things. For Bolingbroke, this was done through the idea of "spirit." Accordingly, he distinguished sharply between actually existing law and the "spirit" underlying law. The actually existing formal legal structure could not give itself its own meaning. That meaning must come from "spirit" alone. "Spirit" would serve, in other words, as the basis for judging existing politicolegal arrangements, including Britain's eighteenth-century common law constitution.

The long sweep of history, for Bolingbroke, was a dance between the antagonistic "spirits" of liberty and faction. This was a Manichaean struggle. As Bolingbroke put it in his "Remarks on the History of England" (1730), "[I]t will remain eternally true, that the spirit of liberty and the spirit of faction are not only different, but repugnant and incompatible: so that the life of either is the death of the other."[36] Accordingly, Bolingbroke marches through the reigns of various monarchs, endorsing one and condemning the other, depending on how favorably disposed

[35] Isaac Kramnick, "Augustan Politics and English Historiography: The Debate on the English Past, 1730–35," *History and Theory* 6, No. 1 (1967): 33–56, at 33–34. The secondary literature on Bolingbroke is vast. The reader is referred to David Armitage's excellent bibliographic essay in Bolingbroke, *Political Writings* (David Armitage, ed.) (Cambridge: Cambridge University Press, 1997).

[36] Bolingbroke, *Remarks on the History of England*, Letter 2, in *Historical Writings* (Isaac Kramnick, ed.) (Chicago: University of Chicago Press, 1972), p. 167.

they were to the "spirit" of liberty.[37] The "spirit" of liberty had won in 1688: "[O]ur ancestors, by keeping this spirit alive and warm, regained [by 1688] all the advantages of a free government, though a foreign invasion had destroyed them, in great measure, and had imposed a very tyrannical yoke on the nation."[38] But the dangers attending the rise of commerce had reinvigorated the "spirit" of faction all over again.

Even though it was possible to thematize history as a struggle between the antagonistic "spirits" of liberty and faction, the difficulty was that it was not easy, especially in Bolingbroke's own day, when the constitutional structure of 1688 remained intact, to distinguish between them. Thus Bolingbroke could write, "[V]irtue and vice are too often confounded, and what belongs to one is ascribed to the other."[39] This was because faction too often treacherously assumed the garb of liberty.[40] The *sub rosa* increase in the power of the Crown and the rise of corruption following the Glorious Revolution, even though it left the formal constitutional structure intact, "bring[s] our liberties, by a natural and necessary progression, into *more real, though less apparent danger*, than they were in before the revolution."[41]

Scholars have long noted a contradiction in Bolingbroke's thought.[42] And it is to this contradiction that I turn. On the one hand, Bolingbroke participated actively in a debate with the Walpole press over England's "ancient constitution." This debate, Isaac Kramnick has suggested, was a reprise of the late-seventeenth-century debate about the origins of Parliament. The debate was played out actively, with Bolingbroke's *Craftsman* adopting the Whig interpretation and the Walpole press advancing the Tory one.[43] At times, in his writings on the "ancient constitution," Bolingbroke strikes a distinctly common lawyerly note. England's

[37] For example, in *Remarks on the History of England*, we are told of the reign of Henry IV: "A spirit of liberty breathes in the laws of this glorious king; and the power and duty of parliaments are set forth, in some of them, with such terms as would never have been passed by a prince who had put the least pedantry, or the least foppery, into his notions of kingship" (Letter 5, p. 183).

[38] Ibid.," Letter 4, p. 181.

[39] Bolingbroke, *Letters on the Study and Use of History*, Letter 2, in *Historical Writings*, p. 16.

[40] Bolingbroke, *Remarks on the History of England*, Letter 2, p. 169. Elsewhere, Bolingbroke writes, "These men insinuate themselves as friends to liberty ... and yet they are almost wholly employed in promoting that which is destructive of liberty, and inconsistent with it, corruption and dependency." Ibid., Letter 7, p. 200.

[41] Bolingbroke, *Letters on the Study and Use of History*, Letter 2, p. 20 (emphasis added).

[42] For a discussion of this contradiction and of Bolingbroke's historical skepticism, see Isaac Kramnick, "Editor's Introduction," in *Historical Writings*.

[43] For an account of this debate, see Kramnick, "Augustan Politics and English Historiography," pp. 40–46.

"ancient constitution" appears "immemorial," seems to be possessed of identity over time. Thus, Bolingbroke states that the Saxon heterotoges, or "public generals," who conquered Britain became kings, "but the supreme power centered in the micklemote, or wittagenmote, composed of the king, the lords, and the Saxon freemen, that original sketch of a British parliament."[44] He continues, "The rights of the people in those days, must have been carried to a very great height.... The principles of the Saxon commonwealth were therefore very democratical; and these principles prevailed through all subsequent changes."[45] At other points, sounding rather more like Sir Matthew Hale, he describes the "ancient constitution" as one built up by slow accretions over time, in the manner of the common law generally: "Thus was the present constitution of our government forming itself for about two centuries and a half; a rough building raised out of the demolitions which the Normans had made, and upon the solid foundations laid by the Saxons."[46]

On the other hand, Bolingbroke also operates with a sharp sense of historical period, one that is utterly at odds with seventeenth-century understandings of the "ancient constitution" and its identity over time. In the *Letters on the Study and Use of History*, Bolingbroke devotes considerable attention to describing what we might recognize as a historical period:

> A new situation, different from the former, begets new interests in the same proportion of difference; not in this or that particular state alone, but in all those that are concerned by vicinity or other relations, as I said just now, in one general system of policy. New interests beget new maxims of government, and new methods of conduct. These, in their turns, beget new manners, new habits, new customs. The longer this new constitution of affairs continues, the more will this difference increase: and although some analogy may remain long between what preceded and what succeeds such a period, yet will this analogy soon become an object of mere curiosity, not of profitable inquiry. Such a period therefore is, in the true sense of the words, an epocha or an era, a point of time at which you stop, or from which you reckon forward.[47]

A "new situation," "new interests," "new maxims of government," "new methods of conduct," "new manners," "new habits," and "new customs": all of these produce an unbridgeable break with the past, mark the point at which one stops or from which one goes forward. For his own European contemporaries, Bolingbroke argues, striking a neo-Harringtonian note,

[44] Bolingbroke, *Remarks on the History of England*, Letter 4, p. 178.
[45] Ibid.
[46] Ibid., p. 180.
[47] Bolingbroke, *Letters on the Study and Use of History*, Letter 6, p. 82.

this new period begins with the end of feudalism at the close of the fifteenth century:

> The end of the fifteenth century seems to be just such a period as I have been describing, for those who live in the eighteenth, and who inhabit the western parts of Europe. A little before, or a little after this point of time, all those events happened, and all those revolutions began, that have produced so vast a change in the manners, customs, and interests of particular nations, and in the whole policy, ecclesiastical and civil, of these parts of the world.[48]

In England, this period begins with the reigns of Henry VII and Henry VIII and the loss of power, prestige, and property by the nobility and the church: "It is from this time that we ought to study the history of our country, ... with the utmost application. *We are not much concerned to know with critical accuracy what were the ancient forms of our parliaments*, concerning which, however, there is little room for dispute from the reign of Henry the Third at least; nor in short the whole system of our civil constitution before Henry the Seventh, and of our ecclesiastical constitution before Henry the Eighth."[49] England's long feudal past has ended; a commercial era has begun. This is an odd assertion, to be sure, by a proponent of the "ancient constitution." It is safe to say that neither Coke nor Hale would have written quite this way.

How do we account for this seeming contradiction, an insistence on a species of continuity (in the form of the temporality of "immemoriality" associated with the "ancient constitution") and an insistence on a species of temporal difference (the sense of a new period that makes everything before 1500 more or less irrelevant for eighteenth-century Europeans living in the age of commerce)? I want to suggest that it is precisely Bolingbroke's distinction between actually existing law and "spirit" that matters here. It is the "spirit" of the "ancient constitution," abstracted from the actual details of early English constitutional structures, that remains constant even as Bolingbroke recognizes that historical periods differ radically from one another, that the feudal has ended and the commercial has begun. Only insofar as it is rendered "spirit" can the "ancient constitution" survive the transformations of history, which Bolingbroke recognizes.

[48] Ibid., p. 83.

[49] Ibid., p. 90 (emphasis added). The same is true of France: "In a word, the constitution is so altered, that any knowledge we can acquire about it, in the history that precedes this period, will serve to little purpose in our study of the history that follows it, and to less purpose still in assisting us to judge of what passes in the present age" (p. 88).

But there is another, still more paradoxical relationship between history and the "ancient constitution." As we have seen, history, for Bolingbroke, is a struggle between the "spirits" of liberty and faction. As a motor of history, the "spirit" of liberty may be invoked to make sense of eighteenth-century Britain's common law constitution and to judge the corruption of the Walpole ministry. History conceived of as the career of the "spirit" of liberty can therefore be brought to bear upon early-eighteenth-century Britain's existing legal structure. But the "spirit" of liberty is itself constituted in terms of nothing other than the common law "ancient constitution." As Bolingbroke puts it: "Whether the Revolution altered our old constitution for the better, or renewed it, and brought it back to the first principles, and nearer to the primitive institution, shall not be disputed here.... A spirit of liberty, transmitted down from our Saxon ancestors, and the unknown ages of our government, preserved itself through one almost continual struggle, against the usurpations of our princes, and the vices of our people."[50] It is the "spirit" of Saxon freedom, itself supplied by the common law, that must be awakened if the post-1688 constitution is not to fall prey to the forces of faction. Thus, even though history thematized as a struggle between the "spirit" of liberty and the "spirit" of faction is used to judge eighteenth-century Britain's common law constitution, the common law "ancient constitution" itself constitutes the "spirit" of liberty. If history is used to make sense of the common law constitution of Bolingbroke's day, the common law itself provides the meaning of history.

Law Between Feudalism and Commerce: The Writings of Lord Kames

In the opening of his *Essay on the History of Civil Society* (1761), one of the key texts of the Scottish Enlightenment, Adam Ferguson (1723–1816) announced that "progress in the case of man is continued to a greater extent than in that of any other animal. Not only the individual advances from infancy to manhood, but the species itself from rudeness to civilization."[51] All men, from the "savage" to the "philosopher," possessed "a principle of progression, and a desire of perfection."[52] Ferguson's reference to the "savage" and the "philosopher" points to one of the central preoccupations of the extraordinary burst of social-historical thought that we associate with the Scottish

[50] Bolingbroke, "A Dissertation upon Parties," in *Political Writings*, p. 82.

[51] Adam Ferguson, *An Essay on the History of Civil Society* (Edinburgh, 1767) (New York: Garland, 1971), pp. 1–2.

[52] Ibid., p. 12.

Enlightenment: the emplotment of history in terms of successive stages. To be sure, different thinkers offered different versions of this emplotment. In his 1762 lectures on jurisprudence, however, Adam Smith provided one of the earliest authoritative models, arguing that "there are four distinct states which mankind pass thro: – 1st the Age of Hunters; 2dly, the Age of Shephards; 3dly the Age of Agriculture; and 4thly, the Age of Commerce."[53] In each stage, society grew closer to peaceful civility. This historical emplotment seemed to correspond to Scotland's own development as a turbulent and bellicose landed aristocracy gave way to a peaceful and commercial society.

It is in the writings of Henry Home, Lord Kames (1696–1782), that we are offered the most systematic instance of Scottish historical thinking as specifically applied to the details of a legal system. Kames was a contemporary and friend of David Hume and Adam Smith and of the generation preceding that of Adam Ferguson, John Millar, and Dugald Stewart. An active participant in the cultural life of mid-eighteenth-century Edinburgh, he was the moving spirit behind the founding of the Physical and Literary Society (later the Royal Society of Edinburgh). Adam Smith famously observed that "we must every one of us acknowledge Kames for our master."[54] Kames was also, of course, a practicing lawyer who eventually ended up serving on Scotland's highest civil court, the Court of Session, as well as on Scotland's highest criminal court, the High Court of Justiciary. Like Smith and other Scottish thinkers, Kames sought to contextualize law in terms of a historical-sociological imagination in which commerce represented a *telos*.

Kames's general view was that law should fit the society that it was intended to govern. But because society was never stationary, law had always to change. As he described it:

> The law of a country is in perfection when it corresponds to the manners of the people, their circumstances, their government. And as these are seldom

[53] Adam Smith, *Lectures on Jurisprudence* (Oxford: Oxford University Press, 1978), p. 14. See also David Spadefora, *The Idea of Progress in Eighteenth-Century Britain* (New Haven, Conn.: Yale University Press, 1990), p. 271. Scholars have discovered a number of antecedents for this emplotment of history in terms of a progression toward commerce and civility, ranging from the Scottish thinker Thomas Blackwell (1701–57) to Montesquieu's (1689–1755) *De l'esprit des lois* (1748) to Turgot's (1727–1781) 1750 discourse at the Sorbonne, "On the Successive Advances of the Human Mind." See Murray Pittock, "Historiography," in *The Cambridge Companion to the Scottish Enlightenment* (Alexander Broadie, ed.) (Cambridge: Cambridge University Press, 2003).

[54] On Kames, see Ian Simpson Ross, *Lord Kames and the Scotland of His Day* (Oxford: Clarendon Press, 1972); see also p. 97.

stationary, the law ought to accompany them in their changes. An institute of law accordingly, however perfect originally, cannot long continue so.... The knowledge, therefore, of the progress of law and of its innovation is essential.[55]

One had to distinguish between those aspects of law that reflected unchanging principles of natural justice and those that were adventitious. Only the latter – which made up the larger part of law – were expected to correspond with, and change along with, "the manners of the people, their circumstances, their government." These could and should be conceived historically. As Kames wrote in the preface to *Historical Law-Tracts* (1758), "Law in particular becomes then only a rational study, when it is traced historically, from its first rudiments among savages ... to its highest improvements in a civilized society.[56]

By far the largest set of historical causes and effects that demanded investigation were those associated with feudalism. As Kames put it, "[F]eudal customs ought to be the study of every man who proposes to reap instruction from the history of the modern European nations."[57] For Kames, as for many mid-eighteenth-century Scottish thinkers, feudal law was the artifact of an outmoded, unnatural, warlike past utterly inconsistent with the modern world of skills, commerce, and peace. He unhesitatingly asserted:

The feudal law was a violent system, repugnant to natural principles. It was submitted to in barbarous times, when the exercise of arms was the only science and the only commerce. It is repugnant to all the arts of peace, and when mankind came to affect security more than danger, nothing could make it tolerable, but long usage and inveterate habit. It behoved however to yield gradually, to the

[55] Lord Kames, *Select Decisions of the Court of Session, from the Year 1752 to the Year 1768* (2d ed.) (Edinburgh, 1799), p. iii.; quoted in David Lieberman, "The Legal Needs of a Commercial Society: The Jurisprudence of Lord Kames," in Istvan Hont and Michael Ignatieff, eds., *Wealth and Virtue: The Shaping of Political Economy in the Scottish Enlightenment* (Cambridge: Cambridge University Press, 1983), p. 209.

[56] Henry Home, Lord Kames, *Historical Law-Tracts* (Edinburgh: A Kincaid, 1761) (1758) (Union, N.J.: Lawbook Exchange, 2000), p. vi. It is interesting that Kames invokes Bolingbroke as an authority for thinking historically and rationally about law. While distancing himself from Bolingbroke politically (an "author, in whose voluminous writings not many things deserve to be copied"), Kames cites Bolingbroke's *Letters on the Study and Use of History* for the proposition that lawyers "must trace the laws of particular states, especially of their own, from the first rough sketches to the more perfect draughts; from the first causes or occasions that produced them, through all the effects, good and bad, that they produced" (p. xi).

[57] Ibid., p. vii.

prevailing love of liberty and independency; and accordingly, through all Europe, it dwindled away gradually, and became a shadow, before any branch of it was abrogated by statute.[58]

Kames's understanding of history as a movement away from feudalism toward commerce went along with a pronounced sense that history was also about moving away from form toward underlying substance, from outward trappings to abstraction. He put it thus:

Religion and law, originally simple, were strangers to form. In process of time, form took the place of substance, and law, as well as religion, were involved in solemnities. What is solemn and important, produceth naturally order and form among the vulgar, who are addicted to objects of sense.... But by gradual improvements in society, and by refinement of taste, forms come insensibly to be neglected, or reduced to their just value; and law as well as religion are verging towards their original simplicity.[59]

The shedding of form, religious as well as legal, was thus also a kind of historical mandate.

The larger legal history that Kames offers in *Historical Law-Tracts* and elsewhere is accordingly one of a movement away not only from feudalism toward commerce, but also from a fetishization of sensible form toward a recognition of substance or abstraction. An important goal of tracing the history of law was to demonstrate, where appropriate, the presence of the past in the present. An existing rule was to be lifted up and shown to belong to a superseded historical stage, typically the feudal. Its historical contingency demonstrated, this became the occasion for suggesting that it should be done away with. It was the sphere of the "social" – intimately linked to "nature" – that was the privileged ground for determining the fitness of rules.

Thematically speaking, Kames's historical account of law takes place in several distinct areas. First, in the context of criminal punishments, Kames finds a diminution over time in the severity or excessiveness of punishments. Particularly "savage and irrational" is the outmoded practice – an effect of excessive and unmitigated resentment – of punishing the innocent along with the guilty (the former often consisting of relations of the guilty individual).[60] Second, in the context of contracts, Kames historicizes the

[58] Ibid., p. 186. Like Bolingbroke, Kames also displays civic humanist themes in decrying the effect of commerce on encouraging luxury and voluptuousness and discouraging "patriotism." See Lieberman, "The Legal Needs of a Commercial Society," p. 222.

[59] Kames, *Historical Law-Tracts*, p. 286.

[60] Ibid., pp. 9–10.

use of formalities in contracts. It was because "the mind of rude people" could not tolerate a naked or abstract promise that solemnities were used in all nations to give conventions a stronger hold on the mind.[61] Third, in the case of property, Kames argues that property began with possession as its ground "because it requires a habit of abstraction, to conceive right or moral power indepedant [*sic*] of natural power; because in this condition, right, being attended with no visible effect, is a mental conception merely. That a man may be deprived of a subject, and yet retain the property, is a lesson too intricate for a savage."[62]

For the most part, Kames's two historical master narratives – feudalism to commerce and form to abstraction – were complementary, part of the same story. Occasionally, however, they could diverge. When they did, the former triumphed. Kames was resolutely unwilling to sanction legal abstractions if they were associated with feudal restrictions on the alienability of real property. An antipathy toward feudal land restrictions remained a preoccupation throughout Kames's legal career. They were part of his historically informed, "rational" commitment to legal reform in Scotland. Thus, in the early *Essays upon Several Subjects Concerning British Antiquities* (1747), Kames argued that feudal land tenures had made sense in a world in which political authority and military service had been tied up with the possession of land. But in the contemporary world, feudal laws served merely to withdraw land from commerce, a "hardship" little noticed "in times of war" but highly undesirable after the emergence of "regular government" in Britain had "made the arts of peace prevail."[63] In *Historical Law-Tracts* (1758), he was vehemently opposed to entails on the ground that property rights, once passed on, must be entire: "For it is the will of the proprietor which must regulate his own succession; and not the will of any other, not even of a predecessor."[64] In *Elucidations Respecting the Common and Statute Law of Scotland* (1777), he maintained that the persistence of legal entails in Scotland represented an unpardonable retreat of reason before legal authority, something that contrasted with the manner in which English judges had manipulated that area of law.[65] In his magnum opus, *Sketches*

[61] Ibid., p. 61.

[62] Ibid., p. 82.

[63] Henry Home, Lord Kames, *Essays upon Several Subjects Concerning British Antiquities* (Edinburgh: A. Kincaid, 1747), pp. 135–140, 155–158.

[64] Kames, *Historical Law-Tracts*, p. 124.

[65] Henry Home, Lord Kames, *Elucidations Respecting the Common and Statute Law of Scotland* (London: Routledge, 1993) (1777), pp. 378–380.

of the History of Man (1774), after showing how entails hindered commerce, industry, improvement, and population, he argued that the persistence of entails threatened the very fabric of political and social life in Britain: "[T]he distribution of land into many shares, accords charmingly with the free spirit of the British constitution; but nothing is more repugnant to that spirit, than overgrown estates in land."[66]

We do not see in Kames's writings any celebration of the authority of the past or of "immemorial" custom. Indeed, in the preface to *Elucidations Respecting the Common and Statute Law of Scotland*, the eighty-one-year-old Kames pronounces utter disdain for "authority": "No science affords more opportunity for exerting the reasoning faculty, than that of law; and yet, in no other science is authority so prevalent."[67] In *Historical Law-Tracts*, custom, the process of law solidifying through repetition, frequently acts to retard historical progress. For Kames, this is a particularly English failing. For example, he argues that trial by battle survived in England long after doubts were entertained about its efficacy because "[c]ustom … and the superstitious notions of the vulgar, preserved it long in force; and even after it became a publick nusance [*sic*] it was not directly abolished."[68] Custom preserves feudal relics in the cumbersome forms of transferring land. Even after landed property had been fully paid for and the purpose of the bargain was that the owner should have unlimited power, "such is the force of custom, that titles behoved to be made up in the feudal form, because no other titles were in use. And thus the purchaser, contrary to the nature of the transaction, was metamorphosed into a vassal, and of consequence subjected to homage, fealty, non-entry, life-rent, escheat, &c.… When the substantial part of the feudal law has thus vanished, it is to be regretted that we should still lie under the oppression of its forms, which occasion great trouble and expence in the transmission of land-property."[69] Custom is to blame as well for preserving feudal relics that impede the full alienability of land and affect the rights of creditors:

> [T]he English, tenacious of their customs, never think of making improvements, or even of supplying legal defects.… In England, at present, land, generally speaking, is absolutely under the power of the proprietor; and yet the ancient practice still subsists, confining execution to the half, precisely as in early times,

[66] Henry Home, Lord Kames, *Sketches of the History of Man* (3 vols.) (Edinburgh: Creech, 1813) (1774), Vol. 3, p. 462.

[67] Kames, *Elucidations*, p. vii.

[68] Kames, *Historical Law-Tracts*, p. 74.

[69] Ibid., pp. 160–161.

when the debtor could dispose of no more but the half. Means however are contrived, indirect indeed, to supply this palpable defect. Any other creditor is authorized to seize the half of the land left out by the first execution, and so without end. Thus, by strictly adhering to form without regarding substance, law, instead of a rational science, becomes a heap of subterfuges and incongruities, which tend insensibly to corrupt the morals of those who make law their profession.[70]

In all these ways, insofar as it points back to a feudal and an excessively form-ridden past, custom is opposed to the logic of history. The English common law, as should be clear, is judged from the perspective of a well-articulated philosophy of history.

However, a judicious measure of reverence for the past, and a commitment to repeating it, might also act to curb the excesses of the inordinate Scottish love of innovation, which – according to Kames – had frequently led to a "relaxation of discipline [and] a profusion of slovenly practice in law-matters."[71] The English attachment to old forms, even as it stands for a vulgar, historically outmoded and costly adherence to solemnities, might paradoxically serve to effectuate the movement of history reasonably well insofar as it guarantees progress in slow, gradual, "insensible" steps. (The suggestion is that the Scots, too eager to embrace change and novelty, are also easily led astray and cannot stay the course.) When Kames describes the historical progression of law, he invariably describes successful change as having taken place slowly, gradually, even imperceptibly. For example, when Kames describes the shift from private punishments of crimes to public punishments, he is essentially describing the common law method, as described by Hale, as the means through which the change occurred: "Steps tending to its completion, were slow, and taken singly, almost imperceptible."[72] There were many small intermediate steps, such as the right to demand monetary compensation, before men became "gradually accustomed to stifle their resentments."[73] It is important to observe that Kames could have been drawing here not only upon an English tradition of customary thought, but also upon a Scottish one. In Lord Stair's *Institutions of the Law of Scotland* (1693), a text all Scottish lawyers were familiar with, praise is bestowed on law "wrung out from … debates upon particular cases," in which "the conveniences and inconveniences thereof,

[70] Ibid., pp. 316–317.

[71] Ibid., p. 323.

[72] Ibid., p. 20.

[73] Ibid., pp. 34–35.

through a tract of time, are experimentally seen." This is contrasted with the method of the legislator whereby "the law-giver must at once balance the conveniences and inconveniences" and therefore "may, and often doth, fall short."[74] Kames shared this relative denigration of statute and did so in terms familiar to any common lawyer:

> Statutes, though commonly made with a view to particular cases, do yet enact in general upon all similar cases; and as man is but short sighted with regard to consequences, 'tis odds but, in remedying one evil, a greater is produced. A court of justice determines nothing in general; their decisions are adapted to particular circumstances.... They creep along with wary steps, until at last, by induction of many cases ... a general rule is with safety formed.[75]

Thus, the common law plays a contradictory role in Kames's account of the historical progression of law. As a substantive body of law intimately identified with feudalism and with English conservatism, the common law impedes the progress of history plotted as a shift from the feudal to the commercial, resulting in the crowding of the emerging commercial world with outmoded and expensive feudal forms. At the same time, however, in proceeding imperceptibly and slowly, the common law method might actually ensure the successful transition from the feudal to the commercial. Kames appears to have shed affiliation to the past *as past*. The common law as a carrier of the accumulated wisdom of previous generations has been rejected in favor of history, reason, and a disdain for authority. Nevertheless, the common law is preserved as a way of doing things, as a bulwark against being too easily swayed – as Kames thinks the Scottish have historically been – by the facile and dazzling appeal of innovation. The common law might be the best way of engineering the shift from feudal to commercial.

Common Law Orthodoxy: Blackstone's Commentaries on the Laws of England

South of the Tweed, history was also a preoccupation of lawyers. As an English lawyer explained in 1774, "[A]n infinite number of questions receive the only light they are capable of from the reflection of history....

[74] James Dalrymple, Viscount of Stair, *The Institutions of the Law of Scotland* (1693) (D. M. Walker, ed.) (Edinburgh, 1981), I.I.15; quoted in Lieberman, "The Legal Needs of a Commercial Society," p. 221.

[75] Kames, *Decisions of the Court of Session*, i, p. iii.; quoted in Lieberman, "The Legal Needs of a Commercial Society," p. 220.

it is necessary to know the original of the matter in question, ... and what has been its progress."[76] The eighteenth century's best-known legal treatise on English law, Sir William Blackstone's *Commentaries on the Laws of England* (1765–1769) – a text that has been described two hundred years after its publication as "the most important legal treatise ever written in the English language" – was no exception to this predilection for historical leaning.[77] The *Commentaries* originated in a set of lectures Blackstone first delivered at Oxford some five years before the appearance of Kames's *Historical Law-Tracts*. They were intended to popularize university education in English law and to educate the landed gentry about English law. Insofar as they served these goals and were widely circulated, they offer an invaluable insight into mid-eighteenth-century orthodox English common law thinking.

All law, for Blackstone, was grounded in a law of nature "co-eval with mankind and dictated by God himself." This law was superior to all human law and could occasionally be uncovered by the law of revelation.[78] However, while all positive laws were thus founded upon the laws of nature and revelation, Blackstone argued, the "indifference" of the law of nature and revelation on many points left positive law considerable leeway to restrict individual liberty "for the benefit of society."[79] This allowed Blackstone to endorse the eighteenth-century constitutional order. Reflecting the lessons of Hobbesian thought, but more importantly the rise of Parliament after 1688, Blackstone derived his famous positivist definition of municipal law as "a rule of civil conduct prescribed by the supreme power in a state, commanding what is right and prohibiting what is wrong."[80] This in turn translated into his controversial statement about the supremacy of Parliament: "If the parliament will positively enact a thing to be done which is unreasonable, I know of no power that can control it."[81] But such statements did not imply any Hobbesian disdain for an "immemorial" and "insensibly" changing common law.

[76] Edward Wynne, *Eunomus: or, Dialogues Concerning the Law and Constitution of England* (4 vols.) (London, 1774), Vol. 1, pp. 59–60; quoted in Lieberman, "The Legal Needs of a Commercial Society," pp. 206–207.

[77] Stanley Katz, "Introduction to Book I," in William Blackstone, *Commentaries on the Laws of England: A Facsimile of the First Edition of 1765–1769* (4 vols.) (Chicago: University of Chicago Press, 1979), Vol. 1, p. iii.

[78] Blackstone, *Commentaries*, Vol. 1, pp. 41–42.

[79] Ibid., p. 42.

[80] Ibid., p. 44.

[81] Ibid., p. 91.

Early in the *Commentaries*, Blackstone observes that the law student has to be taught the various "originals" of English law. Of these, by far the most important is the feudal:

> These originals should be traced to their fountains, as well as our distance will permit; to the customs of the Britons and Germans, as recorded by Caesar and Tacitus; to the codes of the northern nations on the continent, and more especially to those of our own Saxon princes; to the rules of the Roman law, either left here in the days of Papinian, or imported by Vacarius and his followers; *but, above all, to that inexhaustible reservoir of legal antiquities and learning, the feodal law, or, as Spelman has entitled it, the law of nations in our western orb* [emphasis added].[82]

Indeed, Blackstone insists, it is impossible to understand "either the civil constitution of this kingdom ... or the laws which regulate it's [*sic*] landed property" without an understanding of feudal law.[83]

What followed was an exhaustive, even obsessive, survey of English real property law in terms of its various origins, feudal or pre-feudal. For example, Blackstone tells us, "The doctrine of reversions is plainly derived from the feodal constitution."[84] Socage tenures, on the other hand, were "relicks of Saxon liberty; retained by such persons, as had neither forfeited them to the king, nor been obliged to exchange their tenure for the more honourable, as it was called, but at the same time more burthensome, tenure of knight-service."[85] Heriots, another kind of landholding, derived from a Danish custom.[86] And so on.

This obsessive indexing of various bits of law in terms of their origins, feudal or pre-feudal, went along with the apprehension that England was in a commercial age. In other words, feudalism and its aftereffects are clearly recognized from a historical perspective that understands history to be a transition from the feudal to the commercial. Occasionally, Blackstone strikes a Kamesian note when he says that feudal restrictions on the transferability of property are inconsistent with the needs of a commercial economy. Applauding the erosion of "feodal severity" in regard to the alienability of land, Blackstone concludes, "[P]roperty best answers the purposes of civil life, especially in commercial countries, when its transfer and circulation are totally free and unrestrained."[87] Indeed, Blackstone tells

[82] Ibid., pp. 35–36.
[83] Ibid., Vol. 2, p. 44.
[84] Ibid., p. 175.
[85] Ibid., p. 81.
[86] Ibid., p. 97.
[87] Ibid., p. 288.

the new commercial economy has witnessed the rise to prominence of personal property, a species of property more or less entirely disregarded by older writers on the common law.[88] To be sure, scholars have correctly cited Blackstone as evidence of the "continued awkwardness of common lawyers in treating commercial topics."[89] The *Commentaries* are much sounder in discussing real property than personal property. And Blackstone was no jurist like Mansfield, who sought to reshape the common law to fit the needs of merchants through massive importations of continental principles and the consultation of special merchant juries. Nevertheless, it seems difficult to argue that Blackstone was not acutely conscious of living through a momentous historical shift and that he was unaware that the common law should be judged in terms of this historical shift.

Despite a strong historical sensibility that allows him to make sense of law in terms of its feudal origins, however, Blackstone remains wedded to the nonhistorical common law temporality of "immemoriality." To be sure, Blackstone's invocation of "immemoriality" is not, as it was for Coke, an assertion about the absolute identity of the common law over time. Blackstone dismisses the idea that contemporary English customs are the same as those of ancient Britons. Any such assertion, Blackstone cautions, must be taken "with many grains of allowance."[90] Nevertheless, Blackstone invokes the "immemoriality" of the common law repeatedly. Blackstone discusses the seventeenth-century formula describing "immemoriality" thus:

> *[T]he maxims and customs [of the common law] are of higher antiquity than memory or history can reach*: nothing being more difficult than to ascertain the precise beginning and first spring of an antient and long established custom. Whence it is, that in our law, the goodness of a custom depends upon it's having been used time out of mind; or, in the solemnity of our legal phrase, time whereof the memory of man runneth not to the contrary. This it is that gives it its weight and authority; and of this nature are the maxims and customs which compose the common law, or the *lex non scripta*, of this kingdom [emphasis added].[91]

In Blackstone's rendering, a rule may be described as having existed "time out of mind" even though he himself attributes the rule's logic to

[88] "But of later years, since the introduction and extension of trade and commerce, which are entirely occupied in this species of property, and have greatly augmented it's [*sic*] quantity and of course it's [*sic*] value, we have learned to conceive different ideas of it." Ibid., p. 385.

[89] David Lieberman, *The Province of Legislation Determined: Legal Theory in Eighteenth-Century Britain* (Cambridge: Cambridge University Press, 1989), p. 103.

[90] Blackstone, *Commentaries*, Vol. 1, p. 64.

[91] Ibid., p. 67.

feudalism, in other words, to a determinate historical phenomenon. For example, he tells us that the rule that brothers of the half-blood may not succeed to each other's estates "has been determined, time out mind." At the same time, Blackstone insists, the reason of this rule is "the feudal law."[92] The rule thus manages simultaneously to be "feudal" and to have existed "time out of mind." Blackstone also repeats the seventeenth-century idea that English freedoms inhere precisely in "immemorial" customs to which voluntary consent may legitimately be attributed: "[I]t is one of the characteristic marks of English liberty, that our common law depends upon custom; which carries this internal evidence of freedom along with it, that it probably was introduced by the voluntary consent of the people." The loss of custom always implied the loss of liberty. This was illustrated by the fate of Rome: "The Roman law, as practiced in the times of it's liberty, paid also a great regard to custom; but not so much as our law; it only then adopted it, when the written law is deficient."[93]

An emphasis on the common law's customary and "immemorial" nature is part of an insistence on its specificity. The modern reader of the *Commentaries* is powerfully struck by the extent to which Blackstone's world was crowded with complicated, entangled, overlapping, particular, and, most important, multiple customary and prescriptive rights, rights recognized and acquired on the basis of long repetition over time. Blackstone devotes lavish attention to detailing the full range of particular English customs (all "immemorial"), including Kentish gavelkind, borough English, manorial customs, the customs of courts in trading towns and cities, customs of the City of London, the *lex mercatoria*, and so on.[94] Although prescriptive rights were technically different from customs insofar as they attached to individuals, the logic through which prescriptive rights were recognized – repetition over time – was the same. Indeed, Blackstone frequently blurs the difference between customary and prescriptive rights, attributing "immemorial" origins to prescriptive rights relating to commons, franchises, forests, chases, parks, fisheries, and so on.[95]

Blackstone's sense of the specificity and plurality of England's legal regimes translated into a distaste for any facile naturalizing of rights. The pervading sense that the law was the product of a complex and highly

[92] Ibid., pp. 70–71.

[93] Ibid., p. 73–74.

[94] Ibid., Vol. 1, p. 75 *et seq.* The last was *not* technically the common law, but Blackstone includes it under the head of customs because it was "of the utmost validity in all commercial transactions" (p. 75).

[95] Ibid., Vol. 2, pp. 33, 37, 38, 40.

specific past made it possible to resist seeing legal rights as natural, as existing outside time, as being immune to change. What would be seen as natural rights by subsequent American legal commentators were only customs for Blackstone. In his famous discussion of the right of testamentary disposition, for example, Blackstone stated:

> The right of inheritance, or descent to the children and relations of the deceased, seems to have been allowed much earlier than the right of devising by testament. *We are apt to conceive at first view that it has nature on it's side; yet we often mistake for nature what we find established by long and inveterate custom. It is certainly a wise and effectual, but clearly a political, establishment*; since the permanent right of property, vested in the ancestor himself, was no *natural*, but merely a *civil*, right [emphasis in the original].

One could arrive at "wise and effectual" results – for example, rules permitting the transmission of property at death – but it was more correct to think of these as "civil" rather than "natural" rights, as rights that had emerged over time and that could therefore change.[96]

Blackstone's invocation of custom was also, of course, an endorsement of the "insensibility" associated with the common law method.[97] The *Commentaries* is a celebration of the figure of the common law judge. Uniquely equipped to declare the customs of the community and to calibrate change across past, present, and future, common law judges are "the depositary of the laws; the living oracles, who must decide in all cases of doubt." Judges' abilities, in Cokean fashion, were shaped by experience and study and "from being long personally accustomed to the judicial decisions of their predecessors."[98] As such, judges never made new law even as they corrected errors and fitted law to newer ends. The reversal of a judicial error was never the making of new law (as Blackstone's greatest critic, Bentham, would charge), but rather simply proof that the reversed law had never been "the established custom of the realm" and hence law at all. If the common law had faults, Blackstone argued, it was

[96] Ibid., pp. 10–11.

[97] None of this meant that the common law was never supposed to be reformed. Indeed, the scientific study of law was necessary for "improving it's [*sic*] method, retrenching its superfluities, and reconciling the little contrarieties, which the practice of many centuries will necessarily create in any human system." Ibid., Vol. 1, p. 30. Indeed, it was important to study law scientifically precisely in order *not* to be slavishly bound to precedents. Only the lawyer who was properly trained "in solid scientifical method" would be able "to form ... and comprehend any arguments drawn *a priori*, from the spirit of the laws and the natural foundation of justice" Ibid., pp. 34, 32.

[98] Ibid., p. 69.

legislative tampering over the centuries that was to blame.[99] If such tampering, and the inconveniences it caused, had been felt acutely in Coke's day, it was much more pronounced in Blackstone's, "when the statute book is swelled to ten times a larger bulk."[100] The *Commentaries* was, then, equally intended for parliamentarians, who were exhorted to preserve the ancient legacy of the common law, "to watch, to check, and to avert every dangerous innovation, to propose, to adopt, and to cherish any solid and well-weighed improvement; bound ... to transmit that constitution and those laws to their posterity, amended if possible, at least without any derogation."[101]

In celebrating the "insensible" and seamless common law method, Blackstone recognizes – in a way that Hale does not – that common law judges have had to work very hard indeed to produce the effect of "insensibility" as they bridge the gap between feudal and commercial. Kames might reject legal fictions as an outmoded "rude" attachment to form. But Blackstone law endorses them precisely for allowing for a seamless fitting of older doctrines to newer needs:

> When, therefore, by the gradual influence of foreign trade and domestic tranquility, the spirit of our military tenures began to decay, and at length the whole structure was removed, the judges quickly perceived that the forms and delays of the old feudal actions, (guarded with their several outworks of essoins, vouchers, aid-prayers, and a hundred other formidable entrenchments) were ill suited to that more simple and commercial mode of property which succeeded the former, and required a more speedy decision of right, to facilitate exchange and alienation. Yet they wisely avoided soliciting any great legislative revolution in the old established forms, which might have been productive of consequences more numerous and extensive than the most penetrating genius could foresee; but left them as they were, to languish in obscurity and oblivion, and endeavoured by a series of minute contrivances to accommodate such personal actions, as were then in use, to all the most useful purposes of remedial justice.... And, since the new expedients have been refined by the practice of more than a century, and are sufficiently known and understood, they in general answer the purpose of doing speedy and substantial justice, much better than could now be effected by any great fundamental alterations. The only difficulty that attends them arises from their fictions and circuities: but, when once we have discovered the proper clew, that labyrinth is easily pervaded. *[We] inherit an old Gothic castle, erected in the*

[99] "[A]lmost all the perplexed questions, almost all the niceties, intricacies, and delays (which have sometimes disgraced the English, as well as other, courts of justice) owe their original not to the common law itself, but to innovations that have been made in it by acts of parliament." Ibid., p. 10.

[100] Ibid., p. 11.

[101] Ibid., p. 9.

> *days of chivalry, but fitted up for a modern inhabitant. The moated ramparts, the embattled towers, and the trophied halls, are magnificent and venerable, but useless, and therefore neglected. The inferior apartments, now accommodated to daily use, are cheerful and commodious, though their approaches may be winding and difficult* [emphasis added].[102]

The "insensibility" of the common law method allows the eighteenth-century Englishman to enjoy a law that gives him "speedy and substantial justice," but also to experience his past as utterly continuous. Some might call for the English to move out of the Gothic castle of the common law, but the common law judge would rather make the eighteenth-century Englishman at home in it. We are offered various examples of how the common law "insensibly" engineered the shift from feudal to commercial long before the abolition of military tenures during the reign of Charles II. In the context of the emergence of the property rights of villeins, Blackstone writes that the common law recognized villeins' prescriptive rights to transfer property at death: "For the goodnature [*sic*] and benevolence of many lords of manors having, time out of mind, permitted their villeins and their children to enjoy their possessions without interruption, in a regular course of descent, the common law, of which custom is the life, now gave them title to prescribe against their lords."[103] Copyhold tenures similarly emerged "by a long series of immemorial encroachments on the lord" recognized by the common law.[104] When it came to recognizing the importance of commerce, Blackstone could once again emphasize the role of the common law long before the eighteenth century. Indeed, Magna Carta itself, that centerpiece of common law thought, had recognized the rights of foreign merchants. Blackstone states, "[T]he law of England, as a commercial country, pays a very particular regard to foreign merchants in innumerable instances." This is very different from "the genius of the Roman people; who in their manners, their constitution, and even in their laws, treated commerce as a dishonorable employment, and prohibited the exercise thereof to persons of birth, or rank, or fortune."[105]

Less intellectually rigorous than Kames and less philosophically committed to the commercial, Blackstone nevertheless subjects the common law of his day to a historical sensibility that views the movement of history as a movement from the feudal to the commercial. But he simultaneously argues that the common law, armed with the nonhistorical

[102] Ibid., Vol. 3, pp. 268–269.
[103] Ibid., Vol. 2, p. 95.
[104] Ibid.
[105] Ibid., Vol. 1, p. 253.

temporalities of "immemoriality" and "insensibility," is in fact the very motor of history.

Conclusion

In exploring seventeenth-century thinking about the common law and the ways in which such thinking was transformed over the course of the eighteenth century, this chapter sets forth some of the major sources – revealed, I hope, in their dynamism, self-consciousness, and creativity – from which American common lawyers would draw in the late eighteenth and nineteenth centuries. Seventeenth-century common lawyers invoked the nonhistorical common law times of "immemoriality" and "insensibility" with full awareness of the artifice of those times to hold off the encroachments of would-be absolutist monarchs. Temporal indistinction, filled with content as the collective wisdom of multiple generations, served as a bulwark against the royalist idea that law could be made in historical time. By the eighteenth century, as the threat of royal absolutism had vanished, history thematized as a progression from the feudal to the commercial and as a struggle between virtue and faction pervaded British intellectual life. English and Scottish common lawyers subscribed fully to this understanding of history and brought it to bear upon the common law. They sought particularly to identify the impress of feudalism upon the common law. But this did not mean that they were willing to surrender authority over lawmaking to legislatures. Indeed, endorsing the vitality of the common law tradition even as they recognized changes all around them, they argued that the common law was the best method of effecting the movement of history.

In the late eighteenth century, American common lawyers would turn again and again to the writings of Coke, Hale, Bolingbroke, Kames, and especially Blackstone. If Coke, Hale, and Bolingbroke represented that strand of common law thinking that associated the common law with English liberties that Americans so ardently claimed, the writings of Kames stood for the new sciences of society and history applied to law that pointed the path away from the past and toward the future. But it was Blackstone's *Commentaries* that would be by far the most influential text for American common lawyers. Indeed, it is fair to say that, in the immediate postrevolutionary decades, the production of legal knowledge in America consisted in large part of producing a critical relationship to Blackstone's *Commentaries*. Later in life, James Kent would declare that the *Commentaries* had "inspired [him], at the age of 15, with awe" and convinced him to become a lawyer.[106] In 1795, Connecticut's Zephaniah Swift praised Blackstone for having "reduced order out of chaos."[107] Until Blackstone's *Commentaries* appeared, Virginia's leading legal authority, St. George Tucker, observed in 1803, "the students of law in England, and its dependencies, were almost destitute of any scientific guide to conduct their studies."[108] Whether in the form of editions of Blackstone or of treatises modeled on Blackstone's, then, postrevolutionary American legal thinkers from Massachusetts to Virginia felt compelled to confront Blackstone's legal science. What they would have to do, however, would be to make sense of British legal science in terms of the revolution they had lived through, for the American Revolution introduced vocabularies that none of the writers discussed here had entirely prepared Americans for.

[106] *Memoirs and Letters of James Kent* (William Kent, ed.) (Boston: Little, Brown & Co., 1989), p. 18.

[107] Zephaniah Swift, *A System of the Laws of the State of Connecticut* (Windham, Conn.: John Byrne, 1795–1796), Vol. 1, p. 41.

[108] St. George Tucker, ed., *Blackstone's Commentaries with Notes of Reference to the Constitution and Laws of the Federal Government of the United States and of the Commonwealth of Virginia* (5 vols.) (Philadelphia: William Young Birch & Abraham Small, 1803), Vol. 1, Preface, p. iii.

3

Time as Consent

Common Law Thought after the American Revolution

The Loneliness of Consent

Over the past several decades, scholars have been made aware of many of the intellectual sources of the American revolutionary struggle, the period of constitution making, and its aftermath. These include republican thought, Lockean natural rights, Scottish ideas about the shift from the feudal to the commercial, common law thought, and Protestant millennial thought. These various intellectual sources were often mixed in ways that are difficult to separate out. The writings of Bolingbroke, Kames, Blackstone, and others were fully part of this complex universe of ideas.[1]

It is important to emphasize, however, that none of the British writers discussed in the preceding chapter had mapped out the truly innovative political structure that emerged out of the 1787 Philadelphia convention. While eighteenth-century British legal thinkers had imagined government to be constrained by the logic of history, and had sought to subject law to criticism in the name of the logic of history, few had imagined a government in which all three of the traditional orders of government would be subjected to the electoral principle. Accustomed to monarchy and aristocracy, to a world in which birth determined status, eighteenth-century Europeans deemed the constraint of history just one among many.

[1] Bernard Bailyn, *The Ideological Origins of the American Revolution* (enlarged ed.) (Cambridge, Mass.: Belknap Press, 1992); Henry F. May, *The Enlightenment in America* (New York: Oxford University Press, 1976); Gordon Wood, *The Creation of the American Republic, 1776–1787* (Chapel Hill: University of North Carolina Press, 1969); Ernest L. Tuveson, *Redeemer Nation: The Idea of America's Millennial Role* (Chicago: University of Chicago Press, 1968).

It is not surprising, then, that the establishment of a politicolegal structure in America that brought to an end centuries of monarchy and aristocracy resulted in a new and exhilarating sense of the lifting of constraints and of the possibility of remaking the world. At least for a segment of the American population, birth had ceased to be the formal basis of power and privilege. Lifelong subjecthood, traditionally attributed to those born within the protection of the king, was replaced by citizenship, theoretically grounded in volition. Men began to think of themselves as makers of their own political identities, and hence of their own laws, as they had not before.[2] Did this mean, however, that the late-eighteenth-century American politicolegal subject was *entirely* liberated from the fetters of the European past? In what senses did the politicolegal subject remain constrained? In what historical languages would a new sense of liberation and constraint be expressed? What would be the consequences for law in general and for the English common law in particular?

In keeping with this sense of the lifting of constraints, during the revolutionary years and their aftermath, regardless of political and intellectual stripe, Americans understood themselves to be living through a momentous historical shift away from "artificial," "mysterious," dazzling, invisible, nontransparent, nonrational European forms of the exercise of power (which could be, depending on the thinker, the privileges associated with birth, monarchy, feudalism, Roman Catholicism, or religious establishment) and toward "natural," unpretentious, visible, transparent, rational American forms (which could be, depending on the thinker, power grounded in consent, democratic self-government, Protestantism, and freedom of worship). This widespread sense of a historic shift from a world of obscurantism and "mystery" to a world in which clear, logical, and defensible principles could be laid bare was fully part of the demystifying rationalist impulse of the Euro-American Enlightenment and, as such, was not exclusive to Americans of the revolutionary generation. But in the new United States, this Enlightenment vocabulary was specifically joined to arguments about the legitimacy of democratic government and law.

An important and widely embraced implication of understanding the movement of history as a shift away from European "mystery" toward

[2] See James H. Kettner, *The Development of American Citizenship, 1608–1870* (Chapel Hill: University of North Carolina Press, 1978); Holly Brewer, *By Birth or Consent: Children, Law and the Anglo-American Revolution in Authority* (Chapel Hill: University of North Carolina Press, 2005).

American transparency was that law had to be rendered plain, visible, and rational, capable of being viewed and understood and imbibed by the citizens of the new polity. This explains in part the concerted efforts, so prominent in the postrevolutionary decades, to publicize and rationalize law through *writing*, whether in the form of written constitutions, the promulgation of digests and revisions, the standardization and reporting of judicial decisions, or the generation of legal treatises. In March 1791, Federalist U.S. Supreme Court Justice James Wilson, who had been appointed to revise and digest the laws of the Commonwealth of Pennsylvania, put it thus: "[S]implicity and plainness and precision should mark the texture of a law. It claims the *obedience* – it should be level to the *understanding* of all."[3] Wilson subscribed fully to the philosophy of history that saw the shift between England and America as a historic shift from "mystery" to transparency. For too long, he observed, law "has suffered extremely from the thick veil of mystery spread over it in the dark and scholastic ages"; it must now enjoy "the advantages of light, which have resulted from the resurrection of letters."[4] The Federalist politician and lawyer James Kent began his 1794 lecture at Columbia College by striking a similar note: "The human mind, which had been so long degraded by the fetters of the feudal and papal tyranny, has begun to free herself from bondage; and has roused into uncommon energy and boldness." The breaking of the fetters of the European past made it imperative that the structure of American law and government be rendered visible to all:

> [T]he people of this country are under singular obligations, from the nature of their government, to place the study of the law at least on a level with the pursuits of classical learning. The art of maintaining social order, and promoting social prosperity, is not with us a mystery fit only for those who may be distinguished by the adventitious advantages of birth or fortune. The science of civil government has been here stripped of its delusive refinements, and restored to the plain principles of reason.[5]

However, while there was widespread agreement that history was a move away from European "mystery" toward American transparency, and that law had therefore to be rendered plain and accessible to all, such agreement did not by any means imply a universal conviction that politics

[3] *The Works of James Wilson* (James DeWitt Andrews, ed.) (2 vols.) (Chicago: Callaghan and Company, 1896), Vol. 1, p. xxi (emphasis in original).

[4] Ibid., p. xxii.

[5] James Kent, "An Introductory Lecture to a Course of Law Lectures: Delivered November 17, 1794," *Columbia Law Review* 3 (1903): 330–343, at 331.

and law should therefore also be the self-conscious product of an entire population radically ungoverned by the past. James Kent, who claimed in 1794 that American government was not "a mystery fit only for those who may be distinguished by the adventitious advantages of birth or fortune," was a lifelong opponent of universal white male suffrage. During New York's 1821 constitutional convention, Kent would express firm opposition to suffrage expansion on the grounds that it would result in an erosion of private property rights. Neither was there universal agreement that government and law should be unmoored from the prerevolutionary past. Daniel Hulsebosch has written about the deep continuities between prerevolutionary and postrevolutionary governmental structures. Thinkers who opposed the "mystery" associated with prerevolutionary political forms also insisted upon continuity with them. During the 1821 convention at which he opposed universal white male suffrage, for example, Kent also tried, unsuccessfully, to hold off the abolition of New York's Council of Revision, a colonial era official body composed of unelected judges and legislators that could effectively veto legislation.[6]

However, if a commitment to demystifying law as part of a faith that history was a moving away from European "mystery" toward American transparency did not always or necessarily translate into a commitment to what we might take to be a self-conscious, inclusive, present-focused democracy, within certain radical democratic circles that same commitment to demystifying law came to be joined to the controversial figure of the subject of contemporaneous consent. This subject of contemporaneous consent did not, of course, encompass groups such as women, blacks, and Native Americans. Nevertheless, it carried with it the possibility of a thoroughgoing challenge to government and law of precisely the kind that a legal thinker such as James Kent would fear and abhor.

[6] On Kent as an American conservative, see John Theodore Horton, *James Kent: A Study in Conservatism, 1763–1847* (New York: Da Capo Press, 1969). In arguing against the expansion of suffrage, Kent would declare, "Society is an association for the protection of property as well as of life, and the individual who contributes only one cent to the common stock, ought not to have the same power and influence in directing the property concerns of the partnership, as he who contributes his thousands." Nathaniel H. Carter and William L. Stone, *Reports of the Proceedings and Debates of the Convention of 1821 Assembled for the Purpose of Amending the Constitution of the State of New York; Containing All the Official Documents Relating to the Subject, and Other Valuable Matter* (Albany: E. & E. Hosford, 1821), p. 221. On the 1821 New York convention, see Daniel J. Hulsebosch, *Constituting Empire: New York and the Transformation of Constitutionalism in the Atlantic World, 1664–1830* (Chapel Hill: University of North Carolina Press, 2005), Chap. 8.

At the same time, as we shall see, it was itself also limited in various ways that betray continuities with prerevolutionary thought. It is to an exploration of the contours of this subject of contemporaneous consent, accordingly, that I turn.[7]

"Consent" was, of course, one of the master concepts of eighteenth-century politics. The American Revolution had been fought, in an important sense, in its name. But consent also had a venerable history going back long before the Revolution. By the late eighteenth century, it carried different meanings, of which two are significant for our purposes.

In the imaginations of English common lawyers, as we have seen, consent had long been freely attributed to the common law. No express evidence of consent had been considered necessary. As stated in the preceding chapter, Blackstone had claimed that "our common law depends upon custom: which carries this internal evidence of freedom along with it, that it probably was introduced by the voluntary consent of the people."[8] The consent attributed to the common law was imagined to encompass multiple generations, stretching back into the past and out into the future. Not surprisingly, a multigenerational consent to government and law was imbued with the special nonhistorical common law temporality of "immemoriality." In 1783, Richard Wooddeson, one of Blackstone's successors as Vinerian Professor of Law at Oxford, articulated the intimate, mutually constitutive links among custom, consent, and "immemoriality" as follows:

> [G]overnment ought to be, and is generally *considered* as founded on consent.... For what gives any legislature a right to act, where no express consent can be shewn? what, but immemorial usage? and what is the intrinsic force of immemorial usage, in establishing this fundamental or any other law, but that it is evidence of common acquiescence and consent?[9]

But the notion of contemporaneous consent, as it was articulated by radical democratic thinkers in the late eighteenth century and joined to

[7] There were, of course, various species of radical democratic thought in this period that cannot be subsumed within the discussion I offer. See, e.g., Michael Merrill and Sean Wilentz, eds., *The Key of Liberty: The Life and Democratic Writings of William Manning, "A Laborer," 1747–1814* (Cambridge, Mass.: Harvard University Press, 1993). For a discussion of Manning's *Key of Liberty* (1798), see the Prologue to Christopher L. Tomlins, *Law, Labor, and Ideology in the Early American Republic* (Cambridge: Cambridge University Press, 1993).

[8] Blackstone, *Commentaries*, Vol. 1, pp. 73–74.

[9] Richard Wooddeson, *Elements of Jurisprudence: Treated of in the Preliminary Part of a Course of Lectures on the Laws of England* (Dublin: H. Fitzpatrick, 1792), p. 35.

the widely shared commitment to demystifying government and law, was something entirely different. It stood precisely for the possibility of severing ties between generations, forcibly drawing past, present, and future apart. As such, it was sharply at odds with common law understandings of multigenerational attributed consent.

In the hands of radical democratic thinkers, the subject of contemporaneous consent was intended to apply to collectivities rather than to individuals. More important for our purposes, it was internally unstable. In its conceptualization, the subject of contemporaneous consent was simultaneously liberated and constrained. It oscillated freely between (1) the liberating idea that the subject of consent could subject everything to the test of contemporaneous consent, break completely with the past, and remake the present and future repeatedly and at will and (2) the constraining idea that the subject of consent would create a world in which politics and law would end up reflecting an already imagined "nature" or "society," such that the subject of consent would restore man, as it were, to himself. Although both possibilities carried radical consequences when set afloat in the world of late-eighteenth-century political and legal debate, the former authorized an open-ended democratic reimagination of the world, while the latter – often derived, as we shall see, from Scottish ideas – operated as a constraint on democratic reimagination.

Thomas Paine's exhortation to revolution, *Common Sense* (1776), perhaps the best known of the pamphlets of the American Revolution, is an exemplary text in this regard. In urging Americans to rise up against Great Britain, Paine emphasized the urgency of "the present time." As he put it, "The present time ... is that peculiar time which never happens to a nation but once, *viz*. the time of forming itself into a government. Most nations have let slip the opportunity ... of making laws for themselves."[10] Paine's acute sense of the urgency and uniqueness that the present represented for the nation was more than a statement about revolutionary tactics. For many of his readers, it would have been understood to be an argument about America's brief but enormously significant regression to the state of nature of eighteenth-century social contract theory. From this state, Paine argued, an unencumbered man could, on the basis of consent, self-consciously re-create himself.

For Paine, to qualify as one's own, hence to qualify as properly consented to and legitimate, visible and transparent laws would have to

[10] Thomas Paine, *Common Sense*, in *Basic Writings of Thomas Paine* (New York: Willey Book Company, 1942), p. 52.

emerge only in and from that peculiar slice of time known as the present. True consent to such laws could come only from a subject who could offer its consent in and for the present. For Paine, in other words, the subject capable of giving consent to law is *lonely*, imprisoned within its own present, utterly cut off from both past and future. This is the implication and meaning of Paine's celebrated attacks on hereditary right. For Paine, hereditary right is illegitimate – in his words, "unwise, unjust, unnatural" – because future generations have not consented to its transmission into their own times:

[A]s no man at first could possess more public honors than were bestowed upon him, so the givers of those honors could have no power to give away the right of posterity, and though they might say "We choose you for *our* head," they could not, without manifest injustice to their children, say "that your children and your children's children shall *reign* over *ours* for *ever*" [emphasis in original].[11]

In this excerpt, Paine is denouncing hereditary monarchy. However, his argument could potentially be extended to all law. All law had to be the product of the contemporaneous consent of a lonely, temporally truncated subject capable of consenting only in and for its own present. The radical implication was that no law derived from the past was legitimate as such. The present was thus always potentially something like the state of nature, a time from which one could launch a beginning, unencumbered by the weight of the past. As Paine exulted, "We have it in our power to begin the world over again.... The birthday of a new world is at hand."[12]

Even as Paine drew a picture of a subject capable of dramatically recreating the world in the present, however, he sought to pin that subject down, to constrain it. The unencumbered man of the state of nature had never really been unencumbered. Drawing upon Scottish thinkers, Paine drew a sharp distinction between society, described as a function of "our wants," and government, described as a function of "our wickedness." The former was natural; the latter was not. Paine operated with a strong sense of the changeability of government, but with a far weaker sense of the changeability of society. Through a self-conscious transformation of government, he argued, the "genuine mind of man" could be restored to "its native home, society."[13] But what would the laws of society be? If society were naturalized as the "native home" of "the genuine mind of man," could its laws truly be the product of self-conscious design, of a

[11] Ibid., p. 15

[12] Ibid., p. 65.

[13] Thomas Paine, *Rights of Man*, in *Basic Writings of Thomas Paine*, p. 52.

kind of creative and imaginative radical remaking that proceeded from subjecting the world to the test of contemporaneous consent?

In *Common Sense*, Paine did not explore such questions sufficiently. In *Rights of Man* (1791), written fifteen years after *Common Sense*, we discern more clearly Paine's debt to Scottish thinkers such as Kames, who had plotted the movement of history as a shift from a warlike feudal to a peaceable commercial. Paine tells us that, in society, laws would be those "which common usage ordains" and as such would have "a greater influence than the laws of government." Such laws would include laws of trade and commerce grounded in "mutual and reciprocal interest."[14] The spread of commerce would "extirpate the system of war" associated with the feudal-monarchic past and advance "universal civilization."[15]

In Paine's rendering, then, we observe the internal instability of the subject of consent – capable of remaking the world entirely, on the one hand, but restricted to making it so that it matched a given conception of naturalized society, on the other. The idea of contemporaneous consent as a test of the legitimacy of government and law, potentially radical though it is, ends up dissolved into a philosophy of history already imagined by prerevolutionary (and distinctly nonradical) European thinkers.

A similar argument about contemporaneous consent, replete with the same tension between freeing up the subject of consent completely and reigning it in through some conception of society or nature, would be made by a more mainstream figure such as Thomas Jefferson. In a celebrated 1789 letter to James Madison, Jefferson opined:

> The question Whether one generation of men has a right to bind another, seems never to have been started either on this or our side of the water.... I set out on this ground which I suppose to be self-evident, "*that the earth belongs in usufruct to the living*;" that the dead have neither powers nor rights over it. The portion occupied by an individual ceases to be his when himself ceases to be, and reverts to the society [emphasis in original].[16]

Jefferson followed up the above-mentioned statement with the exposition of a complicated scheme based on life expectancies and death rates that would determine precisely how long human laws were to remain in force. This would ensure that, "by the law of nature [i.e., the natural life cycle], one generation is to another as one independant [*sic*] nation

[14] Ibid., pp. 150, 153.
[15] Ibid., p. 210.
[16] Letter to James Madison, September 6, 1789, in Thomas Jefferson, *Writings* (M. D. Peterson, ed.) (New York: Library of America, 1984), p. 959.

to another."[17] One concrete instantiation of this idea was the reversal in Virginia of the English rule of construction according to which, if a statute repealing another was itself repealed, the earlier statute was revived. In Virginia, the law provided that "whensoever one law, which shall have repealed another, shall itself be repealed, the former law shall not be revived without express words to that effect." Virginia's St. George Tucker described the English rule as "certainly inconvenient; since old acts, long since forgotten, might be revived upon the community; affecting their persons and property upon a legal fiction without notice that such was the case."[18] The present generation's consent to its own laws was to be secured. But as the past, present, and future were rendered foreign countries vis-à-vis one another, the subject of contemporaneous consent was rendered lonely, confined to the present, restricted to consenting only for itself, utterly freed from the past and future.

Jefferson repeatedly expressed similar ideas. In an 1801 letter to Joseph Priestley, he condemned "[t]hose who live by mystery and *charlatanerie*," a marker of the old, past-centered power, and eulogized the "newness" of America:

> We can no longer say that there is nothing new under the sun. For this whole chapter in the history of man is new. The great extent of our Republic is new. Its sparse habitation is new. The mighty wave of public opinion which has rolled over it is new.[19]

In 1824, he would repeat this view with breathtaking clarity:

> [Our revolution] presented us an album on which we were free to write what we pleased. We had no occasion to search into musty records, to hunt up royal parchments, or to investigate the laws and institutions of a semi-barbarous ancestry. We appealed to those of nature, and found them engraved on our hearts.[20]

As the reference to appealing to the "laws of nature" and finding them *already* "engraved on our hearts" suggests, however, Jefferson's sense that each generation was free from its predecessor was moored in an understanding of human reality that acted as a check upon radical democratic reimagining. Like Paine's, Jefferson's freeing up of the present from the

[17] Ibid., p. 962.

[18] Act of 1789, c. 9; St. George Tucker, ed., *Blackstone's Commentaries*, Vol. 1, pp. 89–91, n. 19.

[19] Letter to Joseph Priestley, March 21, 1801, in Jefferson, *Writings*, pp. 1085, 1086.

[20] Letter to Major John Cartwright, June 5, 1824, in Jefferson, *Writings*, p. 1491.

claims of the past, the heart of the notion of contemporaneous consent, ended up drawing heavily upon Scottish teachings. Jefferson led the attack on feudally derived landholding forms such as the entail in the Virginia of the late 1770s. Kames had made the case against the entail decades earlier. As such, Jefferson's emphasis on contemporaneous consent as sanctioning a doing away with "mystery and *charlatanerie*" and on being "free to write what we pleased," which could have stood for something quite radical, ended up affirming what mainstream European legal thinkers had been arguing for a while.

Although Paine and Jefferson (but especially the latter) might not have been all that radical in practice, by the early 1790s what I have called the lonely subject of contemporaneous consent appeared to many to be concretely – and terrifyingly – instantiated in the events in France. As the French Revolution entered its radical phase, many in England and America began to think of it as a concerted and self-conscious effort to render the present almost literally a blank canvas, to uproot the past in its entirety so as to inaugurate a brand new order. The French revolutionaries sought to reset the clock and begin time itself anew, proposing a calendar that replaced the Christian year 1792 with the republican *L'an 1*. Hundreds of churches, palaces, and convents were destroyed in France and then all over Europe. Many lost their lives in the process. Although there was no comparable level of physical destruction or bloodshed in the United States, as American domestic politics began to splinter around attitudes toward the French Revolution, calls for a complete break with the past such as those of Paine and Jefferson began to seem more and more worrying. As a result, a range of battles came to be fought around the meanings and implications of the lonely subject of contemporaneous consent who was represented as the fulcrum of the shift from "mystery" to transparency.

One of these battles concerned the presence in America of the English common law. From the perspective of those who believed that government and law should be subjected to the test of contemporaneous consent and that consent should be expressed in writing, the problems with the common law were evident. What was more "mysterious," more a marker of outmoded European forms of power, than a body of unwritten, customary law that rested its legitimacy on the nonhistorical temporalities of "immemoriality" and "insensibility"? What was less the product of contemporaneous consent than a body of law that derived its authority from a repetition of precedent and a boast to bind past, present, and future together effortlessly? Who was more opposed to the will of the people than the common law judge who derided legislation as lacking in the collective wisdom of multiple generations? In the preface to his Connecticut reports (1789–1793), Jesse Root echoed the sentiments of many when he described the temporality of "immemoriality" as a feature of arbitrary governments: "That so long as any one living can remember when they [i.e., customs] began to exist they can have no force or validity whatever, however universally they may be assented to and adopted in practice; but as soon as this is forgotten and no one remembers their beginning, then and not till then they become a law; this may be necessary in arbitrary governments."[21] Legislatures could accomplish openly through written law, many argued, what the fiction of "immemoriality" had once wrought.

The constitutions of most of the new polities, federal and state, were written.[22] This was fully part of a commitment toward moving away from European "mystery" and toward American transparency that was shared by legal thinkers of widely varying political persuasions, from the Federalist James Wilson to the Republican Thomas Jefferson. But were such writings sharp breaks with the past (instantiations of contemporaneous consent and self-sufficient principles) or extensions of the past (transcriptions of unwritten customs and accumulated experience)? The debates of the 1790s over the nature of the written U.S. Constitution and its relationship to the unwritten British one reveal little consensus. Debates over the ontology of the American constitutions led directly to one of the most explosive legal questions of the period, that surrounding the meaning of written legal texts. Could writing – and hence the contemporaneous consent that gave rise to writing – ensure the transparency, legibility, and fixity of its own meaning? Or should written laws be given meaning through unwritten common law? And what was one to make of the vast body of common law that lay outside of the newly demarcated realm of constitutional law? Could everything be subjected to the test of contemporaneous consent, could everything be lifted up and examined, judged in terms of its relevance to the present? All American states,

[21] Jesse Root, "Introduction," in *Report of Cases Adjudged in the Superior Court and Supreme Court of Errors: From July, A.D. 1789 to June, AD 1793* (Hartford, Conn.: Hudson and Goodwin, 1798–1802), p. xii.

[22] For a comprehensive discussion, see Benjamin P. Poore, *The Federal and State Constitutions, Colonial Charters, and Other Organic Laws of the United States* (2 vols.) (Washington, D.C.: Government Printing Office, 1877). Connecticut and Rhode Island were the only original states that did not create new constitutions in the eighteenth century.

whether by statute or otherwise, and with various caveats, "received" the English common law.[23] But this did not end debates about how to establish a relationship to the English legal legacy. Critics called for a legislative reform of the common law or its replacement with a code that would tether it firmly to contemporaneous consent expressed by legislatures.

What is interesting for our purposes is not just how debates over the status of the common law in the postrevolutionary United States were structured around the contours of the subject of contemporaneous consent as the fulcrum of the historical shift from European "mystery" to American transparency, but how the defenders and proponents of the common law deployed the new historical sensibilities to their advantage. Even as the common law's defenders agreed that the law should be subjected to historical critique and demystified, they would argue that the common law embodied the logic of history itself. Some would argue that, where consent was the fulcrum of history, the common law was the most consensual of all possible laws. In doing so, they would blend older common law languages of multigenerational and attributed consent with newer radical democratic languages of contemporaneous consent. In the manner of Kames and Blackstone, other legal thinkers would argue that the common law, entirely by itself, had engineered the historical move from feudal to commercial, and hence from European "mystery" to American transparency. In so doing, they exploited the instability inherent in the idea of the subject of contemporaneous consent, as it oscillated between the possibility of radical democratic reimagining and being hemmed in by Scottish ideas about the logic of history. In constraining the subject of contemporaneous consent, Paine had argued that the ideal society of the future would be governed by "common usage," such that the world of war would be replaced by the world of peaceable commerce. Was the common law *already* that law?

Constitutional Ontologies: Common Law, Writing, and Consent

Eighteenth-century Americans had actively claimed England's "ancient constitution" despite lingering questions about its applicability to the colonies. In the 1720s, New York's attorney general, Joseph Murray,

[23] For an excellent discussion of the reception of the English common law after the American Revolution, see F. W. Hall, "The Common Law: An Account of Its Reception in the United States," *Vanderbilt Law Review* 4 (1951): 791–825.

had argued that New Yorkers' right to form an assembly derived "from the *common Custom and Laws of England*, claimed as an *Englishman's Birth Right*, and as having been such by *Immemorial custom in England*."[24] As the political controversy with Great Britain heated up in the 1760s, Americans once again invoked England's customary constitution. The right of self-taxation, New Yorkers argued, "whether inherent in the People, or sprung from any other Cause, has received the royal Sanction, is the Basis of our Colony State, [and has] become venerable by long Usage."[25] Parliament's assertions of authority over the colonies were dubbed innovations and resisted as a "new and awful Idea of the Constitution."[26] John Philip Reid has shown at great length the extent to which common law ideas were part of the revolutionary struggle.

But in the aftermath of the Revolution, there were also influential arguments that Americans should not blindly obey custom. As Bernard Bailyn has argued in the context of the debates over the ratification of the U.S. Constitution, it was Federalists who argued for a break with, and Anti-Federalists who argued for keeping faith with, tradition, the tradition being that of republicanism.[27] Anti-Federalists had objected to various aspects of the proposed constitutional text – the "Necessary and Proper" Clause, the Supremacy Clause, the reference to Congress's power "to raise and support armies," and the absence of a bill of rights – as an attempt to inject the new American political order with precisely those attributes of "mysterious," overweening power that the Revolution had been fought to check. In response, Federalists argued against facile, unthinking continuity with the republican tradition. The past should not be followed for its own sake. One had to be alive to differences in context and assert the right to make one's present. In other words, Federalists were making an argument about the legitimacy of contemporaneous consent. As James Madison put it in one of the early *Federalist* papers:

> Hearken not to the voice which petulantly tells you that the form of government recommended for your adoption is a novelty in the political world … shut your ears against this unhallowed language. Shut your hearts against the poison which it conveys.… Is it not the glory of the people of America, that whilst they have paid a decent regard to the opinions of former times and other nations, they have not suffered a blind veneration for antiquity, for custom, or for names, to overrule

[24] Hulsebosch, *Constituting Empire*, pp. 63–64 (emphasis in the original).

[25] Ibid., p. 93.

[26] Ibid.

[27] Bailyn, *Ideological Origins of the American Revolution.*

the suggestions of their own good sense, the knowledge of their own situation, and the lessons of their own experience?

... Had no important step been taken by the leaders of the Revolution for which a precedent could not be discovered, no Government established of which an exact model did not present itself, the People of the United States might, at this moment, have been numbered among the melancholy victims of misguided councils, must at best have been labouring under the weight of some other of those forms which have crushed the liberties of the rest of mankind.[28]

Nevertheless, as a result of vigorous debate over the constitutional text, various aspects of England's "ancient constitution" – rights to jury trials in criminal cases, prohibitions on warrantless searches and seizures, bars on double jeopardy – were incorporated and transformed into written fundamental rights in the Bill of Rights. However, the incorporation of aspects of England's "ancient constitution" into America's written constitutions hardly ended discussions of the relationship between the two. By the 1790s, however, the nature of the debate between Federalists and Anti-Federalists had shifted. The former now argued for continuity with the British past; the latter for a break with it.

The discussion must begin with the late eighteenth century's most impassioned defense of British customary constitutionalism under the pressures of revolution, Edmund Burke's *Reflections on the Revolution in France* (1790). To be sure, Burke was responding to the challenges of the French, rather than the American, Revolution (he had been a defender of Americans' rights during their constitutional struggles with Great Britain). But the subsequent American debate over Burke's text reveals a great deal about how Americans in the early 1790s divided on the question of their relationship to their constitutional past.[29]

Burke's great fear was that radicals in France and England bandied about ahistorical principles without any regard for the specific contexts within which such principles had necessarily to be instantiated and which in turn provided the only basis for judging their worth. As he put it, "Circumstances (which with some gentlemen pass for nothing) give in reality to every political principle its distinguishing colour, and

[28] James Madison, Federalist 14, in *The Federalist* (New York: C. Scribner, 1863), pp. 88–89.

[29] Edmund Burke, *Reflections on the Revolution in France*, in *Two Classics of the French Revolution* (New York: Anchor Books, 1989). On Burke's common law sensibilities, see J. G. A. Pocock, "Burke and the Ancient Constitution: A Problem in the History of Ideas," in *Politics, Language & Time: Essays on Political Thought and History* (New York: Atheneum, 1971).

discriminating effect.... Is it because liberty in the abstract may be classed amongst the blessings of mankind, that I am seriously to felicitate a madman, who has escaped from ... his cell, on his restoration to the enjoyment of light and liberty?"[30] For Burke, circumstances gave meaning to principles, mitigating the abstraction of principles by enmeshing them in a temporal, complex, specific world of multiple overlapping claims and interests, a world in many ways close to the common law world Blackstone had described in such detail. Burke's preference for circumstance over principle is a preference for a gradual building up and solidification of government and law over time.

This building up of law over time is described explicitly in terms of the nonhistorical temporality of "insensibility" articulated by common law thinkers such as Hale. Burke argues that the English constitutional order both changes and does not change, is always identical to and different from itself. As such, England's common law order resists the historicist differentiation between old and new, "mysterious" and transparent, ancien régime and new order, that late-eighteenth-century revolutionary thought set such store by. "The spirit of our constitution," Burke claims, is "a sort of immortality through all transmigrations."[31] Indeed, where American legal thinkers of all persuasions repudiated "mystery" as a feature of European power, the proto-romantic Burke embraces "mystery," describing it positively precisely because it allows a breaking down of distinctions between past, present, and future. In its "mystery," Burke argues, the English constitutional order matches "the order of the world" and nature itself. Where thinkers like Paine and Jefferson opposed "mystery" to nature, the Burke sees nature as itself "mysterious":

> Our political system is placed in a just correspondence and symmetry with the order of the world, and with the mode of existence decreed to a permanent body composed of transitory parts; wherein, by the disposition of a stupendous wisdom, moulding together the great mysterious incorporation of the human race, the whole, at one time, is never old, or middle-aged, or young, but in a condition of unchangeable constancy, moves on through the varied tenour of perpetual decay, fall, renovation, and progression. Thus, by preserving the method of nature in the conduct of the state, in what we improve we are never wholly new; in what we retain we are never wholly obsolete.... In this choice of inheritance we have given to our frame of polity the image of a relation in blood; binding up the constitution of our country with our dearest domestic ties.[32]

[30] Burke, *Reflections*, p. 19.

[31] Ibid., p. 34.

[32] Ibid., pp. 45–46.

Given Burke's equation in this excerpt of "our frame of polity" to "a relation in blood," it is not surprising that his preferred metaphor for England's common law constitution is, in the spirit of Coke, "inheritance." Like Coke, Burke describes the English constitutional order as an inheritance in order to embrace and claim the presence of the past.[33] He repeatedly secures the meaning of this idea of inheritance through recourse to the common law property concept of the entail, precisely the legal device through which ancestors controlled the disposition of property down the bloodline (and the landholding form that Kames, Jefferson, and others had attacked so vigorously as an artifact of feudalism). Thus, Burke states, the English "claim and assert our liberties, as an *entailed inheritance* derived to us from our forefathers, and to be transmitted to our posterity; as an estate specially belonging to the people of this kingdom."[34] The English state, for Burke, is "locked fast as in a sort of *family settlement*, grasped as in a kind of mortmain forever."[35]

The representation of government and law as a precious "entailed inheritance" – something derived from the past that is only held temporarily before it is transmitted intact to the future – involves a conception of human political agency implicit in common law modes of thought but completely different from what I have described as the lonely subject of contemporaneous consent associated with radical democratic thought. For Burke, those of the present generation are always only "temporary possessors and life-renters" of the world, a mere conduit between past and future.[36] For Burke, radical democrats in France and England – and, he might have added, America – were driven by nothing other than "a present sense of convenience" or "the bent of a present inclination."[37] This present-oriented "spirit of innovation" was self-regarding and limited: "A spirit of innovation is generally the result of a selfish temper and confined views. People will not look forward to posterity, who never look backward to their ancestors."[38] All great questions, for Burke, necessarily implicated past, present, and future. To have them decided only by the living only for the living – the Jeffersonian idea – excluded important parties from the negotiating table. "Where the great interests of mankind are concerned through a long succession of generations," Burke declares,

[33] Ibid., p. 43.
[34] Ibid., p. 45 (emphasis in original).
[35] Ibid. (emphasis added).
[36] Ibid., p. 108.
[37] Ibid., p. 37.
[38] Ibid., p. 45.

"that succession ought to be admitted into some share in the councils which are so deeply to affect them. If justice requires this, the work itself requires the aid of more minds than one age can furnish."[39] The preceding sentence reveals Burke's debt to Coke. Coke had opposed the encroachments of England's monarch by arguing that a single individual could not possibly possess the undifferentiated collective wisdom of multiple generations embodied in an "immemorial" common law. Burke deploys the same idea against the present-minded revolutionary generation.

The *Reflections* did not pass without immediate response. Intimately involved in revolutionary activities in France, in February 1791 Paine published *Rights of Man: Being an Answer to Mr. Burke's Attack on the French Revolution*. Intended to be a defense of the French Revolution, *Rights of Man* was also written with a keen eye on the American political scene. Paine dedicated the tract to George Washington, expressing the wish that Washington might "enjoy the happiness of seeing the new world regenerate the old."[40]

A large part of Paine's critique of Burke's notion of the English customary constitutional order's "mysterious" incorporation of past, present, and future was a restatement of the presentist, consent-based arguments of *Common Sense*. Burke had lauded the constitutional settlement of 1688 and argued for its binding power. Paine was at pains to attack arguments for continuity with 1688:

> Every age and generation must be as free to act for itself, *in all cases*, as the ages and generations which preceded it.... The parliament or the people of 1688, or of any other period, had no more right to dispose of the people of the present day, or to bind or control them *in any shape whatever*, than the parliament or the people of the present day have to dispose of, bind or control those who are to live an hundred or a thousand years hence [emphasis in original].[41]

However, Paine's most pointed criticisms were directed at Burke's understanding of the term "constitution." In the *Reflections*, Burke had maintained that pre-1789 France had possessed a constitution just as England currently possessed one. By "constitution," Burke had meant exactly what many other eighteenth-century common lawyers might have meant: a common law or customary structure of government that had emerged over time as a result of specific negotiations among the various

[39] Ibid., p. 185.
[40] Paine, *Rights of Man*, unpaginated dedication.
[41] Ibid., p. 4.

branches of government, a series of declaratory acts, and a repetition of past practices that knitted past, present, and future together. By contrast, Paine argued that a constitution that was the proper product of contemporaneous consent had to consist of "principles" – separated out, delineated, visible, and written – rather than of a diffuse Burkean mass of past circumstances. On such a definition, the celebrated "ancient constitution" simply did not exist:

> A constitution is not a thing in name only, but in fact. *It has not an ideal, but a real existence; and wherever it cannot be produced in a visible form, there is none.... It is the body of elements, to which you can refer, and quote article by article, and contains the principles on which the government shall be established.*
>
> Can then Mr. Burke produce the English constitution? If he cannot, we may fairly conclude, that though it has been so much talked about, no such thing as a constitution exists, or ever did exist, and consequently the people have yet a constitution to form [emphasis added].[42]

What followed was a long criticism of unprincipled English parliamentary procedure that, in showing that Parliament was bound by nothing, demonstrated the absence of any English constitution.[43] But Paine had faith that things would change in Great Britain. The French and American Revolutions were bound to have an impact, for "when once the veil [another reference to the "mystery" of European power] begins to rend, it admits not of repair."[44] Indeed, Paine concluded triumphantly, "I do not believe that monarchy and aristocracy will continue seven years longer in any of the enlightened countries of Europe."[45]

Paine's *Rights of Man* was published in the United States by an enterprising publisher who, apparently without authorization, appended as a foreword an excerpt from Jefferson's approving note regarding the book. Jefferson had written, "I am extremely pleased to find ... that something is at length to be publicly said against the political heresies which have sprung up among us. I have no doubt that our citizens will rally a second time to the standard of Common Sense."[46] There was little doubt that Jefferson had John Adams's writings in mind. The letters of "Publicola,"

[42] Ibid., pp. 41–42.

[43] For example, Paine states, "The act by which the English parliament empowered itself to sit for seven years, shows there is no constitution in England. It might, by the same self authority, have sat any greater number of years or for life." Ibid., p. 43.

[44] Ibid., p. 97.

[45] Ibid., p. 141.

[46] Quoted in Lance Banning, *The Jeffersonian Persuasion* (Ithaca, N.Y.: Cornell University Press, 1978), p. 155.

published in the *Columbian Centinel* in June and July 1791, were a response to Paine's *Rights of Man*. Initially, John Adams was thought to be the author, but suspicion eventually – and correctly – centered on his son, John Quincy Adams.[47]

Adams sought to meet head on Paine's argument that the English had to give themselves a constitution because they did not already possess one. If Paine's definition of a constitution as one existing "in a visible form" and that one could quote "article by article" were adopted, Adams asserted, one would be hard pressed to find "in all history, a government that will come within this definition ... previous to the year 1776." But this was clearly absurd. How could one account for the long opposition tradition of eighteenth-century England that had culminated in the American Revolution? The claims made on the basis of "the principles of the English Constitution" by "the most illustrious Whig writers in England" and "the glorious Congress of 1774" rendered Paine's definition utterly illegitimate. Adams went on to make the point more clearly:

> [The British constitution] is composed of a venerable *system* of unwritten or customary laws, handed down from time immemorial, and sanctioned by the accumulated experience of the ages; and of a body of statutes enacted by an authority lawfully competent to that purpose.... I hope they [the English] will never abolish a system so excellent, merely because it cannot be produced in a visible form.... [H]owever frequently [the British constitution] may have been violated by tyrants, monarchical, aristocratical, or democratical, the people have always found it expedient to restore the original foundation, while from time to time they have been successful in improving and ornamenting the building [emphasis in original].[48]

Adams's reference to Britain's common law constitution as an improved and ornamented building resting upon an "original foundation" hearkens to Blackstone's celebrated metaphor of the common law as a constantly refurbished feudal castle. Endorsing the idea of an "immemorial" British constitution, Adams follows up with a notion of attributed and multigenerational consent: "The right of a people to legislate for succeeding generations derives all its authority from the consent of that posterity who are bound by their laws; and therefore the expressions of perpetuity used by the Parliament of 1688, contain no

[47] I draw this information from *The Writings of John Quincy Adams*, Vol. 1: *1779–1796* (Worthington Chauncey Ford, ed.) (New York: MacMillan, 1913), p. 65, n. 1.

[48] Ibid., pp. 74–75.

absurdity; and expressions of a similar nature may be found in all the Constitutions of the United States."[49]

Notwithstanding Adams's vindication of British common law constitutionalism and his rejection of the starkest forms of contemporaneous consent as a test of the legitimacy of law, prominent American legal writers continued to emphasize the creation of written constitutions in America as an important historical break vis-à-vis British practice. But there were divisions on how this break was to be related to its British background.

For some, following Paine, the writing of the U.S. Constitution was a sort of emergence from an unencumbered state of nature in a self-conscious, concrete, visible act of contemporaneous consent that stood by itself. In 1795, Connecticut's Zephaniah Swift wrote, "At the dissolution of our connexion with Great Britain, tho we could not be literally said, to be in a state of nature, yet the states which had been directly dependent on the British crown, were so in a political point of view."[50] The U.S. Constitution, Swift maintained, was "the most illustrious example of a government founded on the voluntary contract of the people, that the page of history has ever recorded."[51] In his famous 1803 "republican" edition of Blackstone's *Commentaries*, Virginia's St. George Tucker spelled out the position more systematically. Blackstone's views about the impossibility of finding "original contracts" had made sense, perhaps, in a world in which "tradition [had supplied] the place of written evidence; where every new construction [had been] in fact a new edict; and where the fountain of power [had been] immemorially transferred from the people, to the usurpers of their natural rights."[52] But this had all changed.

> [T]he American revolution has formed a new epoch in the history of civil institutions, by reducing to practice, what, before, had been supposed to exist only in the visionary speculations of theoretical writers. *The world, for the first time since the annals of its inhabitants began, saw an original written compact formed by the free and deliberate voices of individuals disposed to unite in the same social bonds, thus exhibiting a political phenomenon unknown to former ages* [emphasis added].

Indeed, relying on James Mackintosh's *Vindiciae Gallicae: Defense of the French Revolution* (1791) and reversing Burke's preference for circumstance over principle, Tucker argued that "all the governments that

[49] Ibid., p. 72.

[50] Swift, *A System of Laws of the State of Connecticut*, Vol. 1, p. 12.

[51] Ibid.

[52] St. George Tucker ed., *Blackstone's Commentaries*, Vol. 1, App., p. 4.

now exist in the world, except the United States of America, have been fortuitously formed. They are the produce of chance, not the work of art.... These fortuitous governments cannot be supposed to derive their existence from the free consent of the people."[53] Nothing was clearer: writing was the required evidence that law was the product of contemporaneous consent. Only writing, rather than customary or circumstantial checks and balances between branches of government, truly guaranteed the freedom of the people.[54] This was because only writing could fix what precisely had been consented to. In England, Tucker argued, the liberty of the press was grounded merely "on its not being prohibited." Such liberty could be overridden at any time. In the United States, by contrast, the liberty of the press was protected "by a visible solid foundation" in the constitutional text.[55]

Not all American lawyers shared Tucker's views of the U.S. Constitution as an "original written compact" breaking with the English tradition. Like Blackstone, American common lawyers frequently condemned state of nature and natural rights arguments by pointing out that civil and social rights – that is, rights recognized at common law – were original to man. For example, in his *Dissertations: Being the Preliminary Part of a Course of Law Lectures* (1795), a self-published text based on lectures given at Columbia College, James Kent dismissed state of nature theories precisely because they suggested that "civil society ... was a matter of expediency, rather than the course of our original destination."[56] "Expediency," in the hands of common lawyers, was a pejorative descriptor of the reckless disregard for past and future that the subject of contemporaneous consent displayed (Burke called this a "present sense of convenience"). Kent expressed concern over "the universal passion for novelty" sweeping Europe that "threatens to overturn everything which bears the stamp of time and experience."[57] Kent subscribed instead to the views of Vermont's Nathaniel Chipman, who had argued in his *Sketches of the Principles of Government* (1793) that man was fitted and intended by the great author of his being for society and government.[58] "Our civil

[53] Ibid., p. 15.
[54] Ibid., p. 14.
[55] Ibid., p. 298.
[56] James Kent, *Dissertations: Being the Preliminary Part of a Course of Law Lectures* (New York: George Forman, 1795) (1991), p. 6.
[57] Kent, "Introductory Lecture," p. 343.
[58] Nathaniel Chipman, *Sketches of the Principles of Government* (Rutland, Vt.: From the Press of J. Lyon, 1793), pp. 33–40.

and social rights," Kent maintained, "are our true natural rights."[59] When one looked for the state of nature, from which (for St. George Tucker) the American people had emerged, one found law – and, indeed, the common law – already there.

This view allowed Kent to argue that the common law had undergirded the American Revolution: "[N]o higher evidence need or can be produced of the prevailing knowledge of our rights, and the energy of the freedom of the Common Law, than the spirit which pervaded and roused every part of this Continent on the eve of the late Revolution."[60] Furthermore, Kent argued that Americans, with their written fundamental law, were in no way superior to those who had only an unwritten law. *Contra* Tucker, written law was not the way of the future. Hume had convinced him, Kent observed, "that the present civilized monarchies of Europe [i.e., Great Britain] are governments of laws and not of men, and that under them property is secure, industry encouraged, and the arts flourish."[61] Indeed, the Commons had been able "constantly to meliorate the blessings, and increase the importance of their political condition."[62] Nevertheless, for Kent, there remained "important ... abridgments of freedom" in England, namely religious establishment, hereditary orders, inadequate representation, and the unchecked power of a monarchy that exercised power through the agencies of the nobility, the church, the national debt, and the army.[63] America's "noble experiment" had been to introduce "the principle of representation and responsibility into every part of [the government]."[64]

Kent offers us one instance of how common lawyers in the postrevolutionary decades mingled the language of the common law with the more radical democratic language of America's "noble experiment," insisting upon the self-conscious break that American constitutionalism embodied *and* upon its roots in the common law. A more dramatic version of how American common law thinkers blended newer historical languages with older common law ones is afforded in the writings of U.S. Supreme Court Justice James Wilson. Wilson has been described as having exercised more influence on the structure of the U.S. Constitution than anyone other than James Madison and as having been the principal architect

[59] Kent, *Dissertations*, p. 7.
[60] Kent, "Introductory Lecture," p. 333.
[61] Kent, *Dissertations*, p. 9.
[62] Ibid., p. 14
[63] Ibid., pp. 16–17.
[64] Ibid., p. 17.

of the Pennsylvania Constitution of 1790. Wilson was one of only six men to have signed both the Declaration of Independence and the U.S. Constitution.[65]

Wilson's reflections on the relationship between the written U.S. and Pennsylvania Constitutions and the common law were advanced in a series of lectures delivered at the College of Philadelphia between 1790 and 1792.[66] In the *Lectures*, Wilson promised to investigate "the different parts of the constitution and government of the United States, [which] will lay the foundation of a very interesting parallel between them and the pride of Europe – the British constitution." Wilson's *Lectures* would be self-consciously historical. Particularly in "free countries," Wilson insisted, "[l]aw should be studied and taught as a historical science."[67]

Like Paine, Jefferson, and Tucker, Wilson celebrated America as something unprecedented, something entirely new. In other words, he fully appropriated the radical democratic vocabularies that rested upon a sense of a sharp break with the past. As Wilson put it, "In no other part of the world, and in no former period, even in this part of it, have youth ever beheld so glorious and sublime a prospect before them."[68] This rather Jeffersonian celebration of America's "glorious and sublime," endlessly open future went along with an embrace of the idea of contemporaneous – rather than multigenerational – consent. Wilson articulated it clearly: "All human laws should be founded on the consent of those who obey them."[69] This was not a common lawyerly notion of "immemorial" multigenerational consent attributed to law. Instead, what Wilson called the "revolution principle" supported the view that Americans, in the name of consent, could shrug off precedent "whenever they please":

> This revolution principle – that, the sovereign power residing in the people, they may change their constitution and government whenever they please – is not a principle of discord, rancor, or war: it is a principle of melioration, contentment, and peace.[70]

[65] See Mark David Hall, *The Political and Legal Philosophy of James Wilson, 1742–1798* (Columbia: University of Missouri Press, 1997), p. 1. For a more recent treatment of Wilson, see John Fabian Witt, *Patriots and Cosmopolitans: Hidden Histories of American Law* (Cambridge, Mass.: Harvard University Press, 2007), Chap. 1.

[66] The inaugural lecture appears to have been something of an event. It was attended by the president and vice president of the United States, both houses of Congress, and the president and both houses of the legislature of Pennsylvania.

[67] *The Works of James Wilson*, Vol. 1, p. 3.

[68] Ibid., p. 37.

[69] Ibid., p. 179.

[70] Ibid., p. 18.

Accordingly, like Paine, Wilson argued, *contra* Blackstone and Burke, that Americans were precisely not bound by the constitutional precedent of 1688. Wilson thus comes very close to the radical democratic position.

But such a view cannot be sustained without qualification. For Wilson, America's written constitutions represent an open future, a radical break with the past in the name of the "revolution principle," but simultaneously a return to a distant past. In the manner of an "insensibly" changing common law that collapses identity and difference, America's constitutions are both very new and very old. Wilson secures the blurring of past and future through the familiar Whig narrative of Saxon simplicity and Norman encroachment upon that simplicity. English law was beset with "new and oppressive refinements" that had been "gradually introduced by the Norman practitioners, with a view to supersede (as they did in great measure) the more homely, but the more free and intelligible, maxims of distributive justice among the Saxons."[71] America stood precisely for a shedding of Norman encroachments and a recovery of Saxon originals. As Wilson told his audience, "You will be pleased to hear, that, with regard to ... many ... subjects, we have renewed, in our governments, the principles and the practice of the ancient Saxons."[72] Wilson thus saw the written American constitutions of his day as bearing a marked resemblance to the unwritten Saxon one:

> The original frame of the British constitution, different, indeed, in many important points, from what it now is, and bearing to some of the constitutions which have lately been formed, and established, in America, a degree of resemblance, which will strike and surprise those who compare them together – this venerable frame may be considered as of Saxon architecture.[73]

Wilson saw striking parallels between written American constitutional structures and Saxon customs in the following specific contexts: the resting of the entire government on the elective principle; provisions respecting the adjournment of houses of legislature; the freedom of members of Congress from arrest during their attendance of sessions; the legislative right to make war; the election of the chief executive; the structure of the judiciary; rights to jury trials; the election of sheriffs (under the Pennsylvania Constitution of 1790); and the right to bear arms.[74]

[71] Ibid., pp. xxii–xxiii.

[72] Ibid., Vol. 2, p. 278.

[73] Ibid., Vol. 1, p. 448.

[74] Ibid., Vol. 2, pp. 18, 36, 57–58, 63, 79 *et seq*., 238, 404. James Kent would also see the structure of the postrevolutionary government as being traceable back to Germany. As he

This invocation of the Saxon constitution was not a mere rhetorical nod in the direction of Anti-Federalists chafing under the Federalist administration. For one, drawing analogies between the U.S. and Saxon constitution was a way of arguing for continuity with the past at a time – the time of Burke's *Reflections* – when arguments about continuity had become highly politicized and were openly serving counterrevolutionary ends. More important, the ways in which Wilson used the argument about continuity could not have pleased states' rights Anti-Federalists. In his concurring opinion in *Chisholm v. Georgia* (1793), Wilson agreed with the rest of the U.S. Supreme Court that Article III of the U.S. Constitution authorized the citizen of a state to sue another state in federal court (the decision was subsequently overruled by the passage of the Eleventh Amendment). Wilson saw this provision of the U.S. Constitution as an improvement over the current English constitution and a return to the Saxon:

> In England, according to Sir William Blackstone, no suit can be brought against the King, even in civil matters. So, in that Kingdom, is the law, at this time, received. But it was not always so. Under the Saxon Government, a very different doctrine was held to be orthodox. Under that Government, as we are informed by the Mirror of Justice, a book said, by Sir Edward Coke, to have been written, in part, at least, before the conquest; under that Government it was ordained, and that the King's Court should be open to all Plaintiffs, by which, without delay, they should have remedial writs, as well against the King or against the Queen, as against any other of the people. The law continued to be the same for some centuries after the conquest.[75]

Thus we see, in at least one influential rendering of the relationship between the American constitutions and the Saxon one (advanced by no less than a sitting U.S. Supreme Court justice), that written fundamental law and unwritten common law, even as they could be distinguished in the name of a historical break grounded in ideas of contemporaneous consent, nevertheless remained intimately linked versions of one another. While America's written fundamental law, founded on the "revolution principle," repudiated the past and gestured toward a new and open future, the "revolution principle" ultimately returned America to England's "immemorial" past. This way of plotting the relationship between America's constitutions and the

put it, "It is from the antient Germans that our present ideas of a mixed and representative government are supposed to be derived." Kent, *Dissertations*, p. 12.

[75] *Chisholm v. Georgia*, 2 U.S. 419 (1793), 460.

British constitution underscores how common lawyers combined historical and nonhistorical temporalities. History represented a break with common law continuities, on the one hand, even as it ended up returning to those continuities, on the other.

Written Law and its Unwritten Supplement in the New Polities

Even as they debated the ontology of the American constitutions, American legal thinkers in the late eighteenth and early nineteenth centuries struggled over a related question: how to give meaning to written law in polities considered to be organized on the principle of contemporaneous consent. Notwithstanding the professed faith of republican legal thinkers like St. George Tucker that written texts would ensure their own meaning – and hence secure the boundaries of the contemporaneous consent that had given rise to them – it soon became clear that written texts were capable of engendering as much uncertainty as unwritten ones. If writing was taken to be the only way to ensure that official power did not exceed limits, the problem of supplementing written law with unwritten law was a grave one indeed. It threatened the integrity of contemporaneous consent and muddled the imagined shift from European "mystery" to American transparency.

In its early years, the U.S. Supreme Court hinted at an intimate relationship between the U.S. Constitution and underlying custom when it came to establishing the meaning of the constitutional text. In its 1798 decision in *Calder v. Bull*, the Court limited the scope of the *Ex Post Facto* Clause of the U.S. Constitution to the criminal context in reliance upon the writings of "[t]he celebrated and judicious Sir William Blackstone," his successor Wooddeson, the *Federalist*, and various state constitutions. Domestic custom came to play a specific role in the case. The result was to permit the state of Connecticut – the unwritten constitution of which was described as "composed of its charter, acts of assembly, and usages, and customs" – to pass a legislative resolution permitting appeals in an already adjudicated will dispute in respect of which appeals had previously been legally unavailable. Justice Paterson's concurring opinion would have specifically allowed Connecticut to override the earlier adjudication of the dispute on the ground that Connecticut's legislature possessed "customary judicial capacity," making a legislative overruling of an adjudicated dispute more like the act of an appellate court than like a true *ex post facto* law, thus entirely removing the dispute from possible coverage by the

Constitution's *Ex Post Facto* Clause. Custom – whether resting upon a reading of Blackstone or an acknowledgment of Connecticut's own practices – thus informed the Supreme Court's interpretation of the U.S. Constitution.[76]

But it was by no means clear to all that the federal government should be able to import the common law into its understanding of its own enumerated powers. In the late 1790s, the conflict between Federalists and Anti-Federalists intensified around questions of foreign policy, the suspicion of foreign radicals, and the prosecution of domestic seditious libel. The conflict over Federalist legislation in these areas and over federal common law crimes in general resolved into two related questions: whether Congress possessed common law jurisdiction under the U.S. Constitution and Bill of Rights and whether Article III of the U.S. Constitution conferred common law jurisdiction upon the federal courts. While much of the debate took place in terms of the internal meanings and interrelationships of the clauses of the constitutional text, the question of the relationship between the written text and its unwritten common law background was present in the minds of all parties. At issue, in other words, was whether written principles as products of contemporaneous consent could stand alone or not.

In the spring of 1798, Massachusetts Federalist Congressman Harrison Gray Otis, arguing on behalf of the administration's sedition bill in the House, argued that the common law informed both the U.S. Constitution and state statutes. As he put it, "The people of the individual States brought with them as a birthright into this country the common law of England, upon which all of them have founded their statute law. If it were not for this common law, many crimes which are committed in the United States would go unpunished. No State has enacted statutes for the punishment of all crimes which may be committed."[77] This foundational, interstitial presence of the common law at the level of the states, Otis argued, necessarily extended to the U.S. Constitution. The common law was the background from which the meaning of the constitutional text had to be derived. "When the people of the United States convened for the purpose of framing a federal compact, they were all habituated to this common law, to its usages, its maxims, its definitions." It was natural to conclude then that, in framing the Constitution, "they kept in view the model of the common law, and that a safe recourse may be had to it in

[76] *Calder v. Bull*, 3 U.S. 386 (1798), 391, 392–393, 395.

[77] *Annals of Congress*, House of Representatives, 5C, 2S, 2146.

all cases that would otherwise be doubtful." The very language of the constitutional text had no meaning unless one referred back to the common law:

> Again, what is intended by "cases at law and equity arising under the Constitution,' as distinguished from 'cases arising under the laws of the United States" [the language of Article III]? What other law can be contemplated but common law; what sort of equity but that legal discretion that has been exercised in England from time immemorial, and is to be learnt from the books and reports of that country? [W]hat is to be done with other terms, with trial, jury, impeachment, &c., for an explanation of all which the common law alone can furnish a standard?[78]

The U.S. Constitution, so proudly hailed by many as an original written compact emerging in an act of self-conscious reflection, was thus undergirded, Otis suggested, by an "immemorial" common law.

This argument extended as well to the Bill of Rights. Opponents of the sedition bill had made much of the express language of the First Amendment ("Congress shall make no law abridging the freedom of speech and of the press"). But this language, Otis argued, was merely "a mode of expression which we had borrowed from the only country in which it had been tolerated [i.e., Great Britain]." Its construction, therefore, "should be consonant not only to the laws of that country, but to the laws and judicial decisions of many of the States composing the Union." This freedom consisted of the right to write, publish, and speak one's opinion subject to being answerable for "false, malicious and seditious expression, whether spoken or written." In support of this interpretation of the language of the First Amendment, Otis cited not only Blackstone's *Commentaries*, but also – recognizing that invocations of English authority would make him an easy target of criticism – the laws of various states that had "adopted the definitions of the English law."[79]

Pennsylvania Republican Albert Gallatin responded to Otis's arguments on behalf of the sedition bill by focusing on the self-sufficiency and integrity of the constitutional text. It was necessary to remind the House, he argued, of agreed-upon "Constitutional principles." The language of these principles was "strict and precise; it gave not a vague power, arbitrarily, to create offences against Government." The Constitution had specified the authority of Congress to legislate against certain crimes and no others; it had similarly specified the jurisdiction of the federal courts.

[78] Ibid., 5C, 2S, 2147.
[79] Ibid., 5C, 2S, 2148.

This carefully laid down language excluded common law crimes and federal common law jurisdiction. Furthermore, it was clear. No "immemorial" common law background or supplement was necessary in order to understand the constitutional text. Gallatin contended that Otis was wrong to conclude that the use of technical terms in the constitutional text such as "writ of habeas corpus" implied that federal courts had common law jurisdiction. There was a difference between "the principles of the common law, and the jurisdiction of cases arising under it." Principles of the common law applied only where jurisdiction had been expressly conferred upon federal courts. This did not mean that federal courts had common law jurisdiction generally.[80]

A frequent Republican argument against the common law as an "immemorial" supplement to the constitutional text was that the common law had no temporal priority whatsoever vis-à-vis the U.S. Constitution. It was thus not an antecedent background at all. In the contemporary United States, St. George Tucker argued in his 1803 edition of Blackstone's *Commentaries*, the common law owed its validity not to any inheritance from ancestors, but entirely and exclusively to postrevolutionary acts of reception in the different states.[81] As such, the common law, like the U.S. Constitution, was the product of contemporaneous consent. This argument also made it possible to claim that there was no common law *tout court*. Different jurisdictions had adopted the common law differently. These variations in the common law meant that "we must ... abandon all hope of satisfaction from *any general theory*, and resort to [the colonies'] several charters, provincial establishments, legislative codes, and civil histories, for information."[82] Common law crimes were acceptable in Virginia, Tucker argued, only because the common law had

[80] Ibid., 5C, 2S, 2156–2159. Republican arguments about the limits of federal power took place, of course, within a larger context in which federal extension of power was seen as an encroachment upon the power of the states. The celebrated 1799 declaration of the Virginia General Assembly protested the idea that the common law of England should be part of federal law on precisely such grounds. Given the labor involved in drawing the now-agreed-upon line between federal and state powers, the Virginia General Assembly objected, it was distressing that elements within the federal government were seeking to enlarge federal power by incorporating "in the lump, in an indirect manner, and by a forced construction of a few phrases, the vast and multifarious jurisdiction involved in the common law." Thomas Jefferson and James Madison, *The Virginia Report of 1799–1800, Touching the Alien and Sedition Laws; Together with the Virginia Resolutions of December 21, 1798* (Union, N.J.: Lawbook Exchange, 2004), p. 217.

[81] St. George Tucker, ed., *Blackstone's Commentaries*, Vol. 1, p. 80.

[82] Ibid., App., p. 393.

been explicitly adopted there. This was not the case at the federal level because the common law had not been adopted at that level.

This relocation of the origins of the common law to the present, its transformation from something "immemorial" into a product of contemporaneous consent, made it possible for Tucker to argue that giving meaning to the U.S. Constitution in terms of the common law would represent an overriding of popular consent:

> [A]s every nation is bound to preserve itself, or, in other words, it's independence; so no interpretation whereby it's destruction, or that of the state, which is the same thing, may be hazarded, can be admitted in any case where it has not, in the *most express terms*, given it's consent to such an interpretation [emphasis in original].

The very constitution and acts of legislature, Tucker declared, would be nullities "if the common law of England be paramount thereto."[83] This would have even specific consequences for the states. Among other things, the Virginian wrote, admitting federal common law jurisdiction would override the constitutional and legal recognition of slavery in the states because the English common law did not admit it.[84]

Even as the battle over federal common law jurisdiction raged, however, the U.S. Supreme Court under the chief justiceship of John Marshall actively converted common law background into federal constitutional principle. The case of *Fletcher v. Peck* (1810), the first of the Court's major Contract Clause cases, provides an example.[85] The dispute in *Fletcher* involved a statute passed by the Georgia legislature in 1795 that conveyed large tracts of land to four land companies. A year later, allegations that the companies had bribed legislators surfaced and a newly constituted legislature passed another statute rescinding the conveyances. *Fletcher v. Peck* was set up as a test case in which subsequent purchasers of the lands brought suit to determine the validity of their titles.

At issue was the applicability of the Contract Clause of the U.S. Constitution that prevented states from passing laws "impairing the Obligation of Contracts."[86] But it was not at all obvious that the Contract Clause should govern. Attempting to trace the rather sketchy background of the Contract Clause, G. Edward White has concluded that, "first, it

[83] Ibid., p. 423.
[84] Ibid., p. 425.
[85] 6 Cranch. 87 (1810).
[86] U.S. Const., Art I, Sec. 10.

was designed as one of several restrictions on the power of states to give relief to debtors in periods when the supply of specie was reduced; and, second, that its scope was limited to private contracts."[87] It was not clear, in other words, that the Contracts Clause was ever intended to apply to legislative grants to groups of individuals or whether public contracts (those between the state and individuals) were to be treated as identical, for purposes of constitutional law, to private contracts (those between individuals). For Marshall, however, the governing analogy was contracts between private parties, that is, contracts governed by the common law. As he put it, "Their [referring to conveyees of the original grantees] case is not distinguishable from the ordinary case of purchasers of a legal estate without knowledge of any secret fraud which might have led to the emanation of the original grant. According to the well known course of equity, their rights could not be affected by such fraud."[88] It remained to show that a "grant" was a "contract." Blackstone provided the necessary authority:

> A contract is a compact between two or more parties, and is either executory [to be performed] or executed [performed].... *A contract executed is one in which the object of contract is performed; and this, says Blackstone, differs in nothing from a grant.* The contract between Georgia and the purchasers was executed by the grant.... A grant, in its own nature, amounts to an extinguishment of the right of the grantor, and implies a contract not to reassert that right. A party, is, therefore, always estopped by his own grant [emphasis added].[89]

The general language of the Contract Clause, Marshall continued, was applicable to "contracts of every description," private *and* public. Georgia could not, in other words, rescind the sales of the lands with respect to subsequent purchasers of those lands. Such was the teaching of "those rules of property which are common to all the citizens of the United States, and from those principles of equity which are acknowledged in all our courts."[90] What had once been a set of rules at common law and equity applicable to contracts between private parties had now defined the scope and meaning of the Contract Clause. The common law was thus absorbed into the written text.

[87] G. Edward White, *The Marshall Court and Cultural Change, 1815–1835* (Oxford: Oxford University Press, 1988), p. 601.

[88] 6 Cranch. 87, p. 135.

[89] 6 Cranch. 87, pp. 136–137.

[90] 6 Cranch. 87, p. 134.

This does not mean, however, that the federal courts were able to expand their jurisdiction unchecked in every area. In part, this had to do with the shift in political tide. After the "revolution of 1800," the Sedition Act expired on its own terms. Thereafter, the Federalist position on federal common law crimes began to crumble. In *United States v. Worrall* (1798), Justice Chase, ironically the most vigorous enforcer of the Sedition Act, had declared, "In my opinion, the United States as a Federal government, have no common law; and consequently no indictment can be maintained in their Courts, for offences merely at common law."[91] This position was confirmed in *United States v. Hudson and Goodwin* (1812), when the U.S. Supreme Court declared that it had been "long settled in public opinion" that a person could not be convicted of a federal crime without a statute.[92] In 1813, U.S. Supreme Court Justice William Johnson, on circuit, essentially adopted St. George Tucker's view of the history of the common law in the United States in a case raising the question of whether a person could be punished in admiralty for murder on the high seas. Even though exclusive federal jurisdiction over admiralty cases was guaranteed under the U.S. Constitution, Justice Johnson held that there could be no punishment in the absence of statute in part because there was no single common law from which meaning could be derived. The common law existed only insofar as it had been adopted in the different states.[93]

Even as the Sedition Act expired on its own terms and the federal courts began to capitulate on the question of federal common law crimes, however, during the first decade of the nineteenth century, questions relating to the meaning of written legal texts – and hence to the boundaries of contemporaneous consent – persisted.[94] In states such as Pennsylvania, the fallout of the Sedition Act controversy resulted in attacks on the Federalist-dominated judiciary and then on the common law itself. The demands of Pennsylvania radicals make sense when understood precisely as a repudiation of the common law as a "mysterious" system derived from the past that was seen as occluding contemporaneous consent and

[91] 28 F. Cas. 774 (1798), p. 779.

[92] 7 Cranch 32 (1812). This view prevailed even though several members of the Supreme Court were disposed to reconsider the case four years later. At that time, however, the United States attorney general refused to argue that the *Hudson* case should be overturned, and as a result, the Supreme Court did not reconsider its decision. *United States v. Coolidge*, 1 Wheat. 415 (1816).

[93] *Trial of William Butler for Piracy* (1813?), quoted in Horwitz, *Transformation of American Law, 1780–1860*, p. 15, nn. 39, 48.

[94] After the "revolution" of 1800, the Sedition Act expired on its own terms.

a call for a "simple" system created in the present seen as actualizing it. The radicals demanded, *inter alia*, the creation of a written code of laws free of Latin phrases and technical terms, which they believed would be more consistent with "the plain and simple nature of a Republican form of government"; the simplification of court procedure and the establishment of a system of arbitration to reduce the "sophistication and pretensions" of the legal establishment; and a judiciary more responsive to the wishes of the people.[95]

During the election of 1805, the radicals pressed their case against the common law. They enlisted in their cause none other than Paine, recently returned to America, who now distinguished between what he called "lawyers' law" and "legislative law." The former was "a mass of opinions and decisions, many of them contradictory to each other, which courts and lawyers have instituted themselves, and is chiefly made up of law reports of cases taken from English law books"; the latter was "the law of the land, enacted by our own legislators, chosen by the people for that purpose."[96] The pamphlet *Sampson Against the Philistines* (1805) made much the same point, denouncing lawyers for having turned "simple justice" into a "professional mystery, which has contributed to the oppression and plunder, rather than the happiness and security of the people."[97] In 1808, Pennsylvania Supreme Court Justice Hugh Henry Brackenridge, who had himself not escaped the ire of the radicals when they had attempted to impeach sitting Supreme Court justices, also called for the replacement of the common law by a code.[98] The faith was that written texts produced, to borrow Paine's phrase, "by our own legislators" would secure contemporaneous consent on the strength of language's intrinsic clarity.

Moderate Pennsylvania Republicans responded to radicals' efforts to do away with the common law by insisting, as Federalists had insisted in the Sedition Act debates, that the common law was interstitial and foundational. "Legislative law" – that putatively transparent product of contemporaneous consent that Paine had opposed to common law – was grievously incomplete, a claim with considerable plausibility in the early nineteenth century. It could never deal with "the varying exigencies of

[95] See Richard E. Ellis, *The Jeffersonian Crisis: Courts and Politics in the Young Republic* (Oxford: Oxford University Press, 1971), p. 161.

[96] *The Complete Writings of Thomas Paine* (2 vols.) (Philip S. Foner, ed.) (Binghamton, N.Y.: Citadel Press, 1945), Vol. 2, p. 1004; quoted in Ellis, *Jeffersonian Crisis*, p. 176.

[97] *Sampson against the Philistines*; quoted in Ellis, *Jeffersonian Crisis*, p. 177.

[98] Hugh Henry Brackenridge, *Considerations on the Jurisprudence of the State of Pennsylvania* (Philadelphia, 1808), p. 8.

social life" or "the complicated interests of an enterprising nation." The Society of Constitutional Republicans put forth a lengthy address that was chiefly the work of the moderate Republican Alexander Dallas and that reads like a chiding of radicals:

> It is the common law, generally speaking, not an act of Assembly, that assures the title and the possession of your farms and your houses, and protects your persons, your liberty, your reputation from violence; that defines and punishes offences; that regulates the trial by jury; and (in a word, comprehending all its attributes) that gives efficacy to the fundamental principles of the constitution. If such are the nature and the uses of the common law, is it politic, or would it be practicable, to abandon it? Simply because it originated in Europe cannot afford a better reason to abandon it than to renounce the English and the German languages, or to abolish the institutions of property and marriage, of education and religion, since they, too, were derived from the more ancient civilized nations of the world.[99]

Federalist legal thinkers in Pennsylvania – who were, of course, allied with moderate Republicans on the question of the common law – went even further, attacking the core idea that decontextualized written language could ensure the stability, fixity, and integrity of its own meaning. In other words, they argued that it was always going to be impossible to determine exactly what had been consented to. In 1809, in a pamphlet addressing the proposed abolition of the common law, Joseph Hopkinson sought to reverse the valences of written principles and unwritten supplements, certainty and uncertainty, that were prevalent in radical Republican discourses. One recognizes in Hopkinson's arguments the stamp of common lawyerly derision of legislative efforts going back to Coke and traceable through Kames and Blackstone. Statutes could be "the arbitrary dictates of a single man, or any body of men, who promulge only their own individual sense of right and justice." Furthermore, "the very men who make the law do not all mean the same thing by it." Words themselves could not be trusted: "By turning to a dictionary it will be seen that scarcely a word in our language has a single, fixed, determinate meaning; and, of course,

[99] *Life and Writings of Alexander James Dallas* (George M. Dallas, ed.) (Philadelphia, 1871), p. 222. In 1801, Massachusetts Attorney General James Sullivan made a similar point. He acknowledged that "[t]here have been strong prejudices against what is called the Common Law, from an idea, that it is a system imposed upon us, by a power now foreign to our national existence." James Sullivan, *The History of Land Titles in Massachusetts* (Boston: I. Thomas & E. T. Andrews, 1801), p. 13. But such nativism was misplaced. "We should treat a people with contempt," Sullivan continued," who should be barbarous enough to reject an alphabet, or scale of music, because it had been in use in other countries" (p. 15).

that you will change the sense of a sentence, as you shall adopt one or the other of the various interpretations of the words used in it.... That language is by no means a certain and unquestionable method of conveying and fixing ideas, is proved in every branch of human knowledge."[100] Hopkinson offered example upon example of disputes over the meaning of poetic language, religious texts, contracts, statutes, and constitutions to show that writing in itself meant little when it came to fixing meaning. A code replacing the common law would therefore ensure nothing.

Certainty of meaning emerged, Hopkinson argued, not from written words standing alone, but from interpretations extending over long periods of time, by dint of repetition. It was only the method of the common law, in final analysis, that could confer stability of meaning and hence secure the boundaries of consent, which would necessarily then be multigenerational. The constructions of the common law, Hopkinson argued, "ha[d] been fixed by time, wisdom and experience."[101] Hopkinson related an anecdote about Coke to make the point that the common law was more certain than statutes:

> A statesman told lord Coke, that he meant to consult him on a point of law: If it be common law, said Coke, I should be ashamed if I could not give you a ready answer; but if it be statute law, I should be equally ashamed if I answered you immediately.

In fact, statutes were unsettled "until a course of judicial decision, which in fact is common law, gives them certainty and character."[102] Thus, the diffuse nonhistorical temporality of common law "immemoriality" was required to give body and meaning to the contemporaneous consent instantiated in statutes. In 1802, Federalist Congressman James A. Bayard would make much the same argument, this time in the context of the need to limit judicial discretion: "[S]tripped of the common law, there would be neither Constitution nor Government.... And were we to go into our courts of justice with the mere statutes of the United States, not a step could be taken.... If the common law does not exist in most cases, there is no law but the will of the judge."[103]

[100] Joseph Hopkinson, *Considerations on the Abolition of the Common Law in the United States* (Philadelphia: William P. Farrand, 1809), pp. 23, 31, 25–26.

[101] Ibid., p. 27.

[102] Ibid., p 28.

[103] *Annals of Congress*, 7th Cong., 1st Sess., House, pp. 613–614; quoted in Linda K. Kerber, *Federalists in Dissent: Imagery and Ideology in Jeffersonian America* (Ithaca, N.Y.: Cornell University Press, 1970), p. 154.

Notwithstanding the debates in Pennsylvania over the status of the common law, indictments for common law crimes continued at the state level. The common law was thus a supplement to governments considered to be founded upon written documents grounded in contemporaneous consent. Common law prosecutions of labor combinations began in the first decade of the nineteenth century.[104] In 1806, the presiding judge in the Philadelphia boot and shoemakers' case, Recorder Moses Levy, fended off challenges to the common law as a legitimate basis for prosecuting labor combinations in a republican polity of written laws by praising the common law for its "critical precision" and "consistency." Invoking the temporality of "immemoriality" without naming it, Levy argued that the common law was the result of the "wisdom of ages" and, as such, superior to the "temporary emanations" of legislatures.[105] Counsel for laborers repeatedly argued that common law crimes thwarted the principles of contemporaneous consent on which republican constitutions had been erected, surreptitiously importing a bit of the "mysterious" past in to govern the present. The Irish émigré lawyer William Sampson, in the New York prosecution of journeymen cordwainers, argued:

> In vain [has our constitution] consigned to oblivion so many remnants of antiquated folly [the reference is to English statutes], if ever and again some unsubstantial spectre of the common law were to rise from the grave in all its grotesque and uncouth deformity, to trouble our councils and perplex our judgments. Then should we have, for endless ages, the strange phantoms of *Picts* and *Scots*, of *Danes* and *Saxons*, of *Jutes* and *Angles*, of *Monks* and *Druids*, hovering over us like ... ghosts.[106]

But, like Sampson's arguments in the New York prosecution, such arguments could be unavailing.

[104] Labor combinations were the subject of indictment and prosecution in at least six American states – Pennsylvania, Maryland, New York, Louisiana, Massachusetts, and Virginia – through the first half of the nineteenth century. Legal and labor historians have written a great deal about these highly politicized "conspiracy cases." The authoritative account in this regard is Christopher Tomlins, *Law, Labor, and Ideology in the Early American Republic* (Cambridge: Cambridge University Press, 1993), esp. Chap. 5.

[105] Thomas Lloyd, *The Trial of the Boot and Shoemakers of Philadelphia, on an Indictment for a Combination to Raise their Wages* (Philadelphia: B. Graves, 1806), p. 146.

[106] William Sampson, *Trial of the Journeymen Cordwainers of the City of New-York; for a Conspiracy to Raise their Wages; with the Arguments of Counsel at Full Length, on a Motion to Quash the Indictment, the Verdict of the Jury, and the Sentence of the Court* (New York: I. Riley, 1810), p. 31.

Perhaps the most intellectually rigorous attack on the concept of common law crimes at the state level was John Milton Goodenow's *Historical Sketches of the Principles and Maxims of American Jurisprudence, in Contrast with the Doctrines of English Common Law on the Subject of Crimes and Punishments* (1819).[107] The personal politics of the book had to do with a dispute of long standing between Goodenow and Judge Benjamin Tappan, which eventually ended in a slander suit.[108] But the immediate intellectual impetus was Tappan's 1817 decision in *Ohio v. Lafferty*, which held that English common law crimes could be crimes in Ohio in the absence of specific Ohio legislation.[109]

Whatever one might say of eternal laws, all human laws, Goodenow argued, were necessarily "mere matters of social policy" and, as such, were products of their own time.[110] Fitting law and reason to "the texture of the time in which they are made" took place for Goodenow in terms of a historical progression thematized as a movement toward ever less "mysterious" power.[111] The idea of common law crimes was flatly inconsistent with – that is, anachronistic in terms of – the idea of demystified and transparent American power. It was only in monarchical or aristocratic governments that the principles of the criminal law were the "secrets of the empire."[112] Goodenow specifically extended the attack beyond common law crimes to custom in general. In Goodenow's rendering, in America, where all power was expressed in a public and written form, custom – associated as it was with antiquity, unknown "immemorial" origins, and imperceptible "insensible" change – could not be a source of law. It is worth setting forth his reasoning at some length:

> [W]here a government, like the English government, is founded in custom and usage, and advances in course of time to a regular mode of legislation; but is

[107] John Milton Goodenow, *Historical Sketches of the Principles and Maxims of American Jurisprudence, in Contrast with the Doctrines of English Common Law on the Subject of Crimes and Punishments* (Steubenville, Ohio: James Wilson, 1819) (1821) (Buffalo: William S. Hein & Co., 1975).

[108] Goodenow v. Tappan, 1 *Ohio Reports* 60 (1823). John Milton Goodenow sued Judge Benjamin Tappan for slander for stating that Goodenow was, among other things, an escaped convict and of bad moral character. A jury found in favor of Goodenow and awarded him $600 in damages. On appeal, Tappan argued that the statements were not actionable because they did not directly impugn Goodenow's professional character. The Ohio Supreme Court, in a split decision, refused to grant Tappan a full new trial.

[109] Ohio v. Lafferty, *Tappan* 81 (1817).

[110] Goodenow, *Historical Sketches*, p. 6.

[111] Ibid., pp. 12–13.

[112] Ibid., p. 22.

still guided by its ancient customs, usages and traditions; its *statutory laws* have an uncertain and oscillating standard in the *customary law*.... *But in a government like ours, whose foundation is in written and positive law; untrammeled by custom or tradition; every legislative act, every expression of the people's will, by their agents, has a standard at hand, that never changes; by which the integrity and genuineness of the act may be tested. In such a government, what is not written and published, IS NOT LAW* [first two emphases in original; third emphasis added].[113]

As it turned out, according to Goodenow, it was not just the case that custom could not be a source of law in America. There *was* no custom in America to begin with. America was empty, as it were, of custom. As Goodenow put it, "We have no native common law, no municipal customs, such as is properly so called in England."[114]

An Agent of History? The Common Law and Historical Change

Even as American legal thinkers debated the ontology of their written constitutions and whether the common law could constitute a supplement to written law, they were confronted with the allied question of constructing a relationship to the vast legacy of what had now become a newly deconstitutionalized body of English common law, public and private. All American legal thinkers, regardless of political stripe, agreed with Pennsylvania Supreme Court Judge Hugh Henry Brackenridge that, "[w]ith regard to the common law ... so much of it only, could have been carried by the emigrants to this state, as was applicable to their situation and therefore so much of it only in force."[115] Blackstone himself had earlier made a similar point about the inapplicability of much of the common law to the North American colonies, arguing that "[t]he artificial refinements and distinctions incident to the property of a great and commercial people" were neither necessary nor convenient for "the infant colony."[116] But that did not solve the question of the kind of relationship one established vis-à-vis the common law past.

Republican legal thinkers argued, as did St. George Tucker, that Blackstone's *Commentaries*, indispensable as they were, were a guide

[113] Ibid., p. 40–41.

[114] Ibid., p. 49.

[115] Hugh Henry Brackenridge, *Law Miscellanies: Containing an Introduction to the Study of Law* (Philadelphia: P. Byrne, 1814), p. 37.

[116] Blackstone, *Commentaries*, Vol. 1, pp. 102, 103; cited in Brackenridge, *Law Miscellanies*, p. 47.

only to what the "*law had been*."[117] "The principles of our government," Tucker maintained flatly, are inconsistent with the "principles contained in the *Commentaries*."[118] The former were the product of self-conscious contemporaneous consent; the latter were not. The English common law was the product of unreflective "immemorial usage"; American law was the "principled" result of the "deliberate voice of the legislature."[119] The most comprehensive changes between the common law of England and the new legal regime in Virginia, Tucker argued, were attributable to "the suggestions of political experiment."[120]

Tucker's attempt to organize the historical difference between English and Virginian law in terms of a republican language of consent, principles, and experiments translated into a willingness to dub – one might even call it a delight in dubbing – multiple aspects of the English common law obsolete. To be sure, various rights, privileges, prerogatives, courts, writs, and remedies mentioned by Blackstone were simply not to be found, and had likely never existed, in Virginia.[121] Neither, for that matter, did many of them exist in eighteenth-century Britain. But where Blackstone could often speak of the pastness of the past as simply that, a falling away or a coming into view, for Tucker it was important to account for the pastness of the past in terms of principle, to kill the past definitively, to pronounce its demise. To take the example of writs of attaint, where Blackstone simply highlights their gradual fading from use, Tucker offers a terser footnote: "The writ of attaint

[117] St. George Tucker, ed., *Blackstone's Commentaries*, Vol. 1, Preface, p. v (emphasis in original).

[118] Ibid., pp. iv–v.

[119] Ibid., Vol. 3, App., p. 19.

[120] Ibid., Vol. 1, Preface, p. x.

[121] To offer just a few examples, where Blackstone had mentioned different kinds of rights of commons, Tucker writes that commons of estover were the only type of rights of common known in Virginia. Ibid., Vol. 3, p. 35, n 4. A variety of English common law remedies also did not exist in Virginia, as was the case with a variety of English courts. Ibid., Vol. 4, p. 15. Tucker lists various remedies, such as seizing heriots for distress; ibid., p. 7 (referring to the absence of court-leets and courts baron in Virginia); p. 33 (referring to the absence of courts of *piepoudre* in Virginia); p. 67 (referring to the courts of the king's high commission); p. 68 (the court of chivalry). The proprietors of the Northern-Neck in Virginia had been authorized to set up courts-baron, i.e., manorial courts, by their charters within the limits of their proprietary. However, Tucker remarked that "none of them availed themselves of their authority." Ibid., p. 34, n 2. They had also been authorized to set up a court-leet. Tucker was not sure whether such courts had ever been established but presumed that "the franchise ... was annihilated at the revolution." Ibid., Vol. 5, p. 274, n. 11.

seems *perfectly obsolete* in Virginia."[122] Some English courts that were unimportant even in the England of Blackstone's day such as courts of chivalry that Blackstone nevertheless chooses to detail – perhaps in order to edify his gentlemen readers – were dismissed curtly by Tucker as a "remnant of feudal pomp" that had never existed in Virginia.[123] One gets the sense that Tucker is trying to render the legal landscape of Virginia a blank slate, what Jefferson had described as "an album on which we were free to write what we pleased."

However, at the same time, in keeping with the way in which Paine's and Jefferson's emphasis on an open-ended contemporaneous consent ends up leading the political subject back to a given, constraining conception of nature or society, Tucker suggests that contemporaneous consent results in a recognition of the "naturalness" of various legal principles that are themselves the product of the common law. As discussed in the preceding chapter, Blackstone's acute sense of the specificity and detail of England's legal past had led him to see rights as civil rather than as natural. By contrast, Tucker's adherence to principle allowed him to insist upon those very same rights' naturalness. In his comment on Blackstone's famous observation that the right to transmit property at death was merely custom that had gradually (and, for Blackstone, falsely) acquired the cast of the natural, Tucker registers vehement disagreement. "The notion of property is universal," Tucker insists, "and ... suggested to the mind of man by reason and nature, prior to all positive institutions and civilized refinements." Children's claims to their parents' property did not originate "solely in political establishments"; "*Haeredas successoresque sui cuique liberi* [Every man's children are his heirs and successors] seems not to have been confined to the woods of Germany, but to be one of the first laws in the code of nature."[124] What Blackstone had seen as a common law right had now become a natural one. Of course, what counted as natural remained a subject of disagreement. Where Tucker saw entails as unnatural, Massachusetts Attorney General James Sullivan attributed to the "self-love, incident to the human race," the fact that the people of Massachusetts had preserved the entail.[125]

Thus we see how republican thinkers such as Tucker plotted a relationship to the common law past. In polities where law was supposed

[122] Ibid., Vol. 4, pp. 404–405, n. 1 (emphasis added).

[123] Ibid., p. 105, n. 10.

[124] Ibid., Vol. 3, pp. 10–11n.

[125] Sullivan, *History of Land Titles in Massachusetts*, p. 75.

to be the product of contemporaneous consent, much of the commo law was simply obsolete, inconsistent with America's political "experiment." Where parts of the common law remained relevant, they were re-presented as natural, prepolitical. However, other American legal thinkers – often Federalist – advanced very different representations of the common law past and of the place of the common law in the new polities of America.

In the writings of American common law thinkers, we can discern ways of joining the consent-centered historical sensibilities of the day to older common law temporalities. Newer notions of contemporaneous consent mingle promiscuously with older notions of multigenerational and attributed consent. In thus mingling different temporalities, common law thinkers were able to argue that the common law was the most consensual and experimental of laws, which made it especially fitted to the new, consensual, experimental polities of America. It is also crucial to emphasize the possibilities presented by the internal instability of the subject of contemporaneous consent in the writings of Paine, Jefferson, and Tucker: contemporaneous consent as oscillating between the possibility of radical reimagining, one the one hand, and a return to nature plotted as a shift from the feudal to the commercial, on the other. If contemporaneous consent was nothing other than a return to an already imagined nature, if consent-centered democracy was constrained by nature (or history plotted as a shift from "mystery" to transparency that was really nothing other than an uncovering of nature), the common law could be represented as itself embodying a certain conception of nature and as realizing the logic of history. Tucker himself had suggested that the right to transmit property at death, long recognized by common lawyers, was a natural right. If the common law could do the work of developing natural rights and of accomplishing the shift from feudal to commercial, could it not thereby win a place for itself in the new polities constrained by a metaphysics of history as an uncovering of nature?

Perhaps the most theoretically sustained of the arguments mingling different ideas of consent were contained in U.S. Supreme Court Justice James Wilson's reflections on the common law. In the manner of Scottish thinkers and of Paine, Wilson imagined society to be the natural ground out of which consent could be offered. Society predated civil government and constituted every human subject capable of giving consent. Wilson wrote, "Society is the powerful magnet, which, by its unceasing though silent operation, attracts and influences our dispositions, our desires, our passions, and our enjoyments."[126] This constitutive power of society, insofar as it acted on all its members, underscored the naturalness of democratic consent and made the definitive case for the concentration of power in the people. At the same time, however, it set limits on popular consent.[127]

But if a truly legitimate law could emerge only from the consent of members of a society, what form was that law to take? For Wilson, even as he insists on consent as the only legitimate ground of law, it is the common law – rather than St. George Tucker's "deliberate voice of the legislature" – that constitutes the best evidence of consent and the best instantiation of the social. Wilson argues that insofar as the common law is evidence of consent "practically given," emerging from the silent operations of a naturalized society, it is even more legitimate than laws authorized by express written contemporaneous consent.

> [T]he mode for the promulgation of human laws by custom seems the most significant, and the most effectual. It involves in it internal evidence, of the strongest kind, that the law has been introduced by common *consent*; and that this consent rests upon the most solid basis – experience as well as opinion. This mode of promulgation points to the strongest characteristic of liberty, as well as of law. For a consent thus practically given, must have been given in the freest and most unbiased manner.... If it were asked – and it would be no improper question –who of all the makers and teachers of law have formed and drawn after them the most, the best, and the most willing disciples; it might not be untruly answered – custom.[128]

At first blush, this might seem like nothing other than a traditional common lawyerly argument about the common law's being the most

[126] *The Works of James Wilson*, Vol. 1, p. 253.

[127] There was a broader, and more attractive, universalism associated with Wilson's focus on "society." The naturalness of the "social" – combined with the idea that the ideal social arrangement implied harmony between individual and collective interests – led Wilson to celebrate Lord Mansfield's incorporation of the *lex mercatoria* into English law. As he puts it: "One branch of that law, which since the extension of commerce, and the frequent and liberal intercourse between different nations, has become of peculiar importance, is called the law of merchants. This system of law has been admitted to decide controversies concerning bills of exchange, policies of insurance, and other mercantile transactions, both where citizens of different states, and where citizens of the same state only, have been interested in the event. This system has, of late years, been greatly elucidated, and reduced to rational and solid principles, by a series of adjudications, for which the commercial world is much indebted to a celebrated judge [Lord Mansfield], long famed for his comprehensive talents and luminous learning in general jurisprudence." Ibid., p. 335. This universalism led Wilson to argue that the law of nations should be the rule of decision in the federal courts, a decision anticipating Justice Story's decision in *Swift v. Tyson* decades later. Ibid., pp. 341–342.

[128] Ibid., pp. p. 57–58.

consensual of all laws. However, Wilson mingles newer and older languages. It is noteworthy that, for Wilson, the consent embodied by the common law reflects "experience *as well as* opinion." Earlier generations of English common law thinkers had focused only on custom's ability to embody experience, the accumulated wisdom of past ages. In Wilson's postrevolutionary republican America, the common law also embodies "opinion," an important basis of the new type of government. But Wilson goes further still in his appropriation of the languages of the lonely subject of contemporaneous consent. Where thinkers like St. George Tucker were wont to refer to American polities in the language of "experiment," Wilson argues that the common law is also the product of "experiment":

> The prospect of convenience invites to the first experiment: a first experiment, successful, encourages to make a second. The successful experiments of one man or one body of men induce another man or another body of men to venture upon similar trials. The instances are multiplied and extended, till, at length, the custom becomes universal and established. Can a law be made in a manner more eligible?[129]

However, even as he appropriates these new republican languages of "opinion" and "experiment," *contra* Paine and Jefferson, Wilson insists that the consent embodied in the common law is precisely *not* limited to the human subject's own present or lifetime. Even though the common law is a law of "opinion," "experiment," and "voluntary adoption" – all markers of prevailing notions of contemporaneous consent – the common law for Wilson remains "immemorial," inherited, derived from ancestors: "[O]ur predecessors and ancestors have collected, arranged, and formed a system of experimental law.... This system has stood the test of numerous ages: to every age it has disclosed new beauties and new truths."[130] Indeed, in the manner of a long line of common lawyers from Sir John Davies on, Wilson will argue that the common law affords the best proof of consent precisely because of its ambiguous, nonspecifiable temporality. Because we can never know the "when" of a custom's

[129] Ibid., pp. 183–184. Hugh Henry Brackenridge would go so far as to argue that custom was the equivalent of a legislative act. "When we talk of custom we must remount to some convention; or gathering of the people to originate the rule. Even supposing but two persons in a community, there must be such assent, and so of more; so that I can see nothing in a distinction to be taken between the origin of an unwritten custom and a written law. They are both equally the act of a legislature." Brackenridge, *Law Miscellanies*, p. 84.

[130] *The Works of James Wilson*, Vol. 1, p. 184.

emergence, it becomes possible to dispense with concrete proof of consent and to attribute consent to all actually existing customs:

> Now custom is, *of itself*, intrinsick evidence of consent. How was a custom introduced? By voluntary adoption. How did it become general? By the instances of voluntary adoption being increased. How did it become lasting? By voluntary and satisfactory experience, which ratified and confirmed what voluntary adoption had introduced. In the introduction, in the extension, in the continuance of customary law, we find the operations of consent universally predominant [emphasis added].[131]

We thus see in Wilson's writings how late-eighteenth-century American common lawyers could bring the consent-centered historical sensibilities of their time to bear upon the law and, mingling newer and older notions of consent, argue that that the common law embodied those very same consent-centered historical sensibilities. If, for a thinker like Paine, history was a move from a nonconsensual political to a consensual social, Wilson would argue that the common law was already the best reflection of that consensual social.

All eighteenth-century American common law thinkers shared Paine's, Jefferson's, and Tucker's sense that the feudal had to be left behind. But many did not agree with Tucker that the common law was therefore to be transformed by the legislature into a field for the operation of principles. Although not all late-eighteenth-century American common law thinkers offered carefully reasoned theoretical elaborations of the relationship between common law, consent, and history in the manner of Wilson, certain common law thinkers, in the vein of Kames or Blackstone, wrote as if the common law in America had already accomplished, all by itself, the crucial movement of history from the feudal to the commercial.

Nobody expressed a sense of the common law's role as an agent of history more clearly than Connecticut's Zephaniah Swift. Because Connecticut had no formal common law reception statute, Swift asserted, "The common law of England is obligatory in this state by immemorial usage, and consent, so far as it corresponds with our circumstances and situation."[132] Connecticut courts, furthermore, were the shapers of the boundaries of that "immemorial usage and consent."[133]

According to Swift, the English common law was a law of constant improvement:

[131] Ibid., pp. 88–89.

[132] Swift, *A System of the Laws of the State of Connecticut*, Vol. 1, p. 1.

[133] Ibid., p. 1

> [The common law] establishes one permanent uniform, universal directory, for the conduct of the whole community, and opens the door for a constant progressive improvement in the laws, in proportion to the civilization of their manners, and the encrease of their wealth. [W]hile the legislature were passing acts for general regulations, the courts were polishing, improving, and perfecting a system of conduct, for the minuter subordinate transactions of life, which by the collective wisdom and experience of successive ages, have advanced to the highest pitch of clearness, certainty, and precision.[134]

Swift's representation of the activity of common law courts – that of advancing "the collective wisdom and experience of successive ages" to "the highest pitch of clearness, certainty, and precision" – is of course an endorsement of the "insensible" common law method, one through which improvements are made only by building slowly upon the achievements of the past. These improvements took the form, Swift argues, of nudging society along gradually from the feudal to the commercial. He traces the origin of actions of trespass on the case in England as follows. Initially, all actions grounded in torts had been trespass, replevin, detinue, and deceit. At this stage, there had been little personal property. "[T]he people, being in an agricultural state of society, paid their chief attention to lands." However, "[w]hen [the people] arrived to the commercial state, and the principles of jurisprudence were better understood, as well as personal property largely encreased, it was apparent that new remedies must be devised." Swift then proceeded to trace the slow emergence of trespass on the case.[135] In general, English jurisprudence was praised for the following:

> They have from time to time, devised remedies as the exigencies of mankind required, in a gradual progress from the simplest stages of society, to the complicated interests of commerce, luxury, and the highest refinement of manners. The system of jurisprudence has become so perfect, that it can hardly be expected a case should arise that does not come within the description of specific remedies, well known and established. Yet the same principle ... may still be called into exercise whenever there shall be an occasion.[136]

To be sure, Swift still deemed it important to mark the differences between English rules and American ones. These were all to the advantages of Connecticut, and specifically to the credit of its common lawyers. Connecticut courts had introduced "a vast many improvements ... without any legislative act."[137] For example, Swift stated that there was "much

[134] Ibid., pp. 40–41.
[135] Ibid., Vol. 2, pp. 20.
[136] Ibid., p. 22.
[137] Ibid., Vol. 1, p. 44.

abstruse learning" in England relating to rights of entry on lands that was irrelevant in Connecticut;[138] Connecticut courts had "exploded" the distinction between written and unwritten contracts;[139] the Connecticut writ and process was superior to the "very lengthy and circuitous mode of process" in England[140]; another aspect of Connecticut's process, superior to the English requirement that all writs be returned to the central courts at Westminster Hall, was described as "the offspring of gradual improvement, and cautious innovation";[141] Connecticut courts had replaced all the myriad actions for the recovery of lands in England with just one, the action of disseisin, which was "striking evidence of the propensity of our progenitors, to improve upon and simplify the laws of their native country." In one stroke, they had replaced "an artificial system of law" with a structure "wonderful for its simplicity and beauty."[142]

Like Wilson, then, common law thinkers such as Swift reveal themselves to be acutely aware of the movement of history. However, even as they understand that law has to be subjected to critique in the name of history, they argue that the common law is the best way of effecting the movement of history. If history was a move from a nonconsensual European "mystery" to a consensual American transparency, from the feudal to the commercial, nobody was better equipped to engineer this move than the common law courts. In making such arguments, of course, late-eighteenth- and early-nineteenth-century common lawyers were doing no more than their British counterparts had argued decades earlier.

Conclusion: The Blank Canvas of the Common Law

As stated throughout this chapter, for republican legal thinkers, the non-historical common law temporalities of "immemoriality" and "insensibility" were hallmarks of "mysterious" European power. More important, many agreed with St. George Tucker's argument that, under the technical English legal concept of "immemoriality," there could be neither custom nor prescription in America.[143] Only the legislature, presumably, could create law. This was consistent with Tucker's view that the English

[138] Ibid., Vol. 2, p. 3.
[139] Ibid., p. 6.
[140] Ibid., p. 193.
[141] Ibid., p. 194.
[142] Ibid., p. 68.
[143] St. George Tucker ed., *Blackstone's Commentaries*, Vol. 3, p. 36, n. 7.

common law existed in various American jurisdictions only by virtue of legislative acts of reception.

But it might be interesting to ask how common law thinkers themselves imagined the possibilities of the common law's future in America. We have already seen that American common law thinkers imagined the common law to be a method of effecting the movement of history even as they subjected the English common law to history. At the same time, they were able to argue that the common law was, as the most consensual of all laws, perfectly consistent with America's experimental, consent-based polities. But did this emphasis on the consensual nature of the common law mean that American common law thinkers were receptive to the proliferation of local customs in America?

Occasionally, American legal thinkers, even those opposed to common law sensibilities, recognized that peculiar and local customs had developed in America over time. St. George Tucker remarked that "local circumstances have necessarily introduced a variety of new regulations, which by imperceptible and gradual changes, have lost all resemblance to the British original."[144] Massachusetts's James Sullivan could maintain, "We have also some customs established by general practice, peculiar to ourselves, and which were never known in England: these are law with us by our own consent."[145]

For the most part, however, there was little enthusiastic recognition of local customs, the recognition of which had been such a significant part of Blackstone's legal science. This was, paradoxically, especially true of Federalist and pro–common law thinkers. Even as they actively embraced the common law and wielded the temporalities of "immemoriality" and "insensibility" to their advantage, American common law thinkers appear to have wanted to concentrate the power to declare the customs of the community in the hands of the common law judge, to produce an internally homogeneous legal landscape. Connecticut's Zephaniah Swift, among the era's most enthusiastic proponents of the common law, insisted that "in [Connecticut] we have no local customs, but the citizens are all governed by the same general rule."[146]

Perhaps the sense of America's legal landscape as uniform, internally homogeneous, was nothing other than a version of the clean slate that consent-oriented, present-focused, Jeffersonians and Paine-ites imagined

[144] Ibid., Vol. 1, Preface, p. x.
[145] Sullivan, *History of Land Titles in Massachusetts*, p. 18.
[146] Swift, *A System of the Laws of the State of Connecticut*, Vol. 1, p. 47.

America to be. This suggestion has some plausibility when one looks at judges' self-representation in this period. Here, I examine the writings of James Kent.

Throughout his career as politician, lawyer, and judge, Kent saw himself as a staunch Federalist. As he put it, "I entered with ardor into the Federal politics against France in 1793, and my hostility to the French democracy and to French power beat with strong pulsation down to the Battle of Waterloo."[147] In his activity as a judge sitting on New York's Council of Revision, Kent often incurred the hostility of Democrats for his attack on antiproperty legislation that he frequently dubbed "Jacobinical."[148] Until his death, he fought (often unsuccessfully) to defend the integrity of the judiciary from legislative attack, whether this involved the preservation of the Council on Revision (abolished in 1821), the salaries and tenures of judges, or the maintenance of the distinction between law and equity.

As a Federalist and a common lawyer, Kent despised Jefferson. In 1802, at the height of the Republican attack on the federal judiciary, he wrote in his journal, "The pernicious effects of the violent Jacobinical administration in this [New York] and the United States begin to be sensibly and strongly felt. The best men are no longer in office and government becomes degraded and feeble and threatens to pervert the administration of justice and introduce violence and oppression."[149] The threat was, precisely, the Jeffersonian idea that government and law should be a matter of contemporaneous consent. In 1837, in a letter to Kent, Theodore Dwight offered up a plan for a work he had projected "on the principles and character of Thomas Jefferson." Among the eighteen objections to Jefferson Dwight listed, from "Destitute of veracity" to "Was not a Christian," one was telling: "That one generation of men or of societies cannot make laws or constitutions to bind their successors."[150] Kent's own annotations to Henry St. George Tucker's "Life of Jefferson" revealed similar objections. Kent noted Tucker's "temperate and able discussion of Mr. Jefferson, and [Jefferson's] project that no law, or constitution, or contract [be] binding after nineteen years."[151]

Like other legal thinkers of his generation, Kent was intensely interested in the relationship between law and historical change. Following Montesquieu, Kent argued that "[t]he regulations of the lawgiver should

[147] *Memoirs and Letters of James Kent*, p. 82.
[148] Horton, *James Kent*, p. 239.
[149] Ibid., p. 127.
[150] *Memoirs and Letters of James Kent*, p. 220.
[151] Ibid., p. 222.

always have a steady relation to the state of society, its industry, wealth, trade, morals, genius, extent and connection with other nations."[152] This translated into an intense interest in the shift from the feudal to the commercial. In 1795, commenting on Dugald Stewart's "View of Society," Kent remarked that the book had been "of great use to me in my researches into the genius of feudal policy."[153] On the basis of his reading of Adam Smith, Kent maintained that it was important for laws not to "perplex the industry" of citizens, so that there could be "free circulation of labor and the produce of labor."[154] "[P]roperty," he argued, "should have a free circulation, and free employment, without any of the fetters of entailments and perpetuities."[155]

This interest in getting rid of the feudal and preparing the ground for the commercial made Kent highly open to reforming the common law. Only the very latest common law learning counted. In 1795, in a discussion of the law of nations that could also have been a discussion of common law, Kent argued that, because the law of nations had kept pace with "the cultivation of morals, and the refinements of commerce," only "the modern precedents and writers are deserving of superior attention."[156] Kent was also open to remaking the common law by borrowing from French law writers. He even exploited the pro-French leanings of Republicans to do so. As he explained it:

> Between that time [1798] and 1804, I rode my share of circuits.... I read in that time Valin and Emerigon [authorities on the law of insurance], and completely abridged the latter, and made copious digests of all the English law reports and treatises as they came out. I made much use of the *Corpus Juris*, and as the judges (Livingston excepted) knew nothing of French or civil law, I had immense advantage over them. I could generally put my brethren to rout and carry my point by my mysterious wand of French and civil law. The judges were Republicans and very kindly disposed to everything that was French, and this enabled me, without exciting any alarm or jealousy, to make free use of such authorities and thereby enrich our commercial law.[157]

But if this openness to importing the teachings of French jurisprudence were not enough, Kent sometimes sounds, in his attitude toward law, *precisely* like the despised Jeffersonian lonely subject of contemporaneous

[152] Kent, *Dissertations*, p. 18.
[153] *Memoirs and Letters of James Kent*, p. 239.
[154] Kent, *Dissertations*, p. 19.
[155] Ibid., p. 20.
[156] Ibid., p. 58.
[157] *Memoirs and Letters of James Kent*, p. 117.

consent who jettisons the past, renders the world a blank canvas, and begins afresh. Thus, when Kent was appointed New York's chancellor in 1814, he expressed himself as follows:

> I took the court as if it had been a new institution, and never before known in the United States. I had nothing to guide me, and was left at liberty to assume all such English chancery powers and jurisdiction as I thought applicable under our Constitution. This gave me grand scope, and I was checked only by the revision of the Senate, or Court of Errors.[158]

This language is striking. Kent treats the court as a "new institution ... never before known in the United States." He acknowledges no guide and arrogates to himself "grand scope" to shape it.

In embracing a sense of freedom from the past, pro–common law American judges such as Kent were acting precisely like the subjects of contemporaneous consent that they so feared and despised. For the judiciary's many democratically inclined critics in early-nineteenth-century America, such judicial attitudes were the basis of the argument that the scope of judicial powers had to be limited, that the judiciary had to be rendered subject to the checks of a democracy based on express consent. For our purposes, however, it shows how the engine of history – here the Jeffersonian lonely subject of consent – could be both embraced and rejected. In Kent's understanding of his own vocation as a common lawyer who claims "grand scope" in shaping the law, we find a reinscription of the way the common law was both subjected to history and gave rise to it.

[158] Ibid., p. 158.

4

Time as Spirit

Common Law Thought in the Early Nineteenth Century

The Spirit of the Age

In his massive study of British romantic historicism, the literary scholar James Chandler writes that the early nineteenth century was "the age of the spirit of the age – that is, the period when the normative status of the period becomes a central and self-conscious aspect of historical reflection."[1] The titles of numerous texts from this period testify to the accuracy of this observation for both Britain and America. These include not only famous texts such as William Hazlitt's *The Spirit of the Age* (1825), Thomas Carlyle's essay *Signs of the Times* (1829), and John Stuart Mill's essay *The Spirit of the Age* (1831), but also lesser-known periodicals such as the short-lived, Boston-based *Spirit of the Age* (1833–1834) and the equally short lived, New York–based *Spirit of the Age* (1849–1850). But what precisely did it mean to imagine the movement of history in terms of "the spirit of the age"? For heuristic purposes, I divide the discussion of the "spirit of the age" into a discussion, first, of the concept of the "age" and, second, of the concept of "spirit."

The concept of the "age" was, of course, familiar from long before the early nineteenth century. However, in the early decades of the nineteenth century, owing in large measure to the sense of historical break generated by the late-eighteenth-century revolutions, it was experienced

[1] James Chandler, *England in 1819: The Politics of Literary Culture and the Case of Romantic Historicism* (Chicago: University of Chicago Press, 1998), p. 78. For a study of continental European thought in this regard, see Peter Fritzsche, *Stranded in the Present: Modern Time and the Melancholy of History* (Cambridge, Mass.: Harvard University Press, 2004).

with renewed intensity and articulated with greater precision. The thinker interested in producing the sense of an "age" surveyed an array of coevally existing objects – artifacts, styles, personalities, institutions, ideas – and decided which did or did not belong to the "age." The strategy rested upon the production of a sense of contemporaneity and a sense of anachronism. If some coeval objects belonged together (contemporaneity), other coeval objects did not belong (anachronism). Objects that did not belong to this "age" belonged to another. They were markers of the past or harbingers of the future. As such, they could be cherished, fostered, or earmarked for extinction.

This heightened sense of contemporaneity and anachronism, when inflected by the late eighteenth century's repudiation of "mysterious" prerevolutionary European politicolegal forms (monarchy, feudalism, the Roman Catholic Church, and, for some, the common law), made the "age" a powerfully demystifying concept. Thinkers fitted "mysterious" objects into different "ages" in order to reveal their temporal contingency and cut them down to size. In his *Phenomenology of Spirit* (1807), Hegel, an acute analyst of his own time, described precisely this kind of cutting down to size in his discussion of the contemporary quest for the temporal origins of things:

> If I inquire after their origin and confine them to the point whence they arose, then I have transcended them; for now it is I who am the universal, and *they* are the conditioned and limited. If they are supposed to be validated by *my* insight, then I have already denied their unshakeable, intrinsic being, and regard them as something which, for me, is perhaps true, but also is perhaps not true.[2]

This activity of fitting objects to their "age" to demonstrate their contingency was, therefore, a style of thinking instrumentally.

What early-nineteenth-century thinkers often self-consciously joined to the demystifying concept of the "age" was the concept of "spirit." "Spirit" gave meaning to the age and shaped specific configurations of contemporaneity and anachronism. It thus imbued time with content, history with significance. But the choice of the term "spirit" to name that which gave history significance was not accidental. A word with a long presence in Christian discourses, and an English translation of the German *Geist*, the word "spirit" was popularized, *inter alia*, by a generation of British and American intellectuals who were beginning to discover, share,

[2] G. W. F. Hegel, *The Phenomenology of Spirit* (A. V. Miller, trans.) (Oxford: Clarendon Press, 1977), para. 437 (1807).

and enrich the predilections of German idealism and romanticism. It was an essential part of "spirit" that there was something profound, impalpable, unknowable, even mysterious about it. As Emerson wrote in his "Lectures on the Times":

> The times, as we say – or the present aspects of our social state, the Laws, Divinity, Natural Science, Agriculture, Art, Trade, Letters, have their root in an *invisible spiritual reality*.... Beside all the small reasons we assign, there is a great reason for the existence of every extant fact; a reason which lies *grand and immovable, often unsuspected behind it in silence. The Times are the masquerade of the eternities* [emphasis added].[3]

Where the prerevolutionary European past had been tainted as "mysterious," the turn to "spirit" often meant a turning to that very same prerevolutionary past in order to give the "age" its "mysterious" quality. The term "spirit" was thus put to very different uses from those to which it had been put by eighteenth century thinkers like Bolingbroke and Montesquieu.

How, then, are we to think about the contradictory conjoining of demystifying "age" and mystifying "spirit" in the writings of early-nineteenth-century intellectuals? At the outset, it is important to keep in mind that this conjoining had everything to do with early-nineteenth-century Euro-American intellectuals' self-consciously imagining themselves as occupying a moment *after* the late-eighteenth-century revolutionary moment, of fashioning a complex reaction toward revolutions increasingly seen as legacy, of reconfiguring what were seen as the arid and atomizing mechanistic structures of late-eighteenth-century politicolegal thought by reclaiming the allegedly more holistic, solidaristic, or authoritarian political forms that the eighteenth-century revolutions had displaced. But this attempt to muddy the late eighteenth century's search for clarity and precision did not take the form of attempting to reconstitute the "mysterious" prerevolutionary past in its actuality and integrity, which would have been undesirable and impossible. It took the form rather of "spiritualizing" that prerevolutionary past such that its "spirit" – rather than its actuality – pervaded the "age." Even as early-nineteenth-century thinkers "spiritualized" the past, as we shall see, they continued to adhere to eighteenth-century Scottish ideas about history as a shift from the feudal to the commercial. In the midst of the romantic era's search for "spirit," we discern the shadow of Kames.

[3] Ralph Waldo Emerson, "Lectures on the Times: Read at the Masonic Temple, Boston, December, 1841," in *Essays and Lectures* (New York: Library of America, 1983), p. 153.

There were many different accounts of what constituted the "spirit of the age" in the decades after 1820. This variation made for discussion and debate. For example, if some designated the "spirit of the age" as the relentless advance of the arts and sciences, others such as William Hazlitt saw the "spirit of the age" as a melancholic exhaustion experienced in the light of the artistic and scientific achievements of the past. A plethora of "spirits" thus underlay the passage of historical time. However, by far the most important thematic focus of historical reflection was political democracy itself. As had been the case in the immediate postrevolutionary era, there was no consensus on what democracy meant or what form it should take. Nevertheless, whether in Europe or in America, democracy configured in terms of the "spirit of the age" gave meaning to a whole range of politicolegal forms, institutions, attitudes, and practices that came, as a consequence, to be marked as belonging to the past, present, or future. The paradoxes implicit in the term "spirit of the age" – what I have described as the combination of a demystifying concept (the "age") and a mystifying one ("spirit"), separation and recombination of past and present – were reproduced over and over again.

Democracy's march in early-nineteenth-century America appeared ineluctable. Between 1816 and 1821, six new states entered the Union and provided in their constitutions for universal white male suffrage, breaking with the pattern of almost all original states. Between 1820 and 1830, Massachusetts, New York, and Virginia held constitutional conventions in which they liberalized their own early restrictive suffrage conditions. Suffrage reform shattered the eighteenth century's formal links between landed property and political power. But suffrage reform was only part of the story of the seemingly inexorable advance of democracy. With the presidency of Andrew Jackson came related calls at the state level, increasingly prominent in the 1820s, 1830s, and 1840s and many of them successful, to perfect the power of democratic majorities by codifying the common law, diminishing the hold of vested rights, reducing the power of special interests, increasing the number of elected officials (including judges), recognizing the rights of laboring men, and so on.[4]

[4] One historian has suggested that "something approximating white manhood suffrage had been achieved in most American states prior to 1824." E. Pessen, *Jacksonian America: Society, Personality, and Politics* (Homewood, Ill.: Dorsey Press, 1969), p. 158. On Jacksonian era conventions, see Laura J. Scalia, *America's Jeffersonian Experiment: Remaking State Constitutions, 1820–1850* (DeKalb, Ill.: Northern Illinois University Press, 1999).

Proponents *and* opponents of these emerging styles of popular democracy had recourse to the idea of "spirit" to mystify democracy, although, to be sure, they drew upon very different qualities of the past to "spiritualize." It is significant that the metaphysics of "spirit" – insofar as "spirit" borrowed from the "mysterious" prerevolutionary past – could operate as a limit or constraint on the possibilities of democracy itself. This was recognized by opposing sides of the debate: each saw the other as importing a different undesirable "spiritualized" aspect of the prerevolutionary past into American democracy.

We can see the paradoxical structure of historical thought configured in terms of the "spirit of the age" in the Jacksonian historian George Bancroft's celebration of democracy in overtly "religious" terms. It was hardly new, of course, to detect the hand of God in the unfolding of events in the secular world. This was how several early modern historical thinkers had reconciled their faith with their science. Nor was it especially novel to see history, democracy, and God as mutually reinforcing. The American Revolution had been thus explained by many. But in the early-nineteenth-century writings of Bancroft, there is a difference insofar as religion, explicitly represented as an aspect of a superseded past, comes to lend its "spirit" to democracy.[5]

For the first generation of American historians such as Bancroft, nothing was more erroneous, artificial, false, or "mysterious" – nothing more clearly an index of a superseded undemocratic past – than the Roman Catholic Church. The pejorative word typically used to describe Roman Catholicism, a word going back to the eighteenth century, was "priestcraft."[6] In Rome, on Christmas Eve, 1821, the young Bancroft had watched "the display of pretended devotion" and grown "heartily sick of the mockery of religion, & the tireless profusion of ceremonies,

[5] For an example of early modern thinkers' reconciliation of God and history, see Mark Lilla, *G. B. Vico: The Making of an Anti-Modern* (Cambridge, Mass.: Harvard University Press, 1993). The conjoining of history, democracy, and God in American revolutionary thought is indisputable, notwithstanding scholarly accounts of contemporary histories of the Revolution that have detected in them an increasing emphasis on man's ability to shape the course of his destiny. See, e.g., Lester H. Cohen, *The Revolutionary Histories: Contemporary Narratives of the American Revolution* (Ithaca, N.Y.: Cornell University Press, 1980).

[6] See, e.g., George Bancroft, *History of the United States from the Discovery of the American Continent* (8 vols.) (Boston: Little, Brown & Co., 1854), Vol. 5, p. 3. See also the chapter entitled "Priestcraft and Catholicism" in David Levin, *History as Romantic Art: Bancroft, Prescott, Motley, and Parkman* (Stanford, Calif.: Stanford University Press, 1959), pp. 93–125.

which are intended to inspire the Roman with piety."[7] The battle between Catholicism and Protestantism during the Reformation and after was, Bancroft subsequently argued, nothing but an antecedent to the late-eighteenth-century battle between monarchy and democracy. The Reformation lay at the heart of the American Revolution: "He that will not honor the memory, and respect the influence of Calvin, knows but little of the origin of American liberty."[8]

It is noteworthy, then, that, even as Bancroft celebrated the defeat of Catholicism as a triumph for democracy, he mourned the absence of Catholic faith in the established church in England. Anglicanism was a weak and compromised religion: "The lustre of spiritual influences was tarnished by this strict subordination [of Anglicanism] to the temporal power.... [T]he dean and chapter, at their cathedral stalls, seemed like strangers encamped among the shrines, or lost in the groined aisles which the fervid genius of men of a different age and a heartier faith had fashioned."[9] Lest we see this as mere distaste for Anglicanism expressed by a New Englander, however, it is important to consider Bancroft's following brief encapsulation of modern European history:

> The Catholic system embraced all society in its religious unity; Protestantism broke that religious unity into sects and fragments; philosophy carried analysis through the entire range of human thought and action, and appointed each individual the arbiter of his own belief and the director of his own powers. Society would be organized again; but not till after the recognition of the rights of the individual. *Unity would once more be restored but, not through the canon and feudal law; for the new Catholic element was the people* [emphasis added].[10]

After the disappearance of the possibility of unity under "the canon and feudal law," one of Jacksonian democracy's most prominent intellectual defenders tells us, the people have come to be the "new Catholic element" in America. In Bancroft's rendering, Jacksonian democracy – although it stands opposed to prescription, privilege, nondemocratic authority, "priestcraft" of the Roman Catholic sort, and "mystery" – nevertheless has something very "Catholic," and hence rather "mysterious," about it. Roman Catholicism is rejected in terms of the "age" (it belongs to the superseded historical past), but reclaimed as "spirit." One would be hard

[7] Quoted in Levin, *History as Romantic Art*, p. 100.

[8] George Bancroft, "A Word on Calvin, the Reformer" (1834), in *Literary and Historical Miscellanies* (New York: Harper & Brothers, 1857), p. 406.

[9] Bancroft, *History of the United States*, Vol. 5, p. 35.

[10] Ibid., p. 5.

pressed to find an eighteenth-century thinker such as Jefferson, convinced as he was that democracy was premised on an unequivocal rejection of "mystery," making a similar argument.

Not surprisingly, opponents of this inexorable march of "religious" democracy abounded. During the 1820s, prominent members of the judiciary – Joseph Story in Massachusetts, James Kent in New York, John Marshall in Virginia – allied themselves with the "wrong" side of history, that of resistance to the surge of egalitarian non-property-based suffrage reform.[11] Accordingly, many thinkers came up with their own versions of the "spirit of the age," often equally dependent upon a "spiritualization" of the prerevolutionary past, albeit ones that emphasized different aspects of the past and that sought to reign democracy in. To take just one example, even as Tocqueville represented democracy as historically unstoppable and the ancien régime as irrevocably past, he suggested that the tutelary nature of ancien régime governments might be desirable for young and unfolding democracies. As he put it, the movement toward equality "is already so strong that it cannot be stopped, but ... not yet so rapid that it cannot be guided."[12] In 1845, the Whig legal thinker Rufus Choate expressed a related view. In certain countries, Choate maintained, "the whole political and social order is to be rearranged." But the prerevolutionary order of stasis and oppression had been effectively done away with in America: "[W]ith us the age of this mode and this degree of reform is over; its work is done." What was needed now in America was not more change, but in fact a return to the stasis typically associated with prerevolutionary power. Choate's call was for motionlessness as democracy was advancing all around him: "Government, substantially as it is; jurisprudence, substantially as it is; the general arrangements of liberty, substantially as they are; the Constitution and the Union, exactly as they are, – this is to be wise, according to the wisdom of America."[13]

We are concerned here, of course, with how American common law thinkers created a space for the common law in Jacksonian America

[11] I have already referred to Kent's opposition to suffrage reform in the preceding chapter. For samples of Story's, Kent's, and Marshall's positions, see Merrill Petersen, *Democracy, Liberty, and Property: The State Constitutional Conventions of the 1820s* (Indianapolis: Bobbs-Merrill, 1960), pp. 77–91, 182–184, 360–364.

[12] Alexis de Tocqueville, *Democracy in America* (2 vols.) (Henry Reeve, trans.) (New York: Colonial, 1900), Vol. 1, p. 7.

[13] Rufus Choate, "The Position and Functions of the American Bar, as an Element of Conservatism in the State: An Address Delivered Before the Law School in Cambridge, July 3, 1845," in *The Works of Rufus Choate with a Memoir of His Life* (Samuel Gilman Brown, ed.) (2 vols.) (Boston: Little, Brown & Co., 1862), Vol. 1, pp. 419–421.

through a skillful manipulation of the nonhistorical temporalities of the common law and the historical sensibility of the "spirit of the age." As we shall see, the body of the common law was rigorously set in historical time – or "aged" – by its critics and its defenders, most of whom were inheritors of the eighteenth-century faith in the movement of history from the feudal to the commercial. Neither the common law's critics nor its defenders sought particularly to hang on to aspects of the common law legacy that belonged to what they considered past "ages," especially the feudal. History was thus brought to bear, instrumentally, upon the common law. The debate about the common law in this period was, as in earlier periods, principally about the common law as a method or style of lawmaking. But the common law's blurred temporality of "insensibility," an integral part of its method, was premised upon knitting together past, present, and future. How was this undifferentiated customary temporality, grounded in a past-oriented logic of repetition, to survive a historicist and instrumentalist "aging" of the common law? As we shall see, in the hands of common law thinkers such as Joseph Story and Francis Lieber, the temporality of the common law itself comes to be "spiritualized," to become the "spirit of the age," even as the common law is understood in terms of its relevance to the "age."

The People as "Spirit": the Jacksonian Attack on the Common Law

As the preceding chapter's discussion of the attack on the common law in Pennsylvania suggests, the concept of codification was hardly unknown at the turn of the eighteenth century. Many were familiar with the writings of Bentham and the recent experiences of France, Prussia, and Austria. According to Charles Cook, however, "[i]t was not until 1823 that the American codification movement was actually set in motion by William Sampson's 'Anniversary Discourse' to the New York Historical Society."[14]

[14] Charles M. Cook, *The American Codification Movement: A Study of Antebellum Legal Reform* (Westport, Conn.: Greenwood Press, 1981), p. 106. Cook's book is the authoritative text on American codification for the antebellum period. William Sampson, *Sampson's Discourse, and Correspondence with Various Learned Jurists, Upon the History of the Law, with the Addition of Several Essays, Tracts, and Documents, Relating to the Subject* (Washington, D.C.: Gales & Seaton, 1826). See also Maxwell Bloomfield, "William Sampson and the Codifiers: The Roots of American Legal Reform, 1820–1830," *American Journal of Legal History* 11 (1967): 232–252.

In Sampson's arguments, we observe continuities with late-eighteenth-century consent-centered modes of thought. The common law was roundly condemned for its "mystery," its inconsistency with republican forms, and its flouting of the contemporaneous voice of the people. Sampson wrote firmly:

> [The common law's] stubborn forms will be taught to bend to the convenience and exigencies of the People for whose use it subsists. It will be separated from the rubbish and decay of time and stripped of the parasitical growths that darken and disfigure it.[15]

The Irish émigré Sampson went further when he argued that the common law was in fact not the law of the ancestors of Americans. This was a riposte to the frequent claim of conservative common lawyers from Lord Coke on that the common law was the birthright of "our" ancestors or forefathers. As Sampson put it, "[W]hen a popular orator here declaims to a jury or other assembly, composed of Dutchmen mixed with Israelites and various Gentiles, about the laws and liberties of their Saxon ancestors, probably he is twice mistaken: first, in supposing their ancestors to have been Saxon; and, secondly, in supposing his own to have been freemen."[16]

The answer, for Sampson, lay in codification. "A sister State has already set on foot the experiment of a penal code, and committed its execution to the hands of one of its most capable citizens [the reference is to Edward Livingston's Louisiana code]."[17] Codification could not be resisted on the ground that it was an innovation, the traditional bane of common lawyers, because the Revolution had been all about innovation:

> If the fathers of our Revolution, at the peril of much more than life, ... dared to uproot the three great pillars of the Common Law, the monarchy, the hierarchy, and privileged orders, shall we stand in superstitious awe of unlaid specters; shall we still ... tremble at the thoughts of innovations upon institutions ... which have not half the imposing dignity of those of our ancestors, the red men of the five nations?[18]

It was the task of the present generation, therefore, to work out the anachronism that the common law represented in a republican polity

[15] Sampson, *Sampson's Discourse*, p. 6. For additional criticisms of the common law, see ibid., pp. 5–6, 101.

[16] Ibid., pp. 30–31.

[17] Ibid., p. 37.

[18] Ibid.

and to "giv[e] to all regenerated nations a model of judicial polity equal to that already exhibited in our political institutions."[19]

Sampson's focus on codification as being an actualization of the contemporaneous voice of the people struck a chord among other partisans of codification. In a letter to Sampson, the Louisiana lawyer Charles Watts agreed that "[t]he state of [common] law as a science, and the mode of its administration, are at variance with the spirit of the age and of the people."[20] Thomas Cooper, the president of Columbia College, South Carolina, and a leading proponent of codification in that state as well as an early Benthamite, echoed the view that the law could be rendered properly contemporaneous only through the device of a code. In response to the charge that a code would require judicial interpretation and hence re-create all the problems it was supposed to solve, Cooper offered a Jeffersonian solution: codes would be revised every fifty years:

> It is said the best digest or code we can make, will only serve as a new starting place, and that cases will go on accumulating and reports multiplying, as heretofore. Granted. But is it nothing that we have, or can have if we please, a new starting place every half century, leaving behind us the accumulated rubbish of years' proceedings?[21]

The efforts of Sampson, Cooper, and others publicized codification and placed it firmly on the legislative agenda. In the 1820s, codification appeared to be the wave of the future. Louisiana had adopted a civil code and a code of practice; New York commissioned three lawyers to review the inadequacies of its existing statutes as part of a first step toward codification; and significant codification movements were afoot in Pennsylvania and South Carolina.

According to students of codification in America, however, the codification movement changed course in the 1830s with the rise of Jacksonian democracy insofar as there was an intense focus on common law judges as usurpers of the rights of the people. In order to see this, but also the mystification of the figure of the "people" in Jacksonian discourses, let us turn to the writings of the archetypical Jacksonian reformer, Robert Rantoul, Jr.

Rantoul (1805–1852) was a practicing lawyer and a Democrat member of the Massachusetts House of Representatives, the U.S. House of

[19] Ibid., p. 40.
[20] Ibid., p. 93.
[21] Ibid., p. 53.

Representatives, and the U.S. Senate. Like any able lawyer, he was never loath to invoke the hallowed history of the common law, to say nothing of its nonhistorical temporality of "immemoriality," to serve his ends. In 1842, for example, when Rantoul defended the right to jury trial of the defendants in Dorr's Rebellion, he extolled the tradition of Magna Carta and urged the court "not to throw away a guarantee [jury trials by peers] which had ripened under the varied experience of a thousand years."[22] Rantoul was also, however, a thoroughgoing Jacksonian with a deep-seated suspicion of expansive readings of the U.S. Constitution, the Federalist–Whig judiciary that supported such readings, and the common law that was inevitably, and as a result, joined to the U.S. Constitution. Each of these was to be limited in the name of the "people."

In Rantoul's rendering, the coming of the "people" into its own represented "the spirit of the age." As an agent of history, the people were synonymous with the contemporary "age." Everything inconsistent with the will, preferences, and needs of the people could be represented as an anachronism, a "mysterious" hallmark of the prerevolutionary past, a holdover of a past "age." The principal anachronism was what Rantoul called "the British spirit," which he felt was still dominant in "our literature, our manners and customs, through the whole tone of our society, in the whole tenor and spirit of our laws, and in far too much of our domestic and foreign policy."[23] Not surprisingly, then, Rantoul's pantheon of American heroes consisted of those, each themselves marking an "epoch," who had succeeded in deepening the break with the "charm" – often a synonym for "mystery" – of the British past. As he put it, "There are three great names which mark three distinct epochs in our progress towards a complete independence: Washington who threw off the yoke of British power: Jefferson who broke the charm of British precedents, and British authority: Jackson who cancelled what remained of British institutions, and British policy."[24]

However, even as the people stood for a separation of the contemporary "age" from its predecessor and symbolized a repudiation of the "mystery" or "charm" of British precedents, the people were invested with a "mystery" of their own. This is precisely the "spiritualization" of a repudiated

[22] *Memoirs, Speeches and Writings of Robert Rantoul, Jr.* (Luther Hamilton, ed.) (Boston: John P. Jewett & Co., 1854), p. 27. See also Rantoul's references to Magna Carta in the Thomas Sims case. Ibid., p. 53.

[23] "Oration at Scituate, July 4, 1836," in *Memoirs, Speeches and Writings of Robert Rantoul, Jr.*, p. 252.

[24] Ibid. p. 264.

past that romantic era intellectuals performed in order to imbue the present with meaning. In Rantoul's writings, the people possess a mystical, ineffable, inexorable, unerring, and self-perfecting quality. This quality comprises a potent admixture of egalitarianism, the power to overcome any and every barrier, and the ability to seize the future. "Depend upon it," Rantoul wrote breathlessly in the *Democrat* on November 11, 1834, "the people will ultimately do right."[25] Thus imagined, the people were an object of faith rather than of reason. The problem with Whigs, Rantoul asserted in 1838, was precisely that they had "no faith in the people, no trust in their honesty, or in their capacity for self-government."[26] Faith was precisely what Rantoul possessed in abundance. "We are traveling onward towards perfection," he proclaimed, "and nothing can retard our progress but our own wickedness or our own folly."[27] This sense that the people were traveling toward "perfection" did not by any means imply a rejection of commerce as *telos*. Indeed, the perfection of the people was entirely consistent with a celebration of commerce, the egalitarian and liberalizing virtues of which Rantoul extolled when he claimed that commerce was "the parent of every thing that is valuable in modern civilization, whose blessed fruits are improved manners, comforts, arts, science, intelligence, and liberty."[28]

It should be evident from the aforementioned that, in the writings of Rantoul, even as the prerevolutionary past is rejected in the name of the people on the ground that it relies upon "mystery" and "charm" to work its magic, the American people are themselves invested with "mystery." In what follows, I examine Rantoul's critique of constitutional jurisprudence and common law, on the one hand, and then the celebrated case of *Charles River Bridge v. Warren Bridge* (1837), on the other. Rantoul condemned the Marshall Court's jurisprudence and the common law, even as he and other Jacksonians celebrated the Taney Court's decision in *Charles River Bridge* as a triumph for commerce and the people. But critics of the result in the *Charles River Bridge Case*, most notably Justice Joseph Story, read the case rather differently. As we shall see, in Story's reading of the Court's decision, the people

[25] November 11, 1834, in *Memoirs, Speeches and Writings of Robert Rantoul, Jr.*, p. 153.

[26] November 3, 1838, in *Memoirs, Speeches and Writings of Robert Rantoul, Jr.*, p. 722–723.

[27] "An Address to the Workingmen of the United States of America," in *Memoirs, Speeches and Writings of Robert Rantoul, Jr.*, p. 250.

[28] "Oration at South Reading, July 4, 1832," in *Memoirs, Speeches and Writings of Robert Rantoul, Jr.*, p. 167.

were arrogating to themselves precisely the divine right of kings or, in other words, precisely the "mystery" of a repudiated past, even as they claimed to repudiate monarchy.

Rantoul expressed the Jacksonian view that "the fundamental article in the democratic creed is this – that the general government ought to be strictly confined within its proper sphere."[29] A successor of earlier arguments regarding the boundaries of consent, this view translated into positions on the U.S. Constitution and the common law. Rantoul blamed the Federalists explicitly, and the Marshall Court implicitly, for the view that "*the powers granted to the government IMPLY all other powers which the government may find it convenient to assume*, a doctrine ... practically acted on, and which threatens to make the Constitution a mere dead letter."[30] A retreat from the Federalist position would allow the people – in the form of the states – to work out their own destinies freed from the "artificial" or "British" kinds of power associated with "consolidation." The advantage of having a written constitution was that one could always return to principle over practice. In the name of strict readings of the Constitution, the rights of the states and the people, firm principles, and a faith in a liberalizing and egalitarian commerce, Rantoul opposed all kinds of "consolidation," whether in the form of "unauthorized internal improvements" or the United States Bank, "the most dangerous foe of our liberties."[31]

To this critique of the Marshall Court's constitutional jurisprudence was joined a critique of the common law, made most coherently in Rantoul's famous "Oration at Scituate," delivered on July 4, 1836. Although a revision of the Massachusetts statutes had recently been completed, Rantoul argued, much more had to be done: "We are governed principally, by the common law; and this ought to be reduced, forthwith, to a uniform written code."[32] What followed was an attempt to locate the common law in past "ages" explicitly in order to attack the diffuse nonhistorical common law temporality of "immemoriality" and the supposed backward orientation of common law judges. The common law had "sprung from the dark ages," had its origin in "folly, barbarism and feudality," and had begun "in the time of ignorance."[33] Added to this was a new focus, with

[29] Quotation from article published in the *Gloucester Democrat and Workingmen's Advocate* (1834), in *Memoirs, Speeches and Writings of Robert Rantoul, Jr.*, p. 144.

[30] "Oration at South Reading, July 4, 1832," p. 176 (emphasis in the original).

[31] "Oration at Scituate, July 4, 1836," pp. 148–49.

[32] Ibid., p. 278.

[33] Ibid., p. 279.

a pronounced Benthamite twist, on the common law judge as usurper of the people's power. The common law's uncertainty, unpredictability, arbitrariness, and backward orientation were read in terms of a phrase not to be found in the writings of critics of an earlier generation such as Sampson or Goodenow: "judicial legislation."[34] Unlike legislators, who were responsible to the people, common law judges, their tenure protected and their method susceptible to whim, were bound to nobody. Excessively wedded to repeating precedent, they were able to flout the "the spirit of the age." According to Rantoul:

> [Judges] are sworn to administer common law as it came down from the dark ages, excepting what has been repealed by the Constitution and the statutes, which exception they are always careful to reduce to the narrowest possible limits. *With them, wrong is right, if wrong has existed from time immemorial: precedents are everything: the spirit of the age is nothing....* We must have democratic governors, who will appoint democratic judges, and the whole body of the law must be codified [emphasis added].[35]

The common law's focus on "immemoriality," and on repeating the past, was especially problematic in an "age" in which the people were advancing to perfection. The common law could make sense only in a world of stasis. As Rantoul put it:

> [T]he rapidly advancing state of our country is continually presenting new cases for the decision of the judges; and by determining these as they arise, the bench takes for its share more than half of our legislation.... *If a common law system could be tolerable anywhere, it is only where everything is stationary* [emphasis added].[36]

[34] Ibid., p. 278.

[35] Ibid., p. 281. In arguing against the authority of precedents, Rantoul was, of course, echoing Andrew Jackson himself. In Jackson's 1832 address vetoing the recharter of the United States Bank, he had argued pointedly against an adherence to precedent: "Mere precedent is a dangerous source of authority, and should not be regarded as deciding questions of constitutional power, except where the acquiescence of the people and the States can be considered as well settled." Jackson recognized that precedents were so contradictory that they could point in multiple directions. For this reason, he argued, "there is nothing in precedent ... which, if its authority were admitted, ought to weigh in favor of the act before me." Andrew Jackson's Veto Message Regarding the Second Bank of the United States, July 10, 1832," in Samuel G. Heiskell, ed., *Andrew Jackson and Early Tennessee History* (3 vols.) (Nashville: Ambrose Printing Co., 1921), Vol. 3, p. 302.

[36] "Oration at Scituate, July 4, 1836," p. 282. Rantoul's other major critique was that, in England, the common law made sense only in conjunction with equity. But a court of chancery would not be tolerated in Massachusetts (p. 282).

The solution, accordingly, was clear: "All American law must be statute law."[37] It is hardly surprising, then, as the editor of Rantoul's papers noted, that the one subject Rantoul took "particular pains" to bring before the Massachusetts House of Representatives during his tenure as member from Gloucester was the subject of the codification of the common law.[38] In keeping with Rantoul's rhetoric, codification in the 1830s and beyond was accompanied by widespread attacks on the judiciary and attempts to democratize the legal profession.[39]

Rantoul's criticisms of Federalist–Whig interpretations of the Constitution and of the common law in the name of the rights of the people configured as the "spirit of the age" took various concrete forms. The editor of Rantoul's *Memoirs* described him exuberantly as "an inflexible and eloquent advocate of the rights of man, as above those of property, whether held by individuals, or corporations."[40] Translated into a commitment to the rights of white workingmen, this became a commitment to limiting common law prosecutions of labor combinations that had been going on since the first decade of the nineteenth century.[41] One of Rantoul's most celebrated triumphs was his representation of the

[37] Ibid., p. 282.

[38] *Memoirs, Speeches and Writings of Robert Rantoul, Jr.*, p. 48.

[39] See the discussion in Bloomfield, "William Sampson and the Codifiers," p. 249. Codification itself consisted mostly of partial codification or the passage of revised statutes. Interest in codification began to wane in the 1840s, although it was kept alive in New York well into the late nineteenth century as a result of the efforts of David Dudley Field. Cook, *American Codification Movement*, pp. 185–213.

[40] *Memoirs, Speeches and Writings of Robert Rantoul, Jr.*, p. 20. Rantoul was also a big proponent of free and universal education. "The cry of the age," as he put it, "is for true education" (p. 96). This commitment to universal education was presented as an anticapitalist one. "In a state of general ignorance, the holders of masses of capital have an influence, not only disproportioned to their numbers, but also far beyond the proportion of their wealth, by the control they possess over mercenary talent: but, in a state of general education, the amount of talent developed is far too great to be bought up by any class; a wholesome public opinion makes talent scorn to be mercenary" (p. 137).

[41] See the discussion of common law prosecutions of labor combinations, and William Sampson's role in defending laborers, in the preceding chapter. Rantoul began an 1833 address as follows: "Society, as you very well know, is divided into two classes, – those who do something for their living, and those who do not." "An Address to the Workingmen of the United States of America," pp. 219–220. This concern did not extend to America's slave population. In the above-cited address, Rantoul insisted that he wished "to address [himself] to my fellow-citizens, the workingmen of the United States of America. Not the slave population of the South, for although they may have by nature the same rights which I wish to discuss, yet they are not at present in a situation to enjoy them, and as a practical man, I do not wish to indulge in impracticable theories or visionary speculations, but to offer advice which may ... be carried into action" (pp. 220–221).

defendants in the *Journeymen Boot-Makers Case* (1842), in which the defendant journeymen bootmakers had been indicted for common law conspiracy for having combined to demand higher wages. Rantoul successfully obtained from Chief Justice Lemuel Shaw of the Massachusetts Supreme Judicial Court a ruling that combinations by laborers were not illegal per se.[42] However, Rantoul's preference for the "rights of man" over the "rights of property" also translated into a critique of what he considered special legislation on behalf of corporations, which leads us to a discussion of the *Charles River Bridge Case*.

The Jacksonian fear of special legislation – itself an echo of eighteenth-century republican thought – was that the "yeomanry" would fall under the influence of "great companies," resulting in a subversion of republicanism and a reinstatement of British aristocracy.[43] Committed as they were to commerce as an equalizing force, thinkers such as Rantoul worried that corporations able to capture legislatures would obtain a grip on communal resources for a disproportionate period of time and would end up foreclosing the people's future. This was especially a problem where the people themselves were invested, as they were for Rantoul, with a self-perfecting quality.

> *When once ... one of these corporations obtained an ascendancy in any particular interests, they locked it up from the rest of the community forever....* So that when a power was granted to a corporation to lock up land, although the grant might be limited, the limit was of no avail. A vast portion of the real estate of the Commonwealth [of Massachusetts] was now owned by corporations [Emphasis added].[44]

Rantoul's fear that corporations could "lock up" resources from the rest of the community translated into a dislike of the doctrine of vested rights, which, for Rantoul, was flatly antithetical to the rights of the people to shape its present and future. "The party opposed to the democracy is that which vindicates assumed 'vested rights' to do wrong, which passes and

[42] According to the Court, which in its judgment set aside a long line of American common law conspiracy cases that had held the contrary, there had to be a showing of unlawful purposes or means in order to obtain a conviction for conspiracy. *Commonwealth v. Hunt*, 45 Mass. 111 (1842). For a discussion of the case, see Tomlins, *Law, Labor and Ideology in the Early American Republic*, pp. 199–216.

[43] It was also a fear of paper money as a form of "modern political alchemy." See *Memoirs, Speeches and Writings of Robert Rantoul, Jr.*, p. 355. What was to be resisted, for Rantoul, was "that spirit of speculation and overtrading which over-banking fosters" (p. 362).

[44] Ibid., p. 314.

defends laws for the benefit of the law-making faction of the day, which grants exclusive privileges, and protects the few against the many.... Its rule of legislation is the interest now of the mercantile class, now of the manufacturers, now of the great planters, now of the great capitalists, never of the masses, never of the whole people."[45]

What Rantoul would characterize as the conflict between corporations and the people came to a head, albeit in a complicated way, in the celebrated case of *Charles River Bridge v. Warren Bridge* (1837).[46] In the historiography of American law, the case has come to stand for the difference between the Marshall Court and the Taney Court, the arrogated power of the people versus existing legal entitlements, and, more generally, the problem of how and where to locate the authority to fit law to a changing economy. My interest in this case is a little different. The judicial rhetoric in the case reveals, as we shall see, the imprint of the historical vocabulary of the "spirit of the age." More interestingly, Justice Joseph Story's famous dissent in the case reveals how the majority's position – which in many quarters was read as a victory for the people – could in fact be seen as being imbued precisely with the "spirit" of the undemocratic, prerevolutionary past. From the perspective of its opponents, Jacksonian democracy, invested as it was with the "mystery" of prerevolutionary holistic kinds of power, was capable of riding roughshod over individual rights just as Europe's monarchs had.

The facts of the *Charles River Bridge Case* went back to 1785, when the Massachusetts legislature chartered the Charles River Bridge Company to build a bridge between Boston and Charlestown. For building the bridge and maintaining it, the legislature granted the Charles River Bridge Company the right to collect tolls for forty years, a privilege it extended for an additional thirty years in 1792 as compensation for chartering another bridge across the Charles River. In 1829, however, while the toll rights of the Charles River Bridge were still in force under its charter, the legislature chartered the Warren Bridge Company and authorized it to build a toll-free bridge only a few yards from the old bridge. The impact on the toll revenues of the Charles River Bridge was both predictable and disastrous.

The question, as it was eventually appealed to the U.S. Supreme Court, was how the terms of the charter to the Charles River Bridge Company

[45] Ibid., p. 723.

[46] *Proprietors of Charles River Bridge v. Proprietors of Warren Bridge*, 36 U.S. 420 (1837).

were to be interpreted. This would have implications for the applicability of the Contract Clause of the U.S. Constitution. Was the charter to be read strictly, so that the authorization of the newer Warren Bridge was not a violation of it (in which case there would be no breach of the charter and hence no violation of the U.S. Constitution)? Was the charter to be read more broadly, such that there could be implied in favor of the Charles River Bridge Company the right to have its investment protected from grants to competitors (in which case there would be a breach of the charter and hence a violation of the U.S. Constitution)? By the time the case was argued before the U.S. Supreme Court, the dispute had already become highly politicized. It had been widely construed, in classic Jacksonian terms, as the difference between aristocracy and property (those in favor of protecting the rights of the Charles River Bridge Company) and democracy (those in favor of protecting the rights of the people of Massachusetts to authorize the Warren Bridge Company).

The new chief justice, Roger Taney, formerly Andrew Jackson's attorney general, spoke for the majority. Private property was still sacred and must, declared Taney, be "sacredly guarded."[47] Corporate charters remained contracts under the protection of the U.S. Constitution pursuant to the logic of the *Dartmouth College Case*. However, Taney had recourse to an English common law rule of construction, according to which, in a "bargain between a company of adventurers and the public, the terms of which are expressed in [a] statute, ... the rule of construction ... is now fully established to be this – that any ambiguity in the terms of the contract, must operate against the adventurers, and in favor of the public."[48] This was because "the community" also had rights and the "happiness and well-being of every citizen depends on their faithful preservation." The rights of the public ought not to be surrendered, in other words, on the shaky ground of implication. Following this common law rule of construction, Taney could find nothing in the terms of the charter to the Charles River Bridge Company that prevented the chartering of the Warren Bridge. Thus, there was no violation of the U.S. Constitution's Contract Clause.

This democratic sensibility – a strict reading of the charter on the grounds of safeguarding the rights of the community – was also based on what Taney took to be sound commercial logic, namely, the curbing of corporate monopolies. Implying monopoly rights would set the Court

[47] Ibid., p. 548.
[48] Ibid., p. 558.

against the current of history where commerce was progress and would tie up courts in problems of line drawing that they were ill equipped to handle. If the Court ruled differently, Taney argued, it would both impede development and have to determine, for example, whether old turnpike companies could block the chartering of new railroads. Taney put it thus:

> Let it once be understood, that such charters carry with them these implied contracts, and give this unknown and undefined property in a line of travelling; and you will soon find the old turnpike corporations awakening from their sleep, and calling upon this court to put down the improvements which have taken their place. The millions of property which have been invested in rail-roads and canals, upon lines of travel which had been before occupied by turnpike corporations, will be put in jeopardy; *we shall be thrown back to the improvements of the last century, and obliged to stand still*.... Nor is this all. The court will find itself compelled to fix, by some arbitrary rule, the width of this new kind of property in a line of travel; for if such a right of property exists, we have no lights to guide us in marking out its extent, unless, indeed, *we resort to the old feudal grants* .... This court are not prepared to sanction principles which must lead to such results [emphasis added].

The Court's distaste for resorting to "the old feudal grants" and for being "thrown back to the improvements of the last century" bespeaks its historicist position, its commitment to shedding the feudal past and moving toward the commercial present and future. In a related vein, Justice McLean's concurring opinion declared that English principles long established for the protection of ancient ferries, markets, fairs, and mills from competition – precedents cited by the plaintiffs – were entirely inapplicable to America:

> In this country, there are few rights founded on prescription. The settlement of our country is comparatively recent; and its rapid growth in population, and advance in improvements have prevented, in a great degree, interests from being acquired by immemorial usage. Such evidence of right is found in countries where society has become more fixed, and improvements are in a great degree stationary.

Rantoul had suggested that the common law made sense only in a static country, not in a commercial and future-oriented America imbued with the instinct of perfectibility. McLean argued the opposite. It was "one of the most valuable traits of the common law," McLean observed, that it adopted only rules "adapted to the condition of our country." This is what explained why prescriptive rights based on "immemorial usage" had no place in America. Rights acquired on the basis of prescription were inconsistent, McLean emphasized, with the "spirit of improvement that pervades the whole country."[49]

Although the judges writing for the majority in the *Charles River Bridge Case* had based their ruling precisely upon a common law rule of construction or upon the fact that an American common law had no place for prescriptive rights, in the opinion of many Jacksonian commentators, the *Charles River Bridge Case* stood precisely for a rejection of the manipulable common law method, a repudiation of the claims of the past, and a triumph of the rights of the people. Rantoul was referring to in the *Charles River Bridge Case* when he complained about the unchecked discretion of common law judges. He wrote:

> And suppose the judge prefers the common law to the Constitutions of the State and of the Union; or decides in defiance of a statute; what is the remedy? An astute argument is always at hand to reconcile the open violation of that instrument with the express letter of the Constitution, as in the case of the United States Bank, – or to prove an obnoxious statute unconstitutional, *as would have happened in the case of the Warren Bridge, but for the firmness of Judge Morton* [the judge in the lower court who had ruled for the Warren Bridge Company] [emphasis added].[50]

George Bancroft similarly repudiated prescriptive rights. However, instead of seeing their repudiation as part of the inherent vitality of an American common law, as had Justice McLean in the case, Bancroft saw it as part of the triumph of "justice" over "law": "Prescription can no more assume to be a valid plea for political injustice; society studies to eradicate established abuses, and to bring social institutions and law into harmony with moral right.[51] It was in this vein that Bancroft declared himself to be opposed to what he called the "materialist" vested rights jurisprudence – as distinguished, presumably, from the "spiritualized" rights of the people – that was on the losing side of the *Charles River Bridge Case*. As he put it:

> Instead of saying, It is right, it says, It is established. It asserts an immortality for law, not for justice; it perpetuates established wrong on the basis of a vested right.
>
> This theory, by its very nature, can apply to nothing but material wealth; because mind is always in motion. It is the indefeasible prerogative of humanity

[49] Ibid., pp. 552–553, 563, 563, 583.

[50] "Oration at Scituate, July 4, 1836," p. 281.

[51] George Bancroft, "The Office of the People in Art, Government, and Religion," in *Literary and Historical Miscellanies*, p. 422.

to make progress; the soul cannot be bound down by a fixed contract; error cannot be rendered immutable by an intellectual mortmain; nor the progress of truth restrained by vested rights in opinions.[52]

It should be clear, then, that prominent Jacksonian supporters of the majority position in the *Charles River Bridge Case* saw it as a triumph of commerce and the people over the claims of the past, "immemorial usage," vested rights, and, ultimately, the common law (this was admittedly a simplification of what the case was about). But critics of the *Charles River Bridge* decision told a different story, representing the majority's view as entailing the importation of an aspect of the oppressive prerevolutionary past. For this critical view, let us turn to the dissenting opinion of Justice Joseph Story.

Story was a mainstay of the Marshall Court's pro-Union, pro-commerce, implied rights, and vested rights jurisprudence. As such, his jurisprudential views were in many ways irrevocably opposed to those of thinkers like Rantoul and Bancroft. With the appointment of Roger Taney as chief justice following Marshall's death in 1835, Story experienced a sense of isolation on an altered Supreme Court. In 1837, the same year the *Charles River Bridge Case* was decided, Story described himself somewhat wistfully to Harriet Martineau as being "the last of the old race of judges."[53] Kent Newmyer, whose scholarly account of Story's career and jurisprudence remains the most authoritative to date, describes Story's *Charles River Bridge* dissent thus: "His literally was a voice from the past."[54]

Although Story himself gave his contemporaries to believe that he was "a voice from the past," the past features in contradictory ways in his dissenting opinion. To begin with, Story accuses the majority of representing, indeed of reviving, an undemocratic, prerevolutionary past. He argues that the majority's common law rule of construction – construing grants strictly in favor of the public – had traditionally applied only "to cases

[52] George Bancroft, *An Oration Delivered Before the Democracy of Springfield and Neighboring Towns, July 4, 1836* (Springfield, Mass.: George & Charles Merriam, 1836), pp. 6–7. Elsewhere in the same oration, Bancroft states, "The tory, blaspheming God, pleads the will of heaven as a sanction for a government of force; the whig, forgetting that God is not the God of the dead, appeals to prescription; democracy lives in the consciences of the living" (pp. 10–11).

[53] April 7, 1837, in *Life and Letters of Joseph Story* (William W. Story, ed.) (2 vols.) (Boston: Charles C. Little & James Brown, 1851), Vol. 2, p. 277.

[54] R. Kent Newmyer, *Supreme Court Justice Joseph Story: Statesman of the Old Republic* (Chapel Hill: University of North Carolina Press, 1985), p. 227.

of mere donation, flowing from the bounty of the crown." When a grant had been made upon a valuable consideration, as it allegedly had been in the case of the Charles River Bridge Company, the ordinary common law rule of contract construction applicable to contracts between equal parties should govern. Indeed, Story continued, "Even in the worst ages of arbitrary power, and irresistible prerogative, [Lord Coke and other "venerable sages of the law"] did not hesitate to declare, that contracts founded in a valuable consideration ought to be construed liberally for the subject, for the honor of the crown."[55] In the name of the rights of the public, Story argued, the new Jacksonian majority on the Court was in fact endowing legislatures with the attributes of royal authority:

> Such a claim in favor of republican prerogative is new.... Our legislatures neither have, nor affect to have, any royal prerogatives.... The policy of the common law, which gave the crown so many exclusive privileges and extraordinary claims, different from those of the subject, was founded, in a good measure, if not altogether, upon the divine right of kings, or, at least, upon a sense of their exalted dignity and pre-eminence over all subjects, and upon the notion, that they are entitled to peculiar favor, for the protection of kingly rights and office. Parliamentary grants never enjoyed any such privileges; they were always construed according to common sense and common reason, upon their language and their intent.[56]

Thus, as figured in the *Charles River Bridge* dispute, the people, even as they claimed to break the hold of the "charm of British precedents" (as Rantoul put it), relied precisely upon the attributes of the divine power of the past to realize perfectibility, improvement, and progress. If anything represented a concrete instantiation of Bancroft's claim that the people possessed the "Catholic element" – or of Rantoul's faith that the "people" were utterly infallible – it was this. Story accused the Taney Court of imbuing the people with "the divine right of kings."

At the same time that Story accused Taney of investing the people with an attribute of old power, however, he himself claimed for his own position the protective mantle of the old. His preferred rule – one that would have resulted in rights implied in favor of the Charles River Bridge Company and hence in a violation of the Contract Clause of the U.S. Constitution – was described as follows

> *I stand upon the old law;* upon law established more than three centuries ago, in cases contested with as much ability and learning, as any in the annals of our jurisprudence, in resisting any such encroachments upon the rights and liberties

[55] *Charles River Bridge v. Warren Bridge*, p. 597 (Justice Story, dissenting).

[56] Ibid., p. 602 (Justice Story, dissenting).

of the citizens, secured by public grants. *I will not consent to shake their title deeds, by any speculative niceties or novelties* [emphasis added].[57]

In other words, while the Taney majority was accused of simultaneously engaging in "speculative niceties and novelties" and restoring a superseded "divine power," Story himself claimed to be doing neither. He was being both appropriately "old" and thoroughly democratic. Story also claimed for his rule its own commercial logic. If Taney thought that implying rights on behalf of the Charles River Bridge Company would impede necessary economic progress, Story thought that failing to protect the Company's investment would do the same by acting as a disincentive to future investment: "If the government means to invite citizens to enlarge the public comforts and conveniences, to establish bridges, or turnpikes, or canals, or railroads, there must be some pledge, that the property will be safe." He warned, "No man will hazard his capital in any enterprise, in which, if there be a loss, it must be borne exclusively by himself; and if there be success, he has not the slightest security of enjoying the rewards of that success, for a single moment."[58]

For our purposes, however, the interesting and important questions are as follows: What did it mean for Story to "stand upon the old law" even as he condemned an importation of the attributes of "old" power? What was the place of the common law, as conceived of by one of its most ardent defenders, in the "age of the spirit of the age"?

Constitution, Common Law, and Spirit: the Legal Science of Joseph Story

In November 1829, Joseph Story began an address to the Boston Mechanics' Institute in which he revealed his familiarity with, and his subscription to, the prevailing historical formula of his day: "Much has been said respecting the spirit of our age, and the improvements by which it is characterized. Many learned discussions have been presented to the public, with a view to illustrate this topic."[59] Story then offered his own version:

If I were called upon to state that which, upon the whole, is the most striking characteristic of our age, that which in the largest extent exemplifies its spirit,

[57] Ibid., p. 598 (Justice Story, dissenting).

[58] Ibid., p. 608 (Justice Story, dissenting).

[59] Joseph Story, "Developments of Science and Mechanic Art: A Discourse Delivered Before the Boston Mechanics' Institute, at the Opening of their Annual Course of Lectures, November, 1829," in *The Miscellaneous Writings of Joseph Story* (William W. Story, ed.) (Boston: Charles Little & James Brown, 1852) (1972), p. 475.

I should unhesitatingly answer, that it is the superior attachment to practical science over merely speculative science.[60]

There had been a period, Story continued, "when metaphysical inquiries constituted the principal delight of scholars and philosophers."[61] But this had changed with Francis Bacon's articulation of the method of induction.[62] Bacon's method had taken centuries to establish itself. Its "triumphant adoption," Story maintained, "was reserved as the peculiar glory of our own day."[63] Induction tested all theories against hard facts, thereby saving "a useless consumption of time and thought upon vague and visionary projects."[64] It was the power of this careful, inductive science, Story opined, to identify "the true means to arrive at great ends."[65]

Joseph Story had had a distinguished career as a lawyer, legal scholar, politician, and judge by the time he delivered this address. In the 1830s, following his appointment as Dane Professor of Law at Harvard Law School in 1829, he would distinguish himself even further by writing a number of pioneering treatises, principally devoted to commercial law. He was arguably the most important legal thinker of the second quarter of the nineteenth century in America. Although, as stated in the preceding section, Story self-consciously represented himself as "the last of the old race of judges" after the Marshall Court was succeeded by the Taney Court, Story is better thought of as a jurist for the romantic era in America, as testified by his youthful flirtation with Rousseau and German idealism, his authorship of suggestively titled poems such as "The Power of Solitude" (1804), the quality of his writings and ideas generally, and, not least, his repeated subscription to the romantic vocabulary of the "spirit of the age."

What is noteworthy about Story's identification of inductive, instrumental science as the "spirit of the age" is precisely what he implicitly suggests is *not* the "spirit of the age," namely the explosion and deepening of that democratic, all-encompassing, "religious" democracy that George Bancroft and Robert Rantoul celebrated and that Story saw instantiated in Chief Justice Taney's majority opinion in the *Charles River Bridge*

[60] Ibid., p. 478.
[61] Ibid.,
[62] Ibid., pp. 478–479.
[63] Ibid., p. 479.
[64] Ibid.
[65] Ibid., p. 493.

Case. Alternatively, one might argue, for Story, the excesses of Jacksonian egalitarianism – which he despondently described on Jackson's inauguration on March 2, 1829 as "the reign of King 'Mob'" – were akin to those despised "vague and visionary projects," a flighty democratic version of medieval scholasticism perhaps, that were antithetical to the careful inductive method that constituted the true "spirit of the age."[66]

Political democracy was, of course, critical to Story's understanding of law. Early in his career as a lawyer in Federalist-dominated Essex County, Massachusetts, Story had in fact been a Republican at some cost to himself, although he moved closer to more conservative Federalist–Whig positions by the 1820s. For Story, it was precisely the advent of a certain kind of democracy that was, historically considered, critical to the emergence into prominence of an inductive legal science that could serve as democracy's limiting "spirit." Democracy was a necessary precondition for law to develop independently along scientific lines, but in order for law to develop independently along scientific lines, democracy must itself step back and be constrained. In outmoded arbitrary governments, Story observed, the law "can scarcely be said to have existence as a science"; instead, it "breathes only at the beck of the sovereign ... and assumes no general rules, by which rights or actions are to be governed."[67] By contrast, in democracies, Story maintained, the scientific articulation of law as a collection of principles was the privilege of the jurist, as opposed to that of the politician or layperson. This was also the position James Kent adopted in his famous *Commentaries on American Law* (1826–1830) and was not removed from the claims common lawyers had long made about the advantages of a self-sufficient, spontaneously developing common law that acted to constrain the sovereign. In 1826, despite worries about a more clamorous democracy emerging around him, Story expressed a

[66] Joseph Story to Sarah Story, *Life and Letters of Joseph Story*, March 7, 1829, Vol. 1, pp. 562–563. Elsewhere, Story described Jackson's presidency as akin to being "under the absolute rule of a single man" and as resembling "the last days of the Roman republic, ... when liberty expired with the dark but prophetic words of Cicero." Joseph Story to Judge Fay, February 18, 1834, *Life and Letters of Joseph Story*, Vol. 2, p. 154.

In addition to being the true "spirit of the age," induction was quintessentially Anglo-Saxon, just as speculation was not. "[The] reckless spirit of speculation," Story would write in 1842, "is not indigenous to our soil; nor does it belong to the sober sagacity of the Anglo-Saxon race." Joseph Story, "Literary Tendencies of the Times," in *Miscellaneous Writings*, p. 748.

[67] Joseph Story, "Progress of Jurisprudence," in *Miscellaneous Writings*, p. 200. For Story, this also translated into the fact that the laws of the East had remained stationary, whereas the laws of European nations had undergone "the most extraordinary revolutions" (p. 198).

historical faith – perhaps as much hope as faith – in the rise of science and the cabining of populist democracy. In an essay entitled "Characteristics of the Age," he claimed that the inductive method was "working its way to universality, and interposing checks upon government and people, by means gentle and decisive."[68]

Story's commitment to the method of inductive science over the method of a "vague and visionary" populist democracy was placed at the service of his most unwavering commitment, a faith in the historical inexorability of commerce, one that he shared with many thinkers of this period (including Rantoul) and that derived from the eighteenth century. In its usefulness, intelligence, and liberalization, in its imagined inexorability and universality, commerce was intimately allied with inductive science. Both possessed the same valences. Both were associated with the rise of, yet rested upon a limiting of political democracy. Accordingly, when Story wrote in 1825 that "the law must fashion itself to the wants, and in some sort to the spirit of the age," it was law's facilitation of commerce through the inductive method – and hence its fostering of the "vivifying effect" of commerce *and* inductive science – that Story had in mind.[69] The old common law would have to be subjected to this historical and scientific mandate.

In order for this historical and scientific vision to be realized, however, Story would have to accomplish two things. First, he would have to tether the common law, newly reduced to universal principles, as strongly as possible to the U.S. Constitution. Without this, the spread of scientific principles across America's national space, and hence the realization of the "spirit of the age," would be impossible. Second, he would have to distinguish his historical and scientific method of reducing the common law to principles from the method of legislatures. It is in the contradictions involved in such endeavors, I argue, that we might see the "spiritualization" of the traditional nonhistorical temporalities of the common law.

In order to tether a reformulated common law to the U.S. Constitution, Story was compelled to confront the range of arguments, made in the late eighteenth century but also increasingly aggressively in the 1820s and 1830s (most strongly in the form of nullification), that characterized the

[68] Joseph Story, "Characteristics of the Age," in *Miscellaneous Writings*, p. 341.

[69] Joseph Story, "Growth of the Commercial Law," in *Miscellaneous Writings*, p. 279. The reference to the "vivifying effect" of commerce comes from Story, "Literature of the Maritime Law," in *Miscellaneous Writings*, p. 99.

U.S. Constitution as a compact between the federal government and the states. Arguing that the U.S. Constitution was a compact was, of course, a way of reading the powers of the federal government strictly and of denying where possible the ability of the common law to inform the constitutional text. In order to join the common law to the U.S. Constitution, then, Story had to offer an alternative theory of the Constitution.

Story's celebrated *Commentaries on the Constitution of the United States* (1833), the first major compilation of constitutional jurisprudence published in the United States, was a sustained defense of the Marshall Court's jurisprudence in light of the attacks on the Court recently made public as a consequence of the posthumous publication of Jefferson's *Memoirs* in 1829 (in the *Memoirs*, Jefferson had dubbed Story a "pseudo-republican" and blamed him for bringing about the repeal of the embargo). As part of his attempt to vindicate the politics of the Marshall Court and to combat states' rights theories, Story offered a theory that was a staple of Marshall Court jurisprudence, that the Union had been formed by the people of the colonies taken as a whole rather than by the states. On this reading, the Union and the states were coeval and coexisting sovereigns, each endowed with different powers. The states possessed no necessary priority over the Union. This was shown through a careful tracing of the history of the colonies, the Confederation, and the Constitution.[70]

However, Story also subscribed to an unabashedly Burkean theory of power that saw governmental power as far more profound and encompassing. For him, Burke was, revealingly, "a master-spirit of the last age."[71] In a Burkean mode, Story stressed the inevitability and ubiquity of

[70] As part of his argument, Story would assert that, "antecedent to the Declaration of Independence, none of the colonies were, or pretended to be sovereign states, in the sense, in which the term 'sovereign' is sometimes applied to states," that the colonies did not proclaim their independence severally, and that, from the moment of the Declaration and even before the Confederation, an "exclusive sovereignty" had been established at the center and its supremacy over national measures "universally admitted." Joseph Story, *Commentaries on the Constitution of the United States: With Preliminary review of the Constitutional History of the Colonies and States, Before the Adoption of the Constitution* (2 vols) (2d ed) (Boston: Little & Brown, 1851), Vol. 1, pp. 142, 153–154, 158.

[71] Joseph Story, "Value and Importance of Legal Studies," in *Miscellaneous Writings*, p. 519. In his study of the political culture of the American Whigs, Daniel Walker Howe has drawn attention to the "now-forgotten American vogue of Edmund Burke." Daniel Walker Howe, *The Political Culture of the American Whigs* (Chicago: University of Chicago Press, 1979), p. 211. A good example is Rufus Choate. The American bar, Choate argued in 1845, "helped to withstand the pernicious sophism that the successive generations, as they come to life, are but as so many successive flights of summer flies,

the individual's subjection to power, expressed a suspicion of innovation, and emphasized the importance of discretion, circumstance, embeddedness, implication, compromise, custom, and usage.

According to Story, no contemporary American state had in fact been founded upon the assent of a majority of its population. Thus, governmental power was not created through voluntary contract or contemporaneous consent (grounds of the compact theory), but was ubiquitous, always already there. This was evident if one looked around and saw how subjection to power actually worked. Individuals generally did not assent to the societies they were part of; they were born into such societies subject to their rules. Story put it thus: "The assent of minors, of women, and of unqualified voters has never been asked or allowed; yet these embrace a majority of the whole population in every organized society, and are governed by its existing institutions."[72] The demonstrable imperfection of consent as a ground of authority was true not only of the states, but also of the national government:

> In respect to the American Revolution itself, it is notorious that it was brought about against the wishes and resistance of a formidable minority of the people; and that the declaration of independence never had the universal assent of the inhabitants of the country. So, that this great and glorious change in the organization of our government owes its whole authority to the efforts of a triumphant majority. And the dissent on the part of the minority was deemed in many cases a crime.

Minorities were bound "whether they had assented or not; for the plain reason that opposite wills in the same society, on the same subjects, cannot prevail at the same time." Story went even further: "In a general sense the will of the majority of the people is absolute and sovereign, limited only by their means and power to make their will effectual."[73]

If this emphasis on majoritarian power seems odd coming from someone as concerned to limit popular democracy in the name of science and commerce as Story so manifestly was, it should be stressed that such arguments were directed quite surgically against theories for understanding governmental power through analogies to "municipal contracts between individuals."[74] The most telling proof that Story's arguments against the

without relations to the past or duties to the future, and taught instead that all – all the dead, the living, the unborn – were one moral person." Choate, "The Position and Functions of the American Bar," p. 417

[72] Story, *Commentaries on the Constitution of the United States*, Vol. 1, p. 219.

[73] Ibid., 220–221.

[74] Ibid., p. 221.

compact theory are not so much a vindication of the power of the popular majorities as an argument about the inevitability and permanence of governmental power lies in his endorsement of Blackstone's celebrated and controversial definition of law, a definition that had been repudiated as antirepublican by late-eighteenth-century Federalist jurists such as James Wilson.[75] Story invokes Blackstone thus: "A constitution is in fact a fundamental law or basis of government, and falls strictly within the definition of law, as given by Mr. Justice Blackstone. It is a rule of action, prescribed by the supreme power in a state, regulating the rights and duties of the whole community." Constitutionally recognized rights were not, correspondingly, a matter of contract, of something once possessed and given up, but "a solemn recognition and admission of [those rights], arising from the law of nature and the gift of Providence, and incapable of being transferred or surrendered."[76]

Precisely because governmental power in general was not a creature of contract, but something already existent, much discretion had to be surrendered when it came to the interpretation of the Constitution. This was, of course, the controversial Marshall Court idea of implied powers, so vociferously criticized by Jacksonian intellectuals such as Rantoul. But implied powers were not just about expanding central government. They were also a Burkean common lawyer's corrective to Jeffersonian theories of democracy premised upon the temporal separation of one generation from another. Story made out the case for implied powers thus: "[I]f the whole society is not to be revolutionized at every critical period, and remodeled in every generation, there must be left to those, who administer the government, a very large mass of discretionary powers, capable of greater or less actual expansion, according to circumstances, and sufficiently flexible not to involve the nation in utter destruction from the rigid limitation imposed upon it by an improvident jealousy."[77] In "The

[75] *The Works of James Wilson* (James DeWitt Andrews, ed.) (2 vols.) (Chicago: Callaghan & Co., 1896), Vol. 1, pp. 18–19.

[76] Story, *Commentaries on the Constitution of the United States*, Vol. 1, 227, 228.

[77] Ibid., pp. 301–302. Story had long been a champion of implying powers in favor of government. This was true during his early career on the U.S. Supreme Court, when he was trying cases related to the embargo while on circuit in Massachusetts and refused to hamper enforcing officers by imposing technical restraints. See *U.S. v. Sears*, 27 Fed. Cas. 1006 (No. 16,247) (C.C.D. Mass. 1812). Later, in decisions such as *Brown v. U.S.*, 8 Cranch. 151 (1814), Story would even break with the rest of the Marshall Court on the question of wartime executive powers. As he put it in dissent, "I think that [the President] must, as an incident of the office, have a right to employ all the usual and customary means acknowledged in war." 8 Cranch. 128–129. See also *U.S. v. Bainbridge*, 24 Fed. Cas. 946 (No. 14,497) (C.C.D. Mass. 1816). I derive the discussion in this note from

Science of Government" (1834), Story argues that government is "the science of adaptations – variable in its elements, dependent upon circumstances, and incapable of a rigid mathematical demonstration."[78] The point is clear: implied powers are necessary if society is to maintain continuity as it travels across past, present, and future.

This emphasis on a discretionary, flexible, adaptable, and given governmental power that was supposed to maintain continuity across past, present, and future went along with a common lawyerly repudiation of "innovation" (by which Story undoubtedly means legislative, rather than judicial, innovation). In "Characteristics of the Age" (1826), Story quotes Burke for the following proposition:

> There is not a remark deducible from the history of mankind more important than that advanced by Mr. Burke, that "to innovate is not to reform." That is, if I may venture to follow out the sense of this great man, that innovation is not necessarily improvement; that novelty is not necessarily excellence; that what was deemed wisdom in former times, is not necessarily folly in ours; that the course of the human mind has not been to present a multitude of truths in one great step of its glory, but to gather them up insensibly in its progress, and to

Newmyer, *Supreme Court Justice Joseph Story*. For Newmyer, such decisions "adumbrated a theory of constitutional power that would be Story's hallmark and the Marshall Court's too" (p. 88).

78 Joseph Story, "The Science of Government," in *Miscellaneous Writings*, pp. 616–617. Compromise was all-important. Story celebrated the Constitution's infamous "Three-Fifths Clause" permitting slaves to be counted for purposes of representation as "a real compromise ... for the common good, ... entitled to great praise for its moderation, its aim at practical utility, and its tendency to satisfy the people that the Union framed by all, ought to be dear to all." Story, *Commentaries on the Constitution of the United States*, Vol. 1, p. 443. Irregularity, specificity, and localism were preferable to the sharp lines of theoretical zeal. This is clear when Story discusses state-by-state variations in the right to elect and be elected. "An absolute, indefeasible right to elect or be elected [is] one of mere civil polity, to be arranged upon such a basis, as the majority may deem expedient with reference to the moral, physical, and intellectual condition of the particular State" (p. 405). There was an inevitability of differences among the states, each saturated by the weight of custom. Different states, because of the "natural attachments which long habit and usage had sanctioned," might resist a homogenization of voting (p. 407). Furthermore, relying explicitly on Burke and no doubt hearkening to his pro-property position when it came to suffrage reform, Story doubted whether a system of representative government "could [ever] be safe without a large admixture of different persons and interests" (p. 401, n 2). In England, the House of Commons was founded upon "no uniform principle, either of numbers, or classes or places" (a vociferous complaint of the American revolutionary generation that Story elides); this was different from the uniform principles of territory, population, and taxation adopted in postrevolutionary France, which Burke had shown to be "inconvenient, unequal and inconsistent" (pp. 407–408). There was, in general, "no uniformity of practice, or principle, among free nations in regard to elections" (p. 442).

place them at distances, sometimes at vast distances, as guides or warnings to succeeding ages.[79]

"[I]t is well in all cases to remember the wise recommendation of Lord Bacon," Story continued in the same address, "that men in their innovations would follow the example of time itself; which, indeed, innovateth greatly, but quietly, and by degrees scarce to be perceived."[80]

In Story's preference for truths arrived over long periods of time, his distaste for innovation, and his emphasis on continuity across past, present, and future that facilitates change "by degrees scarce to be perceived," we recognize at work the nonhistorical common law temporalities of "immemoriality" and "insensibility." The U.S. Constitution, and government in general, is imbued with these common law temporalities. We are far from the consent-based theories of Jeffersonians and Jacksonians.

Story's undercutting of the consent-based, contractually grounded, Jeffersonian and Jacksonian vision of a limited governmental power in the name of the profundity, inevitability, discretion, compromise, circumstance prescription, "immemoriality," and "insensibility" associated with governmental power allowed him to turn to the vexed relationship between the U.S. Constitution and the common law. Like the Federalist writers of the 1790s, Story argued that the common law, as "our birthright and inheritance," was foundational to the jurisprudence of the colonies and the United States.[81] This was especially true when it came to giving meaning to various clauses of the U.S. Constitution. To take just one example, in his discussion of the constitutional privileges of Congress, Story stated: "We may resort to the common law to aid us in interpreting such instruments and their powers: for that law is the common rule by which all our legislation is interpreted. It is known, and acted upon and revered by the people. It furnishes principles equally

[79] Story, "Characteristics of the Age," p. 359.

[80] Story, "Value and Importance of Legal Studies," p. 516.

[81] Story, *Commentaries on the Constitution of the United States*, Vol 1, pp. 104–105. On the importance of the common law in colonial Virginia, Story would state, "Indeed, there is no reason to suppose, that the common law was not in its leading features very acceptable to the colonists; and in its general policy, the colony closely followed in the steps of the mother country" (p. 22. Of colonial Massachusetts, he wrote, "They adopted the common law of England as the general basis of their jurisprudence" (p. 28). On colonial New York, "[P]erhaps New York was more close in adoption of the policy and legislation of the parent country before the Revolution than any other colony" (p. 76). Of course, Story also insisted that lands in the Americas had been held of the Crown in free and common socage and not by knight's service (p. 120).

for civil and criminal justice, for public privileges and private rights."[82] This sense that the common law underlay "all our legislation" allowed Story to argue for a federal common law more generally as the necessary jurisprudence of the federal government: "It would be a most extraordinary state of things that the common law should be the basis of the jurisprudence of the States originally composing the Union, and yet a government engrafted upon the existing system should have no jurisprudence at all."[83]

Story's most celebrated and enduring attempt to join the U.S. Constitution and the common law is his opinion in *Swift v. Tyson* (1842), a case widely known to generations of twentieth-century American lawyers as having formalized the (now illegitimate) idea of a "federal common law" in federal diversity jurisdiction cases, that is, cases in which federal courts had jurisdiction over lawsuits in cases in which the parties were citizens of different states. My interest in *Swift v. Tyson* consists in seeing the case as a point of entry in exploring the stark difference between, on the one hand, Story's treatment of the U.S. Constitution, which involves a Burkean language of circumstance, flexibility, adaptation, prescription, and distaste for innovation, and, on the other hand, Story's treatment of the common law, which appears to be a distinctly un-Burkean affair involving universal principles that depend for their recognition upon a fragmentation of the common law into "ages." Let us turn, then, to how Story represents the common law in *Swift* and elsewhere.

According to the 34th section of the Judiciary Act of 1789, the federal courts were instructed that, in diversity jurisdiction cases, "the laws of the several states, except where the constitution, treaties or statutes of the United States shall otherwise recognize or provide, shall be regarded as rules of decision in trials at common law ... in cases where they apply."[84] *Swift* was about the precise meaning of this injunction.

[82] Ibid., p. 585. One might cite other instances. For example, to the extent that "bribery" was an impeachable offense under the Constitution, Story argued, "resort is naturally and necessarily had to the common law; for that, as the common basis of our jurisprudence, can alone furnish the proper exposition of the nature and limits of this offense" (p. 552). For impeachment for political offenses, similarly, resort had to be had to the common law, which was "[t]he only safe guide in such cases" (p. 553).

[83] Ibid., 106, n 1. James Kent would argue similarly: "The Constitution and laws of the United States were made in reference to the existence of common law – the language of the Constitution and law would be inexplicable without reference to the common law." James Kent, *Commentaries on American Law* (4 vols.) (New York: K. B. Clayton, 1832), 336.

[84] 1 Stat. 73 (September 24, 1789); 1 Cong. Ch. 20.

The case involved a suit brought by Swift, as endorsee of a bill of exchange, against Tyson, the acceptor of the bill. The bill had been drawn by Nathaniel Norton and Jairus Keith upon Tyson in Portland, Maine, on May 1, 1836, as consideration for a sale of lands to Tyson. It had been accepted by Tyson in New York. Before its maturity date, the bill had been endorsed to Swift in payment of a preexisting debt. But when Swift presented the bill to Tyson at maturity, Tyson refused to honor the bill on the ground that he had been defrauded by Norton and Keith. All parties were clear that Tyson could have refused to honor the bill, citing fraud, had Norton and Keith presented it to him. The question was whether Tyson could do the same to Swift, who was the holder in due course of the bill. New York law was unclear whether Swift, because he had received the bill in satisfaction of a preexisting debt, could qualify as a holder in due course and therefore evade the consequences of the equities between the original parties.

The consequences of allowing Tyson to dishonor the bill were represented by Swift's counsel as critical to the fate of commerce – and thus of civilization – itself.[85] Not surprisingly, this struck a chord with Story. In his opinion for the Court, Story argued that a ruling for the defendant Tyson would jeopardize commercial transactions in the United States and elsewhere: "Probably, more than one-half of all bank transactions in our country, as well as those of other countries, are of this nature [involving endorsements of bills of exchange in satisfaction of preexisting debts]. The doctrine [urged by the defendant] would strike a fatal blow at all discounts of negotiable securities for pre-existing debts."[86]

Story then read the relevant provision of the Judiciary Act of 1789 to require federal courts in diversity cases to follow only those state laws that were what he called "strictly local" (those involving positive statutes of the state, those relating to real estate, and "local usages of a fixed and permanent operation"). The Act did not apply to "principles established in the general commercial law," which was supposedly at issue in this case. This was a universal law based on no statute in particular. Story described this law as follows: "The law respecting negotiable instruments may be truly declared in the language of Cicero, adopted by Lord

[85] As he put it, "The use of negotiable paper has hardly been of greater service to civilized man, in facilitating the transmission of the equivalent of money, and thus in answering, in some respects, the purposes of money itself, than in preventing hostile proceedings in courts of law for the collection of money due." *Swift v. Tyson*, 41 U.S. (16 Peters) 1, 6 (1842).

[86] Ibid., p. 20.

Mansfield ..., to be in a great measure, not the law of a single country only, but of the commercial world."[87] It was in the name of this transnational and transhistorical principle – in Story's words, "a doctrine so long and so well established ... that it ... requires no authority or reasoning to be now brought in its support" – that Story announced a "federal common law," in the application of which the federal courts were not to be bound by state court judgments.[88] Tyson would have to honor the bill.

The common law joined to the U.S. Constitution in *Swift* was, then, "the general commercial law," "not the law of a single country, but of the commercial world." The lovingly claimed specific ancestral customs of the English play no part here. But if the common law had to be the law of the entire commercial world, the old common law would have to be considerably reworked. It would take effort to reduce it to universal and homogeneous principles. This is exactly the task Story set himself as a scholar of private law. This scientific work of reducing the common law to principles was part of the style of legal scholarship during the second quarter of the nineteenth century, revealed not only in the writings of Story, but also in those of fellow travelers such as James Kent.[89] Story could dismiss legal scholarship that was not self-consciously about principles as "a meagre and loose performance."[90]

As part of the identification of scientific principles based on induction, Story self-consciously and rigorously "ages" – that is, sets into different "ages" – the body of the common law. This historical strategy – fully part of the sensibility of the time – demystifies the traditional common law temporalities of "immemoriality" and "insensibility" and is openly instrumentalist. In "aging" the common law, Story tells his reader what is obsolete and what relevant. In an 1821 address to the Suffolk County bar entitled "Progress of Jurisprudence," Story offered a tripartite division of the history of the common law: first, from the Conquest to the Reformation; second, from the reign of Elizabeth I to the English Revolution; and, finally, from the English Revolution to his own time.[91]

87 Ibid., p. 19.

88 Ibid., pp. 15–16.

89 Story praised Kent for his "untiring research, ... critical exactness, [and] philosophical spirit" Story, "Growth of the Commercial Law," p. 288.

90 Ibid., p. 264. See also Story's 1826 article on Nathan Dane's *General Abridgement and Digest of the American Law*, printed as *Digests of the Common Law*, in *Miscellaneous Writings*, p. 401 ("[N]othing could be more judicious than to give a view of the general principles of each branch of the law, and to illustrate them with cases, and then to proceed to the more minute and subordinate particulars").

91 Story, "Progress of Jurisprudence," p. 200.

What counted as the most significant aspects of the English legal legacy – namely, those relating to the principles of commerce – were of comparatively recent origin, the products of the last or what Story called "the Golden Age of the law."[92] Story cares nothing for the traditional common law wisdom that the common law could not be made. What we are offered is a history precisely of the common law's making, of the common law's authors. Story tells us that the system of equity had come into being only since the reign of Queen Elizabeth; that the law of commercial contracts was, before that period, "either wholly unknown, or, at the most, but very imperfectly understood"; that the law of insurance had "grown up within the latter half of the eighteenth century" and that it had been "almost created by [Lord Mansfield]"; that the doctrine of bailments – "which lies at the foundation of the law of shipments" – was "struck out at a single heat by Lord Holt"; and that Sir William Jones' essay on bailments, which had reduced the law of bailments to its principles, belonged to "our times." Indeed, before the time of Lord Mansfield, Story argued, there were few cases in the reports "which are entitled to much respect, either for their sound interpretation, of principles, or general applicability."[93] Story also tells us that many improvements in the common law were often massive one-time borrowings from continental jurisprudence, a system traditionally derided for its affinity for "system" and its aversion to "circumstance." For example, Story states that the common law had borrowed from the civil law – "this great fountain of rational jurisprudence" – "all that is most valuable and important in its own doctrines of contract."[94]

Thus, in Story's rendering, the common law, insofar as it has been fitted into "ages," populated with innovations and borrowings, created by individual judges, and reduced to principles, does not seem at all imbued

[92] Ibid., p. 203. See also Story, "Growth of the Commercial Law," p. 263, where Story states that "England had made very little progress in commercial law, at so late a period as the commencement of the reign of George the Third."

[93] Ibid., p. 206; "Course of Legal Study," in *Miscellaneous Writings*, pp. 67–68. Story is referring to Lord Holt's decision in *Coggs v. Barnard*, where, according to him, the law of bailments was expounded "with philosophical precision and fullness" (p. 204). Nor is it the case that this rather recent reduction of the common law to principles had been confined to the commercial context. Story was delighted that "[a] spirit of scientific research has diffused itself over the other departments of the common law; contested questions are ... sifted with the most laborious diligence, and the limits of principles established, with a philosophical precision and accuracy, which is rarely observable in the old reports." This was true of the doctrines of uses and trusts, wills and testaments, contingent remainders, executory devises, and legacies (pp. 69–70).

[94] Story, "Growth of the Commercial Law," p. 271.

with the nonhistorical common law temporalities of "immemoriality" and "insensibility." Neither does the common law, as reduced to universal principles governing the commercial world, appear to derive its legitimacy from its antiquity. Indeed, for Story as for Kames, antiquity as the ground of law's legitimacy is suspect. One of the characteristics of Story's own "age," he observed in 1826, was "the bold and fearless spirit of its speculations," which checked "the servile adoption of received opinions, and a timid acquiescence in whatever is established."[95] The ideal vision of the common law for Story is not that of something derived from the past (as it was for Blackstone), but instead that of a vast structure, the legitimacy of which rests upon the aesthetics of its internal ordering, the definition and limits associated with "regular systems" and "general symmetry of parts":

> The modern works do not teach the law in any new and superficial manner.... [T]he principles are now more closely investigated, the problems more fully enunciated, and the boundaries between the known and the unknown more exactly defined. *Instead of sparse and scattered maxims, we have regular systems, built up with general symmetry of parts; and the necessary investigations in new and difficult cases are conducted with more safety, because they are founded on inductions from rules better established, and more exactly limited* [emphasis added].[96]

In highly un-Burkean fashion, in Story's hands, the universal principles of the common law do not allow for the variation and plurality associated with circumstance, adaptation to different settings, or compromise (something that Story insists upon in his reading of the U.S. Constitution). When it came to the commercial law, Story believed firmly that uniformity – in other words, the gradual realization of exact and homogeneous principles – was the wave of the future. Europe was already "approaching to that state, in which the same commercial principles will constitute a part of the public law of all its sovereignties."[97] The commercial law of the Atlantic states had also come to converge in the areas of insurance, shipping, and negotiable instruments.[98] Where the states did not converge – for example, as in the case of the Massachusetts policy of denying days of grace on promissory notes unless expressly provided for – Story

[95] Story, "Characteristics of the Age," p. 350.

[96] Story, "Course of Legal Study," p. 79. Of course, Story was aware of the limitations of the endeavor: "The most that we can hope to do under such circumstances, is, to make nearer and nearer approximations to truth, without our ever being certain of having arrived at it in a positive form." Story, "The Science of Government," p. 615.

[97] Story, "Progress of Jurisprudence," p. 215.

[98] Ibid.

called peremptorily for a legislative act to excise the anomaly, "which has not a single ground, either of convenience, or policy, or antiquity, to recommend it."[99] Of course, universalism was always threatened by the multiplicity of American jurisdictions. Story remarked gloomily that the variation in the common law across the twenty-three common law jurisdictions in the Union meant that the jurisprudence of the states was "perpetually receding farther and farther from the common standard."[100] From his perspective, this was a serious matter: American lawyers might end up becoming provincial experts of "mere state jurisprudence" and set aside "those more enlightened and extensive researches, which form the accomplished scholar, and elevate the refined jurist."[101]

How does one reconcile Story's highly Burkean understanding of the U.S. Constitution, heavily freighted with a common lawyerly language of implication, flexibility, circumstance, adaptation, prescription, hostility to innovation, "immemoriality," and "insensibility," with his representation of the common law itself, which appears to be a matter of scientific principles arrived at after the body of the common law has been aged and peopled with innovations, where uniformity counts for everything and antiquity, circumstance, plurality, and variation for little? One response might be that offered by the Whig legal thinker Rufus Choate, who would see this difference as a simple matter of scale. In 1845, calling conservatism "the one grand and comprehensive duty of a thoughtful patriotism," Choate recognized that conservatism need not apply uniformly at all levels:

> I speak in general, of course, not pausing upon little or inevitable qualifications here and there, – not meaning anything so absurd as to say that this law, or that usage, or that judgment, or that custom or condition, might not be corrected or expunged.... I speak of our general political system; or organic forms; or written constitutions; the great body and the general administration of our jurisprudence; the general way in which liberty is blended with order, and the principle of progression with the securities of permanence; the relation of the States and the functions of the Union.[102]

But Story's reading of the Constitution as being all about circumstance and of the common law as being all about principle – an exact and radical inversion of the ways in which many at the time thought of the two – was

[99] Ibid., p. 216.
[100] Ibid., p. 213.
[101] Ibid., p. 224.
[102] Choate, "The Position and Functions of the American Bar," p. 419.

not, at least for him, the difference between the important and the unimportant, a mere question of greater and lesser scales. If there is one thing that is clear from Story's representations of both the Constitution and the common law, it is that both are deeply felt views for him.

In order to understand the relationship between the utterly different vocabularies Story used to represent the Constitution, on the one hand, and the common law, on the other, it might be more productive to return to Story's own reference to Edmund Burke as "a master-spirit of the last age." In this phrase, we recognize the sense in which Burke, for Story, is both irrevocably past (the "last age") and utterly present ("master-spirit"), utterly irrelevant, and utterly enabling. This impossible conjoining, the very heart of the concept of the "spirit of the age," bears further explication.

On the one hand, Burke is irrevocably past to the extent that he is irrelevant to the Story's proposed scientific reduction of the common law to homogeneous, universal, and abstract principles. Story's emphasis on homogeneous, universal, and abstract principles, his sense that the common law has been authored by individual judges, and his contempt for circumstance and antiquity are not especially common lawyerly. At the very least, they are utterly un-Burkean. They stand for a sharp break not only with the empirical past that Burke represents, but also with a Burkean way of relating to the past. For Story, history is about the facilitation of commerce through the inductive method and Burke, with his solicitude for the past that has come down to him, must be left behind.

On the other hand, Burke is present in the common law – not actually, but "spiritually" – to the extent that it is a highly Burkean reading of the Constitution that allows the homogeneous, uniform, and abstract principles of a reformulated common law to be disseminated, to realize their own homogeneity, uniformity, and abstractness across American national space, and to enable Story – as judge and scholar – to fulfill the mandate of history as the spread of commerce and inductive science. Insofar as it is a particular Burkean reading of the U.S. Constitution that allows the common law to be joined to the Constitution, one could argue that it is the "spirit" of the old common law imbuing the U.S. Constitution that itself makes possible the reduction of the actually existing common law to universal, homogeneous, and abstract principles and its dissemination across America. We see, thus, how the historical sensibility of the "spirit of the age" works in relationship to the old common law. This is, ultimately, a circular relationship. The old common law is "aged," fragmented, and reduced to universal and homogeneous principles in the name of the imperatives of history configured as commerce and inductive science. At the same time, however, the common law temporalities of "immemoriality" and "insensibility" imbue the U.S. Constitution, which operates to facilitate the spread of the scientific common law and thus to enable the realization of the imperatives of history configured as commerce and inductive science. It is these traditional common law temporalities, "spiritualized," that underlie the unfolding of history's logic.

This brings us to the allied question of the relationship between the traditional common law method, with its claim to represent the custom of the community and its affiliation to the past, and the much-vaunted method of induction – for Story, the very "spirit of the age" – through which the common law judge arrives at principles. If the task of the common law judge is to identify abstract, homogeneous, and universal principles, what distinguishes his labor from that of future-oriented legislatures, especially at a time when scientific codification was a subject of considerable public debate? How can Story erect fences around his legal science, in other words, to defend it from the encroachments of legislatures?

Occasionally, Story suggests that legal principles might derive from the responsiveness of the common law judge to the practices of the community. This is the traditional Blackstonian idea of the common law judge as oracle and reader of the community. For Story, the common law possesses the special ability to "partake[e] of the spirit and enterprise of the times."[103] The commercial flowering in the common law during the second half of the eighteenth century, the time when the law began to be set down in principles, was itself a response to the growth of commerce.[104] If the expression that the *lex mercatoria* was part of the common law was anything more than an "idle boast," Story argued, it had to mean "that the general structure of the common law is such, that, *without any positive act of the legislature*, it perpetually admits of an incorporation of those principles and practices, which are from time to time established among merchants, and which ... are proper to be recognized by judicial tribunals."[105]

Kent Newmyer tells us that Story was reputed in his own day for knowing the businesses and trades of the litigants who appeared before

[103] Story, "Progress of Jurisprudence," p. 203.
[104] Ibid., p. 207.
[105] Story, "Growth of the Commercial Law," p. 272 (emphasis added).

him as well as they did.[106] Where Story was baffled by merchant practices or they were themselves unstable, he could – Mansfield-like – consult special juries of informed merchants impaneled from the business community.[107] But Newmyer also tells us, revealingly, that Story "firmly believed that he understood the long-run interests of the business community better than businessmen themselves, and he was convinced that given a chance he could convince them." This belief did not always lead to happy results. Story's attempt to fuse actuarial precision into marine insurance law, for example, generated considerable opposition among the business community.[108]

This idea that, for Story, his principles were often better approximations of mercantile customs than those of merchants themselves – hence that the connection between universal principle and actually existing customs was weak – is reinforced by the fact that, for Story, not all actually existing customs were able to contribute to the building up of principles. Various local customs – for which the old common law, even as expounded by Blackstone, displayed solicitude – were simply in the way, and thus failed to win Story's recognition. Like an earlier generation of American common lawyers, Story repeatedly declares that there are simply no customs local to America or, in the alternative, that such customs are utterly unimportant and unworthy of attention.[109] For example, in his essay "Common Law" for Francis Lieber's *Encyclopaedia Americana*, Story states:

> The common law of England constitutes the general basis of the jurisprudence of all the U. States of America, except only Louisiana, where the civil law prevails. This common law consists only of the first [general customs] and third [ecclesiastical and admiralty] kinds of customary law ..., *there being no local or provincial law existing in any particular country or district of any state, as contradistinguished from that which prevails in the state at large* [emphasis added].[110]

[106] Newmyer, *Supreme Court Justice Joseph Story*, p. 121.

[107] Ibid., p. 122. Newmyer cites two cases: *Harvey v. Richards*, 11 Fed. Cas. 740 (C.C.D.Mass., 1814) and *Peisch v. Dickson*, 19 Fed. Cas. 123 (C.C.D.Mass., 1815).

[108] Ibid., p. 125.

[109] One significant exception that Story mentioned was the Massachusetts practice of allowing a woman to dispose of her real property by a deed with the consent of her husband, whereas in England it had to be done by a process of fine or common recovery. Joseph Story, "Codification of the Common Law: A Report of the Commissioners Appointed to Consider and Report Upon the Practicability and Expediency of Reducing to a Written and Systematic Code the Common Law of Massachusetts, or Any Part Thereof; Made to His Excellency the Governor, January 1837," in *Miscellaneous Writings*, p. 701.

[110] Joseph Story, "Common Law," in Francis Lieber, ed., *Encyclopaedia Americana* (14 vols.) (Philadelphia: Carey, Lea & Carey, 1829–1847), Vol. 3 (1830), p. 394. In Story's

Story's declaration that America is empty of local customs is, of course, entirely of a piece with his larger commitment as a judge, scholar, and educator to produce a homogeneous and scientific national – or even international – common law, uncluttered by a plethora of local practices. But my point is to show that, for Story, not all customs throw up principles worthy of notice. Thus, the legitimacy of judicially articulated principles does not rest in general upon a faithful mapping of actually existing customs even in the favored context of the commercial.

If a grounding in custom is not consistently the basis of the legitimacy of principles, what about principles' relationship to the past? Part of a long line of common lawyers, Story was highly critical of legislation as a method of lawmaking because legislation disregarded the accumulated wisdom of the past. "[M]ore doubts arise in the administration of justice from the imperfections of positive legislation," he maintained, "than from any other source."[111] This had to do with a sense of the rashness of legislation as contrasted with the long time it took to build up law:

> Surely, [legislators] need not be told, how slow every good system of laws must be in consolidating; and how easily the rashness of an hour may destroy what ages have scarcely cemented in a solid form. The oak ... may ... be levelled in an hour.[112]

The traditional common law method, which Story seems in this excerpt to endorse, prided itself on its repetition of the past, on the accumulation of wisdom derived from the past, on the blurring of continuity and change. Is this what distinguishes the modern common law judge, as he articulates principles, from the rash legislator?

But Story is himself contemptuous of the weight of the past. His historicization of the common law, his fitting it into various "ages," and his reduction of it to abstract, homogeneous, and uniform principles bespeaks a turning away from common lawyerly ways of representing the past. He also repeatedly recognizes that the past cannot be repeated. Law is necessarily beset by "uncertainty and doubt." This is not because common law judges abuse their office. Uncertainty does not arise from the "obscurity and fluctuation of decisions, as the vulgar erroneously suppose, but from

essay "Courts" for the same *Encyclopaedia*, we find the following: "[I]n some of the states, there are some customs and peculiarities which grew up in early times. *But they are few, and, in a general sense, unimportant*" (p. 597; emphasis added).

111 Story, "Value and Importance of Legal Studies," p. 514.

112 Ibid., pp. 515–516.

the endless complexity and variety of human actions." Changes in society were forever "silently, but irresistibly, going on."[113]

But this sense that the past has no necessary claim upon us and in any case cannot be repeated does not mean that lawmaking should be surrendered to legislatures. For Story, the common law method remains superior to the method of the legislature. I would argue that the seamless way in which the old common law claimed to bind past, present, and future together becomes relevant to Story not because of any affiliation on his part to the past as past, but rather because of his interest in capturing, securing, and controlling the future and guarding that future from the encroachments of democracy. This is because the future is far too important to be surrendered to the Jeffersonian ideal of each generation's being entirely free to create itself, free from the restraints of legal science itself. The common law's linking of past, present, and future through the method of repetition is retrieved as a way not of slowly building principles over time, but of articulating principles for the present and future in accordance with the historical mandate of commerce and inductive science. Fragmented and historicized in terms of the "age," the common law's traditional affiliation to repeating the past returns, "spiritualized," as a method of managing the future. Story recognized this futural orientation of the common law in a way that someone like Blackstone did not. The common law sought, he tells us, "to measure the future by approximations to certainty, derived solely from the experience of the past."[114] Where an inductive science that yields abstract and universal principles is, for Story, the very the "spirit of the age," the old common law method becomes the "spirit" of that inductive science. This is perhaps what it meant for someone like Story to claim, as he did in the *Charles River Bridge* dissent, to "stand upon the old law" after he had repudiated so much that was old. The past is the "spirit" of the forward-looking principle.

The Political Philosophy of Francis Lieber

Yet another, more openly metaphoric version of the "spiritualization" of the common law is to be found in the writings of the German émigré political and legal theorist Francis Lieber (1798–1872). Perhaps the most important politicolegal theorist of antebellum America, Lieber won the

113 Story, "The Course of Legal Study," p. 70.

114 Joseph Story, "History and Influence of the Puritans," in *Miscellaneous Writings*, pp. 507–508.

approval of various conservative jurists of his time. None of the praises Lieber's *Manual of Political Ethics* (1838–1839) received delighted him more than those of James Kent, who lauded the work in a footnote to a later edition of his *Commentaries*.[115] The connections between Lieber and Story were stronger still. In addition to contributing entries on legal topics to Lieber's *Encyclopaedia Americana* (1829–1833), Story was heavily involved with Lieber's intellectual projects in the 1830s. Story not only recommended the title of Lieber's first major written work, *Manual of Political Ethics*, but even prepared an agenda of the principal topics Lieber should cover. Story, Simon Greenleaf, and Charles Sumner then continued to aid Lieber with suggestions and citations during the writing of the text. It is not surprising that the *Manual*, in the words of Lieber's biographer, ended up resembling a "Whig campaign document."[116] For his part, Lieber dedicated the work to Joseph Story.

No doubt because of an immersion in the traditions of early-nineteenth-century German historical thought, Lieber was inclined to think in terms of world history. In his reading of Western history, which Lieber defined as "the history of all historically active, non-Asiatic nations and tribes," the republican experiments in France and America were accorded special meaning.[117] France and America represented, as it were, the "spirit of the age." As Lieber wrote to Leopold von Ranke:

> In Germany the student of history can study it only in the libraries; in Italy, in retrospection; but in England and America, in its actual existence. And for the present time, of which the key is the democratic principle ... the United States and France seem to be the high-schools of history.[118]

Lieber was extremely conscious of the uniqueness of his "age" as an "age" of democracy. In his *Manual of Political Ethics*, he writes, "Future ages, perhaps will look upon our period as a preeminently political one; as that period in which governments ... became national and popular governments."[119] And in *Civil Liberty and Self-Government* (1854), he

[115] See James Kent, *Commentaries on American Law* (O. W. Holmes, Jr., ed.) (12th ed.) (4 vols.) (Boston: Little, Brown & Co., 1873), Vol. 1, p. 3, note b.

[116] Frank B. Freidel, *Francis Lieber: Nineteenth-Century Liberal* (Baton Rouge: Louisiana State University Press, 1948), p. 164.

[117] Francis Lieber, *On Civil Liberty and Self-Government* (Theodore Woolsey, ed.) (3d ed.) (Philadelphia: J. B. Lippincott Company, 1888) (1853), p. 22, n. 2.

[118] Quoted in Freidel, *Francis Lieber*, p. 88.

[119] Francis Lieber, *Manual of Political Ethics: Designed Chiefly for the Use of Colleges and Students at Law* (2 vols.) (Boston: Charles C. Little & James Brown, 1839), Vol. 2, p. 11.

declared, "Our age ... is stamped by no characteristic more deeply than by a desire to establish or extend freedom in the political societies of mankind. At no previous period, ancient or modern, has this impulse been felt at once so strongly and by such extensive numbers."[120]

History, for Lieber, was necessarily about one "age" ceding to another. Any attempt to resist this movement through an untoward veneration of the old – especially old law – would be disastrous. He put it as follows: "The excellence of all laws depends upon their fitness, that is upon the sound principle judiciously applied to the existing state of things; these things however change in the course of time; real standing still is therefore impossible, and if we do not move onward, if we force the same laws upon changed circumstances, we must ruin the state."[121] Lieber would go so far as to say that laws that did not fit the "spirit of the time" were not worthy of being obeyed. In a striking passage, he states:

> *Laws which are manifestly against the spirit of the times, which cannot be obeyed whatever the law may demand, may and must be disobeyed.* If the government neglects changing the laws according to the change of circumstances, it is not the obligation of the citizen to adhere to the law. Such laws are manifestly fallen in disuse, ... laws which it would be morally impossible to obey [emphasis added].[122]

All this talk of fitting law to its "age," of viewing law as temporally contingent, brought about a change in the view of precedent. A thinker like Story, even though he "aged" the common law, would never openly endorse a disregard for precedent. Story repeated traditional common law learning when he stated, "When once a doctrine is fully recognized as a part of the common law, it forever remains a part of the system, until it is altered by the legislature. A doctrine of the common law settled three hundred years ago is just as conclusive now in a case, which falls within it, as it was then."[123] Lieber, Story's favorite domestic political theorist, was far more forthcoming: "[A precedent] is not absolute. It does not possess binding power merely as a fact, or as an occurrence.... Nor is a precedent unchangeable. It can be overruled. But ... it must be done by the law itself."[124]

What, then, was the status of the common law in Lieber's theory? For all the talk about breaking with the past, fitting law to the "age," and

[120] Lieber, *Civil Liberty*, p. 17.
[121] Lieber, *Manual of Political Ethics*, Vol. 2, pp. 228.
[122] Ibid., p. 302.
[123] Story, "Codification of the Common Law," p. 719.
[124] Lieber, *Civil Liberty*, pp. 208–209.

overturning precedent, Lieber was insistent that in democracies like the United States and Great Britain, as opposed to France, "law is allowed to make its own way."[125] In saying this, Lieber was, of course, echoing the views of Joseph Story, who had similarly insisted upon a certain kind of democracy as necessary for law to exist as an autonomous science but at the same time upon a cabining of democracy so that that autonomous science could develop unimpeded. But how was law to make its own way, independent of the demands of the sovereign, when it had to fit the "spirit of the age" in a dynamic, forward-looking, historically active country?

A powerful metaphoric rendering of the place of the common law in a dynamic American Republic was advanced in Lieber's *On Civil Liberty* (1853), a book that became a leading textbook in American colleges and universities.[126] *Civil Liberty* teems with distinctions. The first relevant distinction is the distinction between ancient and modern notions of liberty. Lieber sets forth this distinction as follows:

> Liberty with the ancients, consisted materially in the degree of participation in government 'where all are in turn the ruled and the rulers.' Liberty, with the moderns, consists less in the forms of authority, which are with them but *means* to obtain the protection of the individual and the undisturbed action of society in its minor and larger circles [emphasis added].[127]

If liberty was once an end in itself, it has now become a means to secure other, private ends. The disillusionment with a publicly instantiated liberty as an end in itself and a recognition of the sphere of the private as a more meaningful sphere for the realization of happiness is a familiar idea in early-nineteenth-century Europe.[128] It could, of course, be seen as a way of cabining liberty's own claims, of making something else – the private, the commercial – more important than liberty.

Another, related set of distinctions Lieber offers – one for which he was celebrated at the time – is the distinction between so-called Anglican and Gallican liberty. Both are different styles of achieving democracy. The content of the distinction is predictable. Anglican liberty is characterized by a network of interlocking institutions, perhaps the most significant of

[125] Francis Lieber, *Legal and Political Hermeneutics, or Principles of Interpretation and Construction in Law and Politics, With Remarks on Precedents and Authorities* (Boston: Charles C. Little & James Brown, 1839), p. viii.

[126] Lieber, *Civil Liberty*, Introduction to the 3d ed. by Theodore D. Woolsey, p. xii.

[127] Ibid., p. 46.

[128] See, e.g., Benjamin Constant, *De l'esprit de conquête et de l'usurpation: Dans leurs rapports avec la civilization européenne* (Paris: Imprimerie Nationale, 1992) (1814).

which is a self-developing common law. Gallican liberty is opposed to something like a self-developing common law:

The idea of a common law, with its own inherent vitality and independence, is, as a matter of course, wholly disavowed by those who follow the French views, and who, as we have seen, strive above all for union of force, and who consider the essence of democracy to consist in absolute equality concentrated in absolute dominion, whether of the majority, or of one to whom the majority has transferred the absolute power – the democratic Caesar. Those American writers, therefore, who take this Gallican or Rousseau's view of democracy, share with French this hostility to the common law. It was rifest at the time of the French Revolution, since which time I believe it may be affirmed that it has greatly subsided. Yet it subsists still, and is occasionally uttered with an energy which surprises those who believe that the severest lesson taught by the first half of the nineteenth century is, perhaps, that absolute democracy has no connection with liberty.[129]

However, according to Lieber, the real difference between Anglican and Gallican liberty – and hence the meaning and weight of a self-developing common law itself – might lie in the fact that Gallican liberty is always confusing means for ends: "Where self-government does not exist, the people are always exposed to the danger that the end of government is lost sight of, and that governments assume themselves as their own ends.... Man is always exposed to the danger of substituting the means for the ends."[130] The Gallican failure to separate out means from ends is accounted for in terms of the French love of form: "[I]t is the exceeding partiality of the French for logical neatness and consistency of form ... – it is this mathematical enthusiasm, if the expression be permitted, applied to the vast field of political practice."[131] Form, for Lieber, is seductive but also dangerous:

The regularity and consistent symmetry, together with the principle of unity, which pervade the whole French government, charm many a beholder, and afford pleasure not unlike that which many persons derive from looking at a plan of a mathematical and regular city, or upon gardens architectonically trimmed. But freedom is life, and wherever we find life it is marked, indeed, by agreement of principles and harmony of development, but also by variety of form and phenomenon, and by a subordinate exactness of symmetry. The centralist, it might be said, mistakes lineal and angular exactness, formal symmetry, and mathematical proportions, for harmonious evolution and profuse vitality. He prefers an angular garden of the times of Louis XIV to an umbrageous grove.[132]

[129] Lieber, *Civil Liberty*, pp. 213–14. Lieber refers to Richard Hildreth's *Theory of Politics*, a text I discuss later. (p. 214, n. 1).

[130] Lieber, *Civil Liberty*, p. 253.

[131] Ibid., p. 284.

[132] Ibid., pp. 393–394.

From this excerpt one can see that Lieber does not fall into the trap of asserting that only the French, afflicted by their inability to distinguish means from ends, are seduced by form ("an angular garden of the times of Louis XIV"). The English and the Americans, who *are* able to distinguish means from ends, are also seduced by form (an "umbrageous grove"). Elsewhere, characterizing "Anglican" institutions as "crescive" or "grown," Lieber writes, "Grown or spontaneous institutions are not ill defined or loosely distinguished from one another on that account; they may be as individualized as a shady tree in the forest."[133] Instrumental means–ends thinking of the Anglo-American sort – which is the kind of historical thinking that fits all law to its "age" and that partakes of the historical sensibility of the time – impossibly takes the form of an "umbrageous grove," where the play of shadow and light makes things simultaneously distinct and indistinct, such that each "age," even as it is separate from another, blends into it. This is a metaphoric spatial realization, I submit, of nothing other than the traditional nonhistorical temporalities of common law "immemoriality" and "insensibility," which began but could not be seen to have begun, which changed but could not be caught in the act of changing. Anglo-Americans are applauded for being able to fit means to ends – to think historically, to match laws to their "age," to disregard precedent where necessary – but are simultaneously applauded for doing it, or urged to do it, in a way that matches the temporality of the common law. The common law returns, as it were, as the "spirit" of a historically grounded instrumentalism itself.

Conclusion: Richard Hildreth on the "Spirit of the Age"

In the foregoing, we see how the historical sensibility of the "spirit of the age" was deployed by a range of mutually opposed thinkers to make sense of the relationship between law and democracy. Thinkers such as Robert Rantoul, Jr., and Joseph Story would, as one might expect, accuse each other of importing into American democracy the "spirit" of an undesirable prerevolutionary past. But this turn to the "spirit" of the prerevolutionary past was the case even if such thinkers are read on their own terms. Committed Jacksonian democrats such as Rantoul and Bancroft would imbue democracy with a "Catholic" quality and endorse an overriding of vested rights in its name. Opponents

[133] Ibid., p. 303.

of Jacksonian democracy such as Joseph Story would seek to limit the reach of democracy in the name of an inductive science committed to the spread of commerce but undergird that inductive science with the "spirit" of the old common law. Common law thinkers such as Story reveal the complex interplay of historical and common law temporalities. In keeping with the contradictions internal to the concept of the "spirit of the age," the old common law would be fitted into different "ages," while its "spirit" was retrieved to enable the logic of history itself.

Not all thinkers in early-nineteenth-century America were seduced, of course, by the historical vocabulary of the "spirit of the age." In order to see this, I turn briefly to an examination of some aspects of the thought of the prodigious Jacksonian era intellectual Richard Hildreth (1807–1865). Hildreth was a Whig journalist, an aggressive polemicist, a practicing lawyer, a prolific historian, and a Benthamite moral and political theorist.[134] His distaste for romantic era metaphysics helps us understand Bancroft, Rantoul, Story, and Lieber in light of their conflicted relationship to the past.

Hildreth learned early, as a Harvard undergraduate interested in government and politics, to scorn "the mists of metaphysical disquisition."[135] A steadfast opposition to what he referred to as "mystical ideas" runs throughout his mature writings. His *Theory of Morals* (1844) contains critical sections entitled "Mystic Hypothesis," "Mystic Theory of Morals," "Amalgamation of the Mystic or Selfish Theories," "Mystic Application of the Doctrine of Selfishness to the Deity,"

[134] For information on Hildreth, I have relied on Donald E. Emerson, *Richard Hildreth* (Baltimore: Johns Hopkins Press, 1946); Peter J. King, *Utilitarian Jurisprudence in America: The Influence of Bentham and Austin on American Legal Thought in the Nineteenth Century* (New York: Garland, 1986); Martha M. Pingel, *An American Utilitarian: Richard Hildreth as a Philosopher* (New York: Columbia University Press, 1948); Arthur M. Schlesinger, Jr., "The Problem of Richard Hildreth," *New England Quarterly* 13 (June 1940): 223–245.

American intellectual historians have long had trouble coming to terms with Hildreth. Sixty years ago, in an article entitled "The Problem of Richard Hildreth," Arthur Schlesinger, Jr., described him as "one of the more enigmatic figures in American intellectual history." Schlesinger, "The Problem of Richard Hildreth," p. 223. This is because Hildreth defies the divisions into which historians have been used to slotting Jacksonian era intellectuals. Although he was described by Frederick Jackson Turner as a "Federalist historian," he struck socialist notes in his vision of democracy, welcomed the disappearance of the Second Bank of the United States, and was an opponent of organized religion, vested rights, and the common law. F. J. Turner, *The United States, 1830–1850: The Nation and Its Sections* (New York, H. Holt, 1935), p. 84.

[135] Quoted in Emerson, *Richard Hildreth*, p. 25.

and so on.[136] The *Theory of Politics* (1853) contains various sections on the "Influence of Mystical Ideas."[137] At one point, Hildreth even projected a pamphlet entitled "A History and Refutation of the Mystical Philosophy."[138] What I am interested in exploring here is not Hildreth's own vast philosophical system, which was projected to cover the entire realm of human experience from morals to aesthetics, but rather his understanding of the way "mystical ideas" worked. One can see Hildreth's diagnosis of the working of "mystical ideas" both in his pointed criticisms of George Bancroft and in his general account of "mystical ideas" in his *Theory of Politics* (1853).

Hildreth recognized that Bancroft combined within his writings a kind of impossible contradiction between demystification and mystification that went beyond mere hypocrisy or self-promotion. This is, of course, what I have characterized as the contradiction of thinking historically in terms of the "spirit of the age." We can see this in Hildreth's account of Bancroft's repudiation of the new "positive" philosophy that was blowing in from France and England in the 1830s and 1840s. In his 1854 address to the New York Historical Society, Bancroft had attacked the new social science precisely for its lack of "spirit":

> Here we are met ... by an afterbirth of the materialism of the last century. A system which professes to re-construct society on the simple observation of the laws of the visible universe, and which is presented with arrogant pretension under the name of the "Positive Philosophy," scoffs at all questions of metaphysics and religious faith as insoluble and unworthy of human attention.[139]

However, even as Bancroft attacked the "positive philosophy" for its inattention to metaphysics, in the very same address, he insisted on the need for a highly scientistic method. Hildreth's critique of Bancroft's contradictory reaction to the "positive philosophy" was as follows: "Now if [Bancroft's own scientistic method] is not precisely the 'positive

[136] See Richard Hildreth, *Theory of Morals: An Inquiry Concerning the Law of Moral Distinctions and the Variations and Contradictions of Ethical Codes* (New York: Augustus M. Kelley, 1971) (1844).

[137] Richard Hildreth, *Theory of Politics: An Inquiry into the Foundations of Governments, and the Causes and Progress of Political Revolutions* (New York: Harper & Bros., 1854), pp. 56, 78, 87.

[138] Quoted in Emerson, *Richard Hildreth*, p. 98.

[139] George Bancroft, "Oration, Delivered Before the New York Historical Society, at its Semi-Centennial Celebration, November 20, 1854," in *Literary and Historical Miscellanies*, p. 505.

philosophy' just before so summarily condemned ..., what is it? Is it possible to make a more precise statement that all knowledge grows out of observation, and is only to be advanced by observation?" The review ends with a scathing judgment of Bancroft's hypocrisy: "If the many are wiser than the few, and the multitude than the philosopher, to what end, pray, does Mr. Bancroft philosophize? Demagogism in politics is an old story, but a demagogue philosopher is something new."[140] The characterization of Bancroft as "something new," folding contradictions into his writings, is entirely of a piece with Hildreth's dissection of "mystical ideas" in his *Theory of Politics*. What he says in the following excerpt refers to theocratic empires, but it applies just as well to metaphysical contemporaries such as Bancroft:

> With respect to the founders of theocratic empires ... the hypothesis, which has been maintained by some writers, of pure hypocrisy and imposture on their part ... is utterly untenable.... Tacitus has set forth the true character of this remarkable class of men in three words: *Fingunt simul creduntque – they feign and believe simultaneously* [emphasis added].[141]

It is "feigning and believing" simultaneously, to borrow from Hildreth, that best describes the historical sensibility that pervaded "the age of the spirit of the age." Of course, we never know exactly *what* is feigned and *what* believed, but we should not make the mistake of accusing Rantoul, Bancroft, Story, or Lieber of hypocrisy. A critical contemporary such as Hildreth gives us a superior point of entry into an ideational world where the "age" demystified and the "spirit" mystified, where "mysterious" past and the demystified present were first rigorously distinguished and then mingled, where Catholicism was rejected as "mystery" in the name of the people and then returned to infuse the people, where a Burkean commitment to circumstance was invoked in favor of non-Burkean principle, where the past was rejected for itself and reclaimed as the "spirit" of the forward-looking principle, where the nonhistorical temporality of the common law was fractured in terms of an instrumentalist "age" and yet retrieved as the "spirit" of a thoroughly practical Anglo-American democracy.

As it turned out, however, Bancroft's lament for the weakening of a historical sensibility founded upon "spirit" was well founded. A combination

[140] Richard Hildreth, "Bancroft vs. Bancroft," *Boston Evening Telegraph*, December 4, 1854; reprinted in Pingel, *American Utilitarian*, pp. 201–203.

[141] Hildreth, *Theory of Politics*, p. 57.

of influences spelled a shift in the mid-nineteenth century to an understanding of the social, political, and historical world in terms of laws modeled on laws of nature imagined as inflexible. As Hildreth put it at the opening of his antislavery polemic, *Despotism in America*, when he discussed the American political experiment, "The consequences likely to flow from the success or failure of this experiment, are doubtless exaggerated; for those universal laws which regulate the feelings and the actions of men, will ultimately produce their necessary effects, in spite of narrow systems of policy and morals, founded upon the success or failure of any single experiment."[142] In the middle years of the nineteenth century, the American experiment was to be relativized in terms of "universal laws."

[142] Richard Hildreth, *Despotism in America; or an Inquiry into the Nature and Results of the Slave-Holding System in the United States* (Boston: Whipple & Damrell, 1840), Introduction, p. 7.

5

Time as Law

Common Law Thought in the Mid-Nineteenth Century

Laws Underlying Laws

The American Civil War is rightly considered a watershed in American history. More than three decades ago, Morton Keller described this watershed in ways that continue to resonate: "On its far side is the young Republic: agrarian, decentralized, living still under the spell of the Revolution and the Founding Fathers, burdened by slavery but exhilarated by the lure of the great undeveloped West. And on its near side is modern America: a nation of cities, factories, immigrants; a society whose controlling realities are not simplicity and underdevelopment but complexity and maturity."[1]

Americans who lived through the Civil War themselves wrote – and how could they not? – as if they had experienced something transformative. Although they did not represent the experience, as Keller did, in terms of an accession to "modernity," they prefigured Keller's observation that the country had lost its youthful innocence and been catapulted into an adulthood marked by complexity and compromise. In *The American Republic* (1865), the Roman Catholic social and political thinker Orestes Brownson wrote that the War had brought the country "to a distinct recognition of itself, and forced it to pass from thoughtlessness, careless, heedless, reckless adolescence to a grave and reflecting manhood."[2] Fourteen years after Appomattox, Henry James struck a similar note.

[1] Morton Keller, *Affairs of State: Public Life in Late Nineteenth Century America* (Cambridge, Mass.: Belknap Press, 1977), p. 1.

[2] Orestes A. Brownson, *The American Republic: Its Constitution, Tendencies and Destiny* (Wilmington, Del.: ISI Books, 2003) (1865), pp. 4, 1–2.

Observing that the Civil War had brought America's naive sense of "its immunity from the usual troubles of earthly empires" to an end, James found that Americans had acquired "a certain sense of proportion and relation, of the world being a more complicated place than it had hitherto seemed, the future more treacherous, success more difficult."[3]

Notwithstanding a widespread sense of the transformative impact of the War on polity and society, however, there were profound intellectual continuities across the middle decades of the nineteenth century. The generation that came of age intellectually in the 1830s and 1840s, and that experienced the War, remained intellectually active after the War. Even though it viewed the War as transformative, it interpreted that transformation from perspectives that themselves remained relatively coherent, that grasped the world in distinct ways. It applied those perspectives to issues not directly related to the War as well. As we shall see, disparate preoccupations of the period – slavery, the prosecution of the War, post-War debates about centralization and decentralization, and midcentury legal science generally – were all approached from similar vantage points.

This was the moment when American thinkers moved away from the eighteenth-century historical vocabulary of the shift from the feudal to the commercial, even as they ceased to rage against British influences in their politicolegal practices. In order to understand how mid-nineteenth-century American thinkers interpreted the historical world, as well as to situate them within the wider Euro-American intellectual context in which they operated, it might be worthwhile to return to George Bancroft's 1850s critique of Comtean "positive philosophy," mentioned in the conclusion to the preceding chapter. Deriding Comteanism as "an afterbirth of the materialism of the last century," Bancroft described it as "a system which professes to re-construct society on the simple observation of the laws of the visible universe." The problem with Comteanism, for Bancroft, was that it "scoff[ed] at all questions of metaphysics and religious faith as insoluble and unworthy of human attention."[4] For a romantic era thinker such as Bancroft, for whom American democracy was imbued, as we have seen, with an ineffable "Catholic element," the scientistic image of the world that Comteans offered was arid, unsatisfactory, impoverished.

[3] Henry James, *Hawthorne* (New York: Harper & Bros., 1901) (1879), pp. 139, 137, 139–140.

[4] Bancroft, "Oration, Delivered Before the New York Historical Society," p. 505.

Notwithstanding such critiques, Comte captured something of the mood of the mid-nineteenth century. Comte's philosophy of history organized historical time in terms of a shift from the theological to the metaphysical to the scientific or "positive." The last stage was intended to herald an all-encompassing science of society (Comte popularized the term "sociology"). Andrew Wernick has written that Comte represents an early version of a "decay of belief in an external yet ineffable superbeing." This waning of belief in a mysterious presence that underlay the human, phenomenal world resulted, Wernick argues, in what could be caricatured as a "totalising scientism, or ... the organized idolatry of *la société*," society as a kind of God substitute.[5]

But Comte's turning away from God toward society is only part of the story. Comte's was equally a turning away from the sphere of the political such as it had been bequeathed to the French by the late-eighteenth-century revolutions. The rocky career of the French Revolution had led to discouragement and despair. For Comte, the intermediate metaphysical stage of history stood, tellingly, for the highly abstract natural rights thinking that had dominated late-eighteenth-century French revolutionary thought. That stage, like the theological, had to be bypassed. For Comte, only the scientific or positive stage, focused as it was on a science of society founded on the knowable "laws of the visible universe" (as Bancroft put it), could be the cure to France's many problems. This was the object of the *philosophie positive*. It is not accidental that socialism – a related scientistic philosophy premised upon a rejection of the formal sphere of bourgeois politics – had its birth in Europe at precisely this time.

Even as American political democracy in the pre-War decades expanded in the form of state constitutional conventions and legislative activity, many American thinkers began to share Comte's scientistic predilection to look for laws that existed beyond or beneath the realm of actually existing politics and law. Since the American Revolution, democratic politics had been imagined not just as an instantiation of social or natural laws, but also as at least potentially allowing social or natural laws to be realized. Scottish thinkers, at least as Americans understood them, had posited social or natural laws against the claims of monarchs, popes, and barons. The inauguration of democratic politics had therefore been

[5] Andrew Wernick, *Auguste Comte and the Religion of Humanity: The Post-Theistic Program of French Social Theory* (Cambridge: Cambridge University Press, 2001), pp. 6, 1.

imagined by thinkers such as Paine and Jefferson, but equally by Robert Rantoul and Joseph Story, as a restoration of man to society and nature, as a political form that would let society and nature run its course. But this was because all these thinkers, in one sense, were haunted by the ghosts of monarchy and aristocracy. By the middle of the nineteenth century, democracy itself, for many Americans, was failing to capture truth.

To some extent, this was because Americans were beginning to experience some of the social and economic problems – for example, an emerging immiserized native-born working class – that they had previously imagined only as the lot of Europeans. A large influx of impoverished Irish Catholic immigrants, many of whom pooled in urban slums, further tested America's sense of its own exceptionalism. However, the principal cause was the escalation of the slavery crisis and the fading of the possibility of entente between North and South.

The intractability of slavery – intractable whether seen from North or South – led American thinkers like nothing else to consciousness of an unbridgeable gap between politics and society, democracy and truth. From the perspective of many in the North, Southern social error in the form of slavery had imbued the political system so thoroughly that the true underlying laws of society were being subverted. From the perspective of many in the South, the argument was reversed. Northern social error in the form of abolitionism – or, for some, the structure of Northern free society generally – had infiltrated the political system so insidiously that the true underlying laws of society were under threat. With a keen eye on European intellectual, political, and social developments, American thinkers in the North and the South began to search for underlying laws, rigorously distinguished from actually existing democratic politics, to explain the fractures of their worlds, to name what they took to be its unalterable truths. Such underlying laws were grounded in categories such as the social or the natural and were frequently analogized to laws governing a static, unchanging, pre-Darwinian nature. As such, the social and the natural were often, if not always, indistinguishable from one another. Imagined as *given*, they served the same purpose: to emphasize the gap between politics and society, to limit what democratic politics could do, and to relativize or cabin the sphere of the political. At the same time, thinkers had to make sense of democratic politics that contravened the underlying laws that they had identified. How to represent a democratic politics that was clearly in violation of truth?

The writings of the Whig social scientist Henry C. Carey (1793–1879), son of the prominent antebellum publisher Mathew Carey and founder of the so-called nationalist school of political economy, afford a point of entry into mid-nineteenth-century antipolitical, scientistic-historicist thought. As one traces Carey's writings from the 1840s to the 1850s, one senses a growing sense of mismatch between the actual state of the world and the natural laws that underlay it.[6]

Sharing Comtean impulses, Carey understood the human, phenomenal world as undergirded by a system of laws. He was utterly convinced that the laws governing the human and nonhuman worlds were the same. As he put it, "[C]loser examination would lead to the development of the great fact, that there existed but a single system of laws – those instituted for the government of matter, in the form of clay and sand, proving to be the same by which that matter was governed, when it took the form of man, or of communities of men."[7] Men and mud, grasped in their essence, followed the same rules.

Even as he insisted upon analogies between the laws governing the human and nonhuman worlds, however, Carey was compelled to recognize that the human world was crowded with instances of nonconformity to its underlying laws. This legitimized his scholarly enterprise. The point of identifying underlying natural and social laws was, after all, to show up existing features of the human world as failing to conform to such laws and to call for their excision. Accordingly, Carey asserted a difference between laws, on the one hand, and "inventions," on the other. "Inventions" were simply contingent artifacts of human history, exceptions that could not claim grounding in any underlying natural or social law. This sense that a law was inevitably accompanied by exceptions

[6] Carey's principal intellectual contribution was his argument contesting Ricardian and Malthusian learning through an exceptionalist reading of American history. Carey's more important works include *Essay of the Rate of Wages: With an Examination of the Causes of the Differences in the Condition of the Labouring Population Throughout the World* (Philadelphia: Carey, Lea & Blanchard, 1835); *Principles of Political Economy* (4 vols.) (Philadelphia: Carey, Lea & Blanchard, 1837–1840); *The Past, the Present and the Future* (Philadelphia: Carey & Hart, 1848); *The Slave Trade, Domestic and Foreign: Why It Exists and How It May be Extinguished* (New York: A. M. Kelley, 1967) (1853); *Principles of Social Science* (3 vols.) (Philadelphia: J. B. Lippincott & Co., 1858–1859); *The Unity of Law: As Exhibited in the Relations of Physical, Social, Mental and Moral Science* (Philadelphia: H. C. Baird, 1872); *The Harmony of Interests: Agricultural, Manufacturing and Commercial* (H. C. Baird, 1872). For accounts of Carey's thought, see Ross, *The Origins of American Social Science*, pp. 44–48; L. L. Bernard and Jessie Bernard, *Origins of American Sociology: The Social Science Movement in the United States* (New York: Russell & Russell, Inc., 1965), Part 4, Chaps. 27–32; Arnold W. Green, *Henry Charles Carey, Nineteenth Century Sociologist* (Philadelphia: University of Pennsylvania Press, 1951).

[7] Carey, *Principles of Social Science*, Vol. 1, Preface, p. vi.

allowed for the construction of a philosophy of history. At various times in human history, laws and exceptions could overcome or occlude one another. The course of human history was that of a progressive realization or recovery of underlying natural and social laws.

The success of a country was to be judged in terms of its conformity to underlying natural or social laws or, alternatively, in terms of the paucity of exceptions it had come up with. In the 1840s, Carey illustrated the point through recourse to the classic distinction between England and France. England respected laws; France was mired in "inventions." Carey described it thus: "The insular position of England has given her peace, and the laws of nature have there been far less habitually set aside than in France." By contrast, the French "have made laws to suit themselves, instead of studying the laws that nature made."[8] At this stage, even though the sectional crisis was well under way, it was still possible for Carey to argue that neither England nor France had given as free reign to underlying natural and social laws as had the United States. The United States had interfered less with underlying laws – or come up with fewer exceptions – than any other country. Today's reader might disagree with Carey's specific applications of the idea of laws and exceptions to American realities. War, for Carey, was an "invention" that contravened the underlying laws of labor and wealth accumulation. Americans were less warlike, he argued, than Europeans.[9] Without discernible irony, he asserted, "By no people have the rights of others been so much respected as by the people of the English colonies of America, now the United States.... [T]hey have never fired a musket but in self-defence."[10] Indeed, Carey argued, nothing showed off the peaceable nature of Americans better than the flourishing of their slave populations. American slaves exercised more rights of "self-government" than most Europeans. Even so, Carey breezily predicted that slavery – as "one of man's weak inventions" – could not endure in America.[11]

By the late 1850s, however, events had shaken Carey's confidence that America gave free reign to underlying natural and social laws. Various developments – the Kansas–Nebraska controversy, the enactment of the fugitive slave law, the 1857 *Dred Scott* decision – made America seem, to Carey, to be more in the grip of "inventions" than ever before. Slavery

[8] Carey, *The Past, the Present, and the Future*, p. 423.
[9] Ibid., p. 309.
[10] Ibid., p. 223.
[11] Ibid., p. 227.

threatened to establish itself not just in the territories, but in the free states themselves. Where earlier it had been possible to argue that America was more successful than England and France in observing underlying natural and social laws, now France and America appeared on a relatively even footing. On the eve of the Civil War, Carey discerned the social and the political to be in conflict with each other in both France and the United States. However, America's future appeared to be more depressing than that of France. "In France, a sound social system is gradually correcting the errors of the political one, with the constant tendency towards increase of freedom; whereas in the United States, social error is gradually triumphing over political truth."[12]

The "social error" was, of course, slavery. Of the United States, Carey asserted, "In no part of the world does the political system – based, as it is, upon the idea of local centers, counteracting the great central attraction – so nearly correspond with that wonderfully beautiful one established for the government of the universe."[13] But the erroneous social system of slavery – in its growing infiltration of the political system – violated this natural law of decentralization. Not surprisingly, Carey argued, the "invention" of War had originated in the South: "[Slavery] is centralization, and hence it is that we see throughout the South, so strong a tendency towards disturbance of the power of association elsewhere. All the wars of the Union have here had their origin."[14]

The prosecution and outcome of the Civil War might have allowed the "invention" or "social error" of slavery, as Carey characterized it, to be done away with, at least formally. From now on, presumably, the natural laws of equality, labor, and accumulation could be realized in both polity and society. But the defeat of the Confederacy by no means ended discussions of the disjuncture between politics, on the one hand, and nature or society, on the other. This was in large part attributable to widespread resistance to the efforts of Radical Republicans to close what they perceived to be the gap between actually existing law and underlying natural law. The politicolegal debates of the post–Civil War period took place, as is well known, around questions of centralization and decentralization. Before the War, thinkers such as Carey had accused the slave South of violating the natural law of decentralization in seeking to spread slavery everywhere. Now parties switched sides. If Radical Republicans

[12] Carey, *Principles of Social Science*, Vol. 2, p. 177.
[13] Ibid., p. 177–78.
[14] Ibid., Vol. 1, p. 52.

emphasized the need for political and legal centralization in order to realize the natural and social law of equality, their Democratic opponents, fearing a centralization of government and citizenship, sought to check Radical Republican impulses precisely in the name of a natural law of decentralization that served as a limit to democratic politics.

Radical Republican centralizing impulses were dealt a significant defeat by the U.S. Supreme Court's 1873 decision in the *Slaughterhouse Cases*, the Court's developing civil rights jurisprudence, and the course of American politics in the 1870s. But the positivist and scientistic language of underlying natural and social laws and their exceptions pervaded other areas of mid-nineteenth-century politicolegal thought. One context was that of the post–Civil War rationalization of government, itself often advanced as a way of curbing the excesses of corrupt, inefficient urban political machines. Another was mid-nineteenth-century legal science. Fully in the grip of thinking in terms of underlying laws and exceptions, mid-nineteenth-century legal thinkers such as Thomas Cooley and Joel Bishop, in contexts ranging from public to private law, sought to make sense of actually existing laws (i.e., statutes and court decisions) in terms of what they identified as underlying laws. The task of the jurisprude, as Bishop saw it, was to delve self-consciously beneath the surface of laws to grasp their subterranean principles. Doctrines, adjudications, and judicial pronouncements that did not conform to the underlying laws he had identified were dubbed, in keeping with the prevailing historical vocabularies, exceptions.

A positivist, scientistic, historicist language of underlying natural and social laws and their accompanying exceptions was thus all-pervasive in the middle decades of the nineteenth century. It straddled the War years and is discernible in context after context. Growing out of a profound sense of crisis in democratic politics that led to the War, it continued long thereafter. It served to cabin the sphere of the political even as, in the guise of ordinary legal science, it sought to cabin the adjudications of judges themselves.

The full weight of this positivist, scientistic, historicist language, as we shall see, was brought to bear upon the common law. Whether in debates concerning slavery, the prosecution of the War, post-War politicolegal arrangements, or general legal science, mid-nineteenth-century legal thinkers subjected the common law to the various underlying natural or social laws they had identified. The common law – like all politics and law – had natural and social laws as its ground and could be judged in terms of them. But even as the common law was subjected to these underlying natural or social laws, as we shall see, legal thinkers would simultaneously argue that the common law also ended up instantiating the very same underlying natural and social laws. Where the movement of history was a progressive uncovering of underlying natural or social laws or a progressive removal of exceptions, in other words, the common law could be represented as already embodying the course of history. Where underlying natural and social laws were imagined as limits to political democracy, furthermore, the common law, to the extent that it was fused with such laws, served as democracy's limit. The reader will observe this pattern repeated in the various contexts this chapter explores: the slavery debates, politicolegal arrangements during and after the War, and mid-century legal science.

Somersett in America: A Fragment of the Antebellum Slavery Debates

Dissatisfied with the trend of American politics and law, both antislavery and proslavery legal thinkers engaged in a search for underlying natural or social laws, although the underlying laws they identified stood in sharp contrast to one another. All law – including the common law – would have to be understood in terms of these underlying natural and social laws. This positing of natural or social laws as a way of making sense of the world – and of emphasizing the gap between politics and its limit – is dramatically revealed in a discrete aspect of the extensive antebellum slavery debates, namely the discussions over the meaning and scope of Lord Mansfield's celebrated 1772 decision in *Somersett v. Stewart*.[15]

The *Somersett* decision was formally about the ability of a master to remove his slave forcibly from England. As such, it neither effected an abolition of slavery in England and the colonies nor invalidated commercial contracts related to slavery. Nevertheless, Lord Mansfield's grandiose statements about the relationships among natural law, common law, and positive law profoundly shaped the subsequent American debate over the legal sources of slavery. Denying that slavery was recognized under the English common law, Mansfield had written, "The state of slavery is of such a nature, that it is incapable of being introduced on any reasons,

[15] *Somersett v. Stewart*, Lofft 1–18, 98 Eng. Rep. 499 (K.B. 1772), reprinted at 20 Howell's State Trials 1. See also William M. Wiecek, "*Somersett*: Lord Mansfield and the Legitimacy of Slavery in the Anglo-American World," *University of Chicago Law Review* 42 (1975): 86–46.

moral or political, but only [by] positive law, which preserves its force long after the reasons, occasion, and time itself from whence it was created, is erased from memory. It is so odious, that nothing can be suffered to support it but positive law."[16] These assertions raised more questions than they answered. Did "positive law" include custom (in Mansfield's rendering, "positive law" was, curiously, imbued with the nonhistorical common law temporality of "immemoriality")? Did "positive law" require that the legislative or executive authority actually establish slavery, rather than merely recognize its existence in slave codes? If slavery was so contrary to natural law, could even "positive law" establish it?[17]

During the late-eighteenth-century emancipations, courts and legislatures in New England, coming up with their own interpretations of *Somersett*, had refused to find evidence of express establishment of slavery in their laws and had held that slavery in their jurisdictions was "merely" a matter of custom or usage. Thus, "mere" custom was distinguished from the "positive law" – and perhaps even the state common law – required to establish slavery.[18] In 1827, however, custom emerged as a powerful legal justification of slavery. In the British case of *The Slave Grace*, Lord Stowell limited the scope of *Somersett* by pointing out, *inter alia*, that slavery had a legitimate origin in "ancient custom," which was "generally recognized as a just foundation of all law" (indeed, it should be noted, this was the foundation of the English common law itself). The point of recognizing custom as a legitimate legal basis for slavery was to lend recognition to colonial slave laws and practices, which might have originated as a matter of custom, without giving them full extraterritorial

[16] *Somersett*, 20 Howell's State Trials, p. 82.

[17] I draw this discussion from William M. Wiecek, *The Sources of Antislavery Constitutionalism in America, 1760–1848* (Ithaca, N.Y.: Cornell University Press, 1977), p. 32.

[18] In the celebrated late-eighteenth-century *Quock Walker* cases that brought about judicial emancipation in Massachusetts, Chief Justice Cushing charged the jury that, although the province had long recognized the presence of slaves and slavery, 'nowhere do we find it [slavery] expressly established"; it had merely been a "usage" acknowledged by the statutes, something that had "slid in upon us." John D. Cushing, "The Cushing Court and the Abolition of Slavery in Massachusetts: More Notes on the 'Quock Walker Case,'" *American Journal of Legal History* 5 (1961): 118–144, quoted in Wiecek, *Sources of Antislavery Constitutionalism in America*, p. 47. Rhode Island's 1784 gradual emancipation statute, invoking the Declaration of Independence, found that "the holding mankind in a state of slavery, as private property, which has gradually obtained by unrestrained custom and the permission of the laws," was repugnant to the principles of the Declaration. Act of 1784, quoted in Wiecek, *Sources of Antislavery Constitutionalism in America*, p. 50.

effect in England, which *Somersett* would not allow. None other than Joseph Story considered this a definitive interpretation of *Somersett*.[19] Custom as a source of law authorizing slavery was also recognized in the United States before the Civil War. In *Miller v. McQuerry* (1853), a fugitive slave case, Justice McLean, on circuit, invoked the nonhistorical common law temporality of "immemoriality" to give slavery the status of something akin to common law in the states that recognized slavery:

> *Usage of long continuance, so long that the memory of man runneth not to the contrary, has the force of law. It arises from long recognized rights, countervened by no legislative action. This is the source of many of the principles of the common law. And this for a century or more may constitute slavery, though it be opposed, as it is, to all the principles of the common law of England.* I speak of African slavery. But such a law can only acquire potency by long usage. Now it may be admitted that in some of the Southern states, perhaps in all of them, there can not be found a statute which contains the words, "And be it enacted that slavery shall exist".... [But] usage, of great antiquity, acquires the force of law. The denial, therefore, that slavery existed by virtue of an express law, or by statute law, which was intended to be denied, was no denial at all [emphasis added].[20]

The last line of this excerpt was a direct contradiction of *Somersett*. If custom could be the legal basis of slavery, no express law – which is how many had come to interpret Mansfield's "positive law" – was required to establish slavery. To argue in terms of the absence of an express law establishing slavery, as many abolitionists were doing following the logic of *Somersett*, did not affect the legality of slavery. Indeed, as an attempt to deny slavery, Justice McLean contended, *Somersett* "was no denial at all."

Notwithstanding decisions like *The Slave Grace* and *Miller v. McQuerry*, the constitutional and legal status of slavery remained subject to debate. In the North, a moderate political abolitionist such as Salmon Chase could concede that, at the time of the framing of the U.S. Constitution, slavery had existed as a matter of positive law in the Southern colonies *and* become "interwoven with domestic habits, pecuniary interests, and legal rights." Having found slavery to be actually existing in the states as a matter of positive law (*Somersett*) *and* custom (*Slave Grace* and *Miller*), Chase argued, the framers had written their egalitarian commitments into national protocols with the understanding that slavery would

[19] *The Slave Grace* (*Rex v. Allen*), 2 Hag. Adm. 94, 166 Eng. Rep. 179 (High Court of Admiralty, 1827); Joseph Story to Lord Stowell, 22 Sept. 1828, *Life and Letters of Joseph Story*, Vol. 1, p. 558.

[20] *Miller v. McQuerry*, 17 F. Cas. 335, 336–337 (1853).

be confined within the slave states existing at the time of the framing. At the same time, Chase could maintain that slaveholding "can have no rightful sanction or support from national authority, but must depend wholly upon State law for existence and continuance."[21] Garrisonians, by contrast, had long been insisting upon disunion and rejected all readings of the U.S. Constitution as an antislavery document.

However, not all antislavery legal thinkers subscribed to Chase's reading of Southern slavery as an admixture of positive law and custom, and hence as something "saved" under both the *Somersett* and *Slave Grace* decisions at least with respect to the old slave states. Neither did they subscribe to a Garrisonian insistence on disengagement. For an example of this third view, but also one that offers an insight into how mid-nineteenth-century antislavery legal thinkers theorized slavery in relation to actually existing law and politics, let us turn to the writings of the radical antislavery Massachusetts lawyer Lysander Spooner (1808–1887). Spooner offers us a clear example of how antislavery thinkers subjected all laws, including any customs believed to sanction slavery, to natural laws believed to underlie existing law and politics.

"Even in a movement that attracted individualists and eccentrics," William Wiecek has written, "Spooner stood out." Spooner was, in fact, something of an anarchist, insistent on shrugging off all manner of legal restraints, whether they related to the minimum number of years of legal education before one could practice law or the federal mail monopoly.[22] For all his eccentricities, however, Spooner's antislavery writings obtained considerable national recognition. Although other radicals such as George F. W. Mellen and William Goodell had advanced antislavery readings of

[21] Salmon P. Chase and Dexter Cleveland, *Anti-Slavery Addresses of 1844 and 1845* (Philadelphia: J. A. Bancroft & Co., 1867), pp. 77, 87.

[22] Wiecek, *Sources of Antislavery Constitutionalism in America*, p. 257. Spooner is often seen as an exemplar of American anarchism. See the discussion in Eunice M. Schuster, *Native American Anarchism: A Study of Left-Wing American Individualism* (Northampton, Mass.: Smith College, Department of History, 1932). Spooner began his legal career in the 1830s by opening a law office in open violation of the Massachusetts requirement of a minimum of three years of legal study (he had completed only two). In the 1840s, he organized the American Letter Mail Company, one of several private mail companies seeking to defeat the federal mail monopoly, only to have his enterprise shut down. In the 1850s, after decades of involvement in antislavery activity, Spooner fell in with John Brown and drafted an antislavery memorandum to be circulated among southern nonslaveholders. After Harpers Ferry, he even hatched plans to rescue Brown. A. John Alexander, "The Ideas of Lysander Spooner," *New England Quarterly* 23 (1950): 200–217, at 202; Lewis Perry, *Radical Abolitionism: Anarchy and the Government of God in Antislavery Thought* (Knoxville: University of Tennessee Press, 1995) (1973), pp. 204–208.

the U.S. Constitution, Spooner's book, *The Unconstitutionality of Slavery* (1845), which went through four editions, was by far the most consistently and thoroughly argued of the three.[23] Widely considered the most prominent antislavery reading of the U.S. Constitution to date, the text moved Wendell Phillips to write a critical review in 1847 to combat some of its ideas.[24] Much admired by Gerrit Smith, *The Unconstitutionality of Slavery* was officially accepted by the Liberty Party in 1849 as "a perfectly conclusive legal argument against the constitutionality of slavery."[25] The American Abolition Society sent the book to every congressman. Spooner's own plans for his work were even more ambitious: he wanted it sent to each one of the nation's thirty thousand lawyers.[26]

At the opening of *The Unconstitutionality of Slavery*, Spooner raises the question "What is law?" Instead of resorting to Hobbesian or common law theories, his answer, revealing affinities to Carey's thought, rests upon analogies to the laws governing the physical world. The word "natural" is emphasized repeatedly:

> The true and general meaning of [law], is that *natural*, permanent, unalterable principle, which governs any particular thing or class of things. The principle is strictly a *natural* one; and the term applies to every *natural* principle, whether mental, moral, or physical.... And it is solely because it is unalterable in its *nature*, and universal in its application, that it is denominated law. If it were changeable, partial or arbitrary, it would be no law. Thus we speak of physical laws; of the laws, for instance, that govern the solar system; of the laws of motion, the laws of gravitation, the laws of light, &c., &c. – Also the laws that govern the vegetable and animal kingdoms, in all their various departments: among which laws may be named, for example, the one that like produces like. Unless the operation of this principle were uniform, universal and necessary, it would be no law [emphasis in the original].[27]

There was no particular difference, for Spooner, between laws governing the human and nonhuman worlds. What gave all true laws their character as laws was permanence and invariability.

[23] G. W. F. Mellen, *An Argument on the Unconstitutionality of Slavery, Embracing an Abstract of the Proceedings of the National and State Conventions on this Subject* (Boston: Saxton & Pierce, 1841); William Goodell, *Views of American Constitutional Law, in its Bearing upon American Slavery* (Utica, N.Y.: Lawson & Chaplin, 1845). I have consulted Lysander Spooner, *The Unconstitutionality of Slavery* (Boston: Bella Marsh, 1860).

[24] Perry, *Radical Abolitionism*, p. 165. Wendell Phillips, *Review of Lysander Spooner's Essay on the Unconstitutionality of Slavery* (Boston: Andrews & Prentiss, 1847).

[25] Schuster, *Native American Anarchism*, p. 145.

[26] Perry, *Radical Abolitionism*, p. 204.

[27] Spooner, *Unconstitutionality of Slavery*, pp. 5–6.

However, only selected man-made laws – something Spooner called "natural law" or "the natural rights of men" – could accede to this level of invariability.[28] Spooner dubbed all other man-made laws "temporary" and "arbitrary," mere artifacts of time (Spooner's term for what Carey would call "exceptions" or "inventions"). Temporary or arbitrary laws were not entitled to obedience: "And, as a merely arbitrary, partial and temporary rule must, of necessity, be of less obligation than a natural, permanent, equal and universal one, the arbitrary one becomes, in reality, of no obligation at all, when the two come in collision. Consequently there is, and can be, correctly speaking, *no law but natural law*."[29]

Spooner's understanding of the world as consisting of an interplay between natural and arbitrary law reflected a coherent philosophy of history. It looked something like this:

> Natural law may be overborne by arbitrary [i.e., contingent] institutions; but she will never aid or perpetuate them. For her to do so, would be to resist, and even deny her own authority. It would present the case of a principle warring against and overcoming itself. Instead of this, she asserts her own authority on the first opportunity. The moment the arbitrary law expires by its own limitation, natural law resumes her reign.[30]

In accordance with this understanding of history, Spooner could argue that, notwithstanding the utter "arbitrariness" of slavery, slaveholders, "through the corrupting influence of their wealth," had nevertheless been able to hold "their slave property in defiance of their constitutions."[31] Similarly, in his *Essay on the Trial by the Jury* (1852), Spooner argued that a range of politicolegal practices in England and America had corrupted the essential nature of the jury.[32] In the interplay of natural and arbitrary laws that history revealed, the arbitrary could often overcome the natural. But Spooner had faith that natural law would be vindicated.

Spooner's understanding of natural law as a standpoint from which to judge all laws was, to be sure, a cabining of political democracy. Like many radical abolitionists, but also like many Americans in this period, Spooner was of the view that the output of democratic majorities was not entitled to respect *as such*. At times, democratic majorities could

[28] Ibid., p. 6.
[29] Ibid., p. 7 (emphasis in original).
[30] Ibid., p. 130.
[31] Ibid., p. 125.
[32] Lysander Spooner, *An Essay on the Trial by Jury* (New York: Da Capo Press, 1971) (1852).

further natural law principles; at others, they could frustrate them. This made Spooner disdainful of the idea that law was whatever a democratic majority said it was. As he wrote in an 1845 letter to his friend George Bradburn, "I do not rely upon 'political machinery' ... because the principle of it is wrong; for it admits ... that under a constitution, the *law* depends on the will of majorities, *for the time being*, as indicated by the acts of the legislature."[33] This distaste for political democracy accounts for Spooner's refusal to belong to the Liberty Party, to the chagrin of someone like Salmon Chase.[34]

It followed that, for Spooner, any actually existing law – constitution, statute, common law principle, or custom – could also be arbitrary and in violation of the natural law underlying it. Not surprisingly, at a time when prominent antislavery voices read the U.S. Constitution as a pact with slavery, Spooner argued that constitutions were not entitled to special regard. As he put it, "[N]atural law tries the contract of government, and declares it lawful or unlawful, obligatory or invalid, by the same rules by which it tries all other contracts between man and man."[35] Because past, present, and future were all to be judged in terms of an invariable natural law, Spooner also had contempt for the weight and density of the past as a ground of law. This made him utterly hostile to arguments that grounded the legitimacy of the common law or custom in its nonhistorical temporalities of "immemoriality" and "insensibility," which in turn shaped his understanding of the legal sources of slavery.

For Spooner, no amount of sanctification by time could save slavery. Accordingly, he completely rejected the idea that slavery might receive the imprimatur of custom or common law. This translated into a strict reading of *Somersett* and a complete rejection of the *Slave Grace* and *Miller* theories about the legal sources of slavery. He described it thus: "Slavery, if it can be legalized at all, can be legalized only by positive legislation. Natural law gives it no other aid. *Custom imparts to it no legal sanction.*"[36]

Given Spooner's hostility to common law temporalities as grounds of law and his insistence on submitting all law to the test of natural law, it is noteworthy that the common law – indeed, custom itself – played an

33 Lysander Spooner to George Bradburn, August 25, 1847, quoted in Perry, *Radical Abolitionism*, p. 200 (emphasis in original).

34 Perry, *Radical Abolitionism*, p. 200.

35 Spooner, *Unconstitutionality of Slavery*, p. 8.

36 Ibid., p. 32 (emphasis added). Even if positive law were to legalize slavery, one imagines that Spooner would dub it "arbitrary," unworthy of respect.

important role in his thought. Following Wendell Phillip's 1847 critique of *The Unconstitutionality of Slavery* on the grounds, *inter alia*, that Spooner's vision of a system based on natural law was uncertain and impracticable, Spooner responded by appending a second part to the text in which he discussed the appropriate nature of the relationship of legislation to natural law. It is here that Spooner revealed himself to be a common lawyer.

Legislatively promulgated laws were valuable, Spooner argued, where they were mere "instrumentalities ... for the purpose of carrying natural law into effect."[37] But for the most part, legislation was to be avoided. Where legislation replicated natural law, it confused matters; where it differed from it, it was arbitrary. Although natural law was a "science" and the legitimate subject of treatises, Spooner maintained, it was also something that was simply and spontaneously picked up as men interacted with each other and that, as such, did not require legislative clarification or intervention:

> Men living in contact with each other, and having intercourse together, *cannot avoid* learning natural law, to a very great extent, even if they would. The dealings of men with men, their separate possessions, and their individual wants, are continually forcing upon their minds the questions, – Is this act just? or is it unjust? Is this thing mine? or is it his? And these are questions of natural law; questions, which, in regard to this great mass of cases, are answered alike by the human mind everywhere.[38]

This description of the inculcation of natural law makes it look suspiciously like custom, which arose, in the accounts of common lawyers, spontaneously, from out of the people themselves. But Spooner goes further, explicitly equating natural law and common law. For all his distaste for legislation, it turns out, the anarchistic Spooner was not ready to do away with common law courts, something that attests to the deep-rootedness of common law thinking even among the radical fringes of the American legal profession at the time. Indeed, Spooner argued that the vast majority of matters dealt with by common law courts in fact conformed to "natural principles." Common law courts might even be the best declarants of a spontaneously arising natural law. Thus:

> It is probable that, on an average, three fourths, and not unlikely nine tenths, of all the law questions that are decided in the progress of every trial in our courts, are decided on natural principles; such questions, for instance, as those

[37] Ibid., p. 140n.
[38] Ibid., p. 141.

of evidence, crime, the obligation of contracts, the burden of proof, the rights of property, &c., &c.

This assertion was immediately followed by an approving reference to, of all texts, Kent's *Commentaries*: "Kent says, and truly, that 'A great proportion of the rules and maxims, which constitute the immense code of the common law, grew into use by gradual adoption, and received the sanction of the courts of justice, without any legislative act or interference. *It was the application of the dictates of natural justice and cultivated reason to particular cases*.'"[39] In other words, for Spooner, the common law – or nine-tenths of it – instantiated natural law. History, understood to be an interplay of natural law and arbitrary law, could be used to judge all law, including the common law. As such, various aspects of the actually existing common law, especially when they could be read as sanctioning slavery, could be judged arbitrary. But where history was plotted as the progressive uncovering of natural law, the common law already embodied natural law and, as such, was itself already the engine of history.

Southern lawyers responded in kind to natural law critiques of slavery such as those advanced by Spooner. George S. Sawyer's *Southern Institutes* (1859) – one of a small number of proslavery treatises to appear before the War – matches the structure of Spooner's thought, albeit with one significant difference.[40] Where Spooner drew upon the model of an unchanging physical nature to express the invariability of underlying natural law, Sawyer invoked an equally unchanging biological nature to the same ends. In this regard, Sawyer resembled other proslavery thinkers of the time.

Slavery was founded on an inequality that was, according to Sawyer, one of the "fixed facts in the philosophy of human nature, beyond the reach of human laws, or remedy by human means" (analogies were to illness, physical disability, and insanity).[41] A sense of "fixed facts in the philosophy of human nature" was the means of testing the legitimacy of

39 Ibid., p. 143n (emphasis in original).

40 George S. Sawyer, *Southern Institutes: or, An Inquiry Into the Origin and Early Prevalence of Slavery and the Slave-Trade: With An Analysis of the Laws, History and Government of the Institution in the Principal Nations, Ancient and Modern, from the Earliest Ages Down to the Present Time. With Notes and Comments in Defence of Southern Institutions* (Philadelphia: J. B. Lippincott, 1858). The other prominent treatise is Thomas R. R. Cobb, *An Inquiry into the Law of Negro Slavery in the United States of America. To which is Prefixed, an Historical Sketch of Study* (Philadelphia: T. & J. W. Johnson & Co and Savannah: W. Thorne Williams, 1858). Although Cobb shares the scientistic historical style of the mid-nineteenth century, he does not, in my view, betray any particular commitment to common law modes of thinking.

41 Sawyer, *Southern Institutes*, p. 14.

actually existing politics and law. Laws that sought to contravene such truths would be, *ab initio*, doomed to failure. Democratic politics, as such, were circumscribed. Much like Spooner's focus on natural law, Sawyer's focus on fixed facts also enabled a coherent philosophy of history that read historical time as an alternate recognition or occlusion of fixed facts. However, for the most part, Sawyer found that history had affirmed his sense of the hard limits to politics and law. He put it thus: "The social, moral, and political, as well as the physical history of the negro race bears strong testimony against them; it furnishes the most undeniable proof of their mental inferiority. In no age or condition has the real negro shown a capacity to throw off the chains of barbarism and brutality that have long bound down the nations of that race; or to rise above the common cloud of darkness that still broods over them."[42]

Even as he turned to history to illustrate the conformity of Southern slavery to "fixed facts in the philosophy of nature," and even as he sought to relativize politics and law in the name of such truths, Sawyer was powerfully committed to the idea of custom. Following the line suggested by the *Slave Grace* and *Miller* cases, Sawyer argued that custom was among "the most potent sources of law." Slavery derived its legitimacy precisely from custom. Furthermore, Sawyer drew upon the languages of the common law to fill out this legitimacy. The "faithful student of history" would find that slavery and the slave trade "came down to us as well authenticated by custom and usage, sanctioned, proved, and improved by the wisdom and experience of ages, as any other right rule for the relation of mankind towards one another."[43] This was precisely because slave customs possessed the power of "immemoriality":

> When customs are so old that the memory of man runneth not to the contrary, their origin is lost in the oracles and mythical edicts of the gods. The feeling of dependence upon the great wisdom and foresight necessary to give validity, force, and effect to the institutions of government and laws among men, has ever induced nations, in their early ages, to attribute their origin to a divine source.[44]

The common law and nature, then, worked together. This had the effect of making customs of slavery universal rather than particular. Writing the ontology of slavery as universal custom provided Sawyer with the tools

[42] Ibid., p. 192.
[43] Ibid., p. 13.
[44] Ibid., p. 17.

to combat the "freedom national, slavery local" argument that had been developed by lawyers such as Salmon Chase. Sawyer could argue:

> Thus the history of the world shows us that slavery and the slave trade are not local, and created only by special laws, as asserted by Justices McLean and Curtis, in their dissenting opinions in the Dred Scott case, but rather that they are originally universal, founded upon immemorial custom and universal principles of international law; and that all free territory, or territory where this right can no longer exist, has originated from some abrogation of this time-honored custom, or some modification of these long-established rights of property and of persons, by the potent arm of legislation.[45]

Thus, it was free territories that had abrogated the twinning of custom and nature that slavery represented; freedom was the exception to the underlying universal law of slavery. This allowed Sawyer to twist Chase's slogan into "slavery national, freedom local." Indeed, Sawyer used the congruence of custom and nature to combat the *Somersett* ruling. Where Lord Mansfield had argued that neither the common law nor nature, but only "positive law," could sustain slavery, Sawyer insisted that the common law and nature together provided the unshakable foundations of slavery. Only "the potent arm of legislation" – that is, Mansfield's "positive law" – could abrogate the dictates of custom and nature. But in doing so, it was erroneous, because slavery, like the family, was "originally universal," part of human sociality itself:

> We maintain directly the reverse of this, viz. that slavery and the slave-trade are not founded on municipal law, but on immemorial custom, incorporated into the ancient and modern code of nations. That the relation of master and slave is as old as the human family; that it rests on the same foundation as that of husband and wife, parent and child, and the distinctive rights of persons and things; that it was originally universal, and sanctioned by law public and private, human and divine; that all exceptions to its prevalence arise from the abrogation of universal custom, by the potent arm of legislation.[46]

From this perspective, it was easy to judge abolitionist legal impulses as contrary to both nature and common law. In Sawyer's reading, slavery, in conforming to nature, had a way of making nature even more natural. Slavery made white men naturally fitted for liberty and white women naturally fitted for domestic pursuits even more fitted to such pursuits.[47] Abolition would reverse this superconformity to nature; it would be an

[45] Ibid., p. 143.

[46] Ibid., p. 308.

[47] Ibid., pp. 373–376.

exception to the underlying law of nature, an abomination. But at the same time, of course, slavery was possessed of the "immemoriality" of the common law. Abolitionist activity that ripped the fabric of custom could equally be dubbed violent in a Burkean sense insofar as it destroyed the harmonious coexistence of different generations simultaneously speaking through custom. It is not surprising, then, to find Sawyer also likening abolitionists to those favorite enemies of nineteenth-century Anglo-American common lawyers, the French revolutionaries:

> The facts that are now transpiring, the history that has been forming around their footsteps, forcibly remind us of the early days of the French Revolution. France had her Robespierre, her Mirabeau, Danton, and Marat.... So the Abolitionists, arrayed in treasonable warfare against the peaceful execution of the laws of the land ... could congregate an infuriated mass ... with minds already wrought up to a pitch of desperation that required but a single spark to explode a magazine, that would have drenched the streets of Boston, like those of Paris, with the blood of her citizens.[48]

What we have in the preceding discussion of Spooner and Sawyer are instances of legal thinkers ranged on opposite sides of the fence. Both are equally moved by the slavery crisis to subject actually existing politics and law to underlying natural laws with a view to positing limits to the different political and legal impulses of the day. Both, however, argue that the common law matches the underlying natural laws they have identified. In a world in which disenchantment with democratic politics in both North and South was expressed in terms of the disjuncture between politics and natural laws, the common law could be a source of solace and hope, a limit to misguided democracy.

Slavery, Sociology, and the Common Law: The Jurisprudence of George Fitzhugh

The proslavery Virginian social thinker George Fitzhugh (1806–1881) has been variously represented as an American forerunner of European fascism, as one of the voices of American antiliberalism, and as the representative of a doomed precapitalist South in an advancing capitalist world.[49] But Fitzhugh is also important for our purposes for the following

[48] Ibid., p. 381.

[49] For a biography, see Harvey Wish, *George Fitzhugh: Propagandist of the Old South* (Baton Rouge: Louisiana State University Press, 1943). Wish sees Fitzhugh as a precursor of fascism. For other prominent treatments of Fitzhugh, see Louis Hartz, *The Liberal Tradition in America: An Interpretation of American Political Thought Since the Revolution* (New York: Harcourt, Brace & Co., 1955); C. Vann Woodward, "George

two reasons. First, his most prominent texts, *Sociology for the South* (1854) and *Cannibals All!* (1857), as well as his numerous essays in periodicals such as *De Bow's Review*, reveal him to be one of the earliest American proponents of understanding law in its social context. Indeed, Fitzhugh's *Sociology for the South* was the first prominent American text to use the new Comtean term "sociology" in its title. Second, Fitzhugh spent the bulk of his working life in Port Royal, Virginia, as a marginally successful trial lawyer. In his writings, a fact little noticed, Fitzhugh not only repeatedly claimed the common law on behalf of the South and Southern institutions, but also confessed that his decades-long career as a rural trial lawyer had had a direct impact on his styles of reasoning and argumentation. In *Cannibals All!* Fitzhugh put it thus:

> [W]e practiced as a jury lawyer for twenty-five years, and thereby acquired an inveterate habit of cumulation and iteration, and of various argument and illustration. But, at the same time, we learned how 'to make out our case,' and to know when it is "made out." The lawyer who observed the Unities in an argument before a jury would be sure to lose his cause; and now the world is our jury, who are going to bring in a verdict against free society of 'guilty.' ... The Exhaustive, not the Artistic, is what we would aspire to. And yet, the Exhaustive may be the highest art of argument. The best mode, we think, of writing, is that in which facts, and argument, and rhetoric, and wit, and sarcasm, succeed each other with rapid iteration.[50]

Fitzhugh's writings afford another instance of how American legal thinkers in the slavery debates intertwined the languages of law and society, actually existing law and underlying (in this case) social law.

For Fitzhugh, in Comtean fashion, "sociology" ultimately stood for the view that the truth inhered not in the political but in the social. Thus, he could state, "Social government is more important than political government; for social government looks into the inmost recesses of society,

Fitzhugh, *Sui Generis*," in George Fitzhugh, *Cannibals All! Or Slaves Without Masters* (C. Vann Woodward, ed.) (Cambridge, Mass.: Belknap Press, 1960) (1857); Eugene D. Genovese, *The World the Slaveholders Made: Two Essays in Interpretation* (Middletown, Conn.: Wesleyan University Press, 1988). On proslavery thought generally, see William Sumner Jenkins, *Pro-Slavery Thought in the Old South* (Gloucester, Mass.: Peter Smith, 1960); Drew Gilpin Faust, *A Sacred Circle: The Dilemma of the Intellectual in the Old South, 1840–1860* (Baltimore: Johns Hopkins University Press, 1977); Michael O'Brien, *Conjectures of Order: Intellectual Life and the American South, 1810–1860* (2 vols.) (Chapel Hill: University of North Carolina Press, 2004); Elizabeth Fox-Genovese and Eugene Genovese, *The Mind of the Master Class: History and Faith in the Southern Slaveholders' Worldview* (Cambridge: Cambridge University Press, 2005).

[50] George Fitzhugh, *Cannibals All!*, p. 239.

and carefully drills, trains, and educates the individual to play the part of subject and of citizen. This neglected, and political government in vain attempts to make a great people of little individuals – a sound whole of rotten parts."[51] By the same token, what was to be feared was not a political revolution but a social one: "Mere political revolutions affect social order but little, and generate but little infidelity. It remained for social revolutions, like those in Europe in 1848, to bring on an infidel age; for, outside slave society, such is the age in which we live."[52]

Like the human body, the social was entirely natural.[53] The naturalness of the social was undergirded, in final analysis, by the naturalness of the inferiority and superiority of men vis-à-vis one other, which ensured a species of social interdependence in which men held property in each other. This species of social interdependence – hence slavery – was a universal law of nature. As Fitzhugh explained it: "Man is a social and gregarious animal [bees and beavers afforded analogies], and all such animals hold property in each other. Nature imposes upon them slavery as a law and necessity of their existence."[54] It is important to emphasize that, even as he turned to Comtean science, Fitzhugh was building upon a long line of Southern defenses of slavery as a social institution.[55]

Even as Fitzhugh claimed to be practicing Comtean "sociology," however, in the manner of romantic era antidemocratic thinkers like Thomas Carlyle, he mourned the gradual fading of a world of reciprocal

[51] George Fitzhugh, "Frederick the Great, by Thomas Carlyle," *De Bow's Review* 29 (1860): 151–167, at 152.

[52] Fitzhugh, *Cannibals All!*, p. 35.

[53] "Social bodies, like human bodies, are the works of God, which man may dissect and sometimes heal, but which he cannot create." Ibid., p. 22.

[54] Ibid., p. 235.

[55] In the 1820s, for example, the South Carolina legislature resisted attempts to tinker with slavery on the ground that slavery was a "system, descended to them from their ancestors, and now inseparably connected with their social and political existence." *State Documents on Federal Relations: The States and the United States* (H. V. Ames, ed.) (Philadelphia: University of Pennsylvania, 1911), p. 208, quoted in Wiecek, *Sources of Antislavery Constitutionalism in America*, p. 141. In 1836, John C. Calhoun defended his position on prohibiting the transmission of abolitionist literature through the mails against charges that such an action would violate the freedom of the press on the ground that slavery was not "just" a property relationship (hence, a creature of law), but also a regulation of "social and political relations." Quoted in Wiecek, *Sources of Antislavery Constitutionalism in America*, p. 176. In his 1858 treatise on slavery, Thomas Cobb defended slavery as follows: "Such a state of society made slavery, in the colonies, a *social institution*. It was upheld and maintained, not for gain solely, but because it had become, as it were, a part of the social system, a social necessity." Cobb, *Inquiry*, p. clx (emphasis in original).

obligations grounded in the subordination of natural inferiors (blacks, women, children, serfs) and deplored the advent of a world characterized by political democracy and laissez-faire thought in which "[m]en were suddenly called on to walk alone, to act and work for themselves without guide, advice or control from superior authority." Fitzhugh thus blended Comte's positivism with Carlyle's nostalgia and transcendentalism.[56]

Fitzhugh's particular conception of the social enabled him to attack the unnaturalness of free societies. In legally separating men from one another, free societies had violated the underlying law of social interdependence or slavery (if Fitzhugh were employing Carey's terminology, he would have dubbed free societies "inventions"). Following Carlyle, Fitzhugh argued that free societies had become unnaturally "ungoverned" as a result of the lifting of all the institutional constraints (feudalism, the church, the monarchy, traditional marriage structures, etc.) that had kept man dependent on man. The result had been considerable suffering for the weakest segments of such societies, especially the working men of the North. As a counterpoint to the diseased liberty of free societies, Fitzhugh offered the image of happy, harmonious, and natural Southern slave societies, which were the best exemplars of the underlying law of social interdependence.[57]

This understanding of natural and unnatural social forms – the law and its powerful exceptions – provided Fitzhugh with a way of reading the history of the West. Fitzhugh did not go very far in expressing admiration for what he saw as the best exemplifications of nature or the social: the Roman Catholic church, feudalism, and monarchy. However, Fitzhugh could, and did, criticize aspects of the thought of the late eighteenth century, especially the ideas of Adam Smith, Jefferson, and the French revolutionaries, for sowing the seeds of what he saw as the unnatural social isolation and anarchism of his own day. But the underlying law of nature or society, for Fitzhugh (as for Lysander Spooner), was continually reasserting itself against the contrivances that political and economic man had set up against it. In *Sociology for the South*, Fitzhugh read the incipient European socialist impulses of the mid-nineteenth century as nothing

[56] George Fitzhugh, *Sociology for the South: or, the Failure of Free Society* (New York: Burt Franklin, 1965) (1854), pp. 10–11. Scholars have long been aware of the antidemocratic romantic thinker Thomas Carlyle's influence on Fitzhugh. As Fitzhugh put it in an 1856 article, "Mr. Carlyle is the profoundest thinker who writes the English language." George Fitzhugh, "The Counter Current, or Slavery Principle," *De Bow's Review* 21 (July 1856): 90–95, at 93.

[57] Fitzhugh, *Sociology for the South*, p. 30.

other than a recognition of the law of social interdependence and, hence, as a return to slavery:

After struggling and blundering and staggering on through various changes, Louis Napoleon is made Emperor. He is a socialist, and socialism is the new fashionable name of slavery. He understands the disease of society, and has nerve enough for any surgical operation that may be required to cure it.... He is now building houses on the social plan for working men, and his Queen is providing nurseries and nurses for the children of working women, just as we Southerners do for our negro women and children. It is a great economy. Fourier suggested it long after Southerners had practiced it.[58]

Similarly, Fitzhugh saw the rise of mutual insurance schemes as the (somewhat flawed) return of slavery: "Domestic slavery is nature's mutual insurance society; art in vain attempts to imitate it, or to supply its place."[59] The same was true of the legal entail, vigorously condemned, as we have seen, in eighteenth-century Scotland and America, that Fitzhugh saw returning in the guise of such things as homestead legislation.[60] In light of all this, Fitzhugh could assert a new direction for history: "[T]owards slavery the North and all Western Europe are unconsciously marching."[61]

Law played a crucial role in Fitzhugh's vision of society and history. He maintained that "[t]he government of law is the natural government of man."[62] But Fitzhugh's sense of "the natural government of man" – which was nothing other than the social – would allow him to judge all actually existing law.

The most severe critiques were reserved for the eighteenth-century constitutions, which had inaugurated the separation of man from man that Fitzhugh saw as the particular problem of his own time. Fitzhugh's

58 Ibid., p. 42.

59 Ibid., p. 168.

60 George Fitzhugh, "The Character and Causes of the Crisis," *De Bow's Review* 24 (1858): 27–32, at 30.

61 Fitzhugh, *Sociology for the South*, p. 45. By the time of *Cannibals All!*, published just a few years later, Fitzhugh was resolutely against socialism as something that had abandoned "religion, family ties, property, and the restraints of justice." But he continued to see socialism as an attempt – albeit a fatally misguided one – to introduce what was best about slavery. The right solution would nevertheless inevitably be found. The underlying natural law would reassert itself: "Society will work out erroneous doctrines to their logical consequences, and detect error only by the experience of mischief. The world will only fall back on domestic slavery when all other social forms have failed and been exhausted." Fitzhugh, *Cannibals All!*, p. 6.

62 George Fitzhugh, "Frederick the Great, by Thomas Carlyle," pp. 151–167, 162.

distance, in this regard, from an earlier generation of Virginian legal thinkers such as St. George Tucker illustrates the dramatic shift from the political to the social that had taken place by the mid-nineteenth century. According to Fitzhugh, the human mind, beginning with Locke and culminating with Jefferson and the French Revolution, had become "extremely presumptuous, and undertook to form governments on exact philosophical principles, just as men make clocks, watches or mills."[63] Written constitutions were just such "clocks, watches or mills." Fitzhugh's denigration of written constitutions grew ever more pronounced over the course of the 1850s. By 1860, distinguishing himself from both states' rights advocates and unionists, he was describing written constitutions as "mere idle figments of the brain."[64] In 1861, he wrote, "The Federal Constitution is by far the most absurd and contradictory paper ever penned by practical men."[65] It was in profound discord with the social, and as such was not deserving of respect.

But it was not just the written constitutions of the eighteenth century that came in for criticism. All laws, including the common law, had the social as ground and could be extinguished by it. Fitzhugh could occasionally sound like a conservative common lawyer committed to the protection of private property: "The institutions of private property in land and hereditary right are ... prescriptive and aboriginal, have existed time out of mind, have been universal with the white man, and have generally prevailed with all races, except the North American Indians and negroes."[66] But at the same time, he could assert that all private property was merely a creature of the social and could, as such, be taken away (in this regard, to be sure, Fitzhugh was also drawing upon a Blackstonian vision of rights as being merely conventional):

> Property is not a natural and divine, but conventional right; it is the mere creature of society and law.... In this country, the history of property is of such recent date, that the simplest and most ignorant man must know, that it commenced in wrong, injustice and violence a few generations ago, and derives its only title now from the will of society through the sanction of law. *Society has no right because it is not expedient, to resume any one man's property because he abuses its possession, and does not so employ it as to redound to public advantage, – but if all*

[63] Fitzhugh, *Sociology for the South*, p. 175.

[64] George Fitzhugh, "Small Nations," *De Bow's Review* 29 (1860): 561–569, at 568.

[65] George Fitzhugh, "The Message, the Constitution, and the Times," *De Bow's Review* 30 (1861): 156–167, at 157.

[66] George Fitzhugh, "The Declaration of Independence and the Republican Party," *De Bow's Review* 29 (1860): 175–187, at 180.

private property, or if private property generally were so used as to injure, instead of promote public good, then society might and ought to destroy the whole institution [emphasis added].[67]

Slave property itself was private only because of "the belief and expectation that such separate property will redound more to public advantage than if all property were common."[68] Thus, all property – by implication, all law, including the common law – was subject to the social.

But even as Fitzhugh would argue that all law, from constitutions to common law, should be subjected to the test of the social, he would argue that the common law, because of the glacial pace of its growth over centuries, was a "discovery" that embodied the "laws and constitution" of society:

Laws, institutions, societies and governments grow, and men may aid their growth, improve their strength and beauty, and lop off their deformities and excrescences, by punishing crime and rewarding virtue. When society has worked long enough, under the hand of God and nature, man observing its operations, may discover its laws and constitution. The common law and the constitution of England, were discoveries of this kind. Fortunately for us, we adopted, with little change, that common law and that constitution. Our institutions and ancestry were English. Those institutions were the growth and accretion of many ages, not the work of legislating philosophers.[69]

Elsewhere, Fitzhugh would write that the common law was "the undefinable tie that binds man to man."[70] It was "a congenital principal of social cohesion and government, the law of man's nature, the higher law, that original and prescriptive law, in which all just 'written law' is to be found in the germ, the vital principle or constitution of the social being, human government."[71] Where the social was truth, and afforded a vantage point from which to judge the political (especially the politics and law of free societies), the common law was the social – and hence, the truth – itself. As such, it was the only true constitution that Americans had ever had. In 1861, in support of the secessionist effort, Fitzhugh was arguing that what distinguished the states from the federal government was that the states' "true constitutions are the common law, which came along with

[67] Fitzhugh, *Sociology for the South*, p. 185.
[68] Ibid., p. 186.
[69] Ibid., p. 176. See also George Fitzhugh, "The Politics and Economics of Aristotle and Mr. Calhoun," *De Bow's Review* 23 (1857): 163–172, at 164–165, 170–171.
[70] Fitzhugh, "The Message, the Constitution, and the Times," pp. 156–167, 158.
[71] Ibid., pp. 156–167, 161.

the first settlers."[72] The states, in other words, realized the social in a way the federal government never could. If free Western societies were moving in the direction of socialism or slavery, the common law had already taken them there.

The Common Law as Possibility as Limit: Law and Governance During and After the War

As suggested by the discussion in the preceding sections, the escalation of the sectional crisis – and the debate over slavery that lay at its heart – gave rise to a profound crisis of faith in American politics that resulted in, and was reflected in, the search for underlying natural and social laws that cabined the sphere of democratic politics. The slavery debates, however, gave way to the crisis of the Civil War, which brought about its own set of debates, in which the question of another underlying natural law – the natural law of national self-preservation – became important. To what extent was the Union to be bound by constitutional restraints as it prosecuted the War? To what extent should the underlying natural law of national self-preservation override actually existing constitutional constraints? Some legal thinkers placed constitutional restraints above the military necessities of prosecuting the War. Others called for a strict subordination of constitutional niceties to the underlying natural law of national self-preservation. In a curious twist, yet others would argue that a more faithful adherence to common law constitutionalism – one in which government was entirely customary, flexible, and capable of action – would be the best mode of effectuating the underlying natural law of national self-preservation. This last argument asserted the ability of the common law to allow the nation to preserve itself in a way that written law – that is, the U.S. Constitution – could not.

The executive, especially the generals on the field, pushed repeatedly at the boundaries of what was legally acceptable as the War progressed. During the second phase of the War, dominated on the Union side by Grant and Sherman, a disregard of constitutional constraints was explicitly justified in the name of national self-preservation. War, Sherman observed, "is simply power unrestrained by constitution or compact." He was ready to undertake whatever it took to preserve the nation: "[S]o important a thing as the self-existence of a great nation should not be

[72] Ibid., pp. 156–167, 158.

left to the fickle chances of war."[73] This willingness to disregard constitutional strictures in the prosecution of the War was accompanied by the occasional denigration of a U.S. Supreme Court that had itself done so much to exacerbate the crisis. In his first inaugural address, for example, Lincoln stated, "[I]f the policy of the government is to be irrevocably fixed by the decisions of the Supreme Court … the people will have ceased to be their own rulers."[74] As it turned out, the wartime Court proved far from obstructionist. From the naval blockade of the South to the emancipation of slaves, it largely acquiesced in the Union's prosecution of the War. In the *Prize Cases* of 1863, which upheld the legality of the blockade, Justice Grier declared, "They cannot ask a court to affect a technical ignorance of the existence of a war, which all the world acknowledges to be the greatest civil war known in the history of the human race, and thus cripple the arm of the government and paralyze its power by subtile definitions and ingenious sophisms."[75]

Nevertheless, as the War advanced, certain Northern legal thinkers began to worry about what they took to be the government's increasingly cavalier attitude toward the Constitution. Harvard Law School's Joel Parker had initially supported the Union cause because he had seen the War as a struggle for the preservation of law. The government itself, therefore, had to be restrained by the Constitution. But the issuance of the Emancipation Proclamation convinced Parker that the War that he had supported as counterrevolutionary was itself becoming revolutionary, spilling beyond the limits of the law. Parker criticized Lincoln's government as "absolute, irresponsible, uncontrollable … a perfect military despotism." He even sought to have Massachusetts radical Senator Charles Sumner ousted by the state legislature.[76] He joined the chorus of antiemancipation, anti-Lincoln Northern voices for the duration of the War.

Other prominent legal thinkers argued, by contrast, that the underlying natural law of national self-preservation should take precedence over the Constitution. The crisis of the War pushed Francis Lieber, antebellum America's foremost proponent of a common law liberty, to what

[73] *Memoirs of General William T. Sherman* (1875) (2d ed.) (2 vols.) (New York: D. Appleton & Co., 1904), Vol. 2, p. 114.

[74] Abraham Lincoln, *First Inaugural Address, March 4, 1861*, in Hutton Webster, ed., *Historical Source Book* (Boston, D. C. Heath and Co., 1920), p. 175.

[75] *Prize Cases*, 67 U.S. 459, 477 (1863).

[76] Joel Parker, *The Domestic and Foreign Relations of the United States* (Cambridge: Welch, Bigelow & Co., 1862), p. 80.

Philip Paludan has called the "eternal verities of natural law."[77] The prosecution of the War, Lieber argued in 1864, should not be held up by the Constitution: "The whole rebellion is beyond the Constitution. The Constitution was not made for such a state of things."[78] Even though Lieber had written in *Civil Liberty* that the power to suspend the privilege of habeas corpus belonged to Congress and not the president, Lincoln's leadership during the early days of the War, when compared with Congress's relative inactivity, led Lieber to approve the president's course and to repudiate his own earlier writings. "A treatise on navigation," he observed, "is not written for a time of shipwreck."[79] Lieber's famous General Orders 100, which provided a guidebook for the Union's troops in the field, has equally been described as based on "natural law ideals."[80]

Yet other legal thinkers, however, called for a return to an older, purer common law constitutionalism precisely in order to effectuate the natural law of national self-preservation and to support the War effort. If the underlying natural law of national self-preservation was at stake, nothing could instantiate this law more effectively than the common law constitution that Americans had abandoned in 1787. England's unwritten common law constitution would thus be a better wartime fundamental law than America's written one. The clearest expositor of this position was Sidney George Fisher (1809–1871), a Pennsylvania gentleman farmer and amateur political and legal theorist, who set forth the argument in his *Trial of the Constitution* (1862).

The issue for Fisher was that the U.S. Constitution, which he dubbed a "new and untried" system, was being subjected for the first time to a severe test and coming up short. By contrast, Fisher maintained, "no such questions have arisen under the English Constitution for nearly two centuries."[81] The reason that the U.S. Constitution had run into difficulties whereas the English common law constitution had not for so long was that the former, unlike the latter, did not sufficiently reflect the fact that "the only safe foundation for government is custom – another name for

[77] Phillip S. Paludan, *A Covenant with Death: The Constitution, Law, and Equality in the Civil War Era* (Urbana, Ill.: University of Illinois Press, 1975).

[78] Francis Lieber to Judge Thayer, February 3, 1864, in Thomas Sergeant Perry, ed., *The Life and Letters of Francis Lieber* (Boston: James R. Osgood & Co., 1882), p. 340.

[79] Quoted in Paludan, *A Covenant with Death*, p. 91.

[80] Ibid., p. 95. *See also* Brainard Dyer, "Francis Lieber and the American Civil War," *Huntington Library Quarterly* 2 (July 1939): 449–465.

[81] Sidney George Fisher, *The Trial of the Constitution* (Philadelphia: J. B. Lippincott & Co., 1862), pp. v–vi.

experience – the best guide in temporal affairs."[82] It was "philosophically true," Fisher asserted, that "all law, in the long run, is and can be nothing but custom."[83] This was the case because only custom, in its capacity to blur continuity and change, to repeat the past yet respond when needed to the imperatives of present and future, effectively instantiated "the natural laws that govern society, which declare that a government is made for a people, and not a people for a government, and that an intelligent people will have a government to satisfy their intelligence."[84] Such "natural laws," true to the style of mid-nineteenth-century thought, were represented as an absolute limit on politicolegal power: they "cannot be resisted by any human contrivances."[85]

If custom was the best way of instantiating the natural limits to government, what was the right institutional mechanism for ensuring that custom could flourish and let underlying natural laws be realized? For Fisher, English parliamentary supremacy, in which Parliament reflected the needs of the people without any formal written limits, was the best way of fostering custom and of bridging past, present, and future. The written U.S. Constitution, with its various checks and balances, perpetually ran the risk of flouting the natural limits to which every government was subject. Written laws, unlike unwritten ones, came in the way of concerted action, which natural law demanded in a time of crisis.[86] Fisher put it thus:

> The difference is that in England the whole power of the people is delegated to Parliament, and the power, therefore, is always ready for action, whilst with us it can only be made available by a difficult and uncertain process, slow, though prompt measures may be important, and uncertain in its results, because the consent of three-fourths of the States or of the people, is necessary before an alteration can be made. The English organic law is the custom of the Government. It is in no danger of sudden and great innovations, for it is in the nature of custom

[82] Ibid., p. 17.

[83] Ibid., p. 18.

[84] Ibid., p. 40.

[85] Ibid., p. 48.

[86] Fisher was dismissive of the "safety valves" built into the U.S. Constitution: "The provision in the Constitution for amending it has been called a safety-valve to prevent the explosion of the passions of the people in revolutionary violence. But the efficacy of a safety-valve depends on the promptness with which it can be opened and the width of its throttle. If defective in either of these, when the pressure of steam is too high the boiler will burst." Ibid., p. 26. A page later, he writes, "The Amendment Article in our Constitution has not preserved us from the civil war.... The safety valve did not work, and the boiler has burst" (p. 27).

or habit to change slowly. It is also in its nature to be constantly changing, according to the age, circumstances and mental condition of an individual or a nation.[87]

The American view that "a written Constitution is and must remain a finality forever, to be interpreted only by itself" flouted underlying natural law. It resulted in an unacceptable static situation, according to which "the people of 1862 must submit to the people of 1787." (It is interesting that Fisher here deploys the arguments of Paine and Jefferson, but in favor of common law rather than in favor of written law.)[88] By contrast, England's common law constitution both avoided "sudden and great innovations" and was "constantly changing, according to the age, circumstances, and mental condition of an individual or a nation."

Fisher's wartime calls for a return to an older, purer English common law constitutionalism to bridge the disjunctures among past, present, and future and to close the growing breach between actually existing American law and the natural law of national self-preservation did not win many adherents. Fisher was, as such, an outlier. Even as he represents the persistent appeal of British common law constitutionalism almost a century after the American Revolution, however, Fisher shows how common lawyers during the War combined common law sensibilities with the natural law sensibilities of the period, such that the common law, shorn of the overlay of written fundamental law, could serve as the best legal framework for the prosecution of the War.

With the conclusion of the War, certain Republicans self-consciously represented themselves as "revolutionaries" for inaugurating a sharp

[87] Ibid., p. 25.

[88] Ibid., pp. 57, 67–68. Fisher also devoted a chapter to comparing the English executive with the American. The English executive, described equally as a product of common law growth, came out looking better. It was "monarchical without arbitrary power and republican without being elective.... It [was] a product of the whole past of the nation, its labors, struggles and dangers, aspirations and achievements through the centuries, and its elements may be traced up through the history of the people to feudalism, to Saxon Arthur and Alfred, nay to their German ancestors described by Tacitus, as in the acorn may be found a miniature picture of the future oak" (p. 203). This account of English executive power supported Fisher's reading that the suspension of habeas corpus was properly within the power of the executive in situations where Parliament was not in session and where "the case demanded instant and secret action" (p. 211). In suspending the writ of habeas corpus, Lincoln displayed continuity with distinguished predecessors: "He did – and the resemblance is worthy noting – precisely what William III did under similar, but far less difficult and perilous circumstances" (p. 231).

break with the past and taking a leap into the future.[89] A great deal of this revolutionary energy was marshaled into ensuring that actually existing law matched underlying natural law. In an 1865 essay entitled "American Political Ideas," Charles Eliot Norton captured the sentiments of many Radical Republicans when he argued that "politics are but a subordinate branch of morals, … and that the government is but a device for the attainment of certain ends."[90] The Civil War amendments to the U.S. Constitution were designed, accordingly, to reflect imagined underlying natural law or moral theories. Furthermore, as Robert Kaczorowski has argued, at least for a time a large number of legal actors – politicians, judges, legal officers, and so on – shared such views.[91]

In the post-War drive to eliminate the disjuncture between actually existing law and underlying natural law, a process inevitably marked by compromise and inconsistency, it was widely understood that all customs contravening such natural law, their antiquity notwithstanding, had to fall away. The venerability of any law was no defense against the imperatives of natural law. Slavery itself, which as we have seen had begun to cloak itself with the mantle of "immemorial" custom, was expunged. The question of what to do about deep-rooted practices of subordination remained. The Civil Rights Act of 1866, a forerunner of the Fourteenth Amendment, sought to establish equality with respect to contract and property rights, "any law, statute, ordinance, regulation, or custom, to the contrary notwithstanding."[92]

[89] Indiana Congressman George W. Julian described the "revolutionary days" of the mid-1860s as follows: "Whole generations of common time are now crowded into the span of a few years. Life was never before so grand and blessed an opportunity. The man mistakes his reckoning, who judges either the present or the future by any political almanac of bygone years. Growth, development, progress, are the expressive watchwords of the hour. Who can remember the marvelous events of the past four years, necessitated by the late war, and then predict the failure of further measures, woven into the same fabric, and born of the same inevitable logic?" Quoted in William Nelson, *The Fourteenth Amendment: From Political Principle to Judicial Doctrine* (Cambridge, Mass.: Harvard University Press, 1988), p. 45.

[90] Charles Eliot Norton, "American Political Ideas," *North American Review* 101 (1865): 559.

[91] Robert J. Kaczorowski, "Revolutionary Constitutionalism in the Era of the Civil War and Reconstruction," *New York University Law Review* 61 (1986): 863–940.

[92] Civil Rights Act of 1866, Section 1, 14 Stat. 27 (1866). Similar language is to be found in the Civil Rights Acts of 1870 and 1871. For a discussion of the status of the category of "custom" in the civil rights legislation of the period, see George Rutherglen, "Custom and Usage as Action Under Color of State Law: An Essay on the Forgotten Terms of Section 1983," *Virginia Law Review* 89 (2003): 925–977.

In Republican circles, this drive to subordinate legal differences and established practices across America to underlying uniform natural laws was clearly seen – and applauded – as a move to centralization. John Draper, chemist, historian, and champion of science over religion, saw centralization as the path to America's future:

> I turn from the hideous contemplation of a disorganization of the Republic, each state, and county, and town setting up for itself, and the continent swarming with maggots bred from the dead body politic. I turn from that to a future I see in prospect – an imperial race organizing its intellect, concentrating it, and voluntarily submitting to be controlled by reason.[93]

Indiana Congressman George Julian stated the Radical Republican ideal clearly: "Nationalizing the South … would tend powerfully to make our whole country homogenous."[94]

Such sentiments played directly into the hands of an emerging opposition. It is conventional wisdom among historians that Radical Republican initiatives were defeated, or at least robbed of their full potential, by a number of coalescing factors: lingering Jacksonian commitments to states' rights and fears of consolidation and corruption; weak commitments to the rights of freedmen, combined with pervasive racism, in both North and South; the desire to reconstitute the Union and to move past a history of division; and the ambitions of parties and individuals. The U.S. Supreme Court has typically shared the blame for the defeat of Radical Republican reform. To be sure, the Chase Court accepted many of the major consequences of the War: the superiority of national over state authority, the end of slavery, and the legitimacy of Congressional Reconstruction. It endorsed a nationalization of citizenship in cases such as *Crandall v. Nevada* (1868), in which it struck down a state head tax on railroad and stagecoach passengers on the ground that "the people of these United States constitute one nation."[95] In the *Slaughterhouse Cases* (1873), however, the Court's first major interpretation of the new Fourteenth Amendment, the scope of the Amendment's "Privileges and Immunities" Clause was curtailed and vitally important civil rights left in state hands. Thereafter, in *United States v. Cruikshank* (1876) and the *Civil Rights Cases* (1883), the Court further immunized private discrimination

93 John W. Draper, *Thoughts on the Future Civil Policy of America* (New York: Harper & Bros., 1865), p. 252.

94 George Julian, quoted in Keller, *Affairs of State*, p. 64.

95 *Crandall v. Nevada*, 73 U.S. 35 (1868).

from state interference, thereby setting the stage for the constitutional sanctioning of segregation in the late nineteenth century.[96]

What is interesting for our purposes in the opposition to Radical Republican centralizing trends is how their (typically Democratic) opponents phrased their opposition. To be sure, post-War Democratic arguments against Republican centralization drew upon older Jacksonian discourses that linked political decentralization to antimonopoly views.[97] But in the middle decades of the nineteenth century, decentralization was frequently expressed as an underlying natural limit to centralizing political power. At the same time, as we shall see, decentralization was invoked as part of a hallowed common law tradition. Underlying natural law and the common law came together to limit the centralizing imperatives of Radical Republicanism.

Before the War, Henry Carey had argued, it should be recalled, that decentralized government, which corresponded to the "wonderfully beautiful [law] established for the government of the universe," had reached its pinnacle with the American system of federal government.[98] Slavery, insofar as it threatened to spill over the boundaries of the slave states, was a violation of this underlying law of decentralization. Decentralization of political power, typically in the form of local self-government, was also naturalized through its association with a naturalized "race." During the War, George Fisher observed that "[t]he dominant passion of the Saxon race is for local self-government."[99] The Democrat Thomas Cooley (1824–1898), striking a similar note, claimed that decentralized government was "part of the very nature of the race to which we belong."[100] This naturalization of decentralization was very much part of the strategy of the Democratic opposition to Radical Republican centralization in the years following the War.

[96] *Slaughterhouse Cases*, 16 Wallace 36 (1873); *United States v. Cruikshank*, 92 U.S. 542 (1876); *Civil Rights Cases*, 109 U.S. 3 (1883).

[97] For example, the famous codifier David Dudley Field criticized the corruption associated with Republican centralization. He found it "quite natural" that Republicans whose theory of government "does not forbid its use for any purpose they deem useful, should seek its intervention in such schemes as require great power or capital.... Not one dollar should Congress or any State legislature hereafter grant to any road, canal, or any other corporation or individual." Field, "Corruption in Politics." *International Review* 4 (1877): 77–96, at 83.

[98] Carey, *Principles of Social Science*, Vol. 2, p. 177–178.

[99] Fisher, *Trial of the Constitution*, pp. 159–60.

[100] Joseph Story, *Commentaries on the Constitution* (2 vols.), Thomas M. Cooley, ed. (Boston: Little-Brown, 1873) Vol. 1, p. 193. These ideas echoed similar ones in Thomas M. Cooley, *A Treatise on the Constitutional Limitations Which Rest Upon the Legislative Power of the States of the American Union* (Boston: Little, Brown & Co., 1868), p. 189.

But even as Democrats opposed to Radical Republican centralization invoked the underlying natural law of decentralization as a limit to government, they turned to the common law to bolster their arguments. An earlier generation of Democrat legal thinkers such as Robert Rantoul, Jr., had disdained the common law. Post-War Democratic legal thinkers such as Thomas Cooley embraced it fervently.

Cooley's revealing titled *Treatise on Constitutional Limitations* (1868), applicable to American constitutions, federal and state, contained an extravagant paean to the common law. The common law was entirely organic. It was nothing less than an "outgrowth of the habits of thought and action of the people" and, as such, was "obviously the best body of laws to which they were suited."[101] But more important, the common law served as a limit to political authority. It had curbed an overreaching power – that of Great Britain – at the time of the American Revolution and would continue to do so in the post–Civil War period.[102]

Cooley insisted that "local self-government is ... a matter of constitutional right and the State cannot abolish it and regulate the local affairs through agents of its own appointment."[103] But in what did this constitutional right to local self-government inhere? In *Constitutional Limitations*, Cooley acknowledged that textual support for local self-government might be weak. However, Cooley argued, "constitutions are to be construed in the light of the common law, and of the fact that its rules are still left in force."[104] And the common law, Cooley argued, had recognized the right to local self-government "immemorially." Local self-government was as old as time itself: "If we question the historical records more closely we shall find that this right of local regulation has never been understood to be a grant from any central authority, but it has been recognized *as of course from the first*."[105] In fact, no historical records were consulted. Like other invocations of "immemoriality," Cooley's was an assertion, an attribution of a mysterious and protective temporality to local self-government. Armed with an "immemorial"

[101] Cooley, *A Treatise on the Constitutional Limitations*, p. 21.

[102] Ibid., p. 24 ("And when the difficulties with the home government sprang up, it was a source of immense moral power to the Colonists that they were able to show that the rights they claimed were conferred by the common law, and that the king and Parliament were seeking to deprive them of the common birthright of Englishmen").

[103] Story, *Commentaries on the Constitution* (Cooley, ed.) Vol. 1, p. 197.

[104] Cooley, *Constitutional Limitations*, p. 60.

[105] Story, *Commentaries on the Constitution* (Cooley, ed.), p. 196 (emphasis added).

right to local self-government that functioned as a supplement to written constitutional texts, Cooley was able to dispense with the problem that the U.S. and state constitutions did not explicitly recognize any right to local self-government. "*[E]ven if not expressly recognized,*" Cooley maintained, all American constitutions were "framed with [local government's] present existence and anticipated continuance in view."[106] There was as well a common lawyerly fear of revolution associated with this commitment to local self-government. Just as Joseph Story had drawn support for centralization from Edmund Burke, Cooley drew support for decentralization from Burke. For Burke, the "fatal defect" (Cooley's phrase) of the French system was that "'[t]he hand of authority was seen in everything and in every place."[107]

In fairness to Cooley, the call for decentralization was not only about defeating Radical Republican centralizing initiatives. Decentralization was a theme at all levels of post-War American governance. State constitutions in the 1870s sought to limit the scope of legislative authority. Illinois forbade its legislature to act in twenty items of local or private concern; Pennsylvania, in forty; California, in thirty-three.[108] The widely emulated Illinois Constitution of 1870 abounded "in negative rather than positive provisions, provisions rather calculated to hedge in powers which have been abused than to establish new ones."[109] The areas enjoined covered a wide range of government functions: social, economic, and political.

The post-War push to decentralize government and to limit its scope went along with a countervailing push to make government more scientific. From the perspective of intellectuals, men of politics – typically those who ran Democratic urban political machines – were constantly flouting the underlying laws of economy and society. In 1876, the scientist Simon Newcomb lamented that governance lay in the hands of "men who are not only ignorant of social laws, but incapable of exact reasoning of any kind whatever."[110] Already in 1870, *The Nation*'s editor, E. L. Godkin, called the trend toward government by commission "the next great political revolution in the western world," one that "will place men's relations in society where they never yet have been placed, under

[106] Cooley, *Constitutional Limitations*, p. 35 (emphasis added).
[107] Story, *Commentaries on the Constitution* (Cooley, ed.), Vol. 1, p. 194.
[108] Keller, *Affairs of State*, p. 112.
[109] "Book Notice," *American Law Review* 5 (1870–1871): 110–113, p. 113.
[110] Simon Newcomb, "Abstract Science in America, 1776–1876," *North American Review* 122 (1876): 88–123, at 122.

the control of trained human reason."[111] If government by commission was the solution, however, it could also be checked by Democratic judges such as Thomas Cooley, who insisted that centrally created, state-level commissions should not violate the rights of local governmental bodies. In a case involving a dispute between a state board of park commissioners and the city of Detroit, Cooley ruled for the city. Furthermore, he analogized the rights of local governments to the rights of individuals. He argued: "[T]hough municipal authorities are made use of in State government, and as such are under complete State control, they are not created exclusively for that purpose, but have other objects and purposes peculiarly local, and in which the State at large ... is legally no more concerned than it is in the individual and private concerns of its several citizens."[112] It was the long history of local self-government, sanctified by the common law, that undergirded this view. And in so doing, it was, of course, also realizing a natural limit to government.

Mid-Nineteenth-Century Legal Science: The Writings of Thomas Cooley and Joel Bishop

Quite apart from the sectional conflict and its aftermath, the middle decades of the nineteenth century were decades of dramatic technological, industrial, and social change. Particularly after the War, as talk of "scientific" government by commission burgeoned around them, common law thinkers felt called upon to make a case for the continued relevance of the common law in a rapidly changing society.[113] In this section, I explore the writings of Thomas Cooley and Joel Bishop, two rather different figures. A prominent judge himself, Cooley celebrated the traditional figure of the common law judge, arguing that the common law judge was better suited than legislatures or legislative commissions to capture rapid social change. Bishop represents a new development on the American legal landscape: a professional treatise writer lacking a judicial or university appointment. As a professional treatise writer, Bishop was at pains

[111] E. L. Godkin, "The Prospects of the Political Art," *North American Review* 110 (1870): 388–419, at 417; "Legislation and Social Science," *Journal of Social Science* 3 (1871): 115–132.

[112] *People v. Common Council of Detroit*, 28 Mich. 228 (1873), 236 (Cooley, J.).

[113] Howard Schweber has argued that the mid-nineteenth century was a period of enormous legal transformation spurred by technological, industrial, and social change. Schweber, *The Creation of American Common Law, 1850–1880: Technology, Politics, and the Construction of Citizenship* (Cambridge: Cambridge University Press, 2004).

to argue that only professional jurisprudes such as himself, as opposed to common law judges, could truly systematize the common law.

Cooley and Bishop fully shared the scientistic temper of the times. Their writings reveal that "normal" legal science in the middle decades of the nineteenth century – that is, legal science dealing with issues other than the sectional conflict and its aftermath – exhibited the same concern with identifying ahistorical underlying natural laws or principles in terms of which existing law could be judged. The common law would be rationalized in keeping with this scientistic style. This would make out the case for its continued relevance in a society buffeted by change and increasingly aware of the need for the rationalization of law and government. Even as they subjected the common law to the test of underlying natural laws, however, both Cooley and Bishop would rely, albeit in different ways, on the nonhistorical temporalities of the common law. Cooley would recognize the need for judicial creativity in the search for underlying natural principles but dissolve judicial creativity into the common law temporality of "insensibility." Bishop would maintain, paradoxically, that the common law, entirely by itself, ended up realizing the very underlying natural principles that he, as jurist, identified. If the common law was rendered an object of scientific contemplation, in other words, it supplied its own temporalities to undergird science.

It was a mistake to believe, Thomas Cooley argued, that the momentous transformations in economy, technology, and society that had taken place in the middle decades of the nineteenth century had reduced the need for common law. Indeed, precisely the opposite was true. As he put it, "Probably popular legislation [Cooley's term for a spontaneously and organically evolving common law] was never so active as now. The reasons for this are all about us – in the wonderful activity of invention and production; in the marvelous expansion of business; in the infinite variety of new conditions to which law must be conformed."[114] Constant change rendered legislative activity outmoded and precedents unsteady. This underscored the importance of the common law judge, who – as a Blackstonian "oracle of the law" – effortlessly "read" the community and grasped its changes. A sitting judge on the Michigan Supreme Court, Cooley illustrated this point with an example drawn from the new context of railroads, an area in which he was perhaps the nation's leading legal authority:

[114] Thomas M. Cooley, "Labor and Capital Before the Law," *North American Review* 139 (1884): 503–516, at 504.

But on all such [new] questions observation and experience are the chief teachers; and the judge, when he comes to deal with them, finds that everybody in any way concerned in railroads has been doing something to enlighten his judgment and solve the legal difficulty. Railroad managers, and conductors, and brakemen, and switchmen; the shippers and receivers of goods; those who travel, and those who go to the trains to receive or dismiss them; the very tramps that jump on and off the moving trains, with occasional loss of foot or arm; in fact, everybody who is concerned in providing or appropriating the comforts and conveniences the railroad affords, has been thinking upon and in some measure doing something to solve the judicial problem; and the judge finds that a store of wisdom has been accumulated by various classes and various interests wherewith he may enlighten his mind. He may even find that this is not only important by way of instruction, but that in fact it has established rules to which railroad managers, as well as the community at large, have already begun to conform, or, at least, have already come to perceive that they must conform when occasion arises for an authoritative declaration of the law in an actual controversy.

The preceding paragraph reveals a highly traditional vision of the role of the common law judge fitted out to suit an entirely new context. To a greater extent than any legislature or commission, Cooley argues, the common law judge is close to the entire people; he grasps the entire social panorama; he is always "taking note of the formation of customs among the people."[115] When the judge speaks, in other words, he is simply articulating what has already come into existence, entirely of its own accord, in the community.

In addition to the common law judge's ability to embody the practices of the community, the common law's long association with decentralization – which we have already seen to be one of Cooley's major political and legal commitments – was also relevant as a way of coping with unprecedented technological, economic, and social change. The political decentralization to which Cooley was so committed in his reading of the post–Civil War constitutions translated into a celebration of the virtues of self-regulation, thereby illustrating the intimate connections between Jacksonian politicolegal thought, its post-War appropriation of common law ideas, and nineteenth-century laissez-faire. Cooley described it thus: "We begin self-government in the family; we establish it in the several towns, cities, counties, and states; and we suffer it to exist, also, in the several trades and occupations." The common law recognized and embraced this legal pluralism, once again as part of its intrinsic ability to recognize what already existed:

Thus, bankers have special rules of their own making for the regulation of their business, common carriers for theirs, telegraph companies for theirs, etc.; and

[115] Ibid., pp. 505–06.

> we must all conform to these rules when having business with those who establish them. This the law does not merely tolerate, but encourages, because those engaged in the business know best what the rules should be, and the rules are made by experts after experience and observation have demonstrated their usefulness. This is legislation by the parties who most of all are competent to deal wisely with the subject; and so long as it is properly limited, the state would be inexcusable if, by the agency of the legislators of less experience and less competency, it were to interfere.[116]

Cooley was thus an enthusiastic supporter of boards of trade and self-instituted judicial tribunals in various trades.

None of this is to say that Cooley was at all averse to the scientific improvement of the common law. Indeed, he was committed to it. Like many common lawyers, however, he was insistent that improvement come internally, only from trained lawyers.[117]

For Cooley, the scientific reform of the common law would take the form of constructing legal "principles" that lay beyond and beneath decided cases. Cooley's legal "principle" was what I have been calling the law underlying the actually existing law (the individual case or adjudication). As he put it, "The case is not the measure of the principle; it does not limit and confine it within the exact facts, but it furnishes an illustration of the principle, which, perhaps, might still have been applied, had some of the facts been different."[118] The judicial craft was not about deciding one case in terms of another, but about establishing the general principle. This construction of principles that lay beyond cases – a method that Cooley *approvingly* labels, in response to Bentham, "judicial legislation" – was "not only more efficient, but also more useful, in establishing the rules by which private rights are to be determined ... than has been the regular and formal enactment of laws."[119] In other words, common law judges, in performing legal science, were better able to rationalize law than legislatures were.

[116] Ibid., p. 508.

[117] "In the improvement of law in its administration, the field must be left to the lawyer almost exclusively. Strong men may sometimes stand apart and condemn, but safe reform must come from within the profession. Those who handle the machinery know best where the jar is, and where worn out wheels need removing and new gearing applied. The natural conservatism of the progression may demand occasional spurring, but in the improvement of the law wisdom requires that haste be made slowly." Thomas M. Cooley, *The State of the Law: A Test of National Progress; Address to the Graduating Class of the Law Department of Michigan University* (Ann Arbor, Mich.: J. Moore, 1877), p. 9.

[118] Thomas M. Cooley, *A Treatise on the Law of Torts or the Wrongs Which Arise Independent of Contract* (Chicago: Callaghan & Co., 1870), pp. 12–13.

[119] Ibid., p. 13.

But Cooley was compelled to recognize that, in the search for underlying principles, common law judges might occasionally be at odds with their more traditional role as declarants of the changing customs of the community. In other words, the imperatives of science might be in tension with an organic mapping of popular practices. This was especially true where cases were entirely unprecedented, which happened often enough, such that there were no already formed customs to guide the judge. In such cases, Cooley declared, "[t]he usage ... must come *after* the decision has established the principle." Indeed, Cooley continued, "With these cases in view, it will be evident that the common law is something *more* than a body of usages; it is that, indeed, but it also embraces the principles which underlie the usages." Thus, even as the common law could be celebrated as standing for the customs and the usages of the people, there was an external point – the principle – that underlay such usages and in fact gave rise to them. Cooley would even claim that "*a very considerable proportion of the common law has had its real origin in judicial action, which has accepted many things for law, and rejected many others, and by a sifting process has made the law what we find it now.*"[120]

This would suggest that the mid-nineteenth-century common law judge was declaring principles that only *eventually* came to underlie individual cases and indeed usages themselves. Far from usages anticipating the declarations of the common law judge, the declarations of the common law judge were anticipating usages. Where did this authority to declare principles come from, particularly in a society with a long history of arguing that the people made their own law? Cooley performs a familiar acrobatics, resorting to the common law fiction that the common law could simultaneously be new and old. He maintains that the principle that the judge constructs in advance of customs is in fact not new at all. Rather, it is one that "from time immemorial ... has constituted a part of the common law of the land, *and ... has only not been applied before, because no occasion has arisen for its application.*"[121] In other words, even as a judge creates a principle for an entirely unprecedented case (say, in the rapidly changing context of railroads), he is drawing from some unknown, but always already existent, recess of the "immemorial" past. This is nothing other than the Blackstonian idea that the common law judge, even as he corrected previous errors and responded to changing circumstances, never made new law.

[120] Ibid., p. 14 (emphasis added in all three quotations).
[121] Ibid., p. 15 (emphasis added).

Equally important, judicially declared principles, even if they are at odds with existing usages, are extended in a way that matches the non-historical common law temporality of "insensibility." Cooley wrote, "In this steady and almost imperceptible change [as principles are developed] must be found the chief advantages of a judicial development of the law over a statutory development."[122] The slow extension of principles – even when principles precede usages – is what gives rise to a "habitual reception and spontaneous obedience." Thus, even though judge-scientists are declaring underlying principles in advance of usages, the temporality of their activity makes people believe that the common law is their own instead of coming from a superior authority (the legislature or a commission). "The people then may be said to be their own policemen; they habitually restrain their actions within the limits of the law, instead of waiting the compulsion of legal process."[123] Thus, Cooley manages to do mid-nineteenth-century legal science and be a highly traditional common law judge all at once. If legal science provides a perspective on the common law, it proceeds from out of the common law itself, relying upon the common law's nonhistorical temporalities for its legitimacy.

An even more striking example of the search for laws underlying actually existing laws might be found in the writings of the legal commentator Joel Prentiss Bishop (1814–1901). Virtually ignored today, Bishop was among the most prominent American legal writers of his day. Lacking a judicial or university appointment, Bishop made his career by systematizing areas of law for the consumption of the legal profession and general public. This gave him an additional incentive, as it were, to emphasize the importance of finding natural laws underlying actually existing laws. Bishop would argue that common law judges, caught up in day-to-day adjudications, were unable to perform this scientific work. Only the professional treatise writer could do so.[124]

[122] Ibid., p. 15.

[123] Ibid.

[124] I was introduced to Bishop by Stephen Siegel, "Joel Bishop's Orthodoxy," *Law and History Review* 13 (1995): 215–259. Historians of family law such as Michael Grossberg and Hendrik Hartog have also turned to Bishop's writings.The corpus of Bishop's writings, stretching from 1850 to 1900, is immense. New editions of his treatises often involved substantial revision (he certainly always claimed they did). The major legal treatises include *Commentaries on the Law of Marriage and Divorce* (first published in 1852; 7 eds.); *Commentaries on the Criminal Law* (first published in 1856; 7 eds.); *Commentaries on the Law of Criminal Procedure* (first published in 1866; 3 eds.); *The First Book of the Law* (1868); *Commentaries on the Law of Married Women* (1871–1875); *Commentaries on the Law of Statutory Crimes* (first published in 1873; 3 eds.); *The Doctrines of the Law of Contracts* (first published in 1878; republished as

In a series of articles published in the *American Law Register* in the mid-1850s, Bishop reveals the outlines of an understanding of law that would never leave his published writings. He began the series by highlighting what he deemed a matter of pressing concern, namely the massive explosion of reported cases. "[W]e have already reported in this country, more cases than are found in the English books; we have thirty-one states, and no tribunal is obliged to follow the decisions in a sister state."[125] This flood of cases, he warned, would only grow greater. What, then, was the lawyer to do? Bishop's advice was telling. "Let [the lawyer] feel below the rubbish of cases for the solid timber of *principle*, and from such material ... let the fabric of our future American Jurisprudence be reared."[126] More emphatically than Thomas Cooley, Bishop insisted that individual cases were not underlying principles or laws. Indeed, it could often be the case that an underlying principle or law could not be found in *any* individual adjudicated case. But this would not make the principle any less a principle.[127]

Commentaries on the Law of Contracts (1887)); *Commentaries on the Written Laws and Their Interpretation* (1882); *Directions and Forms* (1885); *Commentaries on the Non-Contract Law* (1889); *New Commentaries on Marriage, Divorce and Separation* (1891); *New Commentaries on the Criminal Law* (1892); *New Commentaries on the Law of Criminal Procedure* (1895–1896); and *Law in General and as a Profession* (1901). In addition to legal treatises, Bishop published tracts and pamphlets on issues of contemporary concern, the most important of which are *Thoughts for the Times* (1863); *Secession and Slavery* (1864); *The Law of Nolle Prosequi in Criminal Causes* (1876); *Strikes and Their Related Questions* (1886); and *The Common Law and Codification* (1888). He was also a contributor to journals ranging from the *American Law Register* to the *American Law Review*. Biographical information about Bishop can be found in *Central Law Journal* 20 (April 24, 1885): 321–322, and from Charles S. Bishop, "Joel Prentiss Bishop, LL.D.," *American Law Review* 36 (1902): 1–9.

125 Joel P. Bishop, "Law in the United States," *American Law Register* 3 (1854–1855): 60–61, at 60.

126 Ibid., pp. 60–61.

127 "Suppose, then, a proposition is presented to us, and we wish to determine whether it is a principle of our law. Suppose we find, on examination, that it has never been recognized in any of the cases; but suppose we further find, that it will uniformly lead to conclusions which commend themselves as just, and, on bringing it to the test of the cases, find also that wherever it is applicable to the facts it leads to the same results which the judges arrived at by other processes of reasoning. Can one deny that such a proposition is actually a principle of the law? It has in its favor all that any principle has; it conforms to abstract justice, and to the cases which it harmonizes. Surely the fact, that no judge has happened to observe or mention it, cannot affect the question." Joel P. Bishop, "Legal Principles: No. III," *American Law Register* 3 (1854–1855): 252–254 Bishop made this point repeatedly. See, e.g., Joel P. Bishop, *Commentaries on the Law of Criminal Procedure, or Pleading, Evidence, and Practice in Criminal Cases* (Boston: Little, Brown & Co, 1866), Vol. 1, Preface.

In sharp contrast to Cooley, Bishop also denigrated the abilities of the common law judge. He exhibited little commitment to the traditional idea that the common law judge spoke for the community. The common law judge, Bishop observed, was no better equipped than the average lawyer to sniff out the underlying law or principle:

Besides, we should remember that a judge has no better opportunity to know what is a legal principle, than the humblest man in the ranks of the profession. This knowledge depends upon the person's natural capabilities and his experience, study and reflection. We think we have sufficiently shown that Courts do not decide principles, but cases, though, of course, in deciding the latter, they must have a certain recognition of the former.[128]

Bishop even argued that "if a judge, in a case which we know to have been correctly decided, has distinctly laid it down as a principle of law, that does not necessarily establish it as such, though it may go far as evidence to our minds that it is."[129] This self-conscious diminution of the significance of common law adjudication and the common law judge cleared ground for the systematizing jurist, namely Bishop himself. Bishop declared grandly, "The uttering of abstract doctrines is for text-writers."[130] Differently put, "[A] decision should never be deemed a fit guide for the future until it has passed through the hands of a competent jurist."[131] If American lawyers followed this path, "[o]ur jurisprudence will become ... more like the European, but vastly better, departing essentially from the technical and unscientific form it wears in England."[132] Bishop was arguing for a system like the German, in which nonjudicial legal experts – often members of the professoriate – enjoyed considerable prestige in declaring the state of the law.

[128] Joel P. Bishop, "Legal Principles: No. V," *American Law Register* 3 (1854–1855): 381–384, at 383.

[129] Bishop, "Legal Principles: No. III," pp. 252, 253. See also Joel P. Bishop, *Commentaries on the Law of Married Women Under the Statutes of the Several States and at Common Law and in Equity* (2 vols.) (Boston: Little, Brown & Co., 1873), Vol. 1, p. 316.

[130] Joel P. Bishop, *Commentaries on the Law of Marriage and Divorce, with the Evidence, Practice, Pleading, and Forms: Also of Separations without Divorce, and of the Evidence of Marriage in All Issues* (6th ed.) (2 vols.) (Boston: Little, Brown & Co., 1881), Vol. 1, p. xvi.

[131] Bishop, *Commentaries on the Non-Contract Law: And Especially as to Common Affairs not of Contract or the Every-day Rights and Torts* (Chicago: T. H. Flood & Co., 1889), p. 628.

[132] Joel P. Bishop, "Law in the United States," *American Law Register* 3 60, 61 (1854–1855): 60–61, at 61.

Bishop the jurist was acutely aware that underlying laws and principles were to be made and not found. The treatise writer was as much an artist as a scientist. As time went on, Bishop became more and more open about just how subjective the identification of underlying principles was. For example, in the preface to the 1852 edition of his treatise on marriage and divorce, he stated that, although he could have presented the cases "as drift-wood upon the stream of our jurisprudence," he had instead elected to present a "vessel of parts and proportions as symmetrical as it was in my power to build."[133] By the 1880s, he could state, "A jurist work is a picture of the law. Necessarily, therefore, it is taken from a single standpoint, occupied by an eye not double or treble-visioned, and it is drawn by the one skilled hand."[134] While contemporary reviewers hailed Bishop as a "shining mountain," his insistence on offering abstract principles was often criticized for ignoring the specificities of what courts had actually decided, something practitioners – who were his market – needed to know. Indeed, if Bishop saw himself as an artist, reviewers employed the same analogy. The reference was to the pre-Impressionistic style of Camille Corot:

> If we could compare a law book to a landscape painting, we should say that nothing so much resembles Mr. Bishop's books as Corot's paintings. Every one must remember what an entire absence of distinct outline there is in the landscapes of that great master. One gets a dim suggestion of a house, a tree, a hill, an animal; but he is to supply a vast indefiniteness by drawing upon his imagination. So it is with Mr. Bishop's books. They are a cloudy outline of the law; a landscape dimly seen through a fog, or when the sun is eclipsed, or seen by a man whose eyesight is defective.[135]

As Bishop applied the science of identifying underlying principles to the body of the common law, he found himself compelled to confront the common law's historicity. It was a mistake, he argued, to think that the common law had "been nourished and reared by a long line of illustrious

[133] Bishop, *Commentaries on the Law of Marriage and Divorce*, Vol. 1, p. vii (quoting preface to the 1852 ed.).

[134] Joel P. Bishop, "The Common Law as a System of Reasoning, – How and Why Essential to Good Government; What its Perils, and How Averted," *American Law Review* 22 (1888): 1–29, at 19. This article was delivered as an address before the South Carolina Bar Association at Columbia, South Carolina, on December 8, 1887, and subsequently republished as Joel P. Bishop, *Common Law and Codification; or, The Common Law as a System of Reasoning, – How and Why Essential to Good Government; What its Perils, and How Averted* (Chicago: T. H. Flood & Co., 1888).

[135] Review, Joel Bishop, *Directions and Forms*, *American Law Review* 19 (1885): 455–471, at 465.

judges selected from the foremost minds of a learned profession." This was entirely in keeping with Bishop's denigration of the common law judge. Instead:

> [I]t is, in truth, in a large degree uncared for and untamed. If, in fact, it had been nourished and reared by anybody, it would not be as it is now. So hopeful and vigorous a birth as that of the common law was never before known. It has sucked wild berries, frolicked and slept without the care of mother or nurse, careered as the surrounding happenings called it out; and still it is vigorous, yet untutored and unkempt.[136]

Bishop dealt with this wild law by conceiving of the world of legal phenomena as an interplay of underlying laws and exceptions. He thus shared the historical vision of a range of mid-nineteenth-century thinkers, from Henry Carey to Lysander Spooner to George Fitzhugh. With his acute sense of the aesthetics of principles, Bishop insisted that the underlying principle or law should let slip as few exceptions as possible (one reason that reviewers accused him of vagueness).[137] Rather than seeing law as a relatively equally weighted interplay of laws and exceptions, Bishop also preferred, where possible, to see law as an interplay of multiple principles. This corresponded better to the order of the natural world, in which multiple underlying laws interacted with each other.[138]

But Bishop was compelled to admit that, notwithstanding his best ordering efforts, there were undeniably exceptions. There was always something contingent about the common law that could not be reduced to underlying principles. "Unscientific" legislators, judges, and lawyers were continually marring the harmony and uniformity of law that the jurist organized into principles. For example, a principle found to be entirely correct could nevertheless end up conflicting "with a series of adjudications that could not be overthrown"; in such a case, "we should be obliged to admit, that there was an *exception* to the principle."[139] In the case of the law of criminal procedure, for example, Bishop owned up to stating "some doctrines with less confidence of their being harmonious with what judges will hold in future cases, than he sometimes state[d]

[136] Bishop, *Commentaries on the Non-Contract Law*, p. 617.

[137] Joel P. Bishop, "Legal Principles: No. VI," 3 *American Law Register* 3 (1854–1855): 505–507, at 505–506.

[138] Ibid.

[139] Joel P. Bishop, "Legal Principles: No. VII," *American Law Register* 3 (1854–1855): 632–635, at 634 (emphasis in original).

legal propositions."[140] It was history that was responsible for such uncertainties: "The reason of the present uncertainty in the law of criminal procedure, lies partly in its history."[141]

Notwithstanding his willingness to subject the common law to the scientistic-historicist predilections of his time and his recognition that the common law was riddled with exceptions to principles, Bishop urged considerable caution when it came to reforming the common law. This cautious attitude toward reforming the common law stemmed from a profound conservatism. Bishop openly claimed the status of conservative, a man who had escaped what he called "the poison of radicalism and fanaticism."[142] This translated into a Burkean suspicion of the sudden change that came from a sense that the politicolegal subject could remake the world. In his only systematic jurisprudential work, *The First Book of the Law*, Bishop approvingly quoted Burke for the following proposition:

> We are all born in subjection, all born equally, high and low, governors and governed, in subjection to one great, immutable, pre-existent law, prior to all our devises, and prior to all our contrivances, paramount to all our ideas, and all our sensations, antecedent to our very existence, by which are knit and connected in the eternal frame of the universe, out of which we cannot stir. This great law does not arise from our conventions or compacts; on the contrary, it gives to our conventions and compacts all the forms and sanction they can have – it does not arise from our vain institutions.[143]

Bishop's Burkean embrace of the idea of a great law prior "to our conventions and compacts" led to his view that the common law not be casually overridden in the name of principles, including – paradoxically – the principles that he himself was so busily identifying in his role as jurisprude. This was especially true when it came to one of his specialties, the law of marriage, divorce, and women's property rights, an area of considerable ferment in the mid-nineteenth century. Legal reform in

[140] Joel P. Bishop, *Commentaries on the Law of Criminal Procedure or Pleading, Evidence and Practice in Criminal Cases* (2 vols.) (Boston: Little, Brown & Co., 1866), Vol. 1, p. 7

[141] Bishop, *Commentaries on the Law of Criminal Procedure*, Vol. 1, p. 7.

[142] Joel P. Bishop, *Secession and Slavery: or the Constitutional Duty of Congress to give the Elective Franchise and Freedom to all Loyal Persons, in Response to the Act of Secession* (Boston: A. Williams, 1866), p. 40.

[143] Joel P. Bishop, *First Book of the Law: Explaining the Nature, Sources, Books, and Practical Applications of Legal Science, and Methods of Study and Practice* (Boston: Little, Brown & Co., 1868), p. 67.

this area had to take account of community norms because "[t]he habits of a community and the laws by which it is governed will, in some way, adjust themselves to each other, whether we think they ought to do so or not.... [E]xperience proves that the habits make the law, and not the law the habits."[144] And habit itself was in flux. "A part of every community adheres to the old, and a part is pressing forward toward the new. The consequence of which is, that it would be very impolitic for the law now, more so than in any previous age, to establish, as between husband and wife, any uniform rule of property."[145]

Even as Bishop cautioned that underlying principles should not override custom, he also suggested that custom somehow ended up constituting principles. Thus, Bishop could state:

> The law is a system of rules, in a measure technical and artificial, eliminated in the main from judicial decisions, by judges, by legal practitioners, and by text-writers, – added to, modified, perfected, and made more binding from age to age, – the work of multitudes of minds, the growth of centuries. It is composed of what, for the want of a better word, are called "reasons;" but they are not the reasons of able men destitute of legal education, they are "legal reasons." Or, we say it is composed of "principles;" but they are not the principles of honest men who are not lawyers, they are "legal principles."[146]

What Bishop is invoking here on behalf of principles is nothing other than the Cokean "artificial reason" of the common law.[147] But there is a contradictory relationship between Bishop's science and the common law. For Bishop, the individual judicial pronouncement is a mere speck of time; it requires a jurisprude such as himself, positioned outside the courtroom, to make sense of the individual judicial pronouncement in terms of an underlying law or principle. However, when these mere specks of time – described in sweeping common law vocabulary as "the work of multitudes of minds, the growth of centuries" – join up with one another, one arrives – spontaneously – at the very legal principles that the jurisprude identifies. In other words, where underlying legal principles can be used to make sense of the common law, the common law – as it has developed over extended periods of time – itself yields the very same underlying legal principles. Even as Bishop shares the scientific temper of

[144] Joel P. Bishop, *Commentaries on the Law of Married Women*, Vol. 1, p. 674.
[145] Ibid., p. 675.
[146] Ibid., Vol. 2, p. vi.
[147] Bishop was fond of invoking Coke's notion of "artificial reason." See, e.g., Bishop, *First Book of the Law*, pp. 54–55.

the times, his Burkean conservatism makes him argue that the common law itself accomplishes what science could accomplish. This is both an endorsement of the scientific enterprise of rationalizing the common law and an undercutting of the same enterprise. It is as if Bishop pulls himself out of the common law tradition to make sense of it and then dissolves himself into it.

Conclusion

The preceding reveals how a sense of history as consisting of an interplay of underlying laws and their contingent exceptions was applied by legal thinkers in a range of contexts in the mid-nineteenth century: the slavery debates, discussions about the prosecution of the Civil War, post-War debates about centralization and decentralization, and "normal" legal science generally. Such discussions bore tragic consequences for freedmen seeking to vindicate rights of citizenship in what appeared to be a brief moment of promise in the post–Civil War years.

It says a great deal about the future of Reconstruction that George Fitzhugh briefly became a judge in the Freedmen's Court in Richmond, Virginia (Fitzhugh served as judge from October 1865 until the end of 1866).[148] To the extent that the tutelary functions of the Freedmen's Bureau implied a measure of recognition of blacks' inferiority, Fitzhugh approved of the Bureau. He saw it as a vast "Negro Nursery" that rested upon the underlying natural or social law of racial difference. As such, Northerners were now coming to acknowledge what Southerners had long acknowledged:

> This Negro Nursery is an admirable idea of the Federals, which, however, they stole from us. For we always told them the darkeys were but grown-up children that needed guardians, like all other children. They saw this very soon, and therefore established the Freedmen's Bureau; at first for a year, thinking that a year's tuition under Yankee school ma'ams and Federal Provost Marshals would amply fit them for self-support, liberty and equality, and the exercise of the right of suffrage.... At the end of that time, they will discover that their pupils are irreclaimable "*mauvais sujets*" and will be ready to throw up 'in divine disgust' the whole negro-nursing and negro-teaching business, and to turn the affair over to the State authorities.[149]

[148] Wish, *George Fitzhugh*, p. 313.

[149] George Fitzhugh, "Camp Lee and the Freedmen's Bureau," *De Bow's Review (After the War Series II)* (1866): 346–355, at 347.

However, to the extent that Northerners were trying to accomplish more – that is, lay the foundations of a more genuine equality between blacks and whites – Fitzhugh was irrevocably opposed in the name of a conjoined nature and custom: "[I]mmemorial usage, law, custom, and divine injunction, nay human nature itself, have subordinated inferior races to superior races."[150]

Underlying natural laws were also invoked to justify the limits of politics in the context of women's rights. In *Bradwell v. Illinois* (1873), a case in which the U.S. Supreme Court was asked to consider the applicability of the Fourteenth Amendment to an Illinois law that barred women from the practice of law, Justice Bradley, in a concurring opinion, upheld the Illinois law in the following terms, in which the words "nature," "natural," "the nature of things," "the general condition of things," and so on are repeated almost as incantations:

> [T]he civil law, as well as nature herself, has always recognized a wide difference in the respective spheres and destinies of man and woman. Man is, or should be, woman's protector and defender. The natural and proper timidity and delicacy which belongs to the female sex evidently unfits it for many of the occupations of civil life. The constitution of the family organization, which is founded in the divine ordinance, as well as in the nature of things, indicates the domestic sphere as that which properly belongs to the domain and functions of womanhood. The harmony, not to say identity, of interests and views which belong, or should belong, to the family institution is repugnant to the idea of a woman adopting a distinct and independent career from that of her husband.... The paramount destiny and mission of woman are to fulfil the noble and benign offices of wife and mother. This is the law of the Creator. And the rules of civil society must be adapted to the general constitution of things, and cannot be based upon exceptional cases.... In the nature of things it is not every citizen of every age, sex, and condition that is qualified for every calling and position.[151]

Thus, because the Illinois law barring women from the practice of law was a reflection of an underlying "nature herself," the "natural ... timidity" of women, the "divine ordinance," "the nature of things," the "paramount destiny and mission of woman," "the law of the Creator," and "the general condition of things," it could be found constitutional (this was not, to be sure, the only legal basis of the decision). The adoption of the position urged by the law's challenger – an individual with

150 George Fitzhugh, "What's to Be Done with the Negroes?" *De Bow's Review (After the War Series I)* (1866): 577–581, at 580.

151 *Bradwell v. Illinois*, 83 U.S. (16 Wall.) 130 (1872), pp. 141–142 (opinion of Justice Bradley).

ambitions for her sex that exceeded those that society deemed her sex's lot – represented the "exceptional case."

Yet even as an underlying natural law was invoked to demonstrate the correspondence or noncorrespondence of man-made laws to it, it was also clear that the very idea of nature was changing. In 1874, William Cooper, a judge and editor of the Tennessee reports, published a series of articles in the *Southern Law Review* entitled "Modern Theories of Government." The articles, Cooper indicated, were "compiled from notes made in Europe in the year 1863, during a course of political readings resorted to, to relieve the tedium of exile."[152] But the way Cooper began the series itself suggests that the model of nature relied upon by writers such as Carey, Spooner, Sawyer, Fitzhugh, Fisher, Cooley, and Bishop had made a place for something else:

> Modern Geologists are agreed that nothing is so unstable as the surface of our (so-called) "firm-fixed earth." The solid crust on which we tread with so much confidence, and which we have been taught to believe coeval at least with our race, is in a continuous state of oscillation; now rising by a slow and gradual elevation, now sinking by a similarly progressive depression; now lifted by subterranean throes that shake to atoms the 'insubstantial pageants' of human greatness, and, anon, settling in its unstable bed until the waters of the ocean roll over the habitations of man.[153]

Nature itself had acquired a measure of contingency and, as we shall see, a measure of mystery. The late-nineteenth-century models of history in relationship to which legal thinkers would seek to place the common law would, to various degrees, reflect this new sensibility.

[152] William F. Cooper, "Modern Theories of Government: Number One," *Southern Law Review* 3 (1874): 28–46, at 28, n. 1.
[153] Ibid., p. 28.

6

Time as Life

Common Law Thought in the Late Nineteenth Century

The Relations of "Life"

During the last quarter of the nineteenth century and spilling over into the twentieth, as the United States grew into a large-scale industrial economy, it began to experience a new set of problems: mounting capital–labor conflict, massive income inequality, spreading urbanization, and mass immigration. Beginning in the 1870s, in response to such pressures, a variety of groups – farmers, workers, businesses, consumers, reformers – called increasingly stridently for government intervention in economy and society. The federal and state governments responded with a spate of legislation that regulated railroads, utilities, banks, and insurance companies; reigned in monopolies; and sought to reshape capital–labor relations. But there was also considerable opposition to such regulation from a variety of quarters, ranging from those generally distrustful of government to big business interests to a common law–centered bench and bar traditionally hostile to legislation. Increasingly, American democracy would be discussed in terms of the contest between laissez-faire and social democracy, between the immunity of the private sphere from legislative interference and the power of democratic majorities to regulate it.[1]

[1] An astute observer such as James Bryce would argue that it was simplistic to oppose laissez-faire and social democracy in late-nineteenth-century America without paying attention to the differences between discourses and practices. In *The American Commonwealth* (1888), Bryce described Americans' "sentimental" attachment to laissez-faire as being traceable to "such revered documents as the Declaration of Independence and the older State constitutions." Nevertheless, Bryce insisted, "The new democracies of America are just as eager for state interference as the democracy of England, and try their experiments with even more light-hearted promptitude." James Bryce, *The American Commonwealth*

In the late nineteenth century, although there were strands of laissez-faire thought that reached back to the Scottish Enlightenment through Jackson and Jefferson, by far the most significant version of laissez-faire thought, replete with a coherent philosophy of history, was that associated with what we now call Social Darwinism. In his landmark *Social Darwinism in American Thought* (1944), Richard Hofstadter observed, "In some respects the United States during the last three decades of the nineteenth century and at the beginning of the twentieth century was *the* Darwinian country.... Herbert Spencer, who of all men made the most ambitious attempt to systematize the implications of evolution in fields other than biology itself, was far more popular in the United States than he was in his native country."[2] There is much to support this view. Quite in addition to convincing prominent industrialists like Andrew Carnegie of the worth of his ideas, Spencer cast a heavy shadow across America's newly reorganized universities, permeating economics, history, philosophy, political science, and sociology. William James's obituary for Spencer credited him, furthermore, with having "enlarged the imagination and set free the speculative mind of countless doctors, engineers and lawyers, of many physicists and chemists, and of thoughtful laymen generally."[3] If one is to make sense of the late-nineteenth-century debate between laissez-faire and social democracy, we must turn to Spencer's thought.

In turning to Spencer's thought, however, I attempt to do more than present the late nineteenth century's most influential account of laissez-faire. To be sure, Spencer sought to cabin the sphere of political democracy by advancing a teleological philosophy of history that portrayed an autonomously and "unconsciously" functioning industrial society as the future of man. The state – especially the increasingly intrusive regulatory state of the late nineteenth century – was confidently expected to fall away. Such views were undoubtedly popular. But many in Great Britain and America, witness to the ill effects of industrialization and urbanization, would also reject Spencer's conservative politics, especially

(2 vols.) (London: Macmillan & Co., 1888) (1891), Vol. 2, pp. 418–419, 422. Bryce went on to compare the different kinds of state regulation in England and America to show that America enjoyed as much regulation as England.

2 Richard Hofstadter, *Social Darwinism in American Thought* (rev. ed.) (New York: George Braziller, Inc., 1959) (1944), pp. 4–5 (emphasis in original). See also Mike Hawkins, *Social Darwinism in European and American Thought, 1860–1945: Nature as Model and Nature as Threat* (Cambridge: Cambridge University Press, 1997).

3 Quoted in J. D. Y. Peel, *Herbert Spencer: The Evolution of a Sociologist* (New York: Basic Books, 1971), p. 1.

his arguments for political paralysis in the name of a slowly unfolding historical logic. Calls for reform were everywhere.

Spencer's real influence might lie elsewhere: in his turning away from final causes, in his insistence on conceiving of knowledge in terms of the joining up of phenomena, in his modern notion of context, in his appropriation of the Darwinian languages of "life." Such insights and vocabularies would be employed by his admirers and his critics, by William Graham Sumner as much as by Henry George, by conservative common lawyers such as James Coolidge Carter and by critical and skeptical ones such as Oliver Wendell Holmes, Jr. The following discussion of Spencer is intended, then, not only to draw attention to the historical and political sensibilities of late-nineteenth-century laissez-faire, but also to highlight a set of extremely influential insights and vocabularies that could be taken in different directions depending on the thinker.

Herbert Spencer (1820–1903) came from the culture of midcentury middle-class English provincial radicalism.[4] In his intellectual milieu, politics was seen as a sphere of hereditary advantage that placed obstacles in the path of the self-betterment of men of his background. By contrast, the underlying laws of nature or society or economy were considered better ways of getting at the truth. Spencer's early writings thus reveal the same concern with finding underlying social and natural laws – and with identifying exceptions to such laws – that were so much a feature of mid-nineteenth-century thought. However, in one critical respect, Spencer differed from a midcentury thinker like Henry Carey. Where Carey and many other mid-nineteenth-century thinkers posited underlying natural laws as constant and invariable, Spencer insisted on the ubiquity of ceaseless change. In *Social Statics* (1851), he put it thus:

> It is a trite enough remark that change is the law of all things: true equally of a single object and of the universe. Nature in its infinite complexity is ever growing to a new development. Each successive result becomes the parent of an additional influence, destined in some degree to modify all future results....
>
> Strange indeed would it be if, in the midst of this universal mutation, man alone were constant, unchangeable. But it is not so. He also obeys the law of indefinite variation. His circumstances are ever altering, and he is ever adapting himself to them.[5]

[4] Ibid., p. 56.

[5] Herbert Spencer, *Social Statics: or the Conditions Essential to Human Happiness Specified, and the First of them Developed* (New York: Robert Schalkenbach Foundation, 1995) (1851), pp. 31–32.

In other words, for Spencer, man changed constantly because he acquired meaning relationally, in the adaptation to ever changing circumstances. Long before the appearance of Darwin's *Origin of Species* (1859), Spencer operated with an idea of change related to the one Darwin would advance.

We might account for an apparent inconsistency in Spencer's early writings, his simultaneous insistence on subjecting phenomena to inflexible laws and on individualizing phenomena by explaining their origins solely in terms of their antecedents, in terms of the new probabilistic thinking of the mid-nineteenth century that sought to reconcile a sense of randomness (contingency) with a sense of order (noncontingency). The Belgian social scientist Quetelet had demonstrated the deep regularities underlying "free" – hence random, changeable, contingent – actions such as murder and marriage. In his early writings, Spencer relied heavily on Quetelet.

> [C]omplex influences underlying the higher orders of natural phenomena, but more especially those underlying the organic world, work in subordination to the law of probabilities. A plant, for instance, produces thousands of seeds. The greater part of these are destroyed by creatures that live upon them, or fall into places where they cannot germinate. Of the young plants produced by those which do germinate, many are smothered by their neighbors; others are blighted by insects or eaten up by animals; and in the average of cases, only one of them produces a perfect specimen of its species, which, escaping all dangers, brings to maturity seeds enough to continue the race. Thus is it also with every kind of creature. Thus is it also, as M. Quetelet has shown, with the phenomena of human life. And thus was it even with the germination and growth of society. *The seeds of civilization existing in the aboriginal man, and distributed over the earth by his multiplication, were certain in the lapse of time to fall here and there into circumstances fit for their development; and, in spite of all the blightings and uprootings, were certain, by sufficient repetition of these occurrences, ultimately to originate a civilization which should outlive all disasters and arrive at perfection* [emphasis added].[6]

Thus, Spencer was able simultaneously to insist upon temporal contingency and temporal order. Temporal order was discernible only through temporal contingency. The historical world was made up of random, scattered, unpredictable events, each the product of interaction between organism and environment and each individually meaningless. When linked to one another, however, these events revealed the painfully slow arc of movement, the direction of history itself.

[6] Ibid., pp. 372–373.

Precisely because the laws of history could only be traced out of man's many scattered contingent adaptations to his ever varying circumstances, it was also the case that, at any given time, there would always be forms of adaptation that were, as it were, "behind" others, where "behindness" was understood in terms of the direction of history. Henry Carey, operating with a notion of static rather than dynamic laws, would label "exceptions" or "inventions" what Spencer would see as forms of "behindness." Spencer once described nonadaptation as an "evil," but as an "evil" that was entirely ubiquitous: "All evil results from the non-adaptation of constitution to conditions. This is true of everything that lives."[7] Because organisms were always slowly adapting, however, "evil" was also always slowly disappearing. "In virtue of an essential principle of life, this non-adaptation of an organism to its conditions is ever being rectified; and the modification of one or both continues until the adaptation is complete."[8]

This particular understanding of nonadaptation fused with Spencer's antipolitics. Spencer's distaste for the realm of politics was matched by his enthusiasm for the realm of the social, imagined – as so many before him had imagined it – as a sphere in which human communities could function spontaneously and autonomously, without the intervention of the state. But why, then, did the state – and the intrusions of democratic politics – persist? Spencer argued that this was a holdover from a past state:

> Simply because [man] yet partially retains the characteristics that adapted him for an antecedent state. The respects in which he is not fitted to society are the respects in which he is fitted for his original predatory life.... Concerning the present position of the human race, we must therefore say that man needed one moral constitution to fit him for his original state; that he needs another to fit him for his present state; and that he has been, is, and will long continue to be in process of adaptation.[9]

Over the course of the 1850s, Spencer's faith in divine agency dissipated. In his 1857 essay "Progress: Its Law and Cause," he wrote: "[T]he sincere man of science, content to follow wherever the evidence leads him, becomes by each new inquiry more profoundly convinced that the Universe is an insoluble problem. Alike in the external and the internal worlds, he sees himself in the midst of perpetual changes, of which he can

[7] Ibid., p. 54.
[8] Ibid., p. 55.
[9] Ibid., p. 58; see also p. 167.

discover neither beginning nor end.... When, again, he turns from the succession of phenomena, external or internal, to their essential nature, he is equally at fault.... Inward and outward things he thus discovers to be alike inscrutable in their ultimate genesis and nature."[10] The point for Spencer was increasingly that all that seemed graspable was "the succession of phenomena." Their "essential nature" or "ultimate genesis" appeared to have slipped beyond man's reach. It was at this point that Darwin's *Origin of Species* appeared and reinforced something already present in Spencer's thought.

Darwin's work was an attempt to dispel what one might loosely label Christian or Christian-derived notions of creation (separate creation, the fixity of species, etc.) in a highly specific way – through a change of temporal scale. For this change of scale, Darwin relied heavily upon Charles Lyell's *Principles of Geology* (1830–1833), which had offered an account of the age of the earth and showed that the earth was far older than biblical accounts had it. What the change of temporal scale accomplished for Darwin was to render available a greater number of objects, each imagined to represent a specific temporal moment, that could be set in relationship to one another so as to produce a sense of the historicity and changeability of species. Species appeared fixed if one traced their perpetuation only through a few life cycles. Once one expanded or stretched out the timescale and related a larger number of temporally marked objects to one another, however, a slow change became visible. At the same time, Darwin's theory of natural selection, which made this relating of temporally marked objects meaningful in the first place, partook fully of the probabilistic sensibilities of the day. If species changed slowly over time, that change was to be discerned only in the midst of a measure of random, stochastic, contingent variation. It was only from among a welter of differently endowed organisms of the same species, each locked in relationship with its environment, that a more or less average line of change could be apprehended.

In its strictest sense, natural selection was premised against any necessary logic that dictated a course for evolution or the triumph of any particular species. Although Darwin might never entirely have shaken off the legacy of progressionism, he could also state categorically, "I believe ... in no law of necessary development."[11] Perhaps for this reason, the theory

[10] Herbert Spencer, "Progress: Its Law and Cause," *Westminster Review* 67 (April 1857): 445–486 at 485.

[11] Darwin concludes *The Origin of Species* as follows: "Thus, from the war of nature, from famine and death, the most exalted object which we are capable of conceiving, namely,

of natural selection in its integrity was not what became most important to the vast numbers influenced by "Darwinism" in the late nineteenth century. It was the Lamarckian Spencer – and not Darwin – who popularized the term "evolution" to denote the development of life on earth, and despite his praise for Darwin, Spencer was most certainly committed to the idea of progression toward higher states.[12] This is what has made it possible for one scholar of evolution to state, "Much late nineteenth-century evolutionism was non-Darwinian in character.... Perhaps evolutionism triumphed at least in part because it was adapted to the increasingly popular idea of progress."[13] Thus vulgarized, Darwinism made two enormously important, intimately interrelated contributions to the late-nineteenth-century historical sensibility.

First, Darwinism supplied late-nineteenth-century thought with a master metaphor for representing time: a perpetually, inexorably, and silently moving "life." Darwinism accomplished, in so doing, a curious reversal. Its original claim had been to bring history to life. The conclusion of *The Origin of Species* promises prophetically, "Much light will be thrown on the origin of man and his history."[14] It is not a little curious, then, that Darwinism ended up having the effect of configuring history *as* "life." Analogies to biology have been as old in social thought as social thought itself. But where a thinker like George Fitzhugh could point to the gregariousness of beavers and bees as analogies to human sociality, Darwinian "life" as time was writ on a scale far larger than any individual life cycle. It was possessed of immense scale, stretching far back into the past and extending far forward into the future. Precisely because of its massive scale, it was also imagined to elapse unbeknownst to the casual observer (to say nothing of the organism undergoing the changes). As such, even

the production of the higher animals, directly follows. There is grandeur in this view of life, with its several powers, having been originally breathed by the Creator into a few forms or into one; and that, whilst this planet has gone cycling on according to the fixed law of gravity, from so simple a beginning endless forms most beautiful and most wonderful have been, and are being evolved." Charles Darwin, *The Origin of Species By Means of Natural Selection: Or the Preservation of Favored Races in the Struggle for Life and The Descent of Man and Selection in Relation to Sex* (New York: Modern Library, 1993) (1859), p. 374.

12 Peter J. Bowler, *Evolution: The History of an Idea* (3d ed.) (Berkeley: University of California Press, 2003), pp. 8–9. Spencer referred to "Mr. Darwin's great addition to biological science"; he specifically thought of Darwin's theory of natural selection as "raising the hypothesis from a form but partially tenable to a quite tenable form." Herbert Spencer, *The Study of Sociology* (New York: D. Appleton & Co., 1904) (1873), p. 207.

13 Bowler, *Evolution*, p. 23.

14 Darwin, *Origin of Species*, p. 373.

as it was an object of scientific contemplation, Darwinian "life" was invested with a kind of mystery that the easily graspable laws identified by midcentury thinkers such as Carey did not possess.

The vocabulary of "life" and its cessation made possible the same sense of complexity that Spencer had arrived at in *Social Statics* through his emphasis on the imperfection of adaptation. "Life" and "death," even as they were opposed to each other, interpenetrated each other. Objects that could not fully keep up with the imagined pace of "life," or objects that somehow contravened the imagined directionality of "life," could be represented as "dead." The anthropologist E. B. Tylor popularized the related term "survival" (the corresponding Darwinian term was "living fossil"). A survival was something that straddled the boundary between "life" and "death": it had once properly been alive and now should have been dead, but had somehow, inexplicably, lived on. What the survival did, however, was enable one to plot the trajectory of "life" even as it indexed itself as marked for extinction. The documentation of survivals became a cottage industry encompassing not only the efforts of early anthropologists studying non-Western societies, but also antiquaries who studied European societies. This emphasis on locating and timing objects with a view to plotting and confirming the movement of "life" brings us to the other aspect of Darwinism's impact on late-nineteenth-century thought.[15]

Second, precisely because of the immense scale over which Darwinian "life" was projected, the mystery and silence and inexorability of its movement, and the confusing variation out of which it took direction, hard intellectual labor was required in order for its historicity and direction to become visible. This labor consisted in the self-conscious production of relations among objects thought to belong to similar or different times – in other words, a modern notion of context. The fossil record that Darwin needed to make his case was imperfect. Darwin recognized as much, suggesting that new discoveries were needed to fill in the gaps. The need for a missing link created an enormous impetus, indeed an international hunt, to find objects that could be meaningfully related to other objects. Discoveries purporting to be that link were reported from all over Europe. At the same time, the very stochastic and probabilistic nature of Darwinian "life," the fact that a path took a particular direction only in the midst of contingent variation, meant that only the right kinds

[15] On survivals, see Margaret T. Hodgen, *The Doctrine of Survivals: A Chapter in the History of Scientific Method in the Study of Man* (Folcroft, Pa.: Folcroft Library Editions, 1977) (1936).

of relations could permit one to make sense of what would otherwise be only meaningless flux.

Darwin's understanding of a relation was, of course, genealogical – the linking of objects was supposed to confirm the theory of natural selection. But as suggested earlier, natural selection in the strictest sense was not a theory with wide appeal. In more popular discourses, only the very loosest notions of genealogy prevailed. What one was often left with, in a sense, was a chain of objects that floated up for inspection to confirm the passage and direction of time configured as "life." Just as thinkers such as Spencer were rejecting final causes, Darwinism rendered available to them the sense that the meanings of objects were to be sought in other objects, that time was to be plotted, and could be grasped, only by relating objects to one another.

Spencer's writings after the explosion of Darwinism on the intellectual scene remain unchanged in terms of much of their thematic focus and political thrust. There is a more pronounced focus on a mutually interpenetrating "life" and "death." Much more remarkable, however, is the focus on knowledge as the production of relations among objects. For Spencer, the intellectual work of producing relations between phenomena counted as very difficult work indeed. Too many people, he argued, assumed a "simplicity in ... relations among social phenomena."[16] However, as he put it in his massive *Principles of Sociology* (1876–1897), this was a wrong assumption: "[B]efore trying to explain these most involved phenomena, we must learn by inspection the relations of co-existence and sequence in which they stand to one another. By comparing societies of different kinds, and societies in different stages, we must ascertain what traits of size, structure, function, etc., are associated."[17] The first thing one needed in order to relate objects to one another and to discern change – the classic Darwinian strategy – was to acquire the correct temporal perspective, that is, a shift of scale. Thus, Spencer stated, "You must compare positions at great distances from one another in time, before you can tell rightly whither things are tending."[18] For Spencer, the intellectual task of relating phenomena to one other did not, in other words, permit just any phenomenon to be understood in terms of just any other. Instead, the relating of different phenomena to one another, even as it showed up their temporal contingency, revealed distinct regularities in space and time. This finding

[16] Spencer, *Study of Sociology*, pp. 1–2.

[17] Herbert Spencer, *The Principles of Sociology* (New York: D. Appleton & Company, 1925) (3 vols.) (3d ed., 1885; 1876), Vol. 1, pp. 442–443.

[18] Spencer, *Study of Sociology*, p. 95.

of regularity of connection across space or time was presented as a kind of finished object, a coherent whole possessed of parts that could not be tinkered with without incalculable and pernicious consequences.

Ultimately, this establishing of relations between phenomena was a return to Spencer's antipolitics of the 1850s, a cabining of democracy by positing the movement and direction of history configured as "life." Spencer showed, through the hard work of relating objects to one another, that society moved only very slowly, that it could not be remade at will, and that political attempts to remake it were doomed to failure:

> Those who look on a society as either supernaturally created or created by Acts of Parliament, and who consequently consider successive stages of its existence as having no necessary dependence on one another, will not be deterred from drawing political conclusions from passing facts, by a consciousness of the slow genesis of social phenomena. But those who have arisen to the belief that societies are evolved in structure and function, as in growth, will be made to hesitate on contemplating the long unfolding through which early causes work out late results.[19]

This was, of course, an attempt to show the impotence of legislation. It showed "the man of higher type [that he] must be content with greatly-moderated expectations, while he perseveres with undiminished efforts. He has to see how comparatively little can be done, and yet to find it worth while to do that little: so uniting philanthropic energy with philosophic calm."[20]

Spencer's historical faith was that societies moved from a "military" (political) state to an "industrial" (social) state, from arrangements legitimized through violence to arrangements legitimized through peace, from a simple state of a few parts to a complex state of many parts. This view imbued his understanding of law. Spencer was convinced that the large-scale transition in law was (borrowing Sir Henry Maine's 1861 formulation in *Ancient Law*) from "status" to "contract," from law "initiated by political authority" to law "initiated by the *consensus* of individual interests."[21] The latter kind of law constituted the future of society: "[A]s the power of the political head declines – as industrialism fosters an increasingly free population ... there again grows predominant this primitive source of law – the *consensus* of individual interests."[22] The dream, indeed, was of a society that, having dispensed

[19] Ibid., p. 92.
[20] Ibid., p. 367.
[21] Spencer, *Principles of Sociology*, Vol. 2, p. 528.
[22] Ibid..

with the state, operated entirely "unconsciously." Spencer could write, "[A] nation's activities are divisible into two leading kinds of cooperation, distinguishable as the conscious and the unconscious – the one being militant and the other industrial."[23] The former was a holdover from the past, the latter the herald of the future.

A large part of the late-nineteenth-American debate between laissez-faire and social democracy took place around the role of the state. Should the state step in to ameliorate the various problems associated with the transition to industrialism (what Spencer might call "conscious" lawmaking), or should it withdraw and allow the private sphere to function unimpeded (what he might call "unconscious" functioning)? Was history headed where Spencer thought it was heading (in which case "conscious" lawmaking by the state was doomed to failure)? Or was history a less ineluctable movement that called for societies to take control of their futures (which might create a space for "conscious" lawmaking by the state)?

To be sure, the Spencerian dream of an industrial society functioning "unconsciously" was simply that, a dream. Few took seriously the idea that government would vanish completely. It was, instead, a contest about kinds of governance. In the late-nineteenth-century United States, the intrusion of the state into the sphere of the market was an intrusion into a sphere traditionally governed by the common law. To a large extent, the debate between laissez-faire and social democracy was, then, a debate between proponents of democratic control over lawmaking and proponents of the common law. Both the common law's critics and its defenders, I shall suggest, were in the grip of Spencerian vocabulary, although they did different things with it, took it in different directions.

This chapter begins with a discussion of the legal thought of what I label the American historical school. Even as the activities of the regulatory state mounted around them, common law thinkers associated with the American historical school seized upon the historical vocabularies of Spencerism to argue that the common law captured precisely the "unconscious" functioning of "life" that, according to Spencer, legislation would be unable to capture or defeat. A sense of the movement of "life" was produced by splitting off custom from law, such that the gap between law and a constantly evolving custom stood for the passage of time. Custom, in the imaginations of such legal thinkers, underlay all written law. Evidence of spontaneously arisen customs involving property

[23] Ibid., Vol. 3, p. 553.

and contract proved, furthermore, the ontological priority of private law concepts of property and contract at a time when positivist theories of lawmaking were becoming important. Even as they represented the common law as a carrier of Spencerian "life," however, common law thinkers associated with the American historical school continued to adhere to the nonhistorical times of "immemoriality." Once again, then, the common law managed to be different from itself while continuing to be itself.

The chapter then moves to a discussion of the relationship between late-nineteenth-century legal formalism (represented by Harvard Law School's dean, Christopher Columbus Langdell, and a few others) and legal antiformalism (represented by Oliver Wendell Holmes, Jr.). It deconstructs the celebrated distinction between Langdellian legal formalism and Holmesian legal antiformalism. According to Holmes, Langdellian formalism, with its focus on "logic," lacked a historical sensibility. Holmes's own focus on "experience," by contrast, possessed one. I show that both Langdell and Holmes, albeit in different ways, fully absorbed the Spencerian historical sensibility. I further show that the Holmesian category of "experience" depends a great deal on Langdellian "logic." Holmesian "experience" derived its content, in fact, from Langdellian "logic."

Finally, the chapter turns to the emerging late-nineteenth-century critiques of common law thought, ranging from the ideas of Sir Henry Maine, positivist legal thinkers such as John Chipman Gray, and, perhaps most significant, the later Holmes himself. The later Holmes's critique of the common law, as I suggested in Chapter 1, provided a critical intellectual foundation for the Progressive Era critiques that followed.

The Common Law and "Life": The American Historical School

In this section, I examine a cluster of positions constituting what I label the late-nineteenth-century American historical school. Such positions can be discerned in the writings of various legal thinkers, including Philemon Bliss, James Coolidge Carter, John Forrest Dillon, William Gardner Hammond, Christopher Gustavus Tiedeman, and Francis Wharton.[24] Many of these

[24] Philemon Bliss (1813–1889) was a congressman, served on the Missouri Supreme Court, and founded the University of Missouri Law School. James Coolidge Carter (1827–1905) was a prominent corporate lawyer and civil reformer in New York City and an active alumnus of Harvard Law School. John Forrest Dillon (1831–1914) was a lawyer, a judge on the Iowa Supreme Court, and a law professor at Columbia University. William Gardner Hammond (1829–1894) was a professor at the Iowa Law School and later dean of St. Louis Law School. Christopher Gustavus Tiedeman (1857–1902) was a professor

common lawyers were reacting to trends around them, to the expansion of state regulatory authority, and to growing criticism from within and without the legal establishment that the common law was unable to cope with the complexities of America's emerging industrial economy.

In order to make a case for the common law in the late-nineteenth-century industrial polity, such thinkers turned to a Spencerian–Darwinian vocabulary. We observe in their writings a highly specific appropriation of the Spencerian–Darwinian idea of time as "life." A sense of the passage of "life" is produced from out of the common law itself. Bits of law that had once been thought of as belonging to a single time were split off from each other and set ahead and behind each other to produce the effect of the passage of time configured as "life." The relevant bits of law that were separated from each other and then related to each other were law, on the one hand, and custom, on the other. Custom thus came to play a strange new role. It became the carrier, as it were, of "life," "unconsciously" spinning ahead of law, in relation to which law was condemned to Spencerian nonadaptation, to ontological "behindness." At the same time, however, custom was always seen as embodying common law contract and property notions. If custom was seen as being "ahead" of law, in other words, it always also reflected the common law. Thus, the core of common law contract and property, fused with "life" itself, could be described as having arisen "unconsciously." Not surprisingly, we see legal thinkers in late-nineteenth-century America pointing to instances of the spontaneous, "unconscious" emergence of customs of contract and property to emphasize the ontological priority of such notions and hence their immunity from legislative tampering. At the same time, many legal thinkers would argue that only common law judges – as opposed to democratically elected legislatures – could hope to capture the "life" of custom.

One might assume that producing a temporal relation between custom and law as a way of demonstrating the movement of "life" would entail a divorce between custom and the extended common law past. After all, the point of invoking custom for thinkers associated with the late-nineteenth-century American historical school was not – as it had been for Burke – to instill a reverence for the legacy of bygone generations.

at the University of Missouri Law School and the University of the City of New York and dean of the University of Buffalo Law School. Francis Wharton (1820–1899) had a varied career as a lawyer, theologian, priest, law professor at the Boston University Law School, and solicitor of the Department of State. I derive many of these biographical details from David M. Rabban, "The Historiography of Late Nineteenth-Century American Legal History, *Theoretical Inquiries in Law* 4 (July 2003): 541 –578, at 568.

It was to demonstrate a specific relation in the *immediate* temporal vicinity of law, as it were, to show the forward movement of "life," and to make out a case against tampering with it through addle-brained legislation. Many late-nineteenth-century common law thinkers, accordingly, insisted that the weight of custom was not the weight of the past, that custom was less about the past than it was about constantly unfolding "life."

Nevertheless, Burkean ideas died hard. There were certain prominent thinkers associated with the American historical school – notably, James Coolidge Carter – who, even as they associated custom with "life," continued to invoke the older vocabulary in which the common law as custom stood for the accumulated wisdom and experience of multiple generations. In Carter's writings, as we shall see, custom could simultaneously encompass the temporality of Spencerian–Darwinian "life" *and* the traditional nonhistorical temporalities of the common law. Carter shuttled back and forth between these two different and mutually inconsistent temporalities, the one drawn from the historical sensibility of his era, the other the traditional nonhistorical temporality of the common law.

One can begin to discern how custom came to embody "life" by tracing the process through which custom came, during the last third of the nineteenth century, to be progressively divorced from its link with the extended common law past and came more and more to be understood in terms of its immediate temporal relation to law. In part, this divorce of custom from the extended past had to do with the exigencies of life in late-nineteenth-century America. Practices pressing upon courts for recognition as customs arose seemingly spontaneously. More important, associated with new trades, they could point to no venerable lineage. John Lawson's *Law of Usages and Customs* (1881), the only major American treatise from this period on the common law relating to customs, faithfully listed the requirements of the seventeenth-century common law test for a usage to win legal recognition as a custom at variance with the common law.[25] Yet the break between custom and the past in Lawson's treatise could not have been sharper.

Lawson dismissed the common law requirement of antiquity outright as irrelevant to the United States: "[I]t is obvious that the English rule [with respect to the antiquity of a custom] could never have any application here ... for the excellent reason that this country was not discovered until several hundred years [after the legal date that could establish a

[25] John D. Lawson, *The Law of Usages and Customs, With Illustrative Cases* (St. Louis: F. H. Thomas & Co., 1881).

usage's antiquity, i.e., 1189 C.E.]."[26] This was an argument that had been made many times. But what about the requirement that a practice possess continuity – repetition over an extended period of time by a number of individuals – in order to be legally recognized as a custom? We learn from Lawson that the requirement of continuity was also under siege:

> But while a usage of trade or business need not be "ancient," as that word is used in the books, it is nevertheless required that it shall be fully established as a usage of trade or business. And time, it is plain, is one ingredient, at least, necessary to accomplish this. What length of time shall be sufficient can, of course, not be stated in the form of a general rule, but each case must depend upon the various relations of the trade to the public, the exigencies of the business, and the frequency of the repetition of the particular usage in the time within which it may be proved to have existed. Thus, three weeks in the city of New York, where a great number of transactions of the same character take place daily, was considered ... a sufficient length of time to establish a usage in the insurance business restricting the ordinary signification of the word 'storehouse,' as used in a fire policy.[27]

According to American courts, therefore, a usage that had lasted a mere three weeks could possess sufficient continuity to be recognized as a custom of the New York insurance business. We have moved very far away from the old common law requirement that a custom be "immemorial."

This divorce of custom from the extended past was not, however, merely an American phenomenon attributable to a sense of the country's relative youth. A contemporary British treatise on the common law of custom from which Lawson borrowed heavily, J. Balfour Browne's *Law of Usages and Customs* (1881), best expressed the new view of the relationship between custom and the extended common law past. Briefly put, there was to be none. We see here, quite explicitly, how common law thinkers had begun to theorize custom anew.

While admitting that the common law had traditionally required that a usage possess antiquity as a condition for its legal recognition, Browne argued that the real point of the requirement of antiquity was not that a usage be old, but that its origin not be attributable to the act of a single individual on the theory that no single individual could be allowed to create law. In other words, Browne read the common law's concern with a usage's age as a concern that a usage lack an identifiable originator.[28]

[26] Ibid., p. 27.

[27] Ibid., pp. 29–30 (citing *Wall v. East River Ins. Co.*, 3 Duer, 264).

[28] J. H. Balfour Browne, *The Law of Usages and Customs: A Treatise Wherein Is More Particularly Pointed Out When and to What Extent Usages and Customs May Be Set Up as a Defence, and How, as a Matter of Evidence, Their Existence Will Control, Vary, or*

Browne's reading reveals how far custom had come by the 1880s, even in England, to be delinked from the past.

Browne's treatise also makes clear something much more significant – and in this respect it is also followed almost word for word by Lawson's. It reveals not only how custom had separated itself from the past, but also how it had separated itself from law. Custom was now not law itself but something upon which law was founded, something possessed of the ability to mark law's time insofar as it was both prior to and ahead of law. Browne wanted to point out "how large a portion of our law – which may be looked upon as crystallized common-sense, and rational experience – was *at one time*, an amorphous form of heterogeneous custom. Indeed, all laws have been in practice *before* they are put in words."[29] The particular regional or trade customs that had long been recognized by the common law provided they met the requirements of the seventeenth-century common law test were not, strictly speaking, customs at all. Browne put it thus: "These seem to us to be undeserving of the appellation customs, which we would reserve for law when it is being modelled in clay – so to speak – and before it has been transferred to the marble. Custom seems to us to be applicable to the law before it has been recognized as law, but when it is in a condition to claim judicial sanction."[30] The implication, of course, was that law was always "behind" custom.

In its ability to mark law's time, to lie before and ahead of law, custom was explicitly imbued with "life" just as law was somehow always a little "dead." Drawing an analogy between custom and language, Browne argued that, just as German philologists had shown language to pass "from unity to diversity and variety," customs proliferated outward from a common origin.[31] This ability to proliferate endlessly over time was a marker of custom's "life":

> Might we not apply almost the same true words to customs – which in our estimation bear an exactly similar relation to a system of law that dialects do to a language – that the great German philologist [Grimm] has applied to dialects, and say that customs have developed themselves progressively, and that the unity which we find in the history of jurisprudence has been developed into the variety of customs which we find at the present time. *This capability of change in law is not an indication of its inferiority, but of its vitality.* So long as men progress, so

Explain Writings and Agreements (1st U.S. ed. by S. S. Clarke) (Jersey City: Frederick D. Linn & Co., 1881) (1875), p. 16.

29 Ibid., p. 1 (emphasis added).

30 Ibid., pp. 13–14.

31 Ibid., p. 17.

long as new events happen, new trades arise, new commerce floats upon hitherto unsailed seas, new manufactures change the features of our lives, and new and higher principles take the place of those which governed conduct, regulated acts and guided life, so long must we expect progressive change and almost lavish variety in our customs. *When a people is dead, when there are no transactions to be governed, no rights to protect, no interests to regard, the law may remain unchanged, for the law is dead. We have indeed dead laws just as we have dead languages* [emphasis added].[32]

In Spencerian–Darwinian fashion, Browne suggested the movement of "life" – demonstrable through the temporal gap between custom and law – was constant, inexorable: "[T]here is always a slow process of customary regeneration going on, which will be observable to the diligent student of legal history, and which makes up for the gradual decay of law which is going on *pari passu*, and which results from the gradual tendency that almost every fixed enactment has to become obsolete."[33]

But the "life" of custom, for all of its ability to set law in time, was a curious kind of "life." To begin with, custom had always been a legal category. For centuries, as we have seen, it was how the common law had justified itself to itself, selected practices for judicial recognition, and pronounced its superiority vis-à-vis legislation. More important, in Browne's treatise, custom was imagined so that it was a reflection of bits of common law doctrine – contract, property, crime. For example, here is Browne offering an example of the origins of custom that is really the projection of a private property regime:

It must have been understood by men that theft – the act of taking the property of another without his consent – was wrong before they made a law to punish the thief, with the view of preventing similar depredations. But long before men made a law they had bolts to their doors, and if they caught the robber they exercised their right by taking his booty from him and possibly even by inflicting upon him a vengeful punishment. This was not done by one man but by many, and we see in it the embryonic custom out of which the law has developed.[34]

Insofar as custom had become something that constantly gave rise to law and lay before and ahead of it, something in terms of which law could be seen as "dead," something through which time itself could be grasped, it is as if law had produced its own perverse kind of time. If there was an insistence on relating law to custom and thereby producing a sense of the

[32] Ibid., pp. 17–18

[33] Ibid., p. 18.

[34] Ibid., pp. 1–2.

passage of "life," there was a parallel drive to render "life" nothing other than a set of legal precepts known all along.

In the writings of the legal thinkers associated with the late-nineteenth-century American historical school, there is a more or less complete lack of interest in the common law doctrine relating to customs, as well as in specific regional or trade or group customs (the general doctrinal area covered by the Browne and Lawson treatises discussed earlier). The details of customs, understood in the plural, are irrelevant. "Custom" is generalized into a singular and transformed into a temporal object in terms of which law is to be conceived.

American common law thinkers saw custom as giving rise to law all around them. Such customs confirmed the ontological priority of private law concepts of contract and property. One especially arresting image was that of the property customs that had arisen, seemingly spontaneously, among California's Gold Rush mining communities. The image struck a chord even in a positivist like the Harvard Law School professor John Chipman Gray. Gray observed:

> One remarkable instance, however, in late years, of the use of custom as a source of law in matters non-contractual can be found – it is the introduction of miners' customs in California. The discovery of gold brought, in 1849, a large and turbulent population into an almost uninhabited country; the civil authority could be but feebly enforced, and the miners made rules for themselves. These rules related not only to matters of contract, but also to questions of property and possession. They prescribed how possession was to be taken, how much could be taken into possession (four hundred feet by a discoverer and two hundred by a subsequent locator on a lode), and how possession was lost. These rules were adopted into the Law, and, though not formally enacted, they were recognized by the legislature and thus received a statutory sanction as sources of Law.[35]

The image was invoked repeatedly and conjoined with research being conducted on the laws of non-Western societies. For example, in his *Commentaries on Law* (1884), Francis Wharton made the case for custom underlying law by referring, *inter alia*, to the "unconscious action of the community in [Gold Rush California] mining districts," to the customs

[35] John Chipman Gray, *The Nature and Sources of the Law* (2d ed.) (New York: MacMillan Company, 1921), p. 296. Gray's example of mining customs in Gold Rush California was drawn from Gregory Yale's *Legal Titles to Mining Claims and Water Rights in California under the Mining Law of Congress of July, 1866* (San Francisco: Roman & Co., 1867). On Gray, see Stephen S. Siegel, "John Chipman Gray and the Moral Basis of Classical Legal Thought," *Iowa Law Review* 86 (2001): 1513–1599, and "John Chipman Gray, Legal Formalism, and the Transformation of Perpetuities Law," *University of Miami Law Review* 36 (1982): 439–464.

of American Indian tribes, and to the "Asiatic communities, specified by Sir H. Maine."[36] Similarly, in his well-known tract *Of Sovereignty* (1885), Philemon Bliss asserted that even the "rudest societies" exhibited "the primary precepts of the law of contracts" without the command of any sovereign.[37]

As Wharton's characterization of custom suggests, in the 1880s and 1890s, there was a new, explicitly Spencerian–Darwinian lexicon for speaking about custom. Spencer had dreamed of an industrial society functioning "unconsciously." American legal thinkers picked up this language to describe custom. Words such as "unconsciously," "felt," "plastic," "original," "invisible," "universally known," "spontaneous," "instinctive," "mysterious," "irresistible," "habitual," "emanations," "involuntary," "unobserved," and "inarticulate" acquired currency.[38]

This ontological priority of custom was used, predictably, to political ends. The fact that an "unconscious" custom already reflected common law understandings of contract and property could be used to argue against socially redistributive legislation. Legislative initiatives that intruded into the realm of private law would be contrary to "life" itself. Indeed, they would as such be doomed to failure. In 1890, Christopher Tiedeman stated, "[T]he life of a rule of law is derived from its habitual and spontaneous observance by the mass of people." Any lack of correspondence between law and custom could therefore instantly render law a "dead letter."[39]

However, this relationship between law and custom was not simply a matter of the irruption of conservative politics into legal thought

[36] Francis Wharton, *Commentaries on Law, Embracing Chapters on the Nature; the Source; and the History of Law; on International Law; Public and Private; and on Constitutional and Statutory Law* (Philadelphia: Kay & Brother, 1884) (Holmes Beach, Fla.: Gaunt, Inc., 2001), pp. 51, 55, 56.

[37] Philemon Bliss, *Of Sovereignty* (Boston: Little, Brown & Co., 1885), p. 26.

[38] I provide only a single citation for each word, but the same words are repeated across texts and writers. James C. Carter, *The Proposed Codification of Our Common Law: A Paper Prepared at the Request of the Committee of the Bar Association of the City of New York, Appointed to Oppose the Measure* (New York: Evening Post Job Printing Office, 1884), pp. 41, 41, 59, 70; James Coolidge Carter, *Law: Its Origin, Growth and Function: Being a Course of Lectures Prepared for Delivery Before the Law School of Harvard University* (G. P. Putnam's Sons, 1907), p. 21 (quoting Sir John Lubbock), also pp. 78, 153, 153, 155, 249; Christopher G. Tiedeman, *The Unwritten Constitution of the United States: A Philosophical Inquiry into the Fundamentals of American Constitutional Law* (New York: G. P. Putnam's Sons, 1890), p. 9; Wharton, *Commentaries on Law*, pp. iv, 43, 43; Oliver Wendell Holmes, Jr., *The Common Law* (Boston: Little, Brown & Co., 1938) (1881), p. 36.

[39] Tiedeman, *Unwritten Constitution*, p. 6.

(although it was certainly that as well). It also entailed questions of method and stance. How was one to deal with dizzying change, evidence of which was all around one in the late nineteenth century? As thinkers all around them were complaining that common law notions of contract and property were incapable of confronting the complex problems confronting large-scale industrial societies, the thinkers of the American historical school took a different approach, drawing from a long tradition of common law thought. If custom was a marker of the future of law, and law could *never* "catch up," they argued that the best way to deal with this gap was through an interplay of repetition and difference, through a replaying of something that one already knew in order to grasp something one did not. Legislation was to be disdained not only because of its socially redistributive implications, but also because it was "unscientific" to the extent that it attempted blindly to shape an essentially unknown and unknowable future. The superior "scientific" method was to deal with concrete disputes as they presented themselves, in other words, to deal with the future when in some sense it had already been rendered past in the form of a dispute. As such, the invocation of "science" went hand in hand with a romanticization of the traditional incremental and "insensible" temporality of the common law.

These ideas, political and methodological, are present in brilliant outline in the writings of the conservative late-nineteenth-century Mugwump lawyer James Coolidge Carter.[40] Many of Carter's published writings were produced in the context of successfully opposing the codification of New York's civil law in the early 1880s and then endlessly recycled in lectures, addresses, pamphlets, and the like. (Carter's antagonist in the codification debates was David Dudley Field, who had begun his career as a codifier at the height of the Jacksonian passion for codification.)[41] However, for all his awareness of the historical sensibilities of the day, Carter remained a traditional common lawyer. I discuss Carter's thought as an example

[40] On Carter generally, see Lewis A. Grossman, "Langdell Upside-Down: The Anticlassical Jurisprudence of Anticodification," *Yale Journal of Law & Humanities* 19 (2007): 149–219; Lewis A. Grossman, "James Coolidge Carter and Mugwump Jurisprudence," *Law and History Review* 20 (2002): 577–629. For a discussion of Carter's invocation of German legal science, see Mathias Reimann, "The Historical School Against Codification: Savigny, Carter, and the Defeat of the New York Civil Code," *American Journal of Comparative Law* 37 (1989): 95–119.

[41] As Field pointed out, common lawyerly opposition to the codification of New York's civil law was perverse. Common lawyers were opposed not to the collection of statutes into a code, but to the codification of the common law. But statutes had already declared, changed, or repealed the common law. The code in question had, furthermore, been adopted in California and Dakota, and functioned admirably there. David Dudley Field,

of the jostling of different temporalities – nonhistorical common law ones and Spencerian–Darwinian ones – in the late-nineteenth-century American jurisprudence of custom.

In *The Proposed Codification of Our Common Law* (1884), a pamphlet published by the Committee of the Bar Association of the City of New York in an effort to oppose the Field Code, Carter began by invoking a hallowed distinction – that between Anglo-American liberty and European despotism – to oppose common law to code. In the manner of common lawyers traditionally, Carter argued that the distinction ultimately rested upon a relationship to time. The common law had stretched out over a "long succession of centuries," the creation of a class of legal experts; codes were the creature of a mere moment, the creation of arbitrary power.[42]

The difference between common law and code had everything to do with different methods of calibrating change. The common law judge accomplished an effortless blurring of the distinction between new and old (the much revered nonhistorical temporality of "insensibility"). Such successful blending of new and old rested, ultimately, on the common law's insistence on dealing with facts only as they presented themselves on a case-by-case basis. This was "scientific." "Until the *facts* come into existence, the *questions* arising upon such facts cannot be known, and surely cannot be decided."[43] To be sure, Carter insisted at the same time that common law judges never made law: "[T]he judge is never ... *free*. He is bound, in declaring the law of a new case, by established rules just as much as in deciding a case which has been decided a hundred times before. The law of a new case can be determined by him only by building upon the foundation of law already known and declared."[44] By contrast, codes rested upon a presumptuous framing of rules that could never adequately account for the changes of the future. Carter's criticism of codes could equally be extended to legislation:

> Codification ... consists in enacting rules, and such rules must ... from their very nature, cover future and unknown, as well as past and known cases; and so far as it covers future and unknown cases, it is no law that deserves the name. It does not embody justice; it is a mere *jump in the dark*; it is a *violent* framing of rules

A Short Response to a Long Discourse: An Answer to Mr. James C. Carter's Pamphlet on the Proposed Codification of Our Common Law (New York, 1884).

42 Carter, *The Proposed Codification of Our Common Law*, pp. 5–6.

43 Ibid., pp. 32–33 (emphasis in original).

44 Ibid., pp. 29–30.

without reference to justice, which may or may not rightly dispose of the cases which may fall under them [emphasis in the original].[45]

Thus, Carter argued, it was in fact the method of the common law judge, and not the method of the *soi-disant* "scientific" codifier or legislator, that was the more truly "scientific." In light of all this, Carter viewed with alarm "the endeavor of a few men, it might almost be said, of one man [David Dudley Field], to abrogate our system of unwritten law ... and to substitute in its place a scheme of codification borrowed from the systems of despotic nations."[46]

In the foregoing rendering, the temporality of the common law is that of "insensibility." This traditional nonhistorical temporality as a way of producing legitimacy, however, is very different indeed from the temporality of Spencerian–Darwinian "life" with which custom had come to be associated. The effort of many thinkers in the grip of Spencerian–Darwinian ideas, as we have seen, was precisely to effect a divorce between custom and the past. Carter, in this 1884 anticodification pamphlet, cleaves to common law tradition.

But Carter was equally adept at using the historical sensibilities associated with Darwin and Spencer. This is especially true of his posthumously published *Law: Its Origin, Growth and Function* (1907), a text that Carter had planned to deliver as a series of lectures at the Harvard Law School in the spring of 1905.[47]

"Law, Custom, Conduct, Life – different names for almost the same thing – true names for different aspects of the same thing – are so inseparably blended together that one cannot even be thought of without the other," Carter pronounces with a flourish toward the end of this text.[48] Custom has come explicitly to be associated with "life." Custom precedes law, emerging "unconsciously." How is one to capture this "unconscious" law, through common law or legislation? Not surprisingly, Carter argues that common law pronouncements declaring custom capture "life" in a way that legislation can never hope to. Democracy must step back, allow custom to proceed on its own, and allow common law judges to record it. Carter offers us an unabashedly Spencerian argument:

[45] Ibid., p. 33.
[46] Ibid., p. 9.
[47] James C. Carter, *Law: Its Origin, Growth and Function* (New York: G. P. Putnam's Sons, 1907).
[48] Ibid., p. 320.

[When courts declare custom] they find rules already existing, *unconsciously made* by society, the *product*, as it were, of its life; but the written laws which they enforce are rules *consciously made by men* clothed with the legislative power [emphasis in original].[49]

It was specifically private law, for Carter, that was a true reflection of an "unconsciously" proceeding "life," and in a Spencerian vein, he suggested that such law was utterly incapable of being affected by "conscious" legislation: "[T]he whole private law which governs much the larger part of human conduct has arisen from and still stands upon custom, and is the necessary product of the life of society, and therefore incapable of being made at all."[50] Such law had begun "as the product of the automatic action of society" and was "self-created and self-existent."[51]

Precisely because custom stood for a "self-created and self-existent" "life," socially redistributive legislation that interfered with contract and property rights would be "dead." "The *Written Law* is victorious upon paper," Carter warned, "and powerless elsewhere."[52] There were many examples, both in the past and present, of "dead" law. The historical example of sumptuary legislation afforded "a spectacle ... of the impotence of man's conscious effort to overrule the silent and irresistible forces of nature."[53] Of his own day, Carter observed, "There are a vast number of laws on the statute-books of the several States which are never enforced, and generally for the reason that they are unacceptable to the people. There are great numbers of others the enforcement of which, or attempts to enforce which, are productive of bribery, perjury, subornation of perjury, animosity and hate among citizens, useless expenditure, and many other public evils."[54] Examples included antitrust legislation with respect to railroads and civil rights legislation to protect the rights of African Americans.[55]

And yet, at the same time, even in a text so breathtakingly Spencerian, there is a return to the traditional nonhistorical temporality of the common law. For all his turning to the languages of "life" and "unconsciousness," Carter was never able, it would appear, to abandon the association

[49] Ibid., p. 87 (emphasis in original).
[50] Ibid., p. 182.
[51] Ibid., p. 129.
[52] Ibid., p. 213 (emphasis in original).
[53] Ibid., p. 249.
[54] Ibid., p. 3.
[55] Ibid., pp. 206–213, 214–217.

of custom with the weight of the extended past. And this extended common law past was very far from the "scientific" past that was to be plotted, in Spencerian–Darwinian fashion, through the establishment of relations between phenomena. Thus, Carter embraces something like "immemoriality" when he says: "Custom, therefore, is not the accidental, trivial, and meaningless thing which we sometimes think it to be. It is the imperishable record of the wisdom of the illimitable past reaching back to the infancy of the race, revised, corrected, enlarged, open to all alike, and read and understood by all. It was a happy expression of Lord Coke that the wisdom of the law was wiser than any man's wisdom.... What higher or more dignified conception of the study of the law can there be than to make it the task of seeking out, discerning, applying, and extending the principles upon which those grand generalisations of conduct have proceeded which are the fruit of human experience extending through countless ages?"[56]

In Carter's writings, then, the common law could both embody Spencerian–Darwinian "life" and remain thoroughly "immemorial" and "insensible." Where the languages of "life" were used to cabin late-nineteenth-century American democracy, the common law could join with those languages. It did not cease, thereby, to be itself.

The writings of the American historical school played a large role in supporting the conservative constitutional jurisprudence of the late-nineteenth-century federal courts.[57] As the federal and state governments responded to calls for regulation in the late nineteenth century, their efforts were increasingly stymied in the federal courts. With the slavery crisis behind it, the U.S. Supreme Court grew increasingly sympathetic toward business and property interests and ever more assertive in expressing its sympathy. The Court aggressively wielded the U.S. Constitution's Interstate Commerce Clause to limit state efforts to impose taxes and other restrictions on interstate business;[58] reshaped the law of torts and contracts so as to strengthen the legal position of railroads,

[56] Ibid., pp. 127–28; see also p. 144.

[57] Much has been written on the subject of how the late-nineteenth-century U.S. Supreme Court joined the common law to the U.S. Constitution to block all manner of state regulation. See, e.g., Edward A. Purcell, Jr., *Brandeis and the Progressive Constitution: Erie, the Judicial Power, and the Politics of the Federal Courts in Twentieth-Century America* (New Haven, Conn.: Yale University Press, 2000); Horwitz, *The Transformation of American Law, 1870–1960*. I have relied heavily in the succeeding paragraphs on Purcell.

[58] See, e.g., Charles W. McCurdy, "American Law and the Marketing Structure of the Large Corporation, 1875–1890," *Journal of Economic History* 38 (1978): 631–649; *Welton v. Missouri*, 91 U.S. 275 (1875).

manufacturers, and insurance companies;[59] construed the Sherman Anti-Trust Act broadly to prohibit local organizing efforts of labor unions, but narrowly to prevent the federal government from regulating companies that manufactured goods for interstate commerce;[60] and, in 1894, invalidated a minimal federal income tax.[61] As Congress began to expand regulatory activity, the Court also began to check the activities of agencies such as the Interstate Commerce Commission.[62]

A significant part of the Court's pro–big business jurisprudence rested upon the foundation provided by Joseph Story's 1842 decision in *Swift v. Tyson*, a decision that had articulated the idea of a "general law" or a "federal common law" to be declared by the federal courts. Edward Purcell has observed that "[d]uring the second half of the nineteenth century the federal courts ignored state court decisions with increasing frequency. Steadily expanding the scope of the *Swift* doctrine, they developed their own extensive body of independent decisional rules.... By century's end they had inflated the domain of general jurisprudence to encompass most common law subjects, and in 1910 the Supreme Court extended it further to issues of real property law – an area that in the nineteenth century had seemed clearly 'local.'"[63]

Nobody stood for this expansion of federal common law, and its deployment to conservative ends, more steadfastly than Supreme Court Associate Justice David Brewer.[64] For Brewer, the Court's expansive use of *Swift v. Tyson* went along with a broader sense that the U.S. Constitution and the common law were intimately joined. When "interpreting the Constitution," he observed, "we must have recourse to the common

[59] Edward A. Purcell, Jr., *Litigation and Inequality: Federal Diversity Jurisdiction in Industrial America, 1870–1958* (Oxford: Oxford University Press, 1992), 61, 86.

[60] Compare *Loewe v. Lawlor*, 208 U.S. 274 (1908) with *United States v. E.C. Knight Co.*, 156 U.S. 1 (1895).

[61] *Pollock v. Farmers' Loan & Trust Co.*, 157 U.S. 429 (1895).

[62] See, e.g., *Interstate Commerce Commission v. Cincinnati, New Orleans & Texas Pacific Railway Co.*, 167 U.S. 479 (1897); *Johnson v. Southern Pacific Co.*, 196 U.S. 1 (1904).

[63] Purcell, *Brandeis and the Progressive Constitution*, pp. 51–52.

[64] In a series of opinions, Brewer used Story's *Swift v. Tyson* decision to assert federal judicial control over the field of industrial tort law (especially over personal injury claims by employees against their employers), the law of common carriers, the law of insurance, etc. *Baltimore & Ohio Railroad Co. v. Baugh*, 149 U.S. 368 (1893); *Western Union Telegraph Co. v. Call Publishing Co.*, 181 U.S. 92 (1901); *Iowa Life Insurance Co. v. Lewis*, 187 U.S. 335 (1902); *Northern Assurance Co. of London. v. Grand View Building Association*, 183 U.S. 308 (1902). See generally Purcell, *Brandeis and the Progressive Constitution*, "Expanding the Federal Judicial Power: Justice David J. Brewer and the 'General' Common Law."

law."[65] In his landmark opinion in *Kansas v. Colorado* (1907), Brewer went so far as to assert that, while Congress's power was limited and the Tenth Amendment reserved only such powers to the states as were internal to the states, the powers reserved by the Tenth Amendment to "the people" authorized a truly "national" common law that could inform the Constitution. The common law, he argued, "does not rest on any statute or other written declaration of the sovereign"; its "principles" were "in force generally throughout the United States."[66] Not surprisingly, Brewer was aware of Spencerian philosophy. In an 1893 address to the New York State Bar Association, he began by claiming the "philosophy of Plato and Herbert Spencer" as the philosophy of "civilized man."[67]

Perhaps the most notorious instance of common law joined to the Constitution was the doctrine of "substantive due process." In *Allgeyer v. Louisiana* (1897), the Court ruled for the first time that "liberty of contract" was protected under the Due Process Clauses of the Fifth and Fourteenth Amendments and that state and federal legislation could not therefore unduly restrict the contractual freedoms of workers and employers.[68] The Court thereby effectively constitutionalized common law contract rights and set back legislative efforts to regulate working conditions. The case that exemplified this conservative jurisprudence is the now infamous case of *Lochner v. New York* (1905), discussed in Chapter 1, in which the Court struck down as unconstitutional under the Fourteenth Amendment a New York law legislating the length of the work day in the baking and confectionary trades on the ground that the law interfered with freedom of contract.[69] If contract and property rights stood for "life" itself, the U.S. Supreme Court would refuse to let the state interfere with its trajectory.

Custom and ideas of "unwritten" law played an extremely significant role in the burgeoning constitutional law literature during the last third of the nineteenth century. For thinkers associated with the American historical school, a major theme of constitutional commentary was that "written" constitutions rested upon "unwritten" ones, where "unwritten" ones were, not surprisingly, associated with the common law, custom,

[65] *South Carolina v. United States*, 199 U.S. 437, 449 (1905) (Brewer, J.).

[66] *Kansas v. Colorado*, 206 U.S. 46, 96 (1907).

[67] David J. Brewer, *The Movement of Coercion* (Chicago: Building Contractors' Council, 1893), 3.

[68] *Allgeyer v. Louisiana*, 165 U.S. 578 (1897). I have relied for this discussion upon Purcell, *Brandeis and the Progressive Constitution*, pp. 15, 41.

[69] *Lochner v. New York*, 198 U.S. 45 (1905).

and "life." In his *Unwritten Constitution of the United States* (1890), the constitutional theorist Christopher Tiedeman asserted, "[T]he Federal Constitution contains only a declaration of the fundamental and most general principles of constitutional law, while the real, living constitutional law, – that which the people are made to feel around and about them, controlling the exercise of power by government, and protecting the minority from the tyranny of the majority – the flesh and blood of the Constitution, instead of its skeleton, is here, as well as elsewhere, unwritten."[70] The implications were clear – the failure of "written" constitutions to correspond to "unwritten" ones would render the former "lifeless." Quoting Francis Lieber, William Hammond put it thus: "No truth can be clearer to the student of history and law than that a written constitution of any value always presupposes the existence of an unwritten one.... The worthlessness of written constitutions that have not unwritten ones beneath and behind them, is one of the most frequently recurring lessons of the nineteenth century."[71] In 1885, Philemon Bliss echoed the same theme: "The written constitution is a help; but one whose letter is not supported by the unwritten is but chaff."[72] In his 1885 review of Dicey's *Law of the English Constitution*, James Bradley Thayer pointed to the existence of "convention and usage" in the operation of the U.S. Constitution as having the effect of "bringing that wild creature, the political sovereign, into orderly conduct."[73]

The "unwritten" law that gave "life" to "written" law – even where it was recognized to twist the original meaning of the latter – was represented as the emanation of a dynamic society undergoing a constant improvement of morals. Thus, Christopher Tiedeman observed, "It may ... be laid down as a general proposition that a legal rule is the product of social forces, reflecting the prevalent sense of right."[74] This "prevalent sense of right," in true Spencerian–Darwinian fashion, was never stationary. In its "growth and evolution" it could be shown to follow "an easily recognized law of development." However, it is important to emphasize that, for Tiedeman, this constantly improving "prevalent sense of right" was most emphatically *not* shaped by democratic majorities. Legislatures,

[70] Tiedeman, *Unwritten Constitution*, p. 43.

[71] Francis Lieber, *Legal and Political Hermeneutics, or Principles of Interpretation and Construction in Law and Politics, with Remarks on Precedents and Authorities* (William G. Hammond, ed.) (St. Louis: F. H. Thomas & Co, 1880), Note M (note by Hammond), p. 308.

[72] Bliss, *Of Sovereignty*, p. 165.

[73] James Bradley Thayer, *Legal Essays* (Boston: Boston Book Co., 1908), p. 205.

[74] Tiedeman, *Unwritten Constitution*, p. 9.

in other words, had no privilege when it came to declaring it. Just as Joseph Story had argued a half-century earlier in his *Commentaries on the Constitution*, Tiedeman maintained that political democracy was never, in its deepest being, fully representative. Of a population of between 50 and 60 million in the 1880s, Tiedeman observed, only about 11 million had cast votes in presidential elections. The majority had not consented to law, but could nevertheless be compelled to obey it. How did the few command the many? Tiedeman's answer was as follows: "The *moral influence* of the eleven millions over the mass of the forty-nine millions, rather than the possession of the superior physical force, is what secures the subjection of the many to the commands of the few."[75] This emphasis on "moral influence," rather than democratic structures, as the basis of law's legitimacy made it possible to vest the authority to declare the "prevalent sense of right" in ever smaller groups. Tiedeman continued, "Even in the land of democratic rule and of universal suffrage, only a few persons really mould and fashion public opinion. The great body of private law is, by common consent, usually left to be developed by the legal profession."[76] Thus, it was the legal profession – overwhelmingly a body of common lawyers – that was invested with the ability to shape the "unwritten law" on which the U.S. Constitution rested.

This association of dynamic morality, private law, and a relatively restricted legal profession explained why legislatively generated, socially redistributive rules – for example, the New York statute at issue in *Lochner* – could never reflect "the prevalent sense of right" and never be entitled to respect. By contrast, common law notions of contract and property could do exactly that. In his celebrated *Treatise on the Limitations of the Police Power in the United States* (1886), Tiedeman argued that "the unwritten law of this country is in the main against the exercise of police power, and the restrictions and burdens, imposed upon persons and private property by police regulations, are jealously watched and scrutinized."[77]

Understanding constitutional law in terms of a dynamic, ever evolving "unwritten" constitution was deemed, in the final analysis, a mark of modernity. Quoting Rudolf von Jhering's monumental *Geist des Römischen Rechts*, Tiedeman invoked history in support of the assertion

[75] Ibid., p. 118 (emphasis added).

[76] Ibid., p. 9.

[77] Christopher G. Tiedeman, *A Treatise on the Limitations of Police Power in the United States: Considered from Both a Civil and Criminal Standpoint* (St. Louis: F. H. Thomas Law Book Co., 1886), p. 10.

that an excessive attachment to the written word was a sign of backwardness. As language lost its mystical power over people, they began to grasp "the true rules of interpretation" and to reject "a rigid and irrational formalism" in the search for recognizing the "unwritten" foundations of law.[78] Thus, the movement of history – a move away from textualism – itself justified interpreting the U.S. Constitution in terms of its "unwritten" foundation, which was, of course, nothing other than common law contract and property.

Interlude: History, Logic, and Experience Around the Harvard Law School

Many American legal historians have entirely ignored the writings of the American historical school, choosing instead to represent the late-nineteenth-century battle between laissez-faire and social democracy in terms of the battle between legal formalism and legal antiformalism.[79] In this rendering, in the late nineteenth century, laissez-faire legal thought developed an excessively formal and ahistorical style, such that legal decisions could be represented as deductions following from initial premises or as straightforward applications of sharply bounded legal categories. Social democratic legal thought, by contrast, attempted to find a less formal style, insisted that law should be understood in its social and historical context, and questioned the integrity and value of deductive legal reasoning and bounded categories.

For many American legal historians, long before it was projected onto a national screen as a struggle between laissez-faire and social democracy, the formalism–antiformalism battle was played out on more rarefied philosophical terms at the Harvard Law School as it was reorganized after 1870. There is a species of parochialism here, but given the significance of this story in the history of American legal thought, it is worth revisiting. Ranged on the side of legal formalism, or what has been called classical legal thought, tend to be, *inter alia*, Harvard Law School's dean and "founder" of the case method, Christopher Columbus Langdell (1826–1906); Harvard Law School professor, Langdell's protégé, and his successor as dean, James Barr Ames (1846–1910); and Harvard Law

[78] Christopher G. Tiedeman, *A Treatise on Equity Jurisprudence: With Particular Reference to the Present Conditions of Jurisprudence in the United States* (St. Louis: F. H. Thomas Law Book Co., 1893), p. 2.

[79] Exceptions are Lewis Grossman, David Rabban, Stephen Siegel, and Stephen Wilf.

School professor Joseph Henry Beale (1861–1943). Ranged on the side of legal antiformalism or legal pragmatism, and at least gesturing toward social democratic legal thought, tends to be the heroic figure of Oliver Wendell Holmes, Jr. (1841–1935), Civil War veteran, affiliate of the fabled Cambridge Metaphysical Club, to which American philosophical pragmatism traces its origins, and briefly a member of the Harvard Law School faculty before successive judicial appointments to the Massachusetts Supreme Judicial Court and the U.S. Supreme Court.[80]

As already suggested, one of the distinguishing features of late-nineteenth-century Langdellian legal formalism is – supposedly – its extreme ahistoricism, its claim and will to reduce law to a set of formal legal postulates that could be deduced from one other syllogistically in complete disregard of the needs and desires of society and substantive justice, to say nothing of the changeability of law itself. Historical sensibility, we are accustomed to thinking, lies entirely on the side of Holmesian legal antiformalism. This has been a kind of object of faith in the historiography. It is important, therefore, to set forth an example of this received wisdom, and there is no more celebrated example than Langdell's treatment of the "mailbox rule" and Holmes's review of his treatment. The legal question was a simple one. When someone

80 There is an overwhelming literature on both legal formalism and legal antiformalism, on Langdell and Holmes. I offer only a selection I have consulted over the years.On Langdell, see Paul D. Carrington, "Hail! Langdell!" *Law & Social Inquiry* 20 (1995): 691– 760; Thomas C. Grey, "Langdell's Orthodoxy," *University of Pittsburgh Law Review* 45 (1983): 1–53; Bruce A. Kimball, *The Inception of Modern Professional Education: C. C. Langdell, 1826–1906* (Chapel Hill: University of North Carolina Press, 2009); Bruce A. Kimball, "Langdell on Contracts and Legal Reasoning: Correcting the Holmesian Caricature," *Law and History Review* 25 (2007): 345–399; Bruce A. Kimball, "'Warn Students That I Entertain Heretical Opinions, Which They Are Not to Take as Law': The Inception of Case Method Teaching in the Classrooms of the Early C. C. Langdell, 1870–1883," *Law and History Review* 17 (1999): 57–140.

On Holmes, see Albert W. Aschuler, *Law Without Values: The Life, Work and Legacy of Justice Holmes* (Chicago: University of Chicago Press, 2000); Robert W. Gordon, ed., *The Legacy of Oliver Wendell Holmes, Jr.* (Stanford, Calif.: Stanford University Press, 1992); Robert W. Gordon, "Holmes' *Common Law* as Legal and Social Science," *Hofstra Law Review* 10 (1982): 719–746; William P. LaPiana, "Victorian from Beacon Hill: Oliver Wendell Holmes's Early Legal Scholarship," *Columbia Law Review* 90 (1990): 809–833; Mark Tushnet, "The Logic of Experience: Oliver Wendell Holmes on the Supreme Judicial Court," *Virginia Law Review* 63 (1977): 975–1052; Jan Vetter, "The Evolution of Holmes, Holmes and Evolution," *California Law Review* 72 (1984): 343–368; G. Edward White, *Justice Oliver Wendell Holmes: Law and the Inner Self* (Oxford: Oxford University Press, 1993); G. Edward White, "The Integrity of Holmes' Jurisprudence," *Hofstra Law Review* 10 (1982): 633–671; G. Edward White, "The Rise and Fall of Justice Holmes," *University of Chicago Law Review* 39 (1971–1972): 51–77.

accepted a contractual offer by mail, did the acceptance become binding when it was mailed or when it was received by the offeror? This was a matter of some importance in the vastly expanded world of late-nineteenth-century commerce, with its sharp fluctuations of commodity prices, shipments of commodities across the globe, and slow communications.

When Langdell confronted the issue as a law professor in the 1870s, the courts of important jurisdictions were in disagreement. The courts of England and New York had accepted the mailbox rule, according to which an acceptance became binding when it was mailed. The courts of Massachusetts, however, had rejected the rule.[81]

In his *Summary of the Law of Contracts* (1880), Langdell cast the mailbox rule in the form of a "syllogism" and concluded, "The fault of this syllogism is in the major premise, which is untrue."[82] The contract law principle that the offeree had to have knowledge of the offer had its exact and symmetric analogue, he argued, in the principle that the offeror had to have knowledge of the acceptance. Therefore, the mailbox rule – which did not require the offeror's knowledge of the acceptance for the offeree's acceptance to become binding – was wrong as a matter of principle. Unfortunately for Langdell's reputation in the history of American legal thought, he went on to characterize matters as follows:

> It has been claimed that the purposes of substantial justice, and the interests of contracting parties as understood by themselves, will be best served by holding that the contract is complete the moment the letter of acceptance is mailed; and cases have been put to show that the contrary view would produce not only unjust but absurd results. *The true answer to this argument is that it is irrelevant* [emphasis added].[83]

Langdell had more to say on the subject, but it is this language that has survived in the memory of subsequent generations. Langdell had used exactly the same language in the second edition of his *Cases on the Law of Contracts* (1879). Holmes seized upon it in his 1880 review of the second edition in the pages of the *American Law Review*.

81 *Adams v. Lindsell*, 1 B. and Ald. 681, 106 Eng. Rep. 250 (England, 1818); *Mactier's Admin. v. Frith*, 6 Wend. 103 (New York, 1830); McCulloch v. Eagle Ins. Co., 18 Mass. (1 Pick.) 278 (1822).

82 Christopher C. Langdell, *A Summary of the Law of Contracts* (2d ed.) (Boston: Little, Brown & Co., 1880), p. 19.

83 Ibid., pp. 20–21.

At the beginning of his review, Holmes lavished praise upon Langdell's systematizing efforts: "No man competent to judge can read a page of it without at once recognizing the hand of a great master.... It may be said without exaggeration that there cannot be found in the legal literature of this country, such a *tour de force* of patient and profound intellect working out original theory through a mass of detail, and evolving consistency out of what seemed a chaos of conflicting atoms."[84]

But here the praise ended. If Langdell's intellectual rigor was his greatest strength, Holmes observed, it was also his greatest shortcoming. "Mr. Langdell's ideal in the law, the end of all his striving, is the *elegantia juris*, or *logical* integrity of the system as a system. He is, perhaps, the greatest living legal theologian."[85] Holmes went on to quote verbatim Langdell's offending language about the "irrelevance" of considerations of justice or the interests of the parties in deciding upon the validity of the mailbox rule. Holmes continued, "The reader will perceive that the language is only incidental, but it reveals a mode of thought which becomes conspicuous to a careful student."[86]

Holmes used the occasion to set forth his own emerging philosophy of law. This is the first appearance of his famous formulation – since become a mantra of legal modernism – preferring "experience" to "logic" as the "life" of the law. At the same time, Holmes actively claimed "history" for his own view of the law while denying "history" to Langdell's view of the law. It is worth quoting Holmes at some length (the reader should also note Holmes's Spencerian–Darwinian rhetoric):

> If Mr. Langdell could be suspected of ever having troubled himself about Hegel, we might call him a Hegelian in disguise, so entirely is he interested in the formal connections of things, or logic, as distinguished from the feelings which make the content of logic, and which have actually shaped the substance of the law. *The life of the law has not been logic: it has been experience.* The seed of every new growth within its sphere has been a felt necessity.... No one will ever have a truly philosophic mastery over the law who does not habitually consider the forces outside of it which have made it what it is. *More than that, he must remember that as it embodies the story of a nation's development through many centuries, the law finds its philosophy not in self-consistency, which it must always fail in so long as it continues to grow, but in history and the nature of human needs* [emphasis added].[87]

[84] Oliver Wendell Holmes, Jr., Review, in *Collected Works*, Vol. 3, p. 103.

[85] Ibid.

[86] Ibid.

[87] Ibid.

In Holmes's own view, then, Langdell's formalism, grounded in "logic," stood for a repudiation of history, whereas his own antiformalism, grounded in "experience," fully embraced it. Possessed of "life" and capable of "growth," the law, Holmes tells us, "finds its philosophy not in self-consistency, ... but in history." To understand law, furthermore, we must consider "the forces *outside of it*," which, presumably, can also be accounted for as historical.

If we are used to thinking of Langdellian legal formalism as being hermetic and ahistorical, and of Holmesian legal antiformalism as being open to outside influences and historical, we have none other than Holmes, the acclaimed father of American legal antiformalism himself, to thank for it. But might Holmes's self-conscious claiming of the mantle of history for himself and the denial of it to Langdell be overdrawn? How might we evaluate Holmes's own historical imagination? In what follows, I deconstruct the famed distinction between Langdellian legal formalism and Holmesian legal antiformalism, showing not only that both Langdell and Holmes appropriated the Spencerian–Darwinian philosophies of the day, but also that the Holmesian category of "experience" builds upon, and derives from, Langdellian "logic."

The History of "Logic"

For the contemporary American lawyer who turns to the first edition of Langdell's landmark *Selection of Cases on the Law of Contracts* (1871), the experience is somewhat startling.[88] In contrast to so many of the legal texts of the nineteenth century that seem unalterably distant, this one is instantly, even shockingly, recognizable in form. With one major difference (the nearly complete lack of editorial commentary; cases simply and wordlessly follow each other in rough chronological order), it could almost be a contemporary casebook, that staple of legal instruction in American law schools. The 1871 edition of the *Selection of Cases on the Law of Contracts* seems to represent, as such, that very rare thing: a discrete and distinct historical change, a small new step.

Langdell offered sound pedagogic and institutional reasons for his new approach to law school instruction. His 1887 speech to the Harvard Law School Association bespeaks the desire to make law the object of learned

[88] Little, Brown & Co. published the first half of Langdell's *Cases on Contracts* in October 1870. The full first edition appeared in 1871.

study, to break with the English style of legal education by apprenticeship, and to emulate continental European styles and methods. In order to do this, law had to be approached as a "science" that could be mastered only in the university. To the extent that law was an object of scientific study, it depended upon gathering the raw materials out of which a science could be constructed. For Langdell, these consisted of printed materials, "the ultimate sources of all legal knowledge."[89] It was there that students were to obtain their knowledge of legal principles. In this regard, they would be no different from students of the natural sciences:

> We have also constantly inculcated the idea that the library is the proper workshop of professors and students alike; that it is to us all that the laboratories of the university are to the chemists and physicists, the museum of natural history to the zoologists, the botanical garden to the botanists.[90]

Langdell's inductive method with its stress on the importance of cases was thus very different from Joel Bishop's faith in being able to extract timeless principles from underneath the "rubbish of cases." Indeed, Bishop was a critic of Langdell's case method, claiming – on the basis of the famous account of Newton's discovery of gravity – that the case method entailed drowning students in "showers of apples" instead of teaching them "the law of gravitation."[91]

It is in Langdell's insistence on offering the law student nothing but a bare succession of cases following one another in approximate chronological order – an entirely novel idea at the time – that we might discern his affiliation to the Spencerian–Darwinian sense of historical time configured as "life" rendered graspable through the production of relations between phenomena. Langdell is interested precisely in appropriating the form of the imagined movement of "life" for pedagogic ends. I have not been able to find any direct references to "life" or "death" in Langdell's writings. However, the related term "growth" and the emphasis on tracing that "growth" through relating temporally specific phenomena (cases) appear repeatedly. The preface to the first edition of *Selection of Cases on the Law of Contracts* (1871) states:

> Each of these doctrines has arrived at its present state by slow degrees; in other words, it is a growth, extending in many cases through centuries. This growth is

[89] C. C. Langdell, "Harvard Celebration Speech," *Law Quarterly Review* 3 (1887): 118–125, at 124.

[90] Ibid., 124.

[91] Bishop, *Common Law and Codification*, p. 31.

to be traced in the main through a series of cases; and much the shortest and best, if not the only way of mastering the doctrine effectually is by studying the cases in which it is embodied.[92]

There was openly acknowledged artifice in Langdell's construction of the "growth" of doctrine. Not all cases were equally important. It was the task of the casebook editor "to select, classify, and arrange all the cases which had contributed in any important degree to the growth, development, or establishment of ... essential doctrines."[93] In his selection, classification, and arrangement, moreover, Langdell introduced another pedagogic innovation: the inclusion of overruled and conflicting cases. In so doing, we might surmise, he was attempting more or less concertedly to reproduce or capture some of the stochastic and variable nature of Spencerian–Darwinian "life." After all, the movement of Spencerian–Darwinian "life" was seen as involving a stochastic variation that obscured its direction in the short term but that provided – through the assumption of the right temporal perspective – the only infallible means of tracing its arc.

If the unfolding of doctrine was to be grasped through the establishment of relations among cases, in other words, that task was not going to be made easy. In Spencerian–Darwinian fashion, the law student would have to assume the correct temporal scale in order to establish the right relations among cases and to discern the movement of doctrine in the midst of error, contradiction, and aberration. An overruled, contradictory, or aberrant case was thus not merely an "exception" to an underlying natural "law" as it had been for a thinker like Joel Bishop; it was an integral, even crucial, dimension of the "life" of doctrine. It was how doctrine had to be grasped – indeed, the only way in which it could be grasped. Since Langdell himself had artfully chosen the errors, contradictions, and aberrations, it is safe to conclude that presenting a confused set of cases from which the student was to learn represented, for Langdell, a kind of intellectual aesthetic intimately affiliated with the Spencerian–Darwinian historical sensibility of the late nineteenth century. It is not surprising that the first generation of Harvard Law School students confronted with Langdell's method – with the exception of a small devoted

[92] Christopher C. Langdell, *A Selection of Cases on the Law of Contracts. With References and Citations. Prepared for Use As a Text-Book in Harvard Law School* (Boston: Little, Brown, & Company, 1871), Preface, p. vi.

[93] Ibid., p. vii.

band including James Barr Ames – abandoned Langdell's classes en masse for those of his less innovative colleagues.

Langdell's idea of showing the "growth" of doctrine through the artful setting of temporally marked cases in relation to each other did not escape the notice of an editor of the recently founded *American Law Review*: Oliver Wendell Holmes, Jr. What is curious about Holmes's reviews of Langdell's work in the 1870s – up until the famous 1880 review accusing Langdell of being a "theologian" devoid of historical sensibility – is how strongly they acknowledge and applaud nothing other than Langdell's *historical* sensibility. In 1871, for example, Holmes reviewed the first half of Langdell's *Selection of Cases on the Law of Contracts* that had appeared in 1870. He praised the effort effusively:

> Mr. Langdell's scheme is to present without comment the series of cases by which an important principle has been developed, arranged in order of time, and after indicating by the heading of the chapter and section the topic to be illustrated, to leave the rest to the student.... [Holmes then lists the casebook's first set of cases on mutual consent, which includes the English case setting forth the famous mailbox rule.] Thus the important and difficult question as to the *punctum temporis* when parties at a distance, and attempting to contract with each other, become bound, is seen *from the time when it was hardly well enough understood to be asked, up to its final answer upon the maturest deliberation, and by the highest tribunals*. The chronological arrangement, although it may sometimes add to the labor of a beginner, we have found to be most instructive and interesting. *Tracing the growth of a doctrine in this way not only fixes it in the mind, but shows its meaning, extent, and limits as nothing else can. We must mention that we have been struck with the confirmation here afforded ... that judges know how to decide a good deal sooner than they know why* [emphasis added].[94]

In making explicit what Langdell had left implicit, Holmes reveals how thoroughly he himself is in the grip of the reigning Spencerian–Darwinian historical sensibility. "Tracing the growth of a doctrine," says Holmes, "shows its meaning ... as nothing else can." Furthermore, a doctrine cannot be viewed from the moment of time represented by the individual case even by the judge who plays a part in its articulation. It proceeds, in a sense, unbeknownst to the judge, "unconsciously." It can be grasped *only* through the assumption of a temporal scale that makes it possible to see relations among cases. Spencer himself could not have emphasized the importance of scale, or the "unconscious" movement of things, more explicitly.

94 Oliver Wendell Holmes, Jr., Review, *American Law Review* 5 (1871): 534–551, at 539, in *Collected Works*, Vol. 1, p. 243.

It is not a little ironic that Holmes's single criticism of Langdell at this early stage has to do with what Holmes saw as Langdell's excessive commitment *to* a kind of historical complexity, an overblown desire to show the fullness and variation of things, a concerted refusal to simplify:

> It seems as if [Langdell's] desire to give the whole history of the doctrine had led to putting in some contradictory and unreasoned determinations which could have been spared. *Indeed, one surmises that a skeptical vein in the editor* [Langdell] *is sometimes answerable for the prominence given to the other side of what is now settled.* But very likely he had deeper reasons and is right [emphasis added].[95]

In Holmes's own view, Langdell was thus possessed of a "skeptical vein" before he became a "theologian"![96]

Langdell's preoccupation with the idea of the "growth" of law was not by any means limited to his casebooks. The introduction to his *Summary of Equity Pleading* (1877) stressed the "growth" of equity from out of ecclesiastical procedure.[97] And once again, he won the praise of Holmes precisely for his historical sensibility: "If we were to select any part [of the *Summary of Equity Pleading*] as of pre-eminent excellence, we should mention the [historical] introduction. The development of the ecclesiastical procedure as there unfolded, ... and, under the author's hand, even the function of parchment in the time of Lord Eldon becomes instructive."[98]

After almost a decade of nearly unstinting praise for Langdell's historical sensibility as reflected in the form and style of the Langdellian casebooks and summaries, in the above-mentioned 1880 review of the second edition of *Cases on the Law of Contracts*, Holmes suddenly

[95] Ibid.

[96] Holmes's praise continued over the next few years. When the full version of *Selection of Cases on the Law of Contracts* appeared in 1871, Holmes applauded the book for its organization along abstract doctrinal lines. Oliver Wendell Holmes, Jr., Review, *American Law Review* 6 (1871): 34–362, at in *Collected Works*, Vol. 1, p. 273. Holmes was similarly enthusiastic about Langdell's second major casebook, *Cases on Sales* (1872), which also adopted the historical/evolutionary approach of the contracts casebooks. Holmes, Review (1872), p. 145, discussed in Kimball, "Langdell on Contracts and Legal Reasoning," pp. 363–365.

[97] For example, Christopher C. Langdell, *A Summary of Equity Pleading* (Cambridge: Charles W. Sever, 1877), pp. xxvii, xxix.

[98] Holmes, Review (1877), p. 763, quoted in Kimball, "Langdell on Contracts and Legal Reasoning," p. 362. Through a meticulous reading of the changes in Langdell's texts, Bruce Kimball has suggested that there might well have been a direct relationship between Holmes's various reviews and the changes Langdell made as he developed new – or new editions of – casebooks and summaries. When Holmes suggested pruning some cases in the section on forebearance in the contracts casebook, Langdell responded by

changed direction. Langdell was now a "theologian," a Hegelian wedded to "logic," with no sense that the "philosophy" of law lay in its history and that law could be understood only in terms of forces "outside" it. How do we account for this abrupt shift? Can the break between Holmes and Langdell be justified on intellectual grounds? Later in this section, we will explore Holmes's historical sensibility in far greater detail and evaluate his own attempt to ground law in history and in forces "outside" law. We will inquire, specifically, into the sustainability of Holmes's self-conscious sense of being historical and hence different from Langdell. For now, however, based on the foregoing, it is worth emphasizing that, from the perspective of late-nineteenth-century historical sensibility, Langdell's method was thoroughly historical and that he self-consciously sought to render law historical in the very form of his landmark casebooks and summaries. Holmes recognized this fact repeatedly in the 1870s. But this was also widely acknowledged by others. James Barr Ames is an example: "It is a curious fact that Langdell, who was a great logician, taught a doctrine through its historical development."[99] In its own day, Langdellian "logic," it would appear, was not thought to be without history.

Indeed, one could well ask just how "curious" it was to combine "logic" with history at this time. A self-conscious claiming of history was common among many late-nineteenth- and early-twentieth-century legal formalists (this is in contrast to a thinker like Joel Bishop, who rarely claimed the mantle of history). From the perspective of the legal formalists, science was necessarily historical. Deductive logic was spurned; history enabled the discovery of "logic" or "principles." At an address delivered before the St. Louis Congress of Arts and Sciences in 1904, for example, the Harvard law professor Joseph Henry Beale, whose name subsequently became synonymous with the ridiculousness of legal formalism under the pejorative term "Bealism," criticized deductive logic and embraced the historicist legacy of Sir Henry Maine, who was widely

cutting out twenty-five cases from that section in the second edition. When Holmes suggested adding "a full index," Langdell responded by providing a thirteen-page index. Kimball even suggests, more tendentiously, that Holmes might have been responsible for Langdell's evolutionary language. I am skeptical about this last claim. There is no direct evidence for it, the model of the casebook preceded Holmes's reviews, and Holmes had no monopoly whatsoever on evolutionary ideas in the 1870s and beyond. Whatever one makes of Kimball's last claim, however, it would appear that Holmes was not without a hand in shaping the work that he would later criticize as "theological."

99 "Memoir of James Barr Ames," in James Barr Ames, *Lectures on Legal History and Miscellaneous Legal Essays; With a Memoir* (Cambridge, Mass.: Harvard University Press, 1913), p. 8.

taken in the late-nineteenth-century Anglo-American world to have been the first to have sought to historicize law:

> In England a small but important school of legal thinkers have followed the historical method, and in the United States it has obtained a powerful hold.... We are living in an age of scientific scholarship. We have abandoned the subjective and deductive philosophy of the middle ages, and we learn from scientific observation and from historical discovery. The newly accepted principles of observation and induction, applied to the law, have given us a generation of legal scholars for the first time since the modern world began, and the work of these scholars has at last made possible the intelligent statement of the principles of law.[100]

Surely, it is noteworthy that legal formalists rejected those very features of formalism – deductive logic and an absence of historical sensibility – that antiformalists most vehemently criticized.

Some clues as to the relationship between "logic" and history can be found in the writings of Langdell's protégé, colleague, and successor as dean, James Barr Ames. Ames saw himself primarily as a legal historian. As a student, Ames spent an extra year at Harvard Law School, during which time he taught two college courses in history – a history of seventeenth-century England and a history of medieval institutions. As a law professor, Ames devoted himself to painstaking historical research. He went far beyond reported cases and pored over the Year Books (going through Year Books was apparently a summer pastime). Prominent legal historians of the day – Pollock, Maitland, and others – acknowledged the originality of his research. Throughout, he remained a steadfast Langdellian.

As revealed in the cryptic essays from the 1880s on that were gathered in *Lectures on Legal History* (1913), Ames's approach to history was premised on separating – like Darwin, Spencer, and many others – the essential from the inessential in the historical record. The only history worth the name, from his perspective, revealed "the nature of things." The rest was of antiquarian interest. But one could discern "the nature of things" only by going through the archive. In a typical instance, Ames could ask, "Are these doctrines of the old common law accidents of English legal history, or are they founded in the nature of things? Do they chiefly concern the legal antiquarian, or have they also a practical bearing upon the litigation of to-day?"[101] What the hunt through the archives in search of "the nature of things" permitted, in the final instance, was to lift

[100] Joseph Henry Beale, "The Development of Jurisprudence During the Past Century," *Harvard Law Review* 18 (1905): 271–283, at 283.

[101] Ames, "The Nature of Ownership," in *Lectures on Legal History*, p. 192–193.

something out of its own historical context, to retrieve things from history itself and locate them in a chain of unfolding "logic," even as it was recognized that they were to be appropriated only through history. Thus, Ames ended his essay "The Disseisin of Chattels" as follows:

> It is still true that the doctrine of disseisin *belongs not to feudalism alone, but to the general law of property*.... [T]he writer will endeavor to show that this doctrine is *not a mere episode in English legal history, but that it is a living principle, founded in the nature of things, and of great practical value in the solution of many important questions* [emphasis added].[102]

The doctrine of disseisin of chattels, traceable only through meticulous historical research was then simultaneously within and without history. It "belonged" to feudalism *and* to "the general law of property," where "logic" would be allowed to reign. "Logic" and history, then, were intimately linked. There was no "logic" without history; history served to demonstrate the unfolding of "logic" or to prepare the ground for its operation (as we shall see, this was not terribly different from Holmes's own approach).

But if both Langdell and Ames, in different ways, turned to history as the ground for the demonstration of "logic," there was also a recognition in each that history's impact on the law sometimes resisted the operations of "logic." Langdell and Ames operated, in a sense, with a rather modern notion: history intervened against "logic" as pure contingency. For example, Langdell was fully aware that the common law was possessed of a historicity that could not be subsumed into the stable unfolding or "growth" of doctrine no matter how artfully he adorned the narratives in this casebooks with contradiction and error. And this was true not only of public law, but also of the private law that was seen in this period as the appropriate object of logical ordering. At places in Langdell's *Summary of the Law of Contracts*, for example, we see something that would be more fully developed in the writings of Holmes – a sense of the sheer *unreason* of common law doctrine made apparent by tracing the origins of its doctrines. Thus, Langdell discusses how legal consideration came to be transposed from its association with the action of debt to its association with the newer action of assumpsit. On logical grounds, he argued, consideration ought not to have attached to assumpsit. But it had. "But whatever may have been the merits of the question originally, it was long since conclusively settled in the manner stated above; and thus the action

102 Ames, "The Disseisin of Chattels," in *Lectures on Legal History*, p. 191.

of assumpsit modified the old consideration instead of wholly superseding it; but so important were the modifications that the relationship of the new consideration to the old has been almost wholly lost sight of."[103] Here was something "conclusively settled" that could not be accounted for in terms of a working out of "logic" over time. Settled aspects of the law – ones that could not be discarded in the name of "logic" – could be accounted for in terms of nothing but history.

Ames also recognized that considerations of public policy – considerations outside "logic" and "morals" and owing their existence to nothing but history – often infiltrated the private law.[104] As he put it (again sounding rather like Holmes): "The law is utilitarian. It exists for the realization of the reasonable needs of the community. If the interest of an individual runs counter to this chief object of the law, it must be sacrificed. That is why, in the cases just considered and others that will occur to you, the innocent suffer and the wicked go unpunished."[105] The search for "logic," then, went along with a recognition that law, even private law, could never be entirely rationalized. It was recognized by its most ardent proponents to be a partial endeavor, one that could be embarked upon, furthermore, only by a turn to history.

The History of "Experience"

In 1919, Morris R. Cohen inquired of Holmes whether the reading of Voltaire had had any direct influence in producing his famous skepticism. Holmes replied as follows:

[103] Langdell, *Summary of the Law of Contracts*, p. 61.

[104] Thus, in his essay "Law and Morals," Ames states: "On grounds of public policy there are and always will be, on the one hand, many cases in which persons damaged may recover compensation from others whose conduct was morally blameless, and, on the other hand, many cases in which persons damaged cannot obtain compensation even from those whose conduct was morally most reprehensible.... One keeps fierce, wild animals at his peril, and also domestic animals, after knowledge that they are dangerous. By legislation, indeed, in several States, one who keeps a dog must make three-fold compensation, for damage done by the dog, without proof of the keeper's knowledge of its vicious quality. The sheep farmers must be encouraged, even if some innocent persons have to pay dearly for the luxury of keeping a dog. A Massachusetts bank was entered by burglars who carried off and put into circulation a large quantity of bank notes which had been printed but never issued by the bank. The bank had to pay these notes. The bank must safeguard the notes it prints at its peril, to prevent the possibility of a widespreading mischief to the general public. Ames, "Law and Morals," in *Lectures on Legal History*, p. 447.

[105] Ibid., p. 448.

Oh no – it was not Voltaire – it was the influence of the scientific way of looking at the world – that made the change.... My father was brought up scientifically – i.e., he studied medicine in France – and I was not. *Yet there was with him as with the rest of his generation a certain softness of attitude toward the interstitial miracle – the phenomenon without phenomenal antecedents, that I did not feel.* The difference was in the air, although perhaps only a few of my time felt it. *The Origin of Species* I think came out while I was in college – H. Spencer had announced his intention to put the universe into our pockets – I hadn't read either of them to be sure, but as I say it was in the air [emphasis added].[106]

In other words, even though the young Holmes had not read Darwin and Spencer, by his own admission, their science contributed powerfully to his suspicion of "the interstitial miracle – the phenomenon without phenomenal antecedents." Few phrases could capture more succinctly Holmes's debt to Spencer. As expressed in 1919, Holmes's suspicion of "the phenomenon without phenomenal antecedents" is very close indeed to Spencer's 1857 despondent realization that the world was nothing but a "succession of phenomena." However, in one important respect, as we shall see, Homes – along with other members of the Cambridge Metaphysical Club – broke with Spencer. He rejected Spencer's determinism. Holmes summarized the pragmatist suspicion of determinism when, many years later, he described his college friend Chauncey Wright: "Chauncey Wright, a nearly forgotten philosopher of real merit, taught me when I was young that I must not say *necessary* about the universe, that we don't know whether anything is necessary or not."[107]

Generations of legal scholars have intoned the opening lines of Holmes's 1881 masterpiece, *The Common Law*, in which he opposes an ahistorical "logic" to a historical "experience" and claims that only the latter constitutes "the life of the law" (Holmes recycled the language from his 1880 review of Langdell's casebook, quoted earlier).[108] Although the stated target in this opening paragraph is Langdellian "logic," Holmes, as someone opposed to metaphysics of all kinds, was equally, or even more, suspicious of "morals," something he associated with Kantian and Hegelian thought. In the 1860s and 1870s, Holmes's biographer, Mark

[106] Holmes to Cohen, February 5, 1919, quoted in Philip P. Wiener, *Evolution and the Founders of Pragmatism* (Cambridge, Mass.: Harvard University Press, 1949), p. 173.

[107] Holmes to Pollock, August 30, 1929, in *Holmes–Pollock Letters: The Correspondence of Mr. Justice Holmes and Sir Frederick Pollock, 1874–1932* (2 vols.) (Mark DeWolfe Howe, ed.) (Cambridge, Mass.: Harvard University Press, 1941), Vol. 2, p. 252. On Holmes as a pragmatist, see Thomas C. Grey, "Holmes and Legal Pragmatism," *Stanford Law Review* 41 (1989): 787–870.

[108] Holmes, *Common Law*, p. 1.

DeWolfe Howe, informs us, Holmes was beginning to express hostility to the "*a priori* categories of Kant and the conceptual dialectic of Hegel." He was simultaneously "impressed and repelled" by the highly metaphysical investigations of the German historical school of law represented by scholars as diverse as Savigny, Windscheid, Jhering, and Keller.[109] To the extent that Holmes self-consciously wielded history, then, it was against both "logic" *and* "morals" as grounds and explanations of the law.

The argument of *The Common Law* runs roughly as follows. Following a line of antimetaphysical thinking one could trace to Spencer and Darwin, Holmes argues that various areas of the common law – criminal and civil liability, property, contract, and so on – should be interpreted not as straightforward emanations from the ahistorical subjective "internal" intent of the legal actor ("morals") or from "logic," as he claims Kantians or Langdellians might argue, but rather in terms of the law's thoroughly historical setting of external phenomena in relation to each other. These are phenomena surrounding the legal actor and include the legal actor himself as phenomenon. The law's relating of external phenomena has the effect of producing objective external standards through which liability or culpability is determined. For Holmes, everything that is truly vital about the law comes from its ability to select and organize external phenomena into objective external standards by reaching into the realm of "life." "Experience," for Holmes, refers to nothing other than the lessons that law has drawn and continues to draw from "life" that the law then transforms into objective external standards.

Like the thinkers of the American historical school, Holmes operated with a sense of mismatch between law and "life." "Life," he argued, was always spinning ahead of law. Law was always a bit "behind" "life." Also like the thinkers of the historical school, at least in his early writings up to *The Common Law*, Holmes argued that this mismatch took place inside the common law. The common law was at war, temporally speaking, with itself. Condemned to ontological "behindness" vis-à-vis "life," it suffered from a Spencerian problem of nonadaptation. Holmes states:

> The truth is, that the law is always approaching, and never reaching, consistency. It is forever adopting new principles from life at one end, and it always retains old

[109] Mark DeWolfe Howe, *Justice Oliver Wendell Holmes: The Proving Years, 1870–1882* (2 vols.) (Cambridge, Mass.: Harvard University Press, 1963), Vol. 2, p. 151. Mathias Reimann has argued that Holmes's attacks on German legal thinkers were veiled attacks on American contemporaries. Mathias Reimann, "Holmes's *Common Law* and German Legal Science," in Gordon, ed., *The Legacy of Oliver Wendell Holmes, Jr.*, p. 72.

ones from history at the other, which have not yet been absorbed or sloughed off. It will become entirely consistent only when it ceases to grow.[110]

Holmes locates this gap within the common law with a view to making visible a kind of form–substance problem. The form of the law reflects the lessons absorbed from "life" in the past, which might not be relevant today. The substance of the law constitutes lessons from "life" today. Form and substance are locked in a kind of complex temporal dance, the former always "behind" the latter.

How, then, does the common law come to embody "life"? For Holmes, in the vein of James Coolidge Carter, this occurs because of nothing other than the "good sense" of the common law judge who is always able to reach out into "life" and unerringly – more important, "unconsciously" and as a result of "instinctive preferences" – subordinate the claims of "logic" to the claims of "experience," the claims of form to the claims of substance:

> The very considerations which judges most rarely mention, and always with an apology, are the secret root from which the law draws all the juices of life. I mean, of course, considerations of what is expedient for the community concerned. *Every important principle which is developed by litigation is in fact and at bottom the result of more or less definitely understood views of public policy; most generally, to be sure, under our practice and traditions, the unconscious result of instinctive preferences and inarticulate convictions, but none the less traceable to views of public policy in the last analysis.* And as the law is administered by able and experienced men, who know too much to sacrifice good sense to a syllogism, it will be found that, when ancient rules maintain themselves in the way that has been and will be shown in this book, new reasons more fitted to the time have been found for them, and that they gradually receive a new content, and at last a new form, from the grounds to which they have been transplanted [emphasis added].[111]

In other words, when he wrote *The Common Law*, even as he turned to Spencerian–Darwinian thought, Holmes was still very much in the grip of orthodox common law thinking. Even though the law lagged behind "life," the common law judge was "unconsciously" able to drink from "life."[112]

Even at the time of *The Common Law*, however, Holmes differed from thinkers of the American historical school in one significant respect,

[110] Holmes, *Common Law*, p. 36.

[111] Ibid., pp. 35–36.

[112] Morton Horwitz makes this observation about the Holmes of *The Common Law*. Horwitz, *Transformation of American Law, 1870–1960*, p. 125.

namely his lack of faith in Spencerian determinism. The ability of the common law judge to reach into "life" did not mean, for Holmes, that "life" was going somewhere or that it came invested with a particular meaning. Holmes picks up an aspect of the Spencerian corpus – the joining up of phenomena – but rejects Spencerian determinism. The result is an antifoundational, destructive use of history, one that is revealed in Holmes's concerted attempt in *The Common Law* to demolish any claim that the common law's history reveals an uncovering of "logic" or "morals" over time. For Holmes – unlike for many legal thinkers at this time, whether the thinkers of the American historical school or the Harvard formalists – the history of law would "not be straight and its direction not always visible."[113] Accordingly, in *The Common Law* and the texts preceding it, Holmes argues – much as Nietzsche did around the same time in the realm of morals – that the history of common law doctrine is one of mistake, linguistic confusions, and survivals. (As I suggested earlier, this demonstration of the sheer *unreason* of the law was also recognized – although to not nearly quite the same extent by – Langdell and Ames).[114] I will treat each of these in turn.

First, Holmes shows existing common law doctrine to be the result of a surprising number of historical mistakes. Often, these mistakes took the form of a surreptitious or accidental inversion of procedure and substance. The search for the origin of a doctrine frequently revealed this embarrassing truth: "It seems strange that this crude product of the infancy of law should have any importance for us at the present time. Yet whenever we trace a leading doctrine of substantive law far enough back, we are very likely to find some forgotten circumstance of procedure at its source."[115] In *The Common Law*'s chapter on bailment, for example, Holmes shows that the law of bailments hinges upon exactly this inversion: "At first the bailee was answerable to the owner, because he was the only person who could sue. Now it was said he could sue because he was answerable to the owner."[116] In other words, a substantive principle that followed from a procedural one became, through a series of inexplicable contingencies, a procedural principle that followed from a substantive one. This historical

[113] Holmes, *Common Law*, p. 78.

[114] I discuss the similarities between Holmes and Nietzsche in Kunal M. Parker, "The History of Experience: On the Historical Imagination of Oliver Wendell Holmes, Jr.," *PoLAR: Political and Legal Anthropology Review* 26 (2003): 60–85.

[115] Holmes, *Common Law*, p. 253.

[116] Ibid., p. 167.

error in turn was responsible for the idea that common carriers should be subject to strict liability: "[S]trict responsibility is a fragmentary survival from the general law of bailment ... ; and ... the modifications which the old law has undergone were due in part to a confusion of ideas."[117]

Second, a surprising number of existing common law doctrines had resulted from linguistic confusions. For Holmes, the way in which linguistic constructions had shaped substantive doctrine equally reflected a breakdown in reasoning that subverted any claim of the history of the common law to be a history of "logic." In *The Common Law*'s chapter on succession *inter vivos*, Holmes considers the question of succession to easement rights:

> How comes it, then, that one who has neither title nor possession is so far favored? The answer is to be found, not in reasoning, but in failure to reason.... The language of the law of easements was built up out of similes drawn from persons at a time when the *noxae deditio* [under Roman law, an action made available to a person injured by another's slave or son] was still familiar; and then, as often happens, language reacted upon thought, so that conclusions were drawn as to the rights themselves from the terms in which they happened to be expressed.... [M]en's minds were not alert to see that these phrases were only so many personifying metaphors, which explained nothing unless the figure of speech was true....
>
> All that can be said is, that the metaphors and similes employed naturally led to the rule which has prevailed, and that, as this rule was just as good as any other, or at least was unobjectionable, it was drawn from the figures of speech without attracting attention, and before any one had seen that they were only figures, which proved nothing and justified no conclusion.[118]

In other words, a central tenet of the law of real property – the attachments of easements to land – grew out of nothing more than the meanings attached to Roman legal formulas transposed into the common law.

Finally, a large part of common law doctrine consists of survivals, those complex Darwinian phenomena that troublingly straddled the boundary between "life" and "death." In an 1879 article entitled "Common Carriers and the Common Law," Holmes advances his theory of survivals:

[117] Ibid., pp. 180–81. The same inversion of procedure and substance might have taken place, Holmes argues, in the case of the doctrine of consideration in contract law (p. 254).

[118] Ibid., pp. 382–385. The same idea is at work in Holmes's 1891 article on "agency," in which he considers the impact upon the law of agency of Roman legal formulas such as *ex persona domini*: "And the mere habit of using these phrases, where the master is bound or benefited by his servant's act, makes it likely that other cases will be brought within the penumbra of the same thought on no more substantial ground than the way of thinking which the words have brought about." Holmes, "Agency I" (1891), *Collected Works*, Vol. 3, p. 345.

> In form [the law's] growth is logical. The official theory is that each new decision follows syllogistically from existing precedents. But as precedents survive like the clavicle in the cat, long after the use they once served is at an end, and the reason for them has been forgotten, the result of following them must often be failure and confusion from the merely logical point of view. It is easy for the scholar to show that reasons have been misapprehended and precedents misapplied.[119]

The Common Law teems with references to survivals. We learn that "large and important branches of the law … are in fact survivals from more primitive times," that the rule that possessory actions are allowed to bailors is "probably by a survival," and that the rule of strict liability for common carriers "is a fragmentary survival."[120] The idea persists in Holmes's later writings on agency. Thus, the law of agency "must be explained by some cause not manifest to common sense alone; … this cause is, in fact, the survival from ancient times of doctrines which in their earlier form embodied certain rights and liabilities of heads of families based on substantive grounds which have disappeared long since."[121]

In showing that the history of legal doctrine is a history of error, linguistic confusion, and survivals, Holmes emphasizes the apparent randomness rather than the order of Spencerian–Darwinian time configured as "life." As Holmes puts it in "Law in Science and Science in Law" (1899), his object in turning to history is to identify "inflated and unreal explanations, *which collapse at the touch of history*."[122] History serves only to make things collapse; it does not tell us where we are headed. In one sense, Holmes is more Darwinian than Spencerian. At any rate, he reveals a different appropriation of the Spencerian–Darwinian historical sensibility than do the thinkers of the American historical school or the Harvard formalists.

For our purposes, however, what is more interesting – and what, incidentally, reveals the limits of Holmes's antifoundational historical consciousness – is the history, and more specifically the temporality, of "experience" that he sets forth. According to Holmes, as already noted, the law's relating of external phenomena to one another in the process of formulating objective external standards is always based on "what is then understood to be convenient" or on "considerations of what is

[119] Holmes, "Common Carriers and the Common Law" (1879), *Collected Works*, Vol. 3, p. 75.

[120] Holmes, *Common Law*, pp. 37, 174, 180.

[121] Holmes, "Agency I,", p. 341.

[122] Holmes, "Law in Science and Science in Law" (1899), *Collected Works*, Vol. 3, p. 414 (emphasis added).

expedient for the community concerned."[123] The traditional figure of the common law judge is invoked in support of the idea that the common law unerringly reaches into "life" and accomplishes the needful. But it is worth inquiring into how Holmes secures the felt meaning of law as "experience."

In *The Common Law* and in the texts preceding it, Holmes produces the effect of law as "experience" by setting forth before his reader a world simultaneously inside and outside historical time. This is not a world that Holmes's audience in the 1880s or his readers today would necessarily recognize as their own. Yet in another sense it might be very familiar to Holmes's audience in the 1880s, especially to those in each group with some familiarity with the then-emerging world of legal texts, treatises, and pedagogy. This was the world of "experience" constructed out of a legal knowledge in the process of systematizing itself. Let me illustrate what I mean.

In *The Common Law*, "experience," and not subjective internal intent or "logic," is said to furnish the ground for the assignment of legal culpability or liability. Answers to a range of familiar questions – When should the legal actor be held to certain kinds of knowledge? Under what circumstances may the legal actor be privileged to act despite possessing certain kinds of knowledge? And so on – are reduced to what "experience" tells us in each case. Here is an example of what Holmes understands to be "experience":

> Experience as interpreted by the English law has shown that dogs, rams, and bulls are in general of a tame and mild nature, and that, if any one of them does by chance exhibit a tendency to bite, butt, or gore, it is an exceptional phenomenon. Hence it is not the law that a man keeps dogs, rams, bulls, and other like tame animals at his peril as to the personal damages which they may inflict, unless he knows or has notice that the particular animal kept by him has the abnormal tendency which they do sometimes show. The law has, however, been brought a little nearer to actual experience by statute in many jurisdictions.
>
> Now let us go one step further still. A man keeps an unbroken and unruly horse, knowing it to be so. That is not enough to throw the risk of its behavior on him. The tendency of the known wildness is not dangerous generally, but only under particular circumstances. Add to keeping, the attempt to break the horse; still no danger to the public is disclosed. But if the place where the owner tries to break it is a crowded thoroughfare, the owner knows an additional circumstance which, according to common experience, makes his conduct dangerous, and therefore must take the risk of what harm may be done. On the other hand,

[123] Holmes, *Common Law*, pp. 2, 35.

> if a man who was a good rider bought a horse with no appearance of vice and mounted it to ride home, there would be no such apparent danger as to make him answerable if the horse became unruly and did damage. Experience has measured the probabilities and draws the line between the two cases.[124]

One could offer scores of similar examples. Most kinds of "experience" that Holmes offers as grounds for deciding the question of legal liability exist between the historical and the ahistorical, between the recognizable and the remote. Many will strike the reader as stunningly obvious. Consider, for example, the following: (1) when a workman on a housetop throws a heavy beam off the roof and hurts someone, "experience" leads us to consider relevant whether the space below the workman is an empty private yard or a crowded city street[125]; (2) when a man hits someone with a stick, "experience" leads us to consider relevant whether the stick is small and made of wood or large and made of iron[126]; (3) when someone buys a machine for making counterfeit coins, "experience" leads us to consider relevant whether the machine has any conceivable other use[127]; (4) when a man cocks and aims a pistol, "experience" leads us to consider relevant whether there was someone standing in front of the man[128]; (5) when a man rides a horse down a street and causes an accident, "experience" leads us to ask whether the man was spurring, or merely riding, the horse[129]; (6) when someone keeps tigers, bears, or other ferocious animals on his property and these animals escape and cause damage or harm, "experience" has taught us that tigers and bears are alert to find means of escape and will cause damage or harm when they escape; the owner of the tiger or bear should therefore be per se liable[130]; (7) when a barrel falls from a warehouse window and hurts someone, "experience" has taught us that the owner of the warehouse or his employees, because they were in complete control of the barrel, should be held liable for the accident[131]; and (8) when a sane man stands on a railway track and looks at an approaching train until it runs him down, "experience" tells us the man's conduct was imprudent and that the railroad company should not be liable.[132]

124 Ibid., p. 157–158.
125 Ibid., pp. 55–56, 60.
126 Ibid., pp. 59–60.
127 Ibid., p. 67.
128 Ibid., p. 69.
129 Ibid., p. 93.
130 Ibid., pp. 119, 155.
131 Ibid., p. 125.
132 Ibid., pp. 128–129.

In one sense, of course, these instances of "experience" can be located in historical time – the world of men riding down streets and the world of men standing on railroad tracks belong to distinct historical moments. But in another sense, the sheer obviousness of the "experiences" at issue places them outside history – they communicate to us in a seemingly unmediated way across historical time. Even though we no longer ride horses down streets, the experiential lesson that spurring a horse while riding down a crowded street might make a difference to the question of the rider's liability if he caused an accident immediately makes sense. What kind of model is this for talking about "experience"?

To one trained as a lawyer or familiar with the world of legal texts, the temporality of Holmesian "experience" is utterly familiar. What Holmes is offering us as the world of "experience" – the lessons allegedly gleaned from the law's reaching into "life" over the course of history, lessons that allegedly affirm the traditional role of the common law judge – looks suspiciously like instances carefully selected in the first instance by Holmes's "logically" oriented adversaries – Langdell, Ames, and others – as part of the effort to structure the law and to illustrate its various features. What is meant to stand for the forces of "life" in Holmes's text is in fact drawn from the "syllogistic" thought of legal formalists (which, I have been suggesting, was itself far more self-consciously historical than we have been led to believe).

A classic nineteenth-century instance of "syllogistic" legal thought attempting to explain itself, an instance with which Holmes was all too familiar, is the Anglo-Indian codes drafted by Macaulay, Sir James Fitzjames Stephen, and others from the 1830s on. Sections of the Anglo-Indian codes were often accompanied by examples consisting of fact patterns and the application of code provisions to them. Langdell's case method was another, self-consciously historical aspect of the same effort, involving the selection of cases to trace the "growth" of legal principles. What the examples offered by the nineteenth-century codifiers and the cases selected by Langdell and others comprised were precisely instances that were historical, in the sense that they were often selected from real cases, but that managed at the same time to present themselves as illustrations of a system and thus surmount historical specificity. It was the Langdellian James Barr Ames, it should be recalled, who turned to the archives and found something that was simultaneously inside and outside history. The Harvard formalists, in the process of systematizing law, located objects in history *and* lifted objects out of it.

Some of these simultaneously historical and ahistorical objects survive to the present day in law school instruction. For example, all instructors and students of property law today are familiar with the "fact pattern" of *Pierson v. Post*, an early-nineteenth-century New York case involving hunters chasing a fox that illustrates the problem of the acquisition of property rights. It is unclear exactly when *Pierson v. Post* entered the pedagogical canon. Holmes cites it as part of a discussion about the variability of "experience."[133] Similarly, every American law student remembers that the doctrine of *res ipsa loquitur* in tort law is illustrated in first-year torts casebooks through the well-known case of the barrel rolling out of the warehouse window. Holmes also cites this as an example of "experience." There are clues, furthermore, that Holmes constructed his world of "experience" directly out of the illustrations that the systematizers had constructed to elucidate their "theological" thinking. Thus, Holmes cites the following as evidence of the law as "experience": "For instance, a newly born child is laid out naked out of doors, where it must perish as a matter of course. This is none the less murder, that the guilty party would have been very glad to have a stranger find the child and save it." The reference for this instance of "experience" turns out to be Fitzjames Stephen's *Digest of Criminal Law*, Art. 223, Illustration (6).[134] The footnotes of *The Common Law* are full of references to the illustrations that Stephen and the other treatise writers had created to shore up their systematizing efforts. In its peculiar straddling of historical and ahistorical time, Holmes's world of the law as "experience" is little more than the dressed-up world of legal example and illustration constructed and perfected by the very purveyors of "logic" whom Holmes opposed in the name of history.

The foregoing discussion of the relationship between legal formalism and legal antiformalism at the Harvard Law School has been intended to show two things: first, that legal formalists, as much as antiformalists, were in the grip of Spencerian–Darwinian historical thinking; second, that the Holmesian category of "experience," so widely hailed as marking an advance in legal thinking, in fact derives much of its content from the Langdellian category of "logic."

[133] Ibid., pp. 217–218. It is interesting that *Pierson v. Post* might itself have *begun* as a pedagogical exercise in early-nineteenth-century New York. Angela Fernandez, "The Lost Record of *Pierson v. Post*, the Famous Fox Case," *Law and History Review* 27 (2009): 149–178.

[134] Holmes, *Common* Law, p. 53.

The Growing Critique of the Common Law

Thinkers of the American historical school such as Christopher Tiedeman might maintain that "the unwritten law of this country is in the main against the exercise of police power [the source of the state's regulatory authority], and the restrictions and burdens, imposed upon persons and private property by police regulations, are jealously watched and scrutinized."[135] But such assertions were contradicted in the first instance by the fact of burgeoning state regulatory activity. The increasingly assertive role of the state was undergirded by various internal critiques of the common law that came from English and American lawyers trained within the common law tradition.

One very influential one came from none other than Sir Henry Maine. Maine's 1861 thesis that the long sweep of the history of law was from a regime of status to a regime of contract was popular with Spencer and conservative common lawyers generally. But as part of this historical vision, Maine was also firmly of the view that modern, dynamic societies should be governed by legislation rather than by common law. The common law had played its role in law's development, but that time had long since passed. Maine was especially impatient with the common law's pretensions to calibrate change "insensibly" in the name of custom. He put it thus: "We do not admit that our tribunals legislate; we imply that they have never legislated; and yet we maintain that the rules of the English common law ... are coextensive with the complicated interests of modern society."[136] Thinkers associated with the American historical school recognized and criticized Maine's anti–common law bias as an endorsement of the Benthamite–Austinian position. While praising Maine's historical research, James Coolidge Carter expressed regret that Maine "did not devote himself to a systematic and sustained inquiry ... instead of accepting the hypothetical conclusion of Austin."[137]

There were other critiques of the jurisprudence of custom from a positivist perspective. Critics pointed out that the idea of a "mysterious," "inarticulate," "unconscious," "felt" custom that gave rise to law woefully ignored the role of positive law in shaping custom. Such charges were hardly new. Bentham had devoted considerable effort to unmasking what he considered the obscurantist and mystifying pretensions of

[135] Tiedeman, *A Treatise on the Limitations of Police Power*, p. 10.

[136] Maine, *Ancient Law*, p. 27.

[137] Carter, *Law: Its Origin, Growth and Function*, p. 13, n. 1.

common lawyers who had glibly equated the common law with custom. In 1881, William Hammond picked up Bentham's (and Austin's) arguments when he pointed out, "To make the custom enforceable, there must be something to distinguish it from the great mass of unenforceable customs; and it is in that specific difference, not in its general character as a custom, that its legal quality resides."[138] Late-nineteenth- and early-twentieth-century positivists like John Chipman Gray extended the attack, calling the idea that law was founded on custom a "baseless dream."[139] Indeed, if Sir Henry Maine's arguments in *Ancient Law* were taken seriously, Gray pointed out, it was as probable that customs had arisen from judicial decisions as the other way around. (Maine had posited the earliest era of law as one of pure *ex post facto* sovereign decision, the era of Themistes, which had then given rise to the era of custom.)[140] Drawing upon the fact of radical historical change, Gray argued that the idea of a law that existed prior to its declaration was absurd: "When the element of long time is introduced, the absurdity of the view of Law preexistent to its declaration is obvious. What was the law in the time of Richard Coeur de Lion on the liability of a telegraph company to the persons to whom a message was sent?"[141] Furthermore, because law was necessarily conflictual, it did not seem likely that law could have arisen from a univocal and unifying custom. There must have been a source of authority – hence, of power – to have declared winners and losers: "Take for instance, the liability of innkeepers for goods stolen from their inns. This is said to rest on a custom, but it does not seem likely that innkeepers would voluntarily subject themselves to such a liability."[142]

Perhaps the most celebrated critique came from Holmes. As argued earlier, *The Common Law* is a contradictory text. While it reveals an antifoundational use of history in the way in which it uses history to demolish the pretensions of the common law to embody "logic" or "morals," it simultaneously argues that the common law is nevertheless able to drink from "life." In *The Common Law*, the "experience" that is law's ground is built from lessons learned from "life."

Holmes's conception of "experience" changes radically as we move from the 1880s to the 1890s and beyond. In *The Common Law*, there are remarkably few representations of "experience" as unstable. I have been

[138] Lieber, *Legal and Political Hermeneutics*, p. 318 (note by Hammond).

[139] Gray, *Nature and Sources of the Law*, p. 238.

[140] Ibid., p. 297.

[141] Ibid., pp. 98–99.

[142] Ibid., p. 298.

able to identify only one instance in *The Common Law* in which Holmes questions the common law's ability to capture "experience" because of the fundamentally unstable nature of "experience" itself – the rapidly changing standards in questions of medical treatment.[143] By the 1890s, however, after Holmes had spent more than a decade on the bench of the Massachusetts Supreme Judicial Court, we see a very different notion of "experience" emerging in his work. "Experience" grounded in "life" is no longer something that the common law judge can "unconsciously" express. Law requires "conscious" reflection on the needs of society; common law judges were ill equipped for the task. We see this clearly for the first time in Holmes's essay "Privilege, Malice, and Intent" (1894):

> Behind all is the question whether the courts are not flying in the face of the organization of the world which is taking place so fast, and of its inevitable consequences. I make these suggestions, not as criticisms of the decisions, but to call attention to the very serious legislative considerations which have to be weighed. The danger is that such considerations should have their weight in an inarticulate form as unconscious prejudice or half conscious inclination. To measure them justly needs not only the highest powers of a judge and a training which the practice of the law does not insure, but also a freedom from prepossessions which is very hard to attain. It seems to me desirable that the work should be done with express recognition of its nature. *The time has gone by when law is only an unconscious embodiment of the common will. It has become a conscious reaction upon itself of organized society knowingly seeking to determine its own destinies* [emphasis added].[144]

The reader should note that Holmes here reverses the Spencerian valences of "consciousness" and "unconsciousness." He had once praised the "unconscious" ability of the common law judge to drink from "life." He was now arguing that law had to be the product of "conscious reflection," namely legislation. Here we have in microcosm all of the themes that would make Holmes the darling of the Progressive generation – the apprehension that the world was changing so fast that the common law could not keep up with it and, therefore, the conviction that the law should henceforth remain content with serving as no more than a tool through which other kinds of specialized knowledge could act upon society.

In the writings of the 1890s and the early twentieth century, these ideas are filled out in ways familiar to us. As discussed in Chapter 1, in his celebrated essay "The Path of the Law" (1897), Holmes pronounces

[143] Holmes, *Common Law*, p. 123.

[144] Holmes, "Privilege, Malice, and Intent," *Collected Works*, Vol. 3, p. 377.

the death of antiquity as a ground of law's legitimacy: "It is revolting to have no better reason for a rule of law than that so it was laid down in the time of Henry IV. It is still more revolting if the grounds upon which it was laid down have vanished long since, and the rule simply persists from blind imitation of the past."[145] The "immemoriality" of the common law could not serve as a source of legitimacy (as was, of course, implicit in the antifoundational uses to which history had been put in *The Common Law*, but never so explicitly stated). At the same time, we are informed categorically that legal knowledge can no longer hope to encompass "life": "For the rational study of the law the black-letter man may be the man of the present, but the man of the future is the man of statistics and the master of economics."[146] This denigration of legal knowledge is accompanied by a reconceptualization of law's history. If *The Common Law* had presented a dual picture of law as error, confusion, and survivals, on the one hand, and as always drinking greedily (and successfully) from "life," on the other, in "Law in Science and Science in Law" (1899) Holmes claims that the history of the law reveals only "the paucity of original ideas in man," something he compares to "the niggardly uninventiveness of nature … with its few smells or colors or types, its short list of elements, working along in the same slow way from compound to compound."[147] "Life" itself, once dynamic and rich, has become dull. Only "science" – which is sharply distinguished from the law's own ways of knowing – can determine "the relative worth of our different social ends."[148]

Not surprisingly, given this denigration of legal knowledge, of its ability to capture "life," indeed of "life" itself, the model of "experience" is no longer the illustrative case or example that was so much a product of nineteenth-century "syllogistic" legal science. Holmesian "experience" will no longer be that curious world, simultaneously historical and ahistorical, of barrels rolling out of warehouse windows, riders spurring horses down crowded streets, workmen dropping heavy beams off roofs, and so on. That is, of course, a world that has survived in legal pedagogy (as the Langdellian model itself largely has). But for the Holmes of the early twentieth century, even while he earlier declared faith in the ability of the new sciences of economics and statistics to capture "experience," the most

[145] Oliver Wendell Holmes, Jr., "The Path of the Law," p. 399.
[146] Ibid., p. 399.
[147] Holmes, "Law in Science and Science in Law," p. 408
[148] Ibid., p. 420.

authentic kind of "experience" has become a radically privatized one. He finds most of the social philosophies of his day "empty humbug."[149] "Experience" has retreated into the space of the private. Truth is rendered a matter of "experience," to be sure, but a highly personal one: "When I say that a thing is true, I mean that I cannot help believing it. I am stating an experience as to which there is no choice."[150] The point now is that the very private nature of "experience" compels a proceduralist respect for the equal "experience" of others. Furthermore, even though "experience" is represented as emerging in time, the time of "experience" is not so much historical as the time of the natural life cycle rendered coherent and invested with affective meaning:

> [P]roperty, friendship, and truth have a common root in time. One can not be wrenched from the rocky crevices into which one has grown for many years without feeling that one is attacked in one's life. What we most love and revere generally is determined by early associations. I love granite rocks and barberry bushes, no doubt because with them were my earliest joys that reach back through the past eternity of my life. But while one's experience thus makes certain preferences dogmatic for oneself, recognition of how they came to be so leaves one able to see that others, poor souls, may be equally dogmatic about something else. And this again means scepticism.[151]

For the Holmes beloved of the Progressive generation, the model of "experience" has shifted more or less entirely from a matter of knowledge to a matter of roots.

Holmes's "proceduralist" vision of law, the consequence of his view that the common law had to retreat before the advance of the new specialized fields of knowledge of the early twentieth century, is most clearly revealed in his famous dissent in *Lochner v. New York*. Reflecting the evolution of his own views over the course of the 1880s and 1890s, Holmes argued that the U.S. Supreme Court in *Lochner* was usurping the role of the legislature by relying illegitimately upon substantive ideas about freedom. It is here that Herbert Spencer makes his most celebrated appearance in American constitutional discourse:

> This case is decided upon an economic theory which a large part of the country does not entertain. If it were a question whether I agreed with that theory I should desire to study it further and long before making up my mind. But I do

149 Oliver Wendell Holmes, Jr., "Ideals and Doubts" (1915), *Collected Works*, Vol. 3, p. 443.

150 Ibid.

151 Oliver Wendell Holmes, Jr., "Natural Law" (1918), *Collected Works*, Vol. 3, p. 446.

> not conceive that to be my duty, because I strongly believe that my agreement or disagreement has nothing to do with the right of a majority to embody their opinions in law.... The Fourteenth Amendment does not enact Mr. Herbert Spencer's Social Statics.

How, then, was one to decide which infringements on individual liberty amounted to a violation of the Fourteenth Amendment? Holmes's response was as follows:

> General propositions do not decide concrete cases. The decision will depend on a judgment or intuition more subtle than any articulate major premise.... I think that the word liberty in the Fourteenth Amendment is perverted when it is held to prevent the natural outcome of a dominant opinion, unless it can be said that a rational and fair man necessarily would admit that the statute proposed would infringe fundamental principles as they have been understood by the traditions of our people and our law.[152]

One could not reason outward in any straightforward fashion from abstract, formal categories such the "police power" or the "liberty of the individual under the Fourteenth Amendment." This is the meaning of Holmes's celebrated antiformalist pronouncement: "General propositions do not decide concrete cases." Instead, the test of the law's constitutional fitness was to be "fundamental principles *as they have been understood by the traditions of our people and our law*" – in other words, a kind of historical understanding. There is a fundamental undecidability lurking in Holmes's *Lochner* dissent. History serves to demolish substantive theories of right, compelling judges to retreat before the views of democratic majorities. But history – "fundamental principles as they have been understood by the traditions of our people and our law" – must somehow serve as well to control those democratic majorities.

Conclusion

The later Holmes's new understanding of "experience" as privatized and of law as procedural grew out of a profound suspicion of most of the prevailing social philosophies of his day. Holmes's skepticism was evenhanded and could be directed not just at the pretensions of common lawyers and Spencerians, but also at their critics. For legal thinkers of the Progressive Era, however, the Holmesian critique of the common law would be pressed in support of the primacy of social democratic

[152] *Lochner v. New York*, pp. 75–76 (Holmes, J., dissenting).

legislation over common law. Holmes would be claimed, in other words, by a camp increasingly committed to social democracy and opposed to a common law–centered bench and bar.

In 1908, in a well-known article entitled "Common Law and Legislation," the Progressive legal scholar Roscoe Pound complained of the "indifference, if not contempt, with which [legislation] is regarded by courts and lawyers."[153] Common lawyerly ways of ignoring, obstructing, or frustrating socially oriented legislation, Pound argued, ignored the fact that the future of law in America lay in legislation:

> It may be well, however, for judges and lawyers to remember that there is coming to be a science of legislation and that modern statutes are not to be disposed of lightly as off-hand products of a crude desire to do something, but represent long and patient study by experts, careful consideration by conferences or congresses or associations, press discussions in which public opinion is focused upon all important details, and hearings before legislative committees. It may be well to remember also that while bench and bar are never weary of pointing out the deficiencies of legislation, to others the deficiencies of judge-made law are no less apparent. To economists and sociologists, judicial attempts to force Benthamite conceptions of freedom of contract and common law conceptions of individualism upon the public of today are no less amusing – or even irritating – than legislative attempts to do away with or get away from these conceptions are to bench and bar.[154]

This went along with a pointed attack on the pretensions of the common law to express the customs of the community:

> Formerly it was argued that the common law was superior to legislation because it was customary and rested upon the consent of the governed. Today we recognize that the so-called custom is a custom of judicial decision, not a custom of popular action. We recognize that legislation is the more truly democratic form of law-making. We see in legislation the more direct and accurate expression of the general will. We are told that the law-making of the future will consist in putting the sanction of society on what has been worked out in the sociological laboratory [Pound is referring here to the writings of Lester Ward]. That courts cannot conduct such laboratories is self-evident [citations omitted].

Pound ended with a prophetic warning. If the common law did not bend to the will of the public, it would be made to bend: "The public cannot be relied upon permanently to tolerate judicial obstruction or

[153] Roscoe Pound, "Common Law and Legislation," *Harvard Law Review* 21 (1908): 383–407, at 383–384.

[154] Ibid., pp. 383–384.

nullification of the social policies to which more and more it is compelled to be committed."[155]

Nevertheless, perhaps as part of his own growing conservatism, by the 1920s Pound recognized that common lawyers were not just clinging to entrenched common law attitudes, but were appropriating the historical sensibilities of their time. In a series of lectures delivered at Cambridge University in 1922, subsequently published as *Interpretations of Legal History* (1923), he recognized as much:

> This opposition [the judges' opposition to, and consequent invalidation of, redistributive legislation] was not due to class bias or economic associations or social relations of the judges nor to sinister influences brought to bear upon them, as was assumed so freely in the American presidential campaign of 1912, when such decisions were in issue. The judges were imbued with a genuine faith in the tenets of the historical school, especially the political interpretation and the doctrine of progress from status to contract. Hence it seemed to them that the constitutional requirement of due process of law was violated by legislative attempts to restore status and restrict the contractual powers of free men by enacting that men of full age and sound mind in particular callings should not be able to make agreements which other men might make freely.

In other words, the *Lochner* Court – and others like it – was perfectly able to historicize and contextualize law. Adhering to an understanding of the movement of history as one from status to contract, a powerful ideological force after the end of slavery and one wholeheartedly endorsed by Spencer, it had refused to endorse legislation that it saw as going against that historical trend.[156] Pound recognized, furthermore, that the American historical school's understanding of law had given rise to his own contextualized, social democratic understanding of law:

> Finally through its attempt to generalize the phenomena of primitive law and of developed systems by a theory of custom it led to the idea of the legal order as part of a wider social control from which it cannot be dissociated.... This way of thinking did much to help break down the conception of law as something existing of itself and for itself and to be measured by itself; it prepared the way for the functional attitude of the legal science of today.[157]

[155] Ibid., pp. 406–407.

[156] On the ideology of contract in the post-Civil War United States, see Amy Dru Stanley, *From Bondage to Contract: Wage Labor, Marriage, and the Market in the Age of Slave Emancipation* (Cambridge: Cambridge University Press, 1998).

[157] Roscoe Pound, *Interpretations of Legal History* (New York: MacMillan Company, 1923), pp. 62–63, 68.

Taking Pound at his word, one might conclude that the conservative common lawyers of his time participated fully in the historical sensibility of the day and might even have contributed to his own thought. Where that historical sensibility limited the reach of democracy, they could make out a case for the common law in the late-nineteenth-century polity by joining the common law to that historical sensibility. Thus, the common law – in an age in which the inexorable movement of "life" was imagined to check the claims of democracy – was represented as capturing "life" itself. At the same time, it continued to claim the nonhistorical temporalities of "immemoriality" and "insensibility."

One of the goals of this chapter has been to provincialize the Holmesian claim to enjoy a monopoly on historical thought. Different kinds of common law thinkers in the late nineteenth century – those associated with the American historical school, the Harvard formalists, and Holmes himself – appropriated the Spencerian–Darwinian languages of "life" and used them to different ends: conservative, methodological, pedagogical, skeptical. Holmes had no monopoly whatsoever on the critique of the common law either. His uniqueness might lie in embracing the Spencerian concept of producing a sense of the passage of time through the relating of phenomena, but shedding Spencerian determinism. It is not at all clear, however, that those who claimed Holmes would do the same.

7

Conclusion

The seeds of this book have been both a theoretical interest in the relationships among law, democracy, and history and a lingering curiosity about the ways these relationships have been – and continue to be – conceived of in the contemporary American academy.

Let me first set forth the theoretical dilemma. Crudely put, one widely recognized difference between politics and law is their relationship to time. Politics, unlike law, does not depend upon identity over time. Law, in order to be law, appears to depend precisely upon some measure of identity over time. (This identity could inhere in pretended atemporal foundations such as logic, reason, and morality or in a simple but faithful repetition of the past.) Unlike political resolutions of questions, law promises to treat like cases alike, regardless of when they arise in time. The call to historicize and contextualize law – to individuate the legal pronouncement by pinning it down in historical time – is, in this sense, an attempt to break law's pretensions to continuity, to rob it of its claim to identity over time, in short, to politicize it. In the terms in which I began this book, this is precisely the goal of the Holmesian modernist historical enterprise: that of pulling down law's pretense at atemporality by locating it in historical time so as to erode the boundary between law and politics.

As I stated in Chapter 1, this modernist attempt to render law contingent by historicizing it – and hence to show it to be a species of politics – continues to command allegiance within the legal academy and beyond. Robert Gordon, who has written brilliantly about the relationships between law and history for decades, expresses this view clearly. In a 1996–1997 essay entitled "The Arrival of Critical Historicism," Gordon writes:

> So what then is … "critical history" …? I would say it is any approach to the past that produces disturbances in the field – that inverts or scrambles familiar narratives of stasis, recovery or progress; anything that advances rival perspectives (such as those of the losers rather than the winners) for surveying developments, or that posits alternative trajectories that might have produced a very different present – in short any approach that unsettles the familiar strategies that we use to tame the past in order to normalize the present.[1]

It is easy to see that Gordon's representation of the method and goal of "critical history" is very close indeed to what I have described as the Holmesian modernist historical method. Holmes, of course, would not have used quite the same vocabulary; he might also have been suspicious of Gordon's progressive politics. But the similarities remain. A century after Holmes, we continue to attempt to historicize this or that phenomenon to show it to be political, hence changeable, and to begin anew.

The endless modernist recurrence to history to pull down, to render contingent, and to politicize undoubtedly has a great deal to do with progressive scholars' continuing sense of the gap between law and justice. Law must be historicized, shown to the political, in order that it be redone so that justice might finally be done. While I remain sympathetic to the political goals of this historicizing enterprise, I confess that it was a sense of curiosity about alternatives to this now thoroughly conventional practice that led me to ask how relationships among politics, law, and history might have worked before Holmes.

As it turns out, traditional common law thought as it was articulated in the seventeenth century by thinkers such as Coke and Hale had its own language for dealing with the dilemma of reconciling law's claim to identity over time with its need to accommodate difference over time. What I have characterized as the nonhistorical temporalities of "immemoriality" and "insensibility" allowed common lawyers for centuries to collapse identity and difference, such that – to put it in terms of the law–politics distinction – law could do "politics" without ever ceasing to be "law."

The rise of historical thinking in the eighteenth century – centered on the narrativization of history as a shift from feudal to commercial – imbued historical time with meaning, logic, and direction. It gave thinkers ways of

[1] Robert W. Gordon, "Foreword: The Arrival of Critical Historicism," *Stanford Law Review* 49 (1996–1997): 1023–1029, at 1024.

understanding legal phenomena as belonging to this or that period, as markers of the past or as heralds of the future. Legal thinkers from Bolingbroke to Kames to Blackstone would bring this sensibility to bear upon the common law, breaking up its imagined whole body by identifying parts of it as relics of feudalism, others as markers of commerce. But common lawyers such as Blackstone, even as they recognized the imperatives of history and subjected the common law to history, would refuse to dissolve the common law into history, arguing that the common law method – replete with its nonhistorical times of "immemoriality" and "insensibility" – remained the best way of effecting the transition from feudal to commercial.

The American Revolution brought about a new democratic regime, but – Jeffersonian rhetoric notwithstanding – this did not mean that Americans were thereby entirely liberated from the past and able to reimagine an endlessly open future. Indeed, even as it was grounded in a rhetoric of contemporaneous consent, democracy in the writing of Jefferson and Paine – to say nothing of less radical thinkers – was supposed to effectuate the path of an already imagined history, that imagined in important ways by mid-eighteenth-century Scottish thinkers. The same historical narrative remained influential well into the Jacksonian period, even as American thinkers began to imbue democracy with the romantic era rhetoric of "spirit." Once, again, we see American common law thinkers effortlessly deploying historical vocabularies to their ends, using them to historicize the common law, on the one hand, even as they would argue that the common law embodied the direction of history, on the other hand.

As the dominant historical imagination shifted in the mid-nineteenth century, first to the Comtean language of natural and social laws underlying actually existing laws and then to a Darwinian–Spencerian language configuring history as the movement of "life," political democracy – once seen as the medium for the effectuation of underlying social, natural, and historical laws – came increasingly to be seen as an obstacle to the realization of such laws. American common law thinkers, once again, showed themselves to be adept at employing such vocabularies to rethink the common law. And once again, they showed themselves to be adept at shuttling between the times of law and the times of foundational and teleological history.

A few broad conclusions emerge from this book. First, and perhaps most important, we would be wrong to think of the vital presence of the common law in the nineteenth-century American polity as representing in any easy sense an occlusion of democracy. To be sure, from the late eighteenth century on, the common law had numerous critics, from St. George Tucker to William Sampson to Robert Rantoul, Jr., to Sir Henry Maine to

John Chipman Gray to Oliver Wendell Holmes, Jr. Some of these, were committed to the idea that law should be the product of democratic will. But to think of the nineteenth-century common law as antidemocratic implies an imagination of democracy and its possibilities that was not, for the most part, that of nineteenth-century Americans. For nineteenth-century Americans, even as they celebrated it, America's democracy was necessarily constrained in all kinds of ways. An important constraint, for many, was the logic of history. History acted as an imagined limit to what democratic majorities could legitimately do. Other important constraints were the times associated with the common law, mysterious, nonhistorical, premodern times – "immemoriality" and "insensibility" – that kept America tethered to its English past. At a time when the capacities of the American state were relatively weak, American common lawyers combined and recombined the times of the common law and those of history. They subjected the common law to history, thereby updating it in terms of the historical sensibility of their times, but also subjected history to the common law, thereby arguing that the common law was the most effective means of realizing the constraint that history posed. Where history acted as a limit on democracy, they maintained, the common law instantiated that limit.

Second, and following from the preceding point, it should be clear that nineteenth-century American common law thinkers – like their contemporaries generally – were utterly obsessed with understanding law in terms of history. While it is always possible and legitimate to read what lawyers do as politics, from the perspective of nineteenth-century common lawyers themselves, they were performing instead the complex and difficult task of thinking of the common law in relationship to history, engaging with fundamental questions about the relationship between law and history that have continued to perplex and grip us. If one is attentive to their own language, they were engaged neither in a blind repetition of the past nor in a clandestine politics.

Third, from American common lawyers' turn to history, one can conclude that it is not at all clear that a foundational and teleological history ("their" history) is any *less* effective in facilitating reform or producing a sense of the contingency of the world than is an antifoundational one (supposedly "our" history). Thinkers like Lord Kames, James Wilson, Joseph Story, George Fitzhugh, Christopher Columbus Langdell, and James Coolidge Carter were just as able as Oliver Wendell Holmes, Jr. – or those modernists who followed in his wake – to conceive legal reform and legal change. However, in contrast to Holmes and many twentieth-century legal thinkers, they did so in terms of a historical sensibility we would regard as teleological and foundational. Things can be shown to be contingent from the perspective of foundational and teleological history (what Karl Löwith might call a "religious" sensibility) just as easily as they might be from a skeptical one, which should make us more cautious than we often are in hailing the Holmesian, modernist, pragmatist moment as marking the definitive shift in American legal thought. Even the most caricatured logicians of the nineteenth century – Langdell and his circle – sought to conceive of the law in history and recognized its unreason.

Finally, nineteenth-century thinkers did not reduce the common law – or law in general – to politics. Because history possessed logic, meaning, and direction, its purpose was not so much to tear down foundations as to situate phenomena in terms of its own foundations. This might account for why nineteenth-century common lawyers did not end up – as Holmes did – with a sense of ironic despair about the possibilities of reform. Law, for them, was not simply a matter of setting up the procedural rules of the game, as it would become for Holmes.

None of this is at all to suggest a return to the world of nineteenth-century political, legal, and historical thought, even if that were possible. The historical constraints imagined to limit democracy supported the ugliness of slavery and laissez-faire (although also their opposites). There is a reason that the Holmesian tearing down of the wall between law and politics caught fire with the Progressive generation – the common law *was* being used in reactionary ways to stymie attempts to produce a more just society. All I am suggesting is that we examine more carefully the often caricatured way we have represented the world of nineteenth-century political, legal, and historical thought, that we think more carefully about the purported advances of our own thought. One way to confront the dilemma of thinking "after" metaphysics is to examine carefully how the world appeared to work before the alleged end of metaphysics. We might be surprised by the results.

Another way to question the purported advances of our own, post-Holmesian thought is to ask about the career of common law thought in the twentieth century. This is a mammoth subject for another time, another scholar. In what remains of this conclusion, however, I would like to draw attention to a few discrete instances of the irruption of common law thought to illustrate, as it were, the vitality of the tradition in the twentieth century. As we shall see, versions of the common law temporalities of "immemoriality" and "insensibility" show up in the writings of a range of prominent thinkers as efforts to slow the pace of change or to perfect law's correspondence to society or to give disenchanted lawyers a sense of rootedness.

Building upon the writings and judicial pronouncements of Oliver Wendell Holmes, Jr., and others, early-twentieth-century challenges to common law thought traveled, as is well known, under names like Sociological Jurisprudence and Legal Realism. Although there was much variation among the common law's early-twentieth-century critics, the rough outlines of the challenge were clear: common law judges were both too politically conservative and too little qualified to respond to the needs of an increasingly complex and interdependent society. The common law's claims to long continuity, as well as the claims of supposedly "formalist" common law thinkers to reason outward from general propositions to concrete conclusions, were to be repudiated. What mattered was not law "on the books," but law "in action," not law justified on the basis of antiquity, but law as it actually functioned in society. Such challenges were launched sometimes in the name of an antifoundational Holmesian historical consciousness, but more often in the name of a scientific, progressivist, and more foundational historical sensibility. Often the two sensibilities converged without any sense of paradox. These critiques set the stage for the emergence of a different kind of law, one in which the forces of democracy allegedly played a greater role, one generated by legislative bodies, administrative agencies, and scientific experts.[2]

It is not a little ironic, then, that by the 1930s critics of the common law around 1910 should have turned into its staunchest partisans. In order to demonstrate this, I turn to the proceedings of Harvard Law School's suggestively titled "Conference on the Future of the Common Law," held on August 19–21, 1936, as part of the tercentenary of the founding of

[2] There is an extensive literature on early-twentieth-century legal thought, to which the reader is referred. See, e.g., William W. Fisher III, Morton J. Horwitz, and Thomas A. Reed, eds., *American Legal Realism* (Oxford: Oxford University Press, 1993); David Kennedy and William W. Fisher III, eds., *The Canon of American Legal Thought* (Princeton. N.J.: Princeton University Press, 2006); Horwitz, *The Transformation of American Law, 1870–1960*; N. E. H. Hull, *Roscoe Pound and Karl Llewellyn: Searching for an American Jurisprudence* (Chicago: University of Chicago Press, 1997); John Henry Schlegel, *American Legal Realism and Empirical Social Science* (Chapel Hill: University of North Carolina Press, 1995).The differences between pre–World War I "Sociological Jurisprudence" (represented by Pound) and post–World War I "Legal Realism" (represented by Llewellyn), as Morton Horwitz reminded us, might have been more superficial than real, as much the parochial result of personality clashes and careerism as of substantive differences in view point. See Horwitz, *The Transformation of American Law, 1870–1960*, esp. Chaps. 6 and 7.

Harvard College. The conference was convened by none other than Dean Roscoe Pound, who had by the 1930s embarked upon a "conservative" turn, breaking both with certain strands of Legal Realist thought and with the widespread enthusiasm for the consolidating administrative state.[3]

Pound's lecture at the conference was published under the revealing title "What Is the Common Law?" The title itself speaks to the intellectual difficulty of retrieving from under the mass of critiques – critiques that Pound had himself played such a prominent role in articulating – something that could meaningfully be defended as "the common law." Nineteenth-century lawyers had felt little awkwardness in invoking the common law. It had not needed to be defined. But things had changed.

Pound was living, he felt, in a world in which order – but, more important, the sense that order was desirable – was evaporating. As he put it, "Today order in the ordering, system in the adjustment of relations, and checks upon authority operating in accordance with principles logically applied, are under suspicion everywhere."[4] Against this pervasive distaste for order, which one might see as one of the offshoots of a modernist, antifoundational historical sensibility, Pound invoked the common law. But the way he did it is significant.

What the antilegal thinkers of his day ignored, Pound declared, was "the toughness of a taught tradition." As he stated, "A system of law is essentially a taught tradition of ideals, and principles, continuous as long as the course of teaching remains unbroken." The common law was, of course, just such a "taught tradition."[5] But the level of generality at which the idea of the "taught tradition" was pitched allowed Pound to absorb many of the critiques of the common law that he had himself levied decades earlier, while nevertheless hanging on to a certain "essence." Pound described it thus:

> [The common law] is not, then, any body of fixed rules established at any fixed time or by any determinate authority, it is not any body of authoritative permanent or universal premises for legal reasoning, it is not any body of legal institutions, which we may believe is to have a long and distinguished future as an agency of justice among English-speaking peoples. *It is rather a taught tradition of the place of adjudication in the polity of a self-governing people. It is rather a taught tradition of voluntary subjection of authority and power to reason*

[3] For a discussion of Pound's "conservative" turn, see Horwitz, *The Transformation of American Law, 1870–1960*, esp. Chap. 8.

[4] Roscoe Pound, "What is the Common Law?" in *The Future of the Common Law* (Gloucester, Mass.: Peter Smith, 1965), p. 4.

[5] Ibid., p.8.

whether evidenced by medieval charters or by immemorial custom or by the covenant of a sovereign people to rule according to declared principles of right and justice [emphasis added].[6]

Pound does not seem to care a great deal about the integrity of common law knowledge or the privileged position of the common law judge in declaring the customs of the community. The common law does not have to stand for strong contract and property rights. All these aspects of the common law tradition, so dear to Joseph Story, Thomas Cooley, and James Coolidge Carter, seem to have evaporated. The point of the "taught tradition" of the common law is rather that, once all those claims have been given up on, there is still something left over, namely the idea, apparently unique to the English-speaking peoples, that power be chopped up. This was the core of Pound's critique of the administrative state in the name of the common law. As he put it, "There are those today who would think of everything which is done officially as law. Such is not the common-law teaching. Not administration as law but the requiring of administration to conform to rule and form and reason is the common-law ideal."[7] The opposite was the Soviet system: "[I]n the socialist state there can be no law but only administrative ordinances and orders."[8]

However, even as the diffuse idea of the "taught tradition" of the common law allowed Pound to hang on to his own earlier critiques of the substance of the common law while now opposing partisans of the administrative state, Pound was able simultaneously to insist upon a much more conventional fidelity to the past. The attacks upon the common law in his own day, as he saw it, were most definitely attacks upon the past:

> We must not be blind to the attacks upon the common law ... which are going on in every quarter, though, perhaps, most aggressively and persistently in the United States. An era which rejects history is scornful of anything which has its roots in the Middle Ages.[9]

This might be seen as a direct riposte to the Holmesian quip about the undesirability of having no better justification for a rule other than that it was derived from the reign of Henry IV. However, Pound responded, "But a tradition with its roots in the Middle Ages is not without advantages in

[6] Ibid., pp. 10–11.
[7] Ibid., p. 17.
[8] Ibid.
[9] Ibid., p. 19.

the society of today where we seem to be moving towards something very like a new feudalism."[10] The administrative state for Pound – like socialism for George Fitzhugh – was a return to "feudalism." Furthermore, according to Pound, the common law was not divorced from a more substantive link to the past: "[The common law] is rather a traditional technique of finding the grounds of deciding controversies by applying to them principles drawn from recorded judicial experience."[11] We see in Pound, then, yet another instance of common lawyers' managing to live in multiple times at once.

Pound's great antagonist of the 1930s, the Legal Realist Karl Llewellyn, himself proved not to be immune to the pull of common law tradition. We see this in his well-known book, *The Common Law Tradition* (1960).[12] To be sure, Llewellyn distanced himself from what he called the "Formal Style," of which Langdell's legal science was "the American archetype."[13] By the 1960s, however, Llewellyn was equally concerned to respond to what he perceived as a special kind of twentieth-century threat, namely the erosion of lawyers' faith in "any reckonability in the work of our appellate courts, any real stability of footing for the lawyer."[14] The thoroughgoing historicization of law or the reduction of law to a species of politics that had begun in the late nineteenth century had resulted in a kind of cynicism and bewilderment. Disenchanted lawyers had lost confidence in their own skills and in the way the bench would respond to their exercise of these skills. It was important to restore to lawyers faith in their practice, a belief in the relative stability of law, Llewellyn argued, because "[a] right man cannot be a man and feel himself to be a trickster or a charlatan."[15] Accordingly, *The Common Law Tradition*, even as it offered a repudiation of Langdellian formalism and drew upon a range of modern styles of thought (psychology, history, phenomenology, etc.), offered a set of "steadying factors" – or "traditions ... bred in the bone" – that would imbue law with a special stabilizing time, one that would keep law simultaneously inside and outside the anarchy of history, responsive to change and impervious to it.[16] Llewellyn's idea of "steadying factors" – a

[10] Ibid., p. 20.

[11] Ibid., p. 11.

[12] Karl N. Llewellyn, *The Common Law Tradition: Deciding Appeals* (Boston: Little, Brown & Co., 1960).

[13] Ibid., pp. 38–39.

[14] Ibid., p. 3.

[15] Ibid., p. 4.

[16] Ibid., pp. 5, 119.

temporality self-consciously offered as different from that of history, one that ensured continuity even as it guaranteed change – appears in many ways to be analogous to the nonhistorical temporalities of common law. To be sure, it lacks the grandiosity of statements about links to an ancestral past that were a hallmark of nineteenth-century common law thinking and that one sees in the thought of Pound, but in its claim to shield the law from the anarchy of history and politics – even as Llewellyn insists upon an openness to forces outside law – it did something very similar.

If, by 1960, Llewellyn was attempting to hang on to the integrity of the common law tradition in ways not that different from Pound's, larger political, social, and cultural trends in the 1960s and 1970s brought about a revival of Burkean common law thought at the level of constitutional discourse. In large part, this was a response to the forces unleashed by *Brown v. Board of Education* (1954). In 1964, Russell Kirk, a key figure in the reinvigoration of Burkean ideas in the post–World War II period, would insist, in his discussion of the American Revolution, that "[w]e [had] appealed to the prescriptive liberties of Englishmen, not to liberté, égalité, fraternité."[17] But Burke also features in the writings of a trained constitutional thinker like the Yale Law School professor Alexander Bickel, who has been described as the most prominent constitutional theorist of the post–World War II era. Bickel begins his last book, *The Morality of Consent* (1975), by describing two traditions that "diverged in response to the impact of the French Revolution on political thought." These are, according to him, the contractarian tradition associated with Locke and Rousseau, on the one hand, and the Whig tradition associated with Edmund Burke, on the other. The latter, he argues, "is my own model."[18]

In Bickel's own rendering, there was a great deal happening around him that called for a revival of Burke. For one, there was what he perceived to be the utter nihilism of the various social movements of the 1960s, a ferocious insistence on breaking all ties to the past and on opening up a future for reimagination. These were the French revolutionaries or Jeffersonians of Bickel's day. In Bickel's contemptuous view, "Our recent revolutionaries have offered us [nothing but]

[17] Russell Kirk, "Prescription, Authority and Ordered Freedom," in Frank S. Meyer, ed., *What Is Conservatism?* (New York: Holt, Rinehart & Winston, 1964), p. 37.

[18] Alexander Bickel, *The Morality of Consent* (New Haven, Conn.: Yale University Press, 1975), p. 3.

hatred." He went on, "They have offered for the future, so far as their spokesmen have been able to make clear, the Maypole dance and ... a vision of 'liberated' masses adjuring profit, competition, personal achievement, and any form of gratification not instantly and equally available to all." The following pamphlet issued by the Yippies – and quoted extensively by Bickel – must surely have seemed to Bickel to mark out the path to hell:

> Burn your money. You know life is a dream and all our institutions are man-made illusions, effective only because you take the dream for reality. Break down the family, church, nation, city, economy, turn life into an art form and theater of the soul. What is needed is a generation of people who are freaky, crazy, irrational, sexy, angry, irreligious, childish, and mad ... who lure youth with music, pot, and acid ... who redefine the normal.... Burn your houses down and you will be free.

For all his success in "getting" the 1960s, as the historian Laura Kalman informs us, Alexander Bickel was burned in effigy by Yale Law School students.[19]

Bickel's major scholarly concern – indeed, the focus of all his major writings – was the Warren Court. If the Warren Court was not exactly like the Yippies in imagining a future rendered free of all institutional trappings inherited from the past, the Court could nevertheless be likened to the eighteenth-century thinkers who stocked the arsenal of the French revolutionaries. "Like the eighteenth century philosophes," Bickel wrote in *The Supreme Court and the Idea of Progress* (1970), "our Justices ... were rationalists coming after men of faith."[20] Like the rationalists almost two centuries earlier, the bane of all common lawyers, the justices were wreaking havoc. For Bickel, the problem with the Warren Court was precisely that – like the French revolutionaries – it was too seduced by "the idea of progress" to pay attention to the fact that it was engendering serious "discontinuity – open or disguised – in specifics."[21] According to Bickel, the Court was guilty of "a striving for fidelity to a true line of progress," one that led it to "imagine the past and remember the future" and to sweep away recklessly all remnants of the past.[22]

[19] Ibid., p. 140; Laura Kalman, *Yale Law School and the Sixties: Revolt and Reverberations* (Chapel Hill: University of North Carolina Press, 2005), p. 2.

[20] Alexander Bickel, *The Supreme Court and the Idea of Progress* (New York: Harper & Row, 1970), p. 14.

[21] Ibid.

[22] Ibid.

For many in America, the "discontinuity" that Bickel deplored was, of course, a *good* thing. The Warren Court was attempting – through its firm commitment to the "one person, one vote" principle and to implementing desegregation in a range of areas of American life – to enrich and strengthen American democracy, to end historic disfranchisement, and – by admitting into the American body politic a group of hitherto excluded and degraded groups – to increase precisely a measure of needed *difference* between past and future. Bickel's criticisms of the Warren Court, and the solutions he offered, could be seen as arguments for the importance of a Burkean, common lawyerly coexistence of past, present, and future that would break the Court's headlong rush to what Bickel saw as a more and more "presentist" radical democracy. Many of his criticisms were made in the name of different common law "technicalities." One of the most obvious was procedure. As Bickel put it, "[P]rocedural safeguards ... were relatively well-defined by a *less than usually imagined past*"; in other words, they guaranteed a measure of identity between past, present, and future and ensured a kind of common law simultaneity of temporalities.[23] The same argument could be made on behalf of Bickel's famous advocacy of "passive virtues," once again common law "technicalities," devices such as legal standing or ripeness through which the Court would – or *should* – refrain from considering certain constitutional questions to be a prudential matter.

Although he supported the result in *Brown*, Bickel was especially opposed to the Warren Court's voting rights jurisprudence. Like Burke, Story, Tiedeman, and a range of other common law thinkers, Bickel subscribed to the view that suffrage was only a very small part of American democracy, and not even the most important part:

> The Madisonian model of a multiplicity of factions vying against each other and checking each other still more nearly fits our system.... It is perfectly clear as well that, aside from the judges, many other elites that are not immediately and not directly controlled by the electoral process wield power in American government.... Elections are the tip of the iceberg; the bulk of the political process is below. The jockeying, the bargaining, the trading, the threatening and the promising, the checking and the balancing, the spurring and the vetoing are continuous.[24]

Majoritarianism of the Warren Court variety, Bickel conceded, "was heady stuff." But it was, paradoxically, "heady stuff" that would lead

[23] Ibid., p. 32 (emphasis in original).

[24] Ibid., p. 83.

to a rationalistic aridity, to a kind of unaesthetic deintoxication of the public realm. "It is, in truth, a tide flowing with the swiftness of a slogan – whether popular sovereignty, as in the past, or one man, one vote, as in the Warren Court's formulation. The tide is apt to sweep over all institutions, *seeking its level everywhere*."[25] What American democracy will lose in the rapid instantiation of the "one man, one vote" principle, in this unfortunate leveling, Bickel argues, is a measure of "intensity." His hope was that America would revert to a democracy of groups rather than of individuals, groups working simultaneously in a Madisonian/Burkean/technical sense, possessed "of intensities that no ballot can register."[26]

Around the same time, renditions of the common law as instantiating changing knowledge forms continued. In the well-known Priest–Rubin thesis, legal scholars argued that the common law method – what Charles Fried called "a kind of Walrasian *tâtonnement*" but what an older generation of lawyers might have called "insensible" change – best effectuated economic rationality, yet another foundational philosophy in terms of which American democracy would come to be judged.[27] Nor has the old dispute between statute and common law as methods of lawmaking subsided. In 1982, in a book entitled *A Common Law for the Age of Statutes*, the Yale law professor (now federal appellate judge) Guido Calabresi made a case for the common law method by arguing that it could *better* calibrate the twin needs of continuity and change than could democratic legislative activity. Statutes, Calabresi observed, tended rapidly to become obsolete:

> When these laws [statutes] were new and functional, so that they represented in a sense the majority and its needs, the change represented few fundamental problems. *Soon, however, these laws, like all laws, became middle-aged.* They no longer served current needs or represented current majorities. Changed circumstances, or newer statutory and common law developments, rendered some statutes inconsistent with a new social or legal topography.... Despite this inconsistency with the legal landscape, however, such statutes remained effective and continued to govern important areas of social concern [emphasis added].

[25] Ibid., p. 112 (emphasis added).

[26] Ibid., pp. 116–117.

[27] Paul H. Rubin, "Why Is the Common Law Efficient?" *Journal of Legal Studies* 6 (1977): 51–63; George L. Priest, "The Common Law and the Selection of Efficient Rules," *Journal of Legal Studies* 6 (1977): 65–82; John C. Goodman, "An Economic Theory of the Evolution of the Common Law," *Journal of Legal Studies* 7 (1978): 393–406; Charles Fried, "The Laws of Change: The Cunning of Reason in Moral and Legal History," *Journal of Legal Studies* 9 (1980): 335–353, at 335–336.

As a response to this problem of statutes turning "middle-aged," Calabresi offers us a vision of nineteenth-century common law courts. The changes that nineteenth-century courts introduced, Calabresi argues, were "piecemeal and incremental, organic if one wishes, as courts sought to discover and only incidentally to make the ever-changing law."[28] Democratic expressions of law – the people speaking through their representatives in the *present* – age rapidly. As in centuries past, the "insensibly" advancing common law is represented as being able to accomplish the work of history even better than legislative majorities can do. Once again, the common law imagines itself to be a supplement to American democracy.

[28] Guido Calabresi, *A Common Law for the Age of Statutes* (Cambridge, Mass.: Harvard University Press, 1982), pp. 6, 4.

Index